AUGUSTINE AND HIS CRITICS

AUGUSTINE AND HIS CRITICS

Essays in honour of Gerald Bonner

*Edited by Robert Dodaro
and George Lawless*

London and New York

First published 2000
by Routledge
11 New Fetter Lane, London EC4B 4EE

Simultaneously published in the USA and Canada
by Routledge
29 West 35th Street, New York, NY 10001

Routledge is an imprint of the Taylor & Francis Group

Typeset in Garamond
by Curran Publishing Services Ltd
Printed and bound in Great Britain
by Biddles Ltd, Guildford and King's Lynn

British Library Cataloguing in Publication Data
A catalogue record for this book is available
from the British Library

Library of Congress Cataloging in Publication Data
Augustine and his critics / edited by Robert Dodaro and George
Lawless.
288 p. 15.6 x 23.4 cm
Includes bibliographical references and index.
1. Augustine, Saint, Bishop of Hippo. I. Dodaro, Robert, 1955 –
II. Lawless, George.
BR65.A9A83 2000   99–34141
230'.14'092—dc21   CIP

ISBN 0-415-20062-8

CONTENTS

CONTRIBUTORS

Lewis Ayres is Assistant Professor of Theology, Duke University Divinity School, Durham.

Robert Crouse is Emeritus Professor in the Department of Classics, Dalhousie University, and in the University of King's College, Halifax.

Robert Dodaro is Professor in the Patristic Institute, the Augustinianum, Rome.

Hubertus R. Drobner is Professor in the Catholic Theological Faculty of Paderborn.

Daniel W. Hardy, a member of the Faculty of Theology, University of Cambridge, was formerly Van Mildert Professor of Divinity at the University of Durham and later Director of the Center of Theological Inquiry, Princeton.

Carol Harrison is Lecturer in the Faculty of Theology, University of Durham.

Mathijs Lamberigts is Professor in the Faculty of Theology, Catholic University of Leuven.

George Lawless is Professor in the Patristic Institute, the Augustinianum, and Adjunct Professor in the Faculty of Theology, Pontifical Gregorian University, Rome.

Robert A. Markus is Emeritus Professor in the Faculty of History, University of Nottingham.

E. Ann Matter is the R. Jean Brownlee Term Professor in the Department of Religious Studies, University of Pennsylvania, Philadelphia.

John Milbank is the Francis Ball Professor in Philosophical Theology, University of Virginia, Charlottesville.

James Wetzel is Associate Professor of Philosophy and Theology, Colgate University, Hamilton, New York.

Rowan Williams is the Bishop of Monmouth and fomerly Lady Margaret Professor of Divinity in the University of Oxford.

ACKNOWLEDGEMENTS

We would like to thank the series editors, Lewis Ayres and Michel Barnes, for inviting us to publish this volume in their series with Routledge. Lewis Ayres has provided solid, reliable advice throughout the publishing process. Coco Stevenson and others at Routledge have made working on this project the nearest thing to a pleasure that publishing can be. In Rome, Allan Fitzgerald, OSA, and Aldo Bazan, OSA, provided us with hours of technical computer assistance when a 'glitch' threatened the editing process. José Manuel Guirau, OSA, Librarian of the Patristic Institute, contributed valuable assistance by researching certain bibliographical entries for us.

The contribution by John Milbank, 'Sacred Triads: Augustine and the Indo–European Soul', appears here substantially unchanged from its publication in *Modern Theology* 13:4 (October 1997). We gratefully acknowledge the permission of the editors to reprint it here.

ABBREVIATIONS

Editions and translations of Augustine's writings

ACW   *Ancient Christian Writers: The Works of the Fathers in Translation*, ed. J. Quasten, J. C. Plumpe, W. J. Burghart, J. Dillon and D. D. McManus, Westminster Md., 1946–.

BA   *Œuvres de Saint Augustin*, Bibliothèque Augustinienne, Paris, 1936–.

CCL   *Corpus Christianorum Series Latina*, Turnhout, Brepols, 1954–.

CSEL   *Corpus Scriptorum Ecclesiasticorum Latinorum*, Vienna, 1866– .

PL   *Patrologiae Cursus Completus, Series Latina*, ed. J.-P. Migne, Paris, 1841–55.

PG   *Patrologiae Cursus Completus, Series Graeca*, ed. J.-P. Migne, Paris, 1857–66.

FC   *Fathers of the Church*, ed. L. Schopp, R. J. Deferrari, H. Dresler and T. P. Halton, Washington D.C., 1947– .

MiAg   *Miscellanea Agostiniana, Sancti Augustini Sermones post Maurinos Reperti*, Rome, 1930.

WSA   *The Works of Saint Augustine. A Translation for the 21st Century*, ed. J. Rotelle, New York, 1989–.

Cited works of Augustine

Acad.   *De Academicis*. PL 32. CSEL 63. CCL 29. FC 1. ACW 12.

adult. coniug.   *De adulterinis coniugiis*. PL 40. CSEL 41. FC 27.

agon.   *De agone christiano*. PL 40. CSEL 41. FC 2.

an. et or.   *De anima et eius origine*. PL 44. CSEL 60. WSA 1.23.

bapt.   *De baptismo*. PL 43. CSEL 51.

b. uita   *De beata uita*. PL 32. CSEL 63. CCL 29. FC 1.

b. coniug.   *De bono coniugali*. PL 40. CSEL 41. CCL 29 FC 27.

b. uid.   *De bono uiduitatis*. PL 40. CSEL 41. FC 16.

cat. rud.   *De catechizandis rudibus*. PL 40. CCL 46. ACW 2.

ciu.   *De ciuitate Dei*. PL 41. CSEL 40. CCL 47–8. FC 8, 14, 24. H. Bettenson, *Concerning the City of God Against the Pagans*,

London, 1972.

conf.	*Confessiones.* PL 32. CSEL 33. CCL 27. R. S. Pine-Coffin, *Saint Augustine, Confessions*, London, 1961. FC 21. WSA 1.1.
c. Faust.	*Contra Faustum Manicheum.* PL 42. CSEL 25.
cons. eu.	*De consensu euangelistarum.* PL 34. CSEL 43.
cont.	*De continentia.* PL 40. CSEL 41. FC 16.
Cresc.	*Contra Cresconium grammaticum partis Donati.* PL 43. CSEL 52.
diu. qu.	*De diuersis quaestionibus octoginta tribus.* PL 40. CCL 44A. FC 70.
doct. chr.	*De doctrina christiana.* PL 34. CSEL 80. CCL 32. FC 2. WSA 1.11.
en. Ps.	*Enarrationes in Psalmos.* PL 36–7. CCL 38–40.
ench.	*Enchiridion ad Laurentium de fide spe et caritate.* PL 40. CCL 46. ACW 3. FC 2.
ep.	*Epistulae.* PL 33. CSEL 34/1–2, 44, 57, 58. FC 12, 18, 20, 30, 32.
*ep.**	*Epistulae 1*–29*.* CSEL 88. FC 81.
ep. Rm. inch.	*Epistulae ad Romanos inchoata expositio.* PL 35. CSEL 84.
c. ep. Pel.	*Contra dues epistulas Pelagianorum.* CSEL 60. WAS 1.24.
c. ep. Parm.	*Contra epistulam Parmeniani.* PL 43. CSEL 51.
exc. urb.	*De excidio urbis Romae.* PL 40. CCL 46. WSA 3.10.
exp. Gal.	*Expositio epistulae ad Galatas.* PL 35 CSEL 84.
ex. prop. Rm.	*Expositio quarundam propositionum ex epistula apostoli ad Romanos.* PL 35. CSEL 84.
f. et op.	*De fide et operibus.* PL 40. CSEL 41. FC 27. ACW 48.
f. et symb.	*De fide et symbolo.* PL 40. CSEL 41. FC 27.
Gn. adu. Man.	*De Genesi aduersus Manicheos.* PL 34. CSEL 91. FC 84.
Gn. litt.	*De Genesi ad litteram.* PL 34. CSEL 28.1 ACW 41–2.
gr. et. pecc. or.	*De gratia Christi et de peccato originali.* PL 44. CSEL 42. WSA 1.23.
haer.	*De haeresibus.* PL 42. CCL 46. WSA 1.18.
imm. an.	*De immortalitate animae.* PL 32. CSEL 89. FC 2.
Io. eu. tr.	*In Iohannis euangelium tractatus.* PL 35. CCL 36. FC 78, 79, 88, 90, 92.
c. Iul.	*Contra Iulianum.* PL 44. FC 35. WSA 1.24.
c. Iul. imp.	*Contra Iulianum opus imperfectum.* PL 45. CSEL 85.1.
c. litt. Pet.	*Contra litteras Petiliani.* PL 43. CSEL 52.
c. Max.	*Contra Maximinum Arrianum.* PL 42. WSA 1.18.
mor.	*De moribus ecclesiae catholicae et de moribus Manicheorum.* PL 32. CSEL 90. FC 56.
mus.	*De musica.* PL 32. FC 2.
nat. et gr.	*De natura et gratia.* PL 44. CSEL 60. FC 86.
nupt. et conc.	*De nuptiis et concupiscientia.* PL 44. CSEL 42. WSA 1.24.
op. mon.	*De opere monachorum.* PL 40. CSEL 41. FC 16.

pecc. mer.	*De peccatorum meritis et remissione et de baptismo paruulorum.* PL 44. CSEL 60. WSA 1.23.
perf. iust.	*De perfectione iustitiae hominis.* PL 44. CSEL 42. WSA 1.23.
perseu.	*De dono perseuerantiae.* PL 45. FC 86.
qu.	*Quaestiones libri septem = Quaestiones in heptateuchum libri septem.* PL 34. CSEL 28.2. CCL 33.
quant. an.	*De quantitate animae.* PL 32. CSEL 89. FC 2. ACW 9.
reg.	*Praeceptum.* L. Verheijen, *La Règle de saint Augustin*, Paris, Etudes augustiniennes, 1967. English translation: G. Lawless, *Augustine of Hippo and his Monastic Rule*, Oxford, Clarendon Press, 1987.
retr.	*Retractationes.* PL 32. CSEL 36. CCL 57. FC 60.
s.	*Sermon(es).* For a listing of Latin editions, see *Augustinus-Lexikon*, vol. 1, ed. C. Mayer, Basel, Schwabe, 1986–94, c. xxxviii–xxxix. To these should be added *Augustin d'Hippone. Vingt-six sermons au peuple d'Afrique,* ed. F. Dolbeau, Paris, Etudes augustiniennes, 1996. WSA 3.1–11.
s. dom. m.	*Sermo domini in monte.* PL 34. CCL 35. FC 11. ACW 5.
Simpl.	*Ad Simplicianum de diuersis quaestionibus.* PL 40. CCL 44.
spec.	*Speculum.* PL 34. CSEL 12.
spir. et litt.	*De spiritu et littera.* PL 44. CSEL 60. WSA 1.23.
trin.	*De trinitate.* PL 42. CCL 50, 50A. FC 45.
util. ieiun.	*De utilitate ieunii.* PL 40. CCL 46. FC 16. WSA 3.10.
uera rel.	*De uera religione.* PL 34. CSEL 77. CCL 32.
uirg.	*De sancta uirginitate.* PL 40. CSEL 41. FC 27.

Other abbreviations

C. Th.	*Codex Theodosianus*, in *Theodosiani libri XVI cum Constitutionibus Sirmondianis*, ed. T. Mommsen, Berlin, Weidmann, 1904–5; repr. Dublin / Zurich, Weidmann, 1971, pp. 27–906.
C. J.	*Codex Justinianus = Corpus Iuris Civilis*, vol. II, ed. P. Krueger, Berlin, Weidmann, 1954.
C. Sirm.	*Constitutiones Sirmondianae*, in *Theodosiani libri XVI cum Constitutionibus Sirmondianis*, ed. T. Mommsen, Berlin, Weidmann, 1904–5; repr. Dublin / Zurich, Weidmann, 1971, pp. 907–21.

INTRODUCTION

'What I desire for all my works, of course, is not merely a kind reader but also a frank critic'.[1] Augustine did not fear criticism. Nor did he have to search far to find it. It may safely be asserted that from the time he began to write, his *opus* met with both kindly readers and frank critics, often enough together in the same persons. Interest in Augustine's thought on the part of scholars and enquirers engaged in various fields of study has not waned even in our own times. Contemporary philosophers, theologians, spiritual writers, cultural theorists and social scientists take him to task for certain positions of his on issues ranging from human sexuality and the body, gender, personal freedom, religious liberty and the ethics of force, to his concepts of the self and God. Today, more often than not, Augustine's outlook is characterised as 'pessimistic', and he is charged with responsibility for a certain Christian malaise.

Inspired by the eirenic, yet tenaciously scholarly example of Professor Gerald Bonner, to whom this volume is affectionately dedicated, the contributors of *Augustine and his Critics* wished to examine the arguments of certain strident, present-day critics of Augustine in an effort both to respond to the more inaccurate and unfair of these criticisms, and to argue in favour of some of the much-neglected historical, philosophical and theological perspectives that lie behind Augustine's most unpopular convictions. Far from desiring to stifle criticism of Augustine in this way, or to 'whitewash' his controversial positions, the authors gathered here hope to promote a deeper conversation concerning the purposes, direction and, where possible, the contemporary value of the difficult, disputed areas of his thought.

Following an appreciation of Gerald Bonner prepared by Daniel Hardy, Hubertus Drobner opens the volume with a panoramic report on research trends in Augustinian studies over the last decade. His essay offers to specialists and students alike a concise indication of the multifaceted interests in Augustine's work which today command the greatest amount of attention from scholars.

Concern with Augustine's critics, then, begins with Part One of the volume, 'If Plato Were Alive', a phrase rendered famous by Augustine's

1

attempt in *De uera religione* to come to terms with Christianity's debt to the Platonists. Augustine's Platonic heritage constitutes one of the over arching problems for modern critics of his work. This Augustinian, Christian Platonism, still difficult to define precisely, even after a century of research, is a matter which weighs upon every aspect of his thought and lies, sometimes inaudibly, at the foundation of the criticisms of his work considered in each of the essays of this volume. Robert Crouse offers a magisterial account of the most important among the recent efforts to specify the various strands of Platonic influence within Augustine's intellectual and spiritual achievement, and hints strongly in the direction of the need for a wholly new, comprehensive explanation of Augustine's Platonism. Meanwhile, Lewis Ayres and John Milbank present strong, new arguments for refining Augustine's theological and anthropological purposes away from those generally classed or even dismissed as 'Platonist'. Writing on Augustine's trinitarian theology, Ayres takes exception to several recent characterisations of Augustine's trinitarian theology which are popular in North America and the UK, and which associate his theology with a 'Platonic' (read 'other-worldly') over-concern with speculation upon the immanent Trinity at the expense of a sustained, biblical reflection on the historical experience of a triune God intent upon human salvation. Milbank takes up the other principal pole in Augustine's most philosophical investigations – that of the self and its relationship to rule – and argues that Augustine went further even than Plato in replacing the Indo-European mythological, tripartite structure of the soul (and its contingent political theories centred on the ideal of self-government) with something akin to the tripartite structure of love, a move which takes Augustine to the point of subverting Platonic interiority.

This Augustinian 'Order of Love', the heart of Book 15 of the *City of God*, constitutes the theme for Part Two of the volume, which begins with Rowan Williams's highly suggestive – in part, because refreshingly unconventional – reconsideration of Augustine's understanding of evil as the 'privation of the good' (*privatio boni*). Williams unlocks new possibilities in this fundamental direction of Augustine's thought for re-imagining the psychological and religious dynamics involved in self-discovery, reconciliation and relationship to God in a world beset with tragedy.

James Wetzel courageously returns to the choppier philosophical and theological waters surrounding Augustine's doctrines of free will and predestination, long the bane of advocates of Augustine's theology of grace on account of the latter doctrine's seemingly twisted logic and inattention to the divine will in favour of universal salvation. After setting out in remarkably clear terms what he views at stake in the Augustinian position, Wetzel proposes a compromise with the doctrine's hardest aspects, but one that does not reject the entirety of Augustine's concern to hold intact the divine mystery behind the grace of confession.

George Lawless carries many of these themes surrounding Augustine's theology of grace into a focused examination of the several forms of asceticism in his life and thought. Lawless finds a unity in Augustine's ascetical concern for moderation with respect to enjoyment of the body, sexuality, and other material pleasures in his conclusion that, for Augustine, Christian asceticism consisted in the cultivation of ways and means to foster human relationships and render them firm.

E. Ann Matter takes up the highly disputed territory of gender in Augustine's thought, with a thorough review of the most recent scholarly discussions of Augustine's writings on women. Perhaps nowhere else in Augustinian scholarship today are the perspectives of history, philosophy and theology so vital to our attempts to assess the legacy and the value of Augustine's works than in terms of their reception from feminist points of view. Matter navigates among various, differing methods of interpretation of Augustine's views on women in a manner that allows her to outline the strengths of these evaluations, while keeping the historical distance between Augustine's times and our own always before our eyes. Mathijs Lamberigts brings a similar set of skills and sensitivity to bear in his investigation of wide-ranging criticisms of Augustine's views on human sexuality, so many of which are frequently rehearsed in today's popular literature. As he finds no modern critic of Augustine on these questions as courageous in standing up to Augustine as Augustine's younger contemporary, Julian of Eclanum, Lamberigts casts his meticulously detailed presentation and evaluation of Augustine's case largely in terms of Julian's criticisms.

Such is the weight Augustine's times exercised in limiting the horizons of his thought, that the topic itself seemed to warrant examination. Thus, the theme of Part Three of the volume, 'We Are the Times', takes its inspiration from a sentiment expressed in Augustine's *Sermon* 80. In an essay that sets the tone for this section, Robert Markus reopens the question concerning the reasons behind Augustine's abandonment of his earlier view that he lived in divinely privileged, 'Christian times', the era of an evangelisation fulfilled, in exchange for his adoption of a disillusioned, radical agnosticism over God's purposes in human history, and a determination to pursue a 'christianisation' not founded in secular laws and institutional structures supporting the work and values of the Christian religion, but in the interior, spiritual renewal of individual Christians.

In line with this argument, Carol Harrison rejects the judgement that Augustine's rhetorical accomplishments in biblical exegesis and preaching – the heart of his cultural production – exist in unremarkable continuity with the classical sensibilities of late antique Roman culture, and argues instead that they represent an emergent, distinctly Christian aesthetic, informed by and subservient to the aim of promoting in the soul the love of God and neighbour, as witnessed in the life and teachings of Christ. Finally, Robert Dodaro assesses the value of recent criticisms of Augustine's political thought and tactics as authoritarian, elitist and coercive against his goal of liberating individuals from the entire range of ancient philosophies and spiritualities, all of which were captivated for him by an illusion of the self as capable of moral and spiritual self-sufficiency. Dodaro interprets Augustine's rejection of Roman civic virtue, paradigmatically represented in the military and political hero, as being grounded ultimately in imperial society's closure to the possibilities of social reconciliation contained in the experience of pardon as divine gift.

Evidently, a number of urgent, contemporary criticisms of Augustine are not represented in this volume. Augustine's attitudes to war, Jews and ecclesiastical authority are only examples of other of his positions which draw constant fire from modern critics. Selection of the above-mentioned, and exclusion of other topics, are consequences of the availability at the time of qualified contributors and the limit to the length of the volume that could be produced. Routledge are to be thanked for generous consideration given to us in terms of the latter condition.

In addition to the persons named in the Acknowledgements to this book, we would like to thank in particular our contributors for their immediate and overwhelmingly positive response to our invitation to collaborate in this project. In spite of their busy academic and personal lives, they responded as they did both out of love for Augustine and the deepest affection and esteem for Gerald Bonner. For you, Gerald, our most heartfelt, best wishes *ad plurimos annos*!

Robert Dodaro, OSA
George Lawless, OSA
Rome, 28 August 1999
The Feast of St Augustine

Notes

1   Augustine, *trin. 3. proem.* 2; CCL 50.128: 'Sane cum in omnibus litteris meis non solum pium lectorem sed etiam liberum correctorem desiderem'.

1

GERALD BONNER

An appreciation

Daniel W. Hardy

Gerald Bonner has humbly and generously served the tradition of British scholarship with great distinction. Like many others formed in a time before there was so much preoccupation with careers and self-advancement as now, he has maintained an admirable modesty. Not only his work, but also the generosity of his dedication to others has contributed importantly to the scholarship upon which others build today. He richly deserves the tribute paid to him by this book of essays published in his honour.

Gerald was born in London in 1926, one of two sons of Frederick John and Constance Emily Bonner. His father died when he was five, from an injury sustained in an accident in India years before while serving there in the army during the First World War. It was a tragedy not least because it left his family with nothing more than sympathy, for there was no social assistance available. As a teacher, Bonner's mother was poorly paid and had to struggle to support her sons, an achievement that he has never forgotten. She was a member of the Church of England and raised her children as such, and he has always continued in the Church. His schooling from 1936 to 1944 was at the Stationers' Company's School in North London, one of the guild schools that have been so important in British education. It was during that time, when he was thirteen, that his interest in Augustine was first aroused by a sermon.

From 1944 to 1948, he served in the British Army, in the First King's Dragoon Guards (now the Queen's Dragoon Guards). After the conclusion of the Second World War, he served as a wireless operator in Palestine. He then returned to England for officer training, was commissioned in 1947 and served as a second lieutenant in Tripolitania. While there, he visited the ruins of Leptis Magna, a Roman colony that was the birthplace of Septimius Severus, the emperor who began the absolute despotism of the later Roman Empire and who died in Eboracum (York) while subduing parts of Britain not under Roman rule. While in Tripoli, Bonner bought a 1930 Turin reprint of Augustine's *Confessions* adorned by the notes (rather mediocre, as he later thought) of the seventeenth-century German Jesuit, Heinrich Wangnereck.

When he left the army in 1948, he spent a year in civilian employment before going up to Wadham College, Oxford. As one might expect in an ancient university, the School of Modern History made it possible to concentrate on Augustine; there were two final examination papers on him. Gerald Bonner took his finals in 1952. After that came a year's postgraduate research under the supervision of Thomas Corbishley, SJ, then Master of Campion Hall, the Jesuit hall of studies at Oxford. This was a period in England when it was unusual, even among those intending to be university teachers, to engage in postgraduate study. It was a remarkable time to be engaged in such study at Oxford. Corbishley, T. M. Parker of University College and Maurice Bowra, Warden of Wadham, impressed him deeply; and he remained grateful to them ever after.

For a man already in his late twenties in a country still suffering deeply from the effects of the war, employment was also important. In 1953, a rare opportunity came which brought him to leave Oxford, the possibility of work in the Department of Manuscripts at the British Museum. He was to remain there for eleven years. This was not surprising: the department housed one of the finest collections of Western manuscripts, both ancient and modern, in the world. There were a succession of distinguished keepers during his time there including A. J. Collins, Bertram Schofield and T. C. Skeat; and there were always a number of major scholars among its staff from whom one more junior might benefit. However there was also frustration. During the 1950s, the effects of the Second World War were being felt: acquisition of manuscripts had continued during the war, but cataloguing had come to a stop. As a result, the work of the department was too often a routine 'catching up', with less opportunity than before to pursue significant projects. Even such major foundation collections as the Cotton manuscripts needed to be re-catalogued, and still do, but such major tasks could not be attempted. Perhaps Gerald Bonner's most rewarding activity was the sorting and arrangement of the correspondence of the Copticist Walter Ewing Crum (d. 1941) in connection with the writing of his great Coptic dictionary. It provided a fascinating glimpse of one department of ancient learning in modern scholarship.

While serving in the British Museum, Bonner continued his study of Augustine, and published essays – the beginning of a long sequence – began to appear in 1960. His first book was published in 1963, *St Augustine of Hippo: Life and Controversies*; it was later reprinted in a second edition. It was his attendance at the Oxford Patristic Conference in the same year that led to the next phase of his academic life. By chance he met H. E. W. Turner, Van Mildert Professor of Divinity at the University of Durham, who encouraged him to apply for a Lectureship in Church History there in 1964.

Durham is the third oldest university in England (after Oxford and Cambridge), and its Faculty of Theology followed the pattern of scholarship then common in the ancient universities. Although there were also two theological colleges in the university whose staff were sometimes called upon, the faculty itself had nine staff. There was a heavy orientation to biblical studies (six staff), in which Durham had a deservedly high reputation, and much smaller provision for early Christian doctrine and philosophical theology. The addition of Gerald Bonner was a move to consolidate its work in early Church history. What this meant for him was teaching that was both demanding and repetitive, with no opportunity to teach Augustine. Perhaps that was not such a bad thing at the beginning of his university career, since it allowed him a chance to ground his scholarship through serious research.

The faculty was itself an example of the more informal arrangements that prevailed in universities at the time. There was no specific building or offices. Lectures were given in the lecture rooms on Palace Green on the north side of the cathedral, in the area that had been given by Bishop Van Mildert at the university foundation. Tutorials, the weekly personal supervision offered to each student, were in lecturers' homes, while faculty meetings were held in the study of the canon professors in the college on the other side of the cathedral. Such arrangements were becoming increasingly impractical, however, and eventually some old shops in Sadler Street – the narrow main road on to the peninsula where the cathedral and early university buildings were located – were allocated to a few of the staff, Bonner included. They were in doubtful condition, particularly one (not Bonner's) over the former dungeon of the prince bishops of Durham, whose floor was ominously close to giving way. Only in 1973 did Abbey House, adjacent to the cathedral, become the home of the faculty.

Another sign of the development of the faculty was the starting of an alternative degree programme, to include biblical study but also a greater concentration on later studies, both historical and theology *per se*. Still later, a tripartite teaching programme was developed which allowed students to concentrate on the Bible, Church history or theology. Continuing expansion brought staffing into line with this programme. In early Church history, careful attention was given to western and eastern theology. For the West, Gerald Bonner's contribution was pivotal; he created an option on Augustine in the Honours School of Theology. It continues even now, and flourishes under his successor, Carol Harrison. Many students would attest that, in its degree course, Durham provides a grounding in the history and theology of the Christian tradition without parallel in Britain. In this, the scholarship and unfailing care shown in Gerald Bonner's teaching was of the greatest significance. Even by the high standards of the direct, week-by-week tutorial teaching of students that is the hallmark of traditional British university education, his concern for students went far beyond the usual.

There was another, more local, interest at Durham. In the great Norman cathedral spanning the peninsula high above the curving River Wear, were the tombs of the two figures most influential in the Christianity of the North of England, the Venerable Bede (in the Galilee Chapel at the west) and St Cuthbert (behind the high altar at the east). Those unfamiliar with the Celtic form of Christianity which had arrived in the north from Scotland and Ireland may find it difficult to imagine the palpable effect of these two, Cuthbert and Bede, on the 1,000 years of Christian faith and life concentrated in Durham.

When Gerald Bonner came to Durham in 1964, early Northumbrian history was taught only by the indefatigable archaeologist Rosemary Cramp, whose excavations at Wearmouth and Jarrow proved so fruitful. The literary aspect of Northumbrian Christian culture was relatively neglected, however. This led Bonner to try to emulate the tradition of the great Durham scholar, Bertram Colgrave, by examining the spirituality of Cuthbert, Bede and other contemporaries, long before Celtic Christianity had become as popular as it is today. The first evidence of this study was in his 1966 Jarrow Lecture, *St Bede in the Tradition of Western Apocalyptic Commentary*. This was a theme considered unusual at the time, when historical interest dominated Bedan studies, but which has become commonplace thirty years later. It was followed by other essays on Bede's conception of the Christian life, on his place in medieval civilisation, on Anglo-Saxon culture and spirituality and on St Cuthbert's spirituality. He also organised an important conference on Bede in 1973, wrote a catalogue for the 1974 Sunderland Exhibition on Bede, edited a book of commemorative essays for the thirteenth centenary of Bede in 1976, and co-edited a book of essays on St Cuthbert in 1989. Happily today, the Colgrave tradition has now blossomed afresh in Durham through the work of Professor David Rollason.

In 1967, Gerald Bonner married Jane Hodgson, a philologist educated at Bedford College, London. She was a specialist in Early and Middle High German and Gothic Literature, and had been a lecturer at Sheffield University before they married. Throughout their life together, she was content to remain in the background, offering him ungrudging help and encouragement in his work. Her own expertise was often helpful, for example, in comprehending the complicated patterns of speech in theological German, a *Sondersprache* not always intelligible to a self-taught reader. One of her most appreciated contributions was in administering the Bedan Conference held at Durham in 1973, which proved such a notable success. The Bonners have two children, Jeremy and Damaris, born in 1970 and 1976.

Despite his attention to Bede and Cuthbert, Gerald Bonner's primary concern was with Augustine. During his twenty-five years in Durham, he published a great many articles on a wide variety of topics associated with Augustine: his view of the fall and original sin, Pelagius and Pelagianism, his biblical understanding, his Christian humanism, his spirituality as such and its influence on western mysticism, his anti-Donatism, his view of history and society, of church and society, of the eucharist and the Church as

8

eucharistic community, of deification, of man in the image of God and as sinner, of the desire for God and the need for grace, of Christ, of Eve, of women and *amicitia*, of millennarianism, of this world and the hope for the next, etc. These led to a steady stream of requests to write substantial contributions on such topics for various dictionaries, encyclopaedias, and lexicons. In 1987, the first of two collections of Gerald Bonner's essays appeared: *God's Decree and Man's Destiny. Studies on the Thought of Augustine of Hippo*, followed in 1996 by *Church and Faith in the Patristic Tradition. Augustine, Pelagianism, and Early Christian Northumbria.*

Gerald Bonner's writing has special qualities. His deep knowledge of Augustine and the Patristic era, and Cuthbert, Bede and their context allows him to raise probing questions about the easy conclusions reached in current scholarship. Claims tracing modern problems to the heritage of Augustine are rebuffed by close analysis of his thought, and overly simple generalisations about Augustine's religious views are tested and refined. It becomes clear, for example, that Augustine's writings were often corrective to problematic views found in his time. Above all, Bonner can identify and pursue the deep tendencies of Augustine's thought which are so frequently overlooked or misinterpreted, especially his views on the nature of human beings before God. What is particularly significant about Bonner's scholarship is its sensitivity to the religious depth of Augustine and the northern saints, a quality frequently absent from purely historical accounts. His analysis does not soften the demands of Augustine's Christianity, those derived from his certainty of God's absolute power, goodness and justice. Instead, it shows Augustine's position with stunning clarity. These qualities constitute the enduring value of Bonner's writings.

It was not long after his arrival in Durham and the opportunities for research that it brought, before Gerald Bonner's work on Augustine was becoming more widely known. Indeed, the quality of his scholarship was always appreciated more fully among Augustine specialists than at home. In 1970, he was invited to deliver the annual St Augustine Lecture at Villanova University, a prominent university of the Augustinian Order near Philadelphia. He came there through the good offices of Robert P. Russell OSA, whose generosity and friendship he came to value deeply. Russell later introduced to him George Lawless OSA, one of the editors of the present volume, whose research Bonner supervised for a year. Lawless became a lifelong friend.

The value that Durham University attached to Gerald Bonner was evident in his promotion to the position of Reader, a rank reserved for those whose scholarship is considered to be of the highest standard. However, he was guileless, and neither proud nor aloof. Those who knew him at first hand also recognized the extraordinary kindness and generosity that marked his relations with students and fellow academics. With undergraduate students, he took infinite trouble over their essays, writing extensive comment to help

9

them improve. With postgraduates, he combined great care with infectious enthusiasm. Those who met him at conferences often found their way to him later, leaving only after hours – even days – of intensive discussion, help with source-material, etc. He has always been incapable of denying those who come to him. His personal and academic generosity is unlimited.

For a man so generous and so dedicated to research and teaching, life in an English university had become much more difficult by the late 1980s. Hitherto, universities had been funded through a university grant system that protected them from political policies. But now, university grants became an instrument of governmental policy, which came to measure the success of universities by the 'value added' to students, especially in preparing them to meet the needs of a modern industrial society. Universities existed in a climate of financial stringency and constant pressure to improve 'efficiency'. A variety of managerial strategies were imposed; increasingly frequent 'research assessment exercises' to grade university departments on the quantity of their published research, regular staff appraisal, and so on. Day-to-day pressure increased substantially where departments (for such the Faculty of Theology at Durham had become) were already hard-pressed by research and the teaching responsibilities associated with tutorial supervision. By contrast, Gerald Bonner was a gentle and dedicated man who did not respond well to the tensions this brought. With this increasing pressure, he wisely took early retirement in 1989, especially while there was the prospect of a replacement to continue the study of Augustine at Durham.

It was never his intention to retire into inactivity, however. The pace of his scholarship and publications continued, and through the kindness of an old friend and fellow Augustinian, Robert Markus, he was introduced to Sidney Griffith, Chairman of the Early Christian Studies Programme at the Catholic University of America in Washington, D.C. This led to an invitation to teach there, and he subsequently spent three years teaching courses on Augustine, Bede and the Desert Fathers. Between 1992 and 1994, he was joined by Jane and their family. Jeremy remained at the university after the others had returned to England, in order to complete a doctoral dissertation on modern American political history.

Those were good years. Bonner found the Catholic University most congenial. His subject was taken seriously. There were good colleagues, good students and a general atmosphere of friendliness. Furthermore, his scholarship was admired. At his departure, the University presented him with an award named for a most distinguished patristic scholar, the Johannes Quasten Prize for excellence and leadership. It was a signal honour, richly deserved by one who throughout his life had selflessly dedicated himself to Augustinian scholarship.

Invitations to write and teach continue. Since his return to England in 1994, however, Bonner's primary concern has been the study of the Pelagian Controversy. It is work he hopes will be the achievement of his final years.

2

GERALD BONNER
A select bibliography

Daniel W. Hardy

1960

1 'St Augustine's Doctrine of the Holy Spirit', *Sobornost* 4:2, pp. 51–66.

1962

2 '*Libido* and *Concuspiscentia* in St Augustine', in *Studia Patristica*, vol. 6, ed. F. L. Cross = *Texte und Untersuchungen zur Geschichte der altchristlichen Literatur*, vol. 81, Berlin, Akademie-Verlag, pp. 303–14.

1963

3 *St Augustine of Hippo. Life and Controversies*, London, SCM Press.

1966

4 'How Pelagian was Pelagius? An Examination of the Contentions of Torgny Bohlin', in *Studia Patristica*, vol. 9, ed. F. L. Cross = *Texte und Untersuchungen zur Geschichte der altchristlichen Literatur*, vol. 94, Berlin, Akademie-Verlag, pp. 350–8.

1967

5 *St Bede in the Tradition of Western Apocalyptic Commentary*, Jarrow Lecture for 1966, Newcastle, J. and P. Bealls.

6 'Les origines africaines de la doctrine augustinienne sur la chute et le péché originel', *Augustinus* 12, pp. 97–116.

1968

7 'Augustine on Romans 5:12', *Studia Evangelica*, vol. 5 = *Texte und*

Untersuchungen zur Geschichte der altchristlichen Literatur, vol. 103, Berlin, Akademie-Verlag, pp. 242–7.

1970

8 'The Christian Life in the Thought of the Venerable Bede', *Durham University Journal* 63 (= new series 32), pp. 39–55.

9 'Rufinus of Syria and African Pelagianism', *Augustinian Studies* 1, pp. 31–47.

1971

10 '*Quid imperatori cum ecclesia*? St Augustine on History and Society', *Augustinian Studies* 2, pp. 231–51 = review article of R. Markus, *Saeculum. History and Society in the Theology of St Augustine*, Cambridge, Cambridge University Press.

1972

11 *Augustine and Modern Research on Pelagianism*, The Saint Augustine Lecture for 1970, Villanova, Pa., Villanova University Press.

1973

12 'Bede and Medieval Civilization', *Anglo-Saxon England* 2, pp. 71–90.

13 'Anglo-Saxon Culture and Spirituality', *Sobornost* 6:8, pp. 533–50.

14 'Christianity and the Modern World-View', *Eastern Churches Review* 5, pp. 1–15.

1976

15 *Famulus Christi. Essays in Commemoration of the Thirteenth Centenary of the Venerable Bede*, ed. Gerald Bonner, London, SPCK.

1977

16 '*Vera lux illa est quae illuminat*. The Christian Humanism of Augustine', in *Renaissance and Renewal in Christian History*, ed. D. Baker, Oxford, Blackwell, pp. 1–22.

1978

17 'The Church and the Eucharist in the Theology of St Augustine', *Sobornost*, 7:6, pp. 448–61.

1979

18 '"The Holy Spirit Within": St Cuthbert as a Western Orthodox Saint', *Sobornost*, new series, 1:1, pp. 7–22.

1982

19 'The Spirituality of St Augustine and its Influence on Western Mysticism', *Sobornost*, new series, 4:2, pp. 143–62.

1983

20 'Some remarks on Letters 4* and 5*', in *Les lettres de saint Augustin découvertes par Johannes Divjak*. Communications présentées au colloque des 20 et 21 septembre 1982, Paris, Etudes augustiniennes, pp. 155–64.

21 'Martyrdom: its place in the Church', *Sobornost*, new series, 5:2, pp. 6–21.

1984

22 'Augustine's Doctrine of Man: Image of God and Sinner', *Augustinianum* 24, pp. 495–514.

23 'Christ, God and Man, in the Thought of St Augustine', *Angelicum* 61, pp. 268–94.

24 'The Extinction of Paganism and the Church Historian', *Journal of Ecclesiastical History* 35, pp. 339–57.

1985

25 'Abortion and Early Christian Thought', in *Abortion and the Sanctity of Human Life*, ed. J. H. Channer, Exeter, Paternoster Press, pp. 93–122.

1986

26 *St Augustine of Hippo. Life and Controversies*, 2nd edn, Norwich, Canterbury Press.
27 'Adam', in *Augustinus-Lexikon*, vol. 1, ed. C. Mayer, Basel, Schwabe, cc. 63–87.

28 'Augustine's Conception of Deification', *Journal of Theological Studies*, new series, 37, pp. 369–86.

29 'Bede and his Legacy', *Durham University Journal* 78 (new series 47), pp. 219–30.

1987

30 *God's Decree and Man's Destiny. Studies on the Thought of Augustine of Hippo*, Collected Papers, vol. 1, London, Variorum Reprints.

31 'St Cuthbert – Soul Friend', in *Cuthbert: Saint and Patron*, ed. D. W. Rollason, Durham, Dean and Chapter of Durham, pp. 23–42.

32 'Augustine's Attitude to Women and *Amicitia*', in *Homo Spiritalis. Festgabe für Luc Verheijen, OSA zu seinem 70. Geburtstag*, ed. C. Mayer, Würzburg, Augustinus-Verlag, pp. 259–75.

33 'The Desire for God and the Need for Grace in Augustine's Theology', in *Atti del Congresso Internazionale su S. Agostino nel XVI centenario della conversione, Roma, 15–20 settembre 1986*, vol. 1, Rome, Institutum Patristicum «Augustinianum», pp. 203–15.

34 'The Universal Way: St Augustine's Sprituality', *Milltown Studies* 19/20, pp. 7–23.

1988

35 'Augustine: Spiritual Guide', *Augustinian Heritage* 84, pp. 181–201.

36 'Augustine's Doctrine of Man', *Louvain Studies* 13, pp. 41–57.

1989

37 'Augustine and Millenarianism', in *The Making of Orthodoxy. Essays in Honour of Henry Chadwick*, ed. R. Williams, Oxford, Clarendon Press, pp. 235–54.

38 '*Christus Sacerdos*. The Roots of Augustine's Anti-Donatist Polemic', in *Signum Pietatis. Festgabe für C. P. Mayer OSA zum 60. Geburtstag*, ed. A. Zumkeller, Würzburg, Augustinus-Verlag, pp. 325–39.

39 *St Cuthbert. His Cult and Community to AD 1200*, ed. G. Bonner, D. Rollason, and C. Stancliffe, Woodbridge, Boydell Press.

1990

40 'Augustinus: Vita', in *Augustinus-Lexikon*, vol. 1, ed. C. Mayer, Basel, Schwabe, cc. 519–50.

41 'Baptismus paruulorum', in *Augustinus-Lexikon*, vol. 1, ed. C. Mayer, Basel, Schwabe, cc. 592–602.

1991

42 'Schism and Church Unity', in *Early Christianity. Origins and Evolution to AD 600. In Honour of W. H. C. Frend*, ed. I. Hazlett, London, SPCK.

43 'The Doctrine of Sacrifice: Augustine and the Latin Patristic Tradition', in *Sacrifice and Redemption*, Durham Essays in Theology, ed. S. Sykes, Cambridge, Cambridge University Press, pp. 101–17.

44 'The Significance of Augustine's *De Gratia Novi Testamenti*', in *Collectanea Augustiniana. Mélanges T. J. van Bavel*, ed. B. Bruning, M. Lamberigts and J. Van Houtem, vol. 1, Leuven: Augustinian Historical Institute (= *Augustiniana* 40:1–4), pp. 531–59.

1992

45 'Pelagianism and Augustine', *Augustinian Studies* 23, pp. 33–51.

1993

46 'Caelestius', in *Augustinus-Lexikon*, vol. 1, ed. C. Mayer, Basel, Schwabe, cc. 693–4.

47 'Augustine's "Conversion": Historical Fact or Literary Device?', in *Charisteria Augustiniana Iosepho Oroz Reta dicata*, ed. P. Merino and J. M. Torrecilla, vol. 1, Madrid (= *Augustinus* 38), pp. 103–19.

48 'Augustine and Pelagianism', *Augustinian Studies* 24, pp. 27–47.

49 'Pelagianism Reconsidered', *Studia Patristica*, vol. 27, ed. E. Livingstone, Leuven, Peeters, pp. 237–41.

1994

50 'Augustine and Mysticism', in *Collectanea Augustiniana. Augustine: Mystic and Mystagogue*, ed. F. van Fleteren, J. Schnaubelt and J. Reino, New York, Peter Lang, pp. 113–57.

51 'Augustine's Thoughts on this World and Hope for the Next', *Princeton Seminary Bulletin*, Supplementary issue no. 3, pp. 85–103.

52 'Concupiscentia', in *Augustinus-Lexikon*, vol. 1, ed. C. Mayer, Basel, Schwabe, cc. 1113–22.

53 'Religion in Anglo-Saxon England', in *A History of Religion in Britain from Pre-Roman Times to the Present*, ed. S. Gilley and W. J. Shiels, Oxford, Blackwell, 1994, pp. 24–44.

54 'Augustine's Understanding of the Church as a Eucharistic Community', in *St Augustine the Bishop, A Book of Essays*, ed. F. LeMoine and C. Kleinhenz, New York / London, Garland, pp. 39–63.

1996

55 *Church and Faith in the Patristic Tradition. Augustine, Pelagianism, and Early Christian Northumbria*, Collected Papers, Aldershot, Variorum Reprints.

56 'Pelagius/Pelagianischer Streit', in *Theologische Realenzyklopädie*, vol. 26, ed. G. Müller, Paris/Berlin/New York, Walter De Gruyter, cc. 176–85.

57 'Petrus Chrysologus', in *Theologische Realenzyklopädie*, vol. 26, ed. G. Müller Paris / Berlin / New York, Walter De Gruyter, cc 290–1.

1997

58 'Bede – Priest and Scholar', *Milltown Studies* 39, pp. 66–77.

59 'The Figure of Eve in Augustine's Theology', in *Studia Patristica*, vol. 33, ed. E. Livingstone, Leuven, Peeters, pp. 22–34.

60 'Columba of Iona and Augustine of Canterbury', *Sobornost*, new series 19:2, pp. 30–43.

1998

61 'Cupiditas', in *Augustinus-Lexikon*, vol. 1, ed. C. Mayer, Basel, Schwabe, cc. 166–72.

62 'Deificare', in *Augustinus-Lexikon*, vol. 1, ed. C. Mayer, Basel, Schwabe, cc. 265–7.

To appear:

63 'Dic Christi Veritas Ubi Nunc Habitas: Ideas of Schism and Heresy in the Post-Nicene Age', in *The Limits of Ancient Christianity: Essay on Late Antique Thought and Culture in Honor of R. A. Markus*, ed. W. E. Klingshirn and M. Vessey, Ann Arbor, University of Michigan Press.

Many of the above-listed articles have been re-published in two volumes of Gerald Bonner's collected essays, published by Variorum Reprints:

God's Decree and Man's Destiny (1987): Items number 1, 2, 6, 9, 10, 11, 16, 17, 19, 20, 22, 23.

Church and Faith in the Patristic Tradition (1996): Items number 5, 8, 12, 13, 14, 24, 29, 31, 42, 43, 44, 45, 48, 49.

3

STUDYING AUGUSTINE

An overview of recent research

Hubertus R. Drobner

For many centuries, from the Middle Ages to the present, Augustine has remained the most prominent and most widely studied author in western Christianity, second only to biblical writers such as Paul. The roots of this extraordinary phenomenon go back to Augustine's own lifetime, and are in part due to the fact that he did not produce the most immense literary corpus of all western Christianity for solely 'academic' purposes. Already, a good number of his contemporaries considered him to be both the most accomplished theologian and the most trustworthy pastor of their times. The copious number of letters and numerous treatises which Augustine composed on request by enquirers all over the Roman empire bears witness to the high esteem in which his word was held. His works stood in great demand; his sermons were usually recorded by stenographers (*notarii*) and passed on to other bishops. In one famous case, a number of his friends grew impatient with him when, after fourteen years of toiling on twelve books of *De trinitate*, he did not as yet consider his manuscript complete and worth publishing. These 'friends' stole his unfinished manuscript, and copied and distributed it without his knowledge or consent. Only with the greatest difficulty was Augustine then persuaded to complete the enormous task over a period of eight further years. A truly international market existed for Augustine's writings, one that eagerly awaited each new publication of his and sold them as far away as Italy, Spain and Gaul, thus initiating the different strands of transmission of his works.

This appreciation of Augustine's person and work has continued unabated for the last 1600 years. When in around 1450, Gutenberg invented the art of printing, he edited first of all the Bible. But here, too, Augustine yielded the first place only to Scripture. The first patristic work ever printed (Mainz, 1462) was *De vita christiana*, thought at the time to have been written by Augustine, followed by an excerpt of *De doctrina christiana* a year later. Only then did Cicero's *De officiis* and *De oratore* and the works of Lactantius, 'the Christian Cicero', appear in print. After that, it was again the turn of one of

Augustine's most famous and influential works, the *City of God* (Subiaco, 1467). The first complete edition of the works of Augustine was published at Basel in 1506.[1] Five hundred years later, the most recent and comprehensive bibliography on Augustine contains the titles of some 20,000 of a total of about 50,000 estimated publications worldwide, and the annual bibliography published in the *Revue des études Augustiniennes* adds some three to five hundred items to this number each year.[2] The research centre *Cetedoc* in Leuven, Belgium, and the *Augustinus-Lexikon* in Würzburg, Germany, have both prepared CD-ROMs containing the complete works of Augustine, the former including an *Index of Latin Forms*, the latter the most comprehensive Augustinian bibliography.

The fascination Augustine has been exerting over so many people for centuries is best explained by his two most famous books, *Confessions* and *City of God*, both of which belong to the world's heritage of the greatest works in the history of literature, known far beyond the circles of theologians, historians and other scholars. As Augustine himself explains, *Confessions* does not refer only to his sins, but is at the same time a book of praise of God's great goodness, thus applying both meanings of the Latin word *confessio*, 'confession' and 'praise' (*retr.* 2.6). Augustine matured into a powerful, self-conscious writer who united naturally given quick intelligence, sharp analytical capacities, extraordinary comprehension and ingenious thinking with a practical personality formed by many deeply felt and reflected experiences of his own, leading to a profound knowledge of the heart and an unsurpassed understanding of the timeless principles of this world rooted in God.

Confessions and *City of God* are, therefore, by no means only accidentally the most studied of all the numerous works of Augustine, comprising some 15 per cent of all publications concerning Augustine. In second place, but trailing by a long distance, follow the *Sermons* and the *Letters*, adding another 7 per cent between them. Following next are *De trinitate*, *De doctrina christiana*, and his biblical commentaries on John and the Psalms, together sharing a further 8 per cent of scholarly literature devoted to Augustine. This statistic reveals a fundamental feature of all Augustinian scholarship: it is by no means evenly distributed. Those eight treatises have been edited, translated and studied many times over, while some of the remaining 109 works of Augustine have largely been neglected. The *Quaestiones euangeliorum* are the least studied, with only four entries in the bibliography.[3]

Of course, one is entitled to ask if this selection is not wholly justified. If two handfuls of rightly famous works correctly and fully represent the thoughts of Augustine, why bother with the remainder? It is exactly this question, however, that in recent times has raised serious doubts. Scholars are also discovering that Augustine's doctrinal, and, especially, his polemical treatises represent only a partial view of his entire theology, given the fact that in them he sought to defend the true faith in what amounts at times to extreme terms. Yet in his pastoral writings and, in particular, in his sermons to the faithful, he avoided the relentless polemic witnessed so often in his doctrinal treatises. As a result, his explanations of doctrinal matters in the sermons and other, lesser-known works offer new, more balanced formulations for many of his theological positions. Scholars are only now beginning to tap these works, but are doing so at great profit. What follows is a brief *aperçu* of current research trends in Augustinian thought.[4]

Confessions

It is understandable that the 1,600[th] anniversaries of Augustine's conversion and baptism in 1986/87 witnessed a particularly large number of studies on the *Confessions*, a number which then fell off during the years following the anniversaries to its usual, though consistently remarkable, level. The *Confessions* have preserved their central place of interest in Augustinian research because they provide such an extraordinary insight into Augustine's personality, his early life and interior development, thereby seemingly revealing even his psychological condition. However it is at this point that scholarly discussion begins.[5] Are the *Confessions* really to be regarded as an autobiography and, if so, what does one say about Books 10–13 which are certainly not autobiographical at all, but, rather, philosophical and theological? If Augustine wishes merely to 'confess', that is, to recall his search for God and the errors he committed on the way to his final conversion, why does he add Book 9 which recounts his sojourn at Cassiciacum, his baptism in Milan, and the life and death of his mother Monica? On the other hand, if the *Confessions* are not to be understood as an account of his personal history, how should we judge the reliability of the facts given therein? Take, for example, the 'garden scene' of Augustine's conversion (*conf.* 8.12.29). Are accounts such as this to be taken literally or symbolically? These deliberations bear directly on the structure of the *Confessions*. What is the main topic of them and what are merely 'digressions' and 'appendices'? Does the book represent a unity at all or does it disintegrate in two or three sections that could just as easily have been published separately? Is Augustine's life the unifying theme, or is it God, or is the whole of the narrative constituted by a dialogue between Augustine and God? Or must the whole rather be understood in the light of the Trinity?

One will rightly think that there are many questions and deplorably few answers, but this characterises exactly the basic situation of the studies on the *Confessions*: 'boundless research' has been done (Herzog 1984: 215), but 'little consensus reached' (Feldmann 1989: 28). The answer to this apparent paradox seems to be that such a profound work of a genius like Augustine will never be completely exhausted and will never invite a simple and unified answer. Each generation will see it on the basis of its own premises and therefore read it differently. A splendid example for this perspective is the epoch-making study of the *Confessions* by Pierre Courcelle, who understood

Augustine's conversion process in the intellectual light of his reading of both Cicero's *Hortensius* and Neoplatonic philosophy. In more recent years, scholars have tended to view Augustine's religious and cultural experiences as constituting the decisive driving forces behind his conversion.[6] Attention over the last decade has focused especially on his early works, those written before he became a priest in AD 390/91, as contributing to our knowledge of the young Augustine, his thought and development.

Apart from the personal data about Augustine reported by the *Confessions*, Book 11 has always attracted special attention as a treatise on the fundamental human questions, 'What is time, and how does it relate to the eternity of God?', or, in other words, 'What relationship do God's temporal creation and the human race which is a part of it have to their eternal creator?'. The most important new results in interpreting Book 11 culminate in the recognition that it 'is not primarily, a systematic treatise on the much discussed topics "creation, eternity, and time" (that it is only in second place). Primarily it is the attempt to understand more clearly the human and the divine way of being'.[7]

City of God

It is Augustine's own description which best introduces the other of his great works that keeps attracting no less attention than the *Confessions*: the *City of God*, written in the aftermath of the first ever sack of Rome, carried out by the Visigoths under Alaric on 24 August AD 410:

> The first five books refute those who want human affairs to prosper, who believe that the veneration of the numerous gods whom the pagans used to worship is indispensable for this end, and who argue that the present evils are caused and abound chiefly because this cult is forbidden. The following five books speak out against those who declare that the life of mortals has never been and will never be free of those evils, sometimes great and sometimes small, varying from time to time, from place to place, and from person to person, while they dispute the usefulness of the veneration of numerous gods for the future life after death by offering sacrifice to them. These ten books refute therefore those two opinions contradicting Christian religion. Lest, however, someone reproaches us that we only refute the opinions of others without asserting our own, the second part of this work does so, comprising twelve books, though in the first ten books we also assert our own opinion where it is necessary, and refute the opposing arguments in the latter twelve. The first four of the following twelve books contain the origin of the two cities, one being God's and the other one of this world; the next four treat

their growth or development, and the third and last set of four describe their aims.

(retr. 2.43)

Thus, the first part of this work constitutes an attack on the traditional connection between the welfare of the Roman empire and its veneration of the traditional gods, while the second half presents an extended exposition of a Christian theology of history. For these reasons, the *City of God* has been studied over centuries chiefly for its political, social and historical theology. More recent studies have returned to the question of the structure of the *City of God* in an effort to understand its relationship to the development of Augustine's concept of 'history'.[8] Fascinated with Augustine's attempt to respond to and complete Varro's account of a tripartite theology (*theologia tripartita*: natural, ethical, civil), Basil Studer examines Augustine's Porphyrian-inspired application of historical studies (*cognitio historialis*) to the Scriptures with the aim of deepening the significance of 'sacred history' (*historia sacra*).[9] Equally concerned with the structure of Augustine's text, Johannes van Oort has undertaken a comprehensive analysis of the sources of the *City of God* in Jewish–Christian apocalyptic literature and thought.[10] In his synthesis of the place and meaning of history in the *City of God*, Gaetano Lettieri considers Augustine's 'theology of history' to be more suitably conceived as an 'ecclesiology of history' or, better, a 'christology of history'.[11] This view seems to support the observations made later in this essay that christology appears to be not only the centre of Augustine's thought, but, intrinsically, its method.

New discoveries

Twice during the last two decades, Augustinian scholarship was roused by spectacular discoveries of authentic writings of Augustine hitherto lost. In 1981, Johannes Divjak added twenty-nine new letters to the 270 known so far, twenty-six of them from the pen of Augustine, two addressed to him, and one by Jerome. In 1990, François Dolbeau, searching for pseudo-Augustinian writings in a newly published catalogue of the municipal library in Mainz, came across twenty-six new sermons ascribed to Augustine. The reading of the texts, however, raised serious doubts about their authenticity. Dolbeau succeeded in proving their Augustinian authorship by recourse to the *Indiculum* of Augustine's works compiled by his friend and first biographer, Possidius.[13] Since then, Dolbeau has continued to search for new sermons, and has found three more, together with a new fragment, while remaining confident that, with the help of modern computerised data banks, further discoveries are to be expected.[14]

The chances for further discoveries should, in fact, be excellent, given that, from the time of the Maurist edition of Augustine's sermons, the complete texts of 184 new sermons and nine fragments have been discovered. At present, 559 Augustinian sermons are recognized as authentic. However, in view of the fact that in nearly forty years of ministry as priest and bishop Augustine preached every Saturday and Sunday (and every day during the Lenten and Easter seasons), as well as on the feast of saints, and on some days even twice, he must have preached far beyond 4,000 sermons, and presumably many more than 559 of them were recorded and published.[15]

Letters

Divjak's discovery triggered renewed scholarly interest in the comparatively little-studied corpus of Augustine's letters, particularly in his correspondence with his great contemporary Jerome, who had retired from the bustle of Rome to a contemplative life in Bethlehem, where he translated the Bible into Latin.[16] In the end, a correspondence between Augustine and Jerome resulted in a total of nineteen letters.

The two main topics of this correspondence are the canon of the Old Testament, and the dispute between Peter and Paul in Antioch over the question whether Christians converted from the gentiles should be obligated to observe Jewish law (Gal 2: 11–14). This latter issue had troubled the Fathers for a long time, and two basically different interpretations developed in the East and West. Jerome followed the eastern tradition in assuming that Peter and Paul only feigned a quarrel for the sake of the argument in order to convince both parties. The western tradition, on the other hand, did not whitewash the reality of the disagreement between them, but, rather, took it as a good example of how to resolve problems in the church. According to this tradition, the exemplary humility which Peter showed, having been rightly reproached for his error, did not impair his supreme authority but enhanced it, as witnessed also by the fact that Paul never doubted it. To Augustine, the idea that the apostles would engage in dissimulation was much more abhorrent than the conclusion that they might not have completely agreed on occasion. The practical application which Augustine made of both the argument between Peter and Paul and of resolution is shown in one of his sermons, recently discovered in Mainz, where he treats the matter at length as a shining example of the relationship between the bishop and his flock.[17]

Bible and exegesis

Having received a first-class literary education and, as he himself records, already excelling in the art of rhetoric at school (*conf.* 1.17.27), the reading of Cicero's *Hortensius* at the age of eighteen initiated Augustine's search for the 'true philosophy' (*conf.* 3.4.7). Monica's influence over the religious formation of her son at an early age may have later led him to the Scriptures in order to seek Christ. The Bible, however, repelled him at first because of a 'crudeness of style' that made it 'not worthy to be compared to the high standards of Cicero' (*conf.* 3.5.9), but also because of the often barbaric stories of the Old Testament that seemed to reveal the God of these books as, likewise, uncultivated. Manichaeism thus persuaded him at that stage of his life because it explained away the Old Testament as not belonging to the Father of Jesus Christ, but to a different, evil demiurge (*conf.* 3.6.10–11). Only much later did Augustine recognise logical inconsistencies in the Manichaean system, but even then the Scriptures did not disclose themselves to him immediately. Eleven years later (AD 384), the homilies of the bishop of Milan, Ambrose, and the instructions of one of his priests, Simplicianus, eventually opened him to an acceptable understanding of the Scriptures, thereby leading him to a spiritual interpretation of them in the light of Platonic philosophy (*conf.* 5.14.24). His reading of St Paul completed his conversion in the famous garden scene: 'Let us live decently as people do in the daytime: no drunken orgies, no promiscuity or licentiousness, and no wrangling or jealousy. Let your armour be the Lord Jesus Christ; forget about satisfying your bodies with all their cravings' (Rom 13:13–14; see *conf.* 8.8.19). When Augustine became a priest early in AD 391, he first of all requested a leave of absence to prepare his ministry by studying the Scriptures (*ep.* 21.1–3).

By this time, Jerome had already begun the Latin translation of the Bible that was to become the *Vulgata*, the popular, standard edition in the West. Jerome, however, only completed his translation around AD 404/5, and it took still much more time to be generally distributed and accepted throughout the western church. Augustine, as we know from his *ep.* 28 addressed to Jerome, received a first draft of a part of Jerome's translation of the Old Testament three years after his ordination as priest in 394/5. Augustine thus usually read one of those 'Old Latin' translations which the *Vetus-Latina-Institut* in Beuron, Germany, after the pioneering work of Petrus Sabatier (1743), has been reconstructing since 1951.

Anne-Marie La Bonnardière earned herself unfading merits in studying Augustine's biblical text and usage in the seven fascicles of her *Biblia Augustiniana*: from the Old Testament, Deuteronomy, the historical books, Proverbs, Wisdom, Jeremiah, and the twelve minor prophets; from the New Testament, 1–2 Thessalonians, Titus, and Philemon.[18] Much remains to do in order to complete these analyses, but, above all, one has to cope with a basic problem. As with all Fathers of the Church, Augustine knew and quoted most of the Bible by heart; he never read a sermon from a prepared manuscript. There are many instances where he quotes the same phrase several times and always a little differently, not changing the meaning but only the word order, or where he adds synonyms to suit his rhetoric or symbolism. It is probably impossible to establish the definitive 'Augustinian Bible text', but a complete list of his biblical quotations and their different forms would aid immensely those seeking to understand his theology, because his texts – as with those of virtually all the Fathers of the Church –

are impregnated with biblical vocabulary, allusions and images that are often recognisable only if one knows precisely with which words he quoted different biblical phrases.

De doctrina christiana

Augustine's most prominent work on exegetical method are his four books on Christian doctrine, comprising the fundamentals of biblical hermeneutics. When Augustine composed his *Retractationes* in AD 426/27, he came across the unfinished and unpublished *De doctrina christiana* (begun in 397 and completed only to Book 3.25.35), and decided to complete it before continuing with the *Retractationes*, a decision resulting in a division within the former work into two parts written with an interval of nearly thirty years (*retr.* 2.4.1).

Recent research into *De doctrina christiana* has focused upon three primary themes:

- Augustine's theory relating the acts of 'enjoying' (*frui*) and 'using' (*uti*) objects surrounding us
- his theory of signs (*signa*), and
- his critique of the rules of Tyconius.

1   The theory of 'enjoying' (*frui*) and 'using' (*uti*) corresponds to the fundamental question of difference between creator and creation.[19] Earlier in this century, Augustine's position was taken to suggest that the triune God, being the sole eternal good, was, therefore, the only reality (*res*) which creation might justly enjoy. According to this reading, all created goods, including persons, serve as instruments in an 'enjoyment' reserved exclusively to God. A number of recent studies have daringly sought to develop the hermeneutical contexts of Augustine's remarks.[20]

2   In his theory of signs (*signa*), Augustine fundamentally distinguishes between the existence of things-in-themselves (*res*) and the function of signs (*signa*) which refer to another reality beyond themselves, as, for example, smoke is usually understood as a sign of fire.[21] Natural signs, being part of creation, automatically always point to their creator by their very nature. God, however, also wanted to reveal himself by intentionally set signs, in word and in sacrament. Recent studies of Augustine's understanding of signs in *De doctrina christiana* have attempted to delineate his theory more completely and to demonstrate more precisely his view of its role in scriptural interpretation.[22]

3   Book 3 (30.42–37.56) treats the exegetical rules which a Donatist theologian turned dissident, Tyconius (c. AD 330–90), presented in his 'Book of Rules' (*Liber regularum*). While reproaching Tyconius personally

for not having completely severed his links with the Donatist sect, and criticising his rules for not achieving their author's claim that they would resolve nearly all the problems in the biblical texts, Augustine nevertheless explains the rules at length and applies them in his comprehensive *Enarrationes in Psalmos*. Scholars have recently turned their attention to Augustine's appropriation of Tyconius's rules both in an effort to detail more completely his appropriation of the rules and to gain further insight into the overall structure of Augustine's scriptural hermeneutics.[23]

Expositions on the Psalms

'[Christ] prays for us being our priest, he prays in us being our head, and we pray to him being our God . . . we therefore pray to him, through him, and in him' (*en. Ps.* 85.1). These well-known words of Augustine comprise both the intention and the method of the first complete commentary on the Psalms ever compiled in Christianity. The two most recent, comprehensive studies of the *Enarrationes* reflect its christocentric intention and method.[24]

Although King David's Psalms were the daily prayer of the church, for a Christian they made sense only in a christological perspective, as, indeed, the entire Old Testament was and is understood by the church, in part, as preparation and prophecy of Christ's incarnation and saving work. In understanding Augustine's approach to the Psalms, however, we have a task far more complicated than that of interpreting an Old Testament prophet as he speaks about Christ. Augustine applies a particular exegetical method which he learned at school, one that had played a major role in the interpretation of Homer's songs. In order to disclose the deeper meaning of a statement that might be plainly unfitting (*ineptum*) if ascribed to its grammatical subject, the exegete asks, 'Who is actually speaking in this verse?', 'Whom does this particular utterance fit (*aptum*)?'. If this question is applied to the verses of the Psalms, the answer nearly always is Christ, especially in view of the tradition that Christ, while hanging on cross, prayed in the words of Psalm 21:1 'My God, my God, why have you forsaken me?'. It is this tradition that Augustine generalises in order to arrive at the exegetical principle, 'when a prophet speaks in his own person (*ex persona sua*), the Lord himself speaks through him, dictating to him the truth he speaks' (*en. Ps.* 56.13). Following, however, Tyconius' first rule 'concerning the Lord and his body' (*de domino et corpore eius*), Christ has always to be understood in an ecclesial sense as the 'complete Christ' (*Christus totus*), head and body of the church. Thus, Augustine comments, 'You will rarely find phrases in the Psalms, that do not refer to Christ and the church, or to Christ alone, or to the church alone, of which we are members, too' (*en. Ps.* 59.1)

Always, or nearly always let us hear the voice of Christ from the Psalm in such a way that we do not only look upon that head, that is the one mediator between God and humanity, the man Jesus Christ (1 Tim 2:5) . . . but let us consider Christ as head and body, a human being totally complete.

(en. Ps. 58.1.2)

Applying this comprehensive christological–ecclesiological 'rule' to interpret the Psalms, Christ might speak as Son of God, thus as head of the church (*ex persona capitis*), or as a human being (*ex persona hominis/carnis*), or the entire human race (*ex persona generis humani*), or even as his body, the church (*ex persona corporis*). The determination of which of these alternatives applies in a specific case depends upon the context, that is, on which interpretation is the most fitting (*aptum*) given the context.

Hence the *Enarrationes in Psalmos* should be read as a book of christological prayer and studied under the perspective of both the exegetical techniques employed (Fiedrowicz 1997) and the prayerful life of Augustine and his community reflected by it (Vincent 1990).

Christology

Although Augustine's trinitarian theology was the subject matter of one of his major treatises and has always met with great interest, his christology was, in the past, mostly disregarded by scholars as largely traditional. This judgement owed a great deal to Adolf von Harnack's view that when Tertullian, in *Adversus Praxean* 27.11, first introduced the notion of 'person' to Christian theology he thus directly and inevitably shaped the formula of the 'hypostatic union' in the Calcedonian creed. Only after Harnack's authoritative opinion was much revised by scholars has Augustinian research investigated more deeply the specific christology of Augustine's works. In doing so, they have had to confront as a basic difficulty the fact that, in contrast with the Trinity, Augustine never devoted a single treatise to Christ.

One of the questions that arises for scholars as a result of this lack of a serious Augustinian christological treatise in an era when christological controversies, together with trinitarian disputes, clearly formed the centre of Christian theological discussion is whether the triune God, and not Christ, forms the core of Augustine's theology.[25] Passages of Augustine's writings in which he speaks directly and at some length about Christ are scattered through his *opus* without any particular, systematic treatment ever emerging. As a result, scholars tend to speak of Augustine's 'doctrine of Christ' primarily through a series of treatments of diverse motifs: 'Christ the physician' (*Christus medicus*), 'the Mediator' (*Christus mediator*), 'the example or model'

(*Christus exemplum*), 'the homeland and the way' (*Christus patria et via*), and so on. Yet reading the works of Augustine in their entirety, one notes that his discussions of Christ seem all too numerous and important to be in any way marginalised in the context of his overall intellectual vision. Almost paradoxically, in view of its attention to scattered christological themes, recent Augustinian research supports the centrality of the mystery of Christ over that of the Trinity in Augustine's thought as a whole. However, this answer begs a more important question: does the juxtaposition of the Trinity and Christ as alternative emphases in Augustine's thought arise as a consequence of our own preoccupation with a modern division of theology into different 'tracts', a theological method that may not be faithful to Augustinian or patristic ways of thinking in the first place? It is true that the Trinity forms an explicit subject of Augustine's theology while Christ does not. Yet, while after over twenty years of toiling on his tractate *De trinitate* Augustine concludes that 'we speak of three persons not in order to declare that, but rather lest we be silent' (*trin.* 5.9), he never has to say the same thing about Christ. Christ simply pervades all of Augustine's theology as a ubiquitous and familiar subject.

The key to understanding Augustine's approach to Christ may be found in a set of christological distinctions which the bishop of Hippo introduces explicitly. Speaking with reference to the Scriptures, he observes that

> our Lord Jesus Christ . . . is understood and called in three different ways . . . the first refers to his being God and to his divinity that is equal to and coeternal with the Father . . . the second is that the same Christ is both God and man . . . mediator and head of the Church . . . the third is the total Christ (*Christus totus*) in the fullness of the church, that is, head and body.
>
> (*s.* 341.2).

Thus, the Scriptures reveal Christ as the divine Logos, as the incarnate Son in Jesus of Nazareth, *and* as the church understood in its most spiritual form.

Goulven Madec is aware of these distinctions, but subordinates them under the general heading 'titles and functions of Christ', and then classes them with other names and metaphors for Christ such as: 'form of God – form of a slave', 'Jesus – Christ', 'physician', 'saviour', 'merchant', 'bread of the angels – milk of the infants'.[26] In the context of this discussion concerning the place of Christ in Augustine's thought, it is doubtful whether this fundamental threefold division ought to be reduced in importance to the titles attributed by Scripture to Christ. Recent studies support the conclusion that more clarity is achieved if this christological distinction is seen as the foundation of Augustine's thought in general, rather than as some marginal consideration. If the fullness of the Godhead is present in Christ, if by his incarnation, death and resurrection he saved all people, uniting them to his divinity, and if the church is his body, how can we think or talk about anything in heaven or on earth apart from Christ? Moreover, for Augustine, all that we know about Christ is exclusively transmitted by the Scriptures and by the church, Christ's body. How then can anyone ever speak about Christ apart from him?

It probably never entered Augustine's mind to make Christ an object of a sustained theological treatise, because he regarded him as the condition, the author and the method of all his thinking. Christ is necessarily omnipresent in a way that is not true for God the Father and the Holy Spirit, not, at least, in quite the same way. There always remains some distance between them and their creation, but not for the incarnate Son. Of course, Augustine stresses repeatedly that the whole Trinity is always present in the Son and that the actions of the three persons can never be separated (see, for example, *c. Max.* 2.17.1), but Christ alone is the means and the condition even of his thinking about the Trinity.

Accordingly, recent research is helping us to understand that those treatises that outline the role Christ played in Augustine's life, in his moral and spiritual development (such as the *Confessions* or passages of other works such as *De utilitate credendi*), may come closer to indicating the fullness of Augustine's reflections on Christ than even those of his writings, which at times focus more explicitly on Christ, but do so with specific speculative philosophical or theological purposes in mind (such as *ciu.* 10 or *trin.* 4). It may seem that something similar could be claimed for Christians in general in terms of the role that Christ plays in their lives, but the important point in approaching Augustine must be the understanding that Christ is not so much an object of his speculation, but the source and method for his philosophical and theological thinking. Here it should be sufficient to recall the function of Christ as the interior teacher (*magister interior*), the knowledge and wisdom of God (*scientia et sapientia dei*) in Augustine's illuminationist approach to knowledge. In this respect, one will not find a traditional christology in the works of Augustine as we have come to understand the term through recent centuries, but only the whole Christ (*Christus totus*) who pervades the entirety of his thought, thereby drawing it into a unity that Augustinian scholarship has yet to understand fully as such.

Theology of grace

Recent research into Augustine's theology of grace seems largely to confirm the general conclusions outlined above concerning Augustine's christocentric method. Following J. Patout Burns' research, scholars have continued for the most part to examine Augustine's theology of grace in relation to both the developing accounts of the role of Christ in his thought and the increasingly historical investigations concerning the Pelagian controversy.[27] Thus, Basil Studer, Joanne McWilliam and Robert Dodaro have reopened the question as to what extent serious christological issues lay at the root of the disputes over grace between Augustine and his adversaries.[28] In this regard, it seems that, for Augustine, the human capacity to make moral decisions that are just requires the intervention of grace upon the soul, and that, from the outset of the Pelagian controversy, the model for the communication of that graced knowledge of justice was provided by the union of natures in the one person of Jesus Christ:

> religious knowledge, as in the case of justice, can not stand *beside* love any more than the two natures of Christ can be said to stand beside one another without any communication 'between' them. It is this anticipation of a later, Chalcedonian doctrine which led Augustine to register a cautious, somewhat muted disapproval of Pelagian christology.[29]

Basing his study on a complete analysis of 1 Cor 1:31 'Let him who boasts, boast in the Lord', and 1 Cor 4:7 'What do you possess that was not given you? And if you received it as a gift, why take the credit to yourself?', Pierre-Marie Hombert demonstrates that, for Augustine, grace and the predestination of every human being are inevitably rooted in the humanity of Christ.[30] In Christ's person every human being receives sanctifying grace, in Christ's predestination to salvation human beings receive their own saving predestination. Augustine's understanding of the intimate union of the two natures of divinity and humanity in the one person of Christ forms the core of his theology of grace. Moreover, because the principal aim of Augustine's understanding of grace is its function in leading the faithful to humility, it is the 'humble Christ' (*Christus humilis*) in whom and with whom they achieve predestination.

This cluster of issues surrounding Augustine's theology of grace in the context of the Pelagian controversy appears to offer a most promising field of further studies, not so much as one special research topic apart from others, but as 'a meeting point of the theology of God's economy, christology, soteriology, ecclesiology, theology of grace, and spirituality'.[31]

Conclusion

Scholarly papers in the humanities are normally expected to be published in one of the the five major European languages: English, French, German, Italian and Spanish. This norm also holds for Augustinian studies, but there are significant exceptions to it which are worth knowing. There are a considerable number of Polish translations and studies on Augustine, but *'Polonia non leguntur'*, as, in fact, most scholars – including the author of these lines – lack the knowledge to do so. The same is true for Danish, Romanian, Croatian or Japanese publications. Evaluating the whole of Augustinian scholarship, however, one must become aware of the fact that there is far more material than the average scholar will be able to read, and while it is true that those five modern languages comprise over 90 per cent of all current publications on Augustine, there still remains a margin of valuable contributions to the field rarely taken into consideration.

The dawn of the third Christian millennium brings with it a more international and, therefore, greater cross-cultural collaboration in the development of research methods in Augustinian studies. While it is difficult to characterize, without unfair generalisations, national approaches to Augustinian research, certain patterns of interests, methods and mentalities continue to distinguish the geographical regions in which the majority of studies in Augustine are published. Looking broadly over the last decade or so, German and Austrian studies in Augustine still tend to stress lexicographical concerns, while southern Mediterranean research continues to be conducted along very traditional scholastic and philological lines. Two tendencies can be observed regarding recent North American work in Augustine: an ongoing production of English translations, and a strong commitment to interpretation rooted in current issues and trends from both the social sciences and literary criticism. Finally, much French Augustinian research abstracts ideas from texts in order to form a mental view of the reality that the texts describe. In doing this, such studies generally portray a picture which is essentially correct, but difficult to demonstrate through methods involving textual analysis. If these very broad impressions are in some way accurate, they also suggest a number of strengths to be shared reciprocally across cultural boundaries to the advantage of future generations of Augustinian scholars.

Notes

1 See A.-G. Hamman, *L'épopée du livre. Du scribe à l'imprimerie*, Paris, Perrin, 1985, pp. 143–54.

2 This electronic bibliography is featured in a CD-ROM, the CAG = *Corpus Augustinianum Gissense*, ed. C. Mayer, Basel, Schwabe, 1996.

3 'Questions on the Gospels'. See PL 35.1321–64.

4 With up to 500 annual publications on Augustine, it is plainly impossible to survey briefly the present state of research. The following essay will depart from the last ten issues of the Augustinian bibliography in the *Revue des études augustiniennes* in order to introduce some of the major subjects of research over the last decade. Moreover, the thorough overviews of recent scholarly literature included in several essays published elsewhere in this volume allow me to refer the reader to these discussions for treatment of Augustine and Platonism (by Robert Crouse), the Trinity (by Lewis Ayres), women (by E. Ann Matter), sexuality (by Mathijs Lamberigts) and monasticism (by George Lawless). For a more complete picture of Augustinian research than can be afforded by the essays of this volume, the reader is referred to the CAG CD-ROM mentioned above, n. 2, as well as to the annual bulletin published in the *Revue des études augustiniennes*, Paris, Institut des Études augustiniennes, 1955ff., and to the following bibliographies: R. Lorenz, 'Augustinusliteratur seit dem Jubiläum

von 1954', in *Theologische Rundschau* 25 (1959), pp. 1–75; idem, 'Zwölf Jahre Augustinusforschung (1959–1970)', in *Theologische Rundschau* 38 (1973/74), pp. 292–333; ibid., 39 (1974/75), pp. 95–138, 253–86, 331–64; ibid., 40 (1975), pp. 1–41, 97–149, 227–261; C. Andresen, *Bibliographia Augustiniana*, Darmstadt, Wissenschaftliche Buchgesellschaft, ²1973, C. Andresen (ed.), *Zum Augustin-Gespräch der Gegenwart I-II*, Darmstadt, Wissenschaftliche Buchgesellschaft, 1975–81; T. L. Miethe, *Augustinian Bibliography, 1970–1980. With Essays on the Fundamentals of Augustinian Scholarship*, Westport, Conn./ London, Greenwood Press, 1982.

5 See E. Feldmann, 'Literarische und theologische Probleme der *Confessiones*', in *Internationales Symposion über den Stand der Augustinus-Forschung*, ed. C. Mayer and K.-H. Chelius, Würzburg, Augustinus-Verlag, 1989, pp. 27–45, and R. Herzog, 'Non in sua voce. Augustins Gespräch mit Gott in den Confessiones – Voraussetzungen und Folgen', in *Das Gespräch. Poetik und Hermeneutik II*, ed. K. Stierle and R. Warning, Munich, Fink, 1984. For a general look at the scholarly literature on *conf.*, see R. Severson, *The Confessions of Saint Augustine. An Annotated Bibliography of Modern Criticism, 1888–19x95*, Westport, Conn., Greenwood, 1996.

6 P. Courcelle, *Recherches sur les Confessions de saint Augustin*, Paris, Etudes augustiniennes, ²1968.

7 E. P. Meijering, *Augustin über Schöpfung, Ewigkeit und Zeit. Das elfte Buch der Bekenntnisse*, Leiden, E. J. Brill, 1979, at p. 115.

8 See, for example, C. Müller, *Geschichtsbewußtsein bei Augustinus*, Würzburg, Augustinus-Verlag, 1993. Further recent work on *ciu.* is available in five collections of essays: *The City of God. A Collection of Critical Essays*, ed. D. F. Donnelly, New York, Peter Lang, 1995; *Il De civitate Dei. L'opera, le interpretazioni, l'influsso*, ed. E. Cavalcanti, Rome, Herder, 1996; *Interiorità e intenzionalità nel De civitate Dei di Sant'Agostino*, ed. R. Piccolomini, Rome, Institutum Patristicum «Augustinianum», 1991; *Il mistero del male e la libertà possibile: III. Lettura del De civitate Dei di Agostino*, ed. L. Alici, R. Piccolomini and A. Piccretti, Rome, Institutum Patristicum «Augustinianum», 1996; *History, Apocalypse and the Secular Imagination: New Essays on Augustine's City of God*, ed. M. Vessey, K. Pollmann and A. Fitzgerald, Bowling Green, Ohio, Philosophy Documentation Center, 1999 (= *Augustinian Studies* 30:2, 1999). Helpful for an overview of other, less recent scholarly literature on *ciu.* is D. Donnelly and M. A. Sherman (eds), *Augustine's De civitate Dei. An Annotated Bibliography of Modern Criticism, 1960–1990*, New York, Peter Lang, 1991. See also the studies cited in G. J. P. O'Daly, 'Ciuitate dei (De-)', in *Augustinus-Lexikon*, vol. 1, ed. C. Mayer, Basel, Schwabe, 1986–94, cc. 969–1010. This article is also an excellent point of departure for an understanding of *ciu.*

9 B. Studer, 'La *cognitio historialis* di Porfirio nel *De civitate Dei* di Agostino (*civ.* 10,32)', in *La narrativa cristiana antica. Codici narrativi, strutture formali, schemi retorici*, Rome, Institutum Patristicum «Augustinianum», 1995, pp. 529–53.

10 J. van Oort, *Jerusalem and Babylon. A Study into Augustine's* City of God *and the Sources of his Doctrine of Two Cities*, Leiden, E. J. Brill, 1991.

11 G. Lettieri, *Il senso della storia in Agostino d'Ippona. Il 'saeculum' e la gloria nel* De civitate Dei, Rome, Borla, 1988.

12 The Latin texts are available in CSEL 88. For an English translation, see *Saint*

Augustine, Letters, vol. 6 (1*–29*), tr. R. B. Eno, Washington, Catholic University of America Press, 1989. For scholarly studies on the new letters, see especially *Les lettres de saint Augustin découvertes par Johannes Divjak*, Paris, Etudes augustiniennes, 1983.

13 See F. Dolbeau, Augustin d'Hippone, *Vingt-six sermons au peuple*, Paris, Etudes augustiniennes, 1996. The sermons have been translated into English by E. Hill, *Sermons III/11, The Works of Saint Augustine. A Translation for the 21st Century*, ed. J. E. Rotelle, New York, New City Press, 1997.

14 See *Revue des études augustiniennes* 40 (1994), p. 299.

15 According to P.-P. Verbraken, 'Lire aujourd'hui les Sermons de saint Augustin', *Nouvelle Revue Théologique* 119 (1987), pp. 829–39, at p. 830, Augustine is thought to have preached 8,000 times. We may, therefore, possess relatively few of his sermons, only one out of fourteen.

16 A most helpful, recent survey of the recipients and contents of Augustine's letters is provided by F. Morgenstern, *Die Briefpartner des Augustinus von Hippo. Prosopographische, Sozial – und Ideologiegeschichtliche Untersuchungen*, Bochum, N. Brockmeyer, 1993. On Augustine's correspondence with Jerome, see C. White, *The Correspondence (394–419) between Jerome and Augustine. A Translation with Introduction and Notes*, Dyfed, Wales, Edwin Mellen Press, 1990; and R. Hennings, *Der Briefwechsel zwischen Augustinus und Hieronymus und ihr Streit um den Kanon des Alten Testaments und die Auslegung von Gal. 2,11–14*, Leiden, E. J. Brill, 1994.

17 *S.* 162 C (= *s. Dolbeau* 10 = *s. Moguntinus* 27); see H. R. Drobner, 'Augustins *sermo Moguntinus* über Gal 2,11–14. Einleitung, Übersetzung und Anmerkungen', in *Theologie und Glaube* 84 (1994), pp. 226–42.

18 A.-M. La Bonnardière, *Biblia Augustiniana*, 7 fascicles, Paris, Etudes augustiniennes, 1960–75. See also *Saint Augustin et la Bible*, ed. A.-M. La Bonnardière, Paris, Etudes augustiniennes, 1986.

19 See *doctr. chr.* 1.4.4; 1.22.20; 1.31.34–5 in the edition CSEL 32.

20 Here we can cite only some of the most recent studies: O. O'Donovan, '*Usus* and *Fruitio* in Augustine, *De doctrina christiana* I', *Journal of Theological Studies*, new series, 33:2 (1982), pp. 361–97; W. R. O'Connor, 'The *uti/frui* Distinction in Augustine's Ethics', *Augustinian Studies* 14 (1983), pp. 45–62; T. van Bavel, 'The Double Face of Love in Augustine', *Augustinian Studies* 17 (1986), pp. 169–81; W. Schoedel, 'Augustine on Love: A Response', *Augustinian Studies* 17 (1986), pp. 183–5; L. Verheijen, 'Le premier livre du *De doctrina christiana* d'Augustin: Un traité de «télicologie» biblique', in *Augustiniana Traiectina*, ed. J. den Boeft and J. van Oort, Paris, Etudes augustiniennes, 1987, pp. 169–87; R. D. Williams, 'Language, Reality and Desire in Augustine's *De doctrina*', *Literature and Theology* 3 (1989), pp. 138–50; R. Canning, *The Unity of Love for God and Neighbour in St Augustine*, Heverlee-Leuven: Augustinian Historical Institute, 1993, pp. 79–115.

21 See *doctr. chr.* 2.1.1.–2.4.5, in the edition CSEL 32.

22 Most recent studies include C. Kirwan, *Augustine*, London, Routledge, 1989, pp. 35–59; A. Louth, 'Augustine on Language', *Literature and Theology* 3 (1989), pp. 151–8; C. Ando, 'Augustine on Language', *Revue des études augustiniennes* 40 (1994), 45–78; J. Rist, *Augustine: Ancient thought baptized*, Cambridge, Cambridge University Press, ²1995, pp. 23–40; D. Dawson, 'Sign Theory, allegorical reading and the motions of the soul' in De doctrina christiana: *A Classic of Western Culture*, ed. D. W. H. Arnold and P. Bright, Notre Dame, Ind., Notre Dame University

Press, 1995, pp. 123–41; K. Pollmann, Doctrina Christiana. *Untersuchungen zu den Anfängen der christlichen Hermeneutik unter besonderer Berücksichtigung von Augustinus, De doctrina christiana*, Fribourg, Universitätsverlag, 1996, pp. 147–96; R. A. Markus, *Signs and Meanings. Word and Text in Ancient Christianity*, Liverpool, Liverpool University Press, 1996; B. Stock, *Augustine the Reader. Meditation, Self-Knowledge, and the Ethics of Interpretation*, Cambridge, Mass., The Belknap Press of Harvard University Press, 1996, especially pp. 196–204. See Markus, op. cit., pp. 120–4, for references to important, earlier scholarship on this topic.

23 See K. B. Steinhauser, *The Apocalypse Commentary of Tyconius. A History of Its Reception and Influence*, Frankfurt, Peter Lang, 1987; P. Bright, *The Book of Rules of Tyconius. Its Purpose and Inner Logic*, Notre Dame, Ind., Notre Dame University Press, 1988; and M. Dulaey, 'La sixième Règle de Tyconius et son résumé dans le *De doctrina christiana*', *Revue des études augustiniennes* 35 (1989), pp. 83–103.

24 See M. Vincent, *Saint Augustin maître de prière d'après les 'Enarrationes in Psalmos'*, Paris, Beauchesne, 1990; M. Fiedrowicz, *Psalmus vox totius Christi. Studien zu Augustins* Enarrationes in Psalmos, Freiburg, Herder, 1997.

25 See B. Studer, *The Grace of Christ and the Grace of God in Augustine of Hippo: Christocentrism or Theocentrism?*, tr. M. J. O'Connell, Collegeville Minn., Liturgical Press, 1997.

26 G. Madec, 'Christus', *Augustinus-Lexikon*, vol. 1, ed. C. Mayer, Basel, Schwabe, cc. 845–908, at cc. 869–76.

27 J. P. Burns, *The Development of Augustine's Doctrine of Operative Grace*, Paris, Etudes augustiniennes, 1980. See also A. Trapè, *Agostino: Introduzione alla Dottrina della Grazia, I: Natura e grazia*, Rome, Città Nuova, 1987; *II: Grazia e libertà*, Rome, Città Nuova, 1990; R. H. Weaver, *Divine Grace and Human Agency. A Study of the Semi-Pelagian Controversy*, Macon Ga., Mercer University Press, 1996; J. Lössl, *Intellectus gratiae. Die erkenntnistheoretische und hermeneutische Dimension der Gnadenlehre Augustins von Hippo*, Leiden, E. J. Brill, 1997, whose account, although historically comprehensive in relation to all the controversies in Augustine's life, also devotes enormous attention to Augustine's doctrine of grace in connection with the Pelagian controversy (see especially pp. 119–44, 187–96, 245–410).

28 B. Studer, 'Sacramentum et exemplum chez saint Augustin', in *Recherches augustiniennes* 10 (1975), pp. 87–141, especially pp. 124–39: 'Un thème anti-pélagien?'; J. McWilliam, 'The Christology of the Pelagian Controversy', in *Studia Patristica*. Papers presented at the Tenth International Conference on Patristic Studies held in Oxford 1979, vol. 17:3, ed. E. Livingstone, Leuven, Peeters, 1982, pp. 1221–44; R. Dodaro, 'Sacramentum Christi: Augustine on the Christology of Pelagius', in *Studia Patristica*. Papers presented at the Eleventh International Conference on Patristic Studies held in Oxford 1991, vol. 27, ed. E. Livingstone, Leuven, Peeters, 1993, pp. 274–80. Christology was first examined in relation to the Pelagian controversy by T. J. van Bavel, *Recherches sur la christologie de saint Augustin. L'humain et le divin dans le Christ d'après saint Augustin*, Fribourg, Editions universitaires, 1954.

29 Dodaro, op. cit., p. 280.

30 P.-M. Hombert, *Gloria gratiae. Se glorifier en Dieu, principe et fin de la théologie augustinienne de la grâce*, Paris, etudes augustiniennes, 1996.

31 Hombert, op. cit., p. 488.

Part I

IF PLATO WERE ALIVE

Augustine, *True Religion* 3.3

4

PAUCIS MUTATIS VERBIS
St. Augustine's Platonism

Robert Crouse

Nebridius of Carthage, dear friend and often companion of Augustine, was delighted to find Augustine's letters full of Plato and Plotinus, as well as full of Christ: *'illae mihi Christum, illae Platonem, illae Plotinum sonabunt'*.[1] That conjunction, however, which Nebridius found so pleasant and so edifying, has been a major problem for modern students of Augustine. For well over a century now, no aspect of Augustinian studies has been more marked by controversy than the question of his 'Platonism', and the vast body of scholarly literature devoted to the subject leaves many of the issues unresolved.

Still far from settled, for example, is the whole matter of his Platonic sources. Were his initial readings, the notorious *platonicorum libri* of Book 7 of the *Confessions*, texts from Plotinus, or were they perhaps Plotinian texts with Porphyrian commentaries?[2] Debate about those alternatives has been prolific, but inconclusive, and, as Andrew Smith remarks, it now seems unlikely that the exact nature of those books will ever be clarified.[3]

Beyond those early readings, how much did he eventually come to know of the texts of Plato, of Plotinus, of Porphyry and other pagan Platonists? Did he know anything, for example, of Iamblichus, who is mentioned in the *City of God*?[4] How much of his knowledge of Platonism came from Cicero, from Varro, and from doxographies?[5] How much of it was an already Christian Platonism, from Ambrose, Origen, and other Greek and Latin Fathers?[6] All of these questions have been extensively studied and debated, with incomplete and more or less inconclusive results.

As Gerald Bonner observes, 'the discovery of Neoplatonism was unquestionably a major event in the history of Augustine's intellectual development', but troublesome questions continue to arise about the extent and character of that philosophy in his thought and writings.[7] The thesis advanced most dramatically by Prosper Alfaric, in 1918, to the effect that the young Augustine was initially converted to Neoplatonism rather than to Christianity, was widely criticised and has undergone many modifications, but the basic problem has not disappeared.[8] Seeing Neoplatonism and

Christianity as opposed or only externally related positions, should one think of Augustine as a Christian whose thought was more or less deeply influenced by Platonism, employing Neoplatonic conceptual forms as '*Denkmittel*' for the understanding and expression of Christian doctrine?[9] Or should one rather think of him as simultaneously Platonist and Christian, effecting a genuine synthesis of Christian and Neoplatonic positions, understood as sharing 'a profound common ground'?[10]

Must one, perhaps, regard him, rather, as a critic of pagan Platonism, choosing with careful discretion those elements which would be consistent with Christian doctrine?[11] Was he, perhaps, especially in his later career, not only critical, but even 'anti-Platonic'?[12]

Alternatively, might one see in Augustine's Platonism a transformation, or 'conversion' of Neoplatonic theology in terms of principles of Christian doctrine: a Christianising of Platonism rather than a Platonising of Christianity?[13] Or was it, perhaps, solely a religious, and not a philosophical difference that marked for Augustine the distance between pagan Platonism and Christianity?[14]

Behind these varied proposals lie various presuppositions, about both the history of Christian doctrine and the history of Platonism. Thus, as Eckard König observes, much of the controversy about Augustine's conversion rests upon the assumption that Christian belief and Neoplatonic philosophy were simply alternative and opposed ways of thinking: 'If one saw him as a philosopher, his Christianity would be more or less a secondary matter; if one saw him as a Christian, his philosophy could be, at best, instrument and aid to understanding'.[15] However, that assumption about Christianity and philosophy as alternatives is simply one aspect of a much more pervasive presupposition that has governed the history of Christian doctrine (both Catholic and Protestant) for several centuries: the thesis that Christianity has been distorted, or, at least, radically modified by various compromises with Hellenistic culture.

Although the idea of the 'Hellenising' of Christianity is commonly associated with the name of Adolf Harnack, the standpoint is, in fact, much older. It goes back at least as far as the Catholic humanist Guilielmus Budaeus' *De transitu Hellenismi ad Christianismum*, published in Paris in 1535, and reached a high point with the publication (anonymously) of M. Souverain's *Le Platonisme devoilé*, in 1700, in which the theology of the Fathers is represented as a transformation of the purity and simplicity of primitive Christianity into essentially pagan dogma.[16]

That long-standing interpretative paradigm, which Johannes Hessen describes as the '*Lieblingsproblem*' of modern theology, has been refined in twentieth-century scholarship by attempts to define more precisely the differences between Hellenic modes of thought, on the one hand, and Hebraic (and therefore 'authentically Christian') modes on the other.[17] The consequence has been to liberate the gospel message from Hellenic 'distortions'.[18]

Thus, Greek thought is said to be static, Hebrew thought dynamic; Hebrew categories historical, Greek categories metaphysical; Greek theology concerned with abstract principles, Hebrew theology with a living person; Hellenic culture concerned with rational order, Hebrew religion concerned with righteous will; and so on. In terms of such discriminations, attempts are made to formulate systems of 'Biblical' theology in opposition to the 'metaphysical' theology of the Fathers, and patristic doctrine comes to be regarded as an illicit mixture of theology (conceived of in late medieval fashion as *sola fide*) and philosophy (*sola ratione*).

A prime example of such anti-Hellenic, or anti-Platonic criticism of Augustine is Anders Nygren's vastly influential work on *Eros und Agape* (still, after more than half a century, 'an indispensable reference point'), in which Augustine's '*caritas* synthesis' is represented as an illegitimate amalgam of Platonic and Christian concepts, destined to distort western Christian thought and piety for a thousand years.[20] For Nygren, Augustine's blending of the Platonic *eros* motif with the very different, indeed, contradictory Christian conception of *agape* was a crucial '*Knotenpunkte*' in the whole spiritual development in which classical culture and Christianity were amalgamated.[21] But in as much as, according to Nygren, the human aspiration of *eros* and the divine gift of *agape* stand in mutual contradiction, Augustine's synthesis is impossible, and, in Nygren's view (as Victorino Capánaga puts it) we find ourselves '*en presencia de la contradiccion grandiosa y fatal del pensamiento de Agustín*'.[22]

Nygren's position, although frequently criticised by John Burnaby and others, on many grounds, continues to be popular, because it is so neatly consistent with the anti-Hellenic temper of twentieth-century Christian thought.[23] However, the argument leads at least by way of implication, beyond the issue of Hellenism to a more universal theological question. As Luigi Pizzolato points out, it is really an argument about the relation of nature to grace, and Augustine's 'synthesis' expresses his conviction that grace does not destroy nature, but perfects it.[24] *Eros* and *agape* are not simply conflated in *caritas*: *eros* is elevated and transfigured by grace, not destroyed, but redeemed. '*Amor tuus migret*': 'Your love migrates', says Augustine, and finds its focus in God.[25] '*Venit Christus mutare amorem*': 'Christ came to transform love'.[26] For Augustine, it is a matter of *dilectio ordinata*: love re-ordered by grace.[27]

J. J. O'Donnell calls Nygren's work 'the most outspokenly Protestant criticism of Augustine in this century'.[28] However, Nygren's anti-Platonic standpoint is by no means unique, nor is it uniquely Protestant. Robert O'Connell, for example, who has argued most consistently for a strong doctrinal influence of Plotinus in Augustine's *intellectus fidei*, also sees that influence at odds with biblical Christianity: 'The whole question of the framework for his understanding of Scripture is now the issue'; and he refers to 'the possibility Du Roy and Mandouze are far from alone in suggesting:

that the "faith" Augustine claimed to understand was frequently a "faith" already "understood" in the light of prior thought – commitments of questionable relevance to that faith'.[29] 'Finally', says O'Connell, giving the whole issue contemporary reference, 'we must seriously examine the possibility that the "understanding" Christians are being urged to accept bears all too many kinship features with the understanding to be found in Neoplatonism'.[30]

While Nygren and many other anti-Hellenic historians of doctrine, both Protestant and Catholic, have criticised Augustine for distorting Christianity by his Platonism, other scholars have criticised his Platonism on quite different grounds. Heinrich Dörrie, for example, in his many important studies of late Platonism, has insisted that Neoplatonism in the fourth and fifth centuries was a closed theological and religious system, utterly incompatible with Christianity; that no synthesis was possible, and that the apparent approval of aspects of Neoplatonic doctrine on the part of Augustine and other Christians was simply an 'apologetic fiction', which Augustine corrected in his *Retractationes*.[31] That view is at least shared to some extent by Paul Aubin, with respect to trinitarian doctrine, where he advises '*la plus grande prudence*' in evaluating apparent parallels between Augustine and Plotinus.[32]

Other critics suggest that Augustine's Platonism involves misrepresentations, or, at least, misunderstandings of his Platonic sources. Étienne Gilson, for example, encountering 'unsettled questions' in the doctrine of Augustine, remarks that 'one source of them would seem to be Augustine's use of the doctrine of Plotinus'.[33] In particular, says Gilson, 'everything leads us to believe that he always mistook Plotinus' emanation for the Christian notion of creation'.[34] The critical point, which is a very serious one, rests, of course, upon the assumption that the difference between 'emanation' and 'creation' is clear: an assumption that more recent studies of Neoplatonism and Christian doctrine would call into question. As Jean Trouillard remarks, '*contrairement à des préjugés assez repandus, ni les identifications ni les oppositions sommaires ne résistent à l'examen*'.[35]

Still other critics find Augustine's synthesis of Platonic and Christian doctrine full of inconsistencies and mutually contradictory positions. Thus, Kurt Flasch, perhaps the most outspoken of such critics, calls Augustine's doctrine 'a nest of contradictions' ('*ein Nest von Widersprüchen*').[36] Observing the wide diversity of Augustinian interpretations in subsequent centuries, Flasch suggests that we must trace that diversity to divergent starting-points in Augustine's works, which can no longer be represented (as, for example, by Gilson) as a 'monolithic block', but as embodying all those contradictions which later emerge in the Augustinian tradition.[37] Fundamental among the contradictions, from Flasch's standpoint, is Augustine's attempt to hold the philosophical legacy of classical antiquity, involving convictions about divine justice and human rationality, together with a completely unjust and irrational doctrine of sin and grace.[38] Thus, Platonic doctrines (even if in a somewhat confused form) are maintained, but together with theological principles antithetical to, and destructive of, those doctrines. That is, according to Flasch, Augustine's conflict (der Zwiespalt Augustins).[39]

Flasch's argument certainly depends upon a naïve representation of Augustine's doctrine of grace, as several critics have indicated; but it also depends upon questionable presuppositions about the history and character of Platonism.[40] He accuses Augustine of contradicting the philosophical conception of an ethical God, in favour of a doctrine of divine inscrutability, of establishing a religious authority hostile to reason, of destroying the ancient philosophy of nature, and of demolishing the ancient ideal of rational man, compos sui.[41] However, even if that catena of doctrines could be taken as representative of the philosophical theology of classical Greece, which is, at least doubtful, it is impossible as a representation of the Platonism of Augustine's time (that is, post-Plotinian Neoplatonism). In comparison with the philosophical and religious positions of Iamblichus, for example, the doctrines of Augustine seem remarkably sober and rational.[42]

For an understanding of Augustine's Platonism, and a just evaluation of its significance, the great advances during recent decades in the study of the history of pagan Platonism are of crucial importance.[43] Those advances, which provide an ever more full and precise account of the Platonic theology and religious doctrines of Augustine's pagan predecessors and their successors, enable us to measure more accurately both the extent of his dependence upon that tradition and the originality of his Christian resolution of certain of its dilemmas. No longer can pagan Platonism be looked upon as simply a 'secular' philosophy, providing only linguistic and conceptual apparatus for the formulation of Christian doctrine; there is a commonality of theological concerns, theoretical and practical, with certain radical differences in solutions.

Giovanni Reale, in a remarkable essay on 'the final spiritual message of antiquity in the metaphysical and theurgical thought of Proclus', observes that while pagan Platonism after Plotinus moves in the direction of 'systematic complication', Christian Platonism moves in an opposite direction, towards 'systematic simplification'.[44] The systematic complication of Platonism was necessary precisely in relation to certain theological dilemmas about meditation. As John Dillon remarks, in regard to Iamblichus and the doctrine of henads, 'All of his very complicated systematising of the Realm of the One . . . is prompted by the desire to bridge the great gap between a completely transcendent First Principle and everything subsequent to it'.[45] However, by such a procedure the gap is never truly bridged, and the complication must be infinite. Theurgic mysteries must take over where theology fails: philosophy demands liturgical consummation.[46]

Christian Platonism approaches the same dilemmas in regard to mediation (in creation and redemption) very differently, in terms of the theology of Nicaea and Constantinople, and the christology of Ephesus and Chalcedon. Augustine's anti-Arian formulation of trinitarian doctrine owes much to both pagan and Christian predecessors, a good deal perhaps to Porphyry (especially if he is the author of the fragmentary *Commentary on the Parmenides*) and his remarkable conflation of Platonic and Aristotelian theology.[47] Whatever the sources, the formulation in which the antithesis between ontology and henology is transcended, and God is understood as a unity of co-equal and co-eternal moments of being, knowing and willing, is an original and profoundly important revision of Platonic theology in Christian terms. The logical necessity (and the futility) of mediating hierarchies is done away with,[48] and the way is open for an understanding of mediation in which divine and human natures are seen as personally united without confusion.

In accordance with that resolution of the question of mediation, Augustine's Christian Platonism assigns an enhanced role and scope to intellect. Certainly, in pagan Platonism, *nous* has a high place in the divine hierarchy and in the human soul, yet the ascent to God demands a faculty of soul beyond intellect, where union is sought by way of the religious *praxis* of the mysteries, above understanding.[49] For Augustine, there is no such faculty. Certainly, faith precedes understanding, and understanding precedes faith, in the 'hermeneutic circle', but ultimately, union with the triune God is a contemplative union in memory, understanding and love.[50] Thus, faith is, for Augustine, not a distinct faculty, nor a substitute for intellect, but the salvation of intellect.[51] It is not the contradiction or the destruction of Platonism, but its conversion and redemption.

Goulven Madec has frequently argued that, for Augustine, Platonism was completed, or fulfilled in Christianity: '*Le platonisme s'accomplit dans le christianisme*'.[52] In the eyes of Augustine, according to Madec, Platonism suffered from a fatal contradiction between a good theology and a bad religion; only Christianity could bring coherence between theory and religious practice; the deficiencies were not metaphysical, but religious.[53] Surely, Madec is right, that, for Augustine, Christianity fulfilled the aspirations of Platonism; but the fulfilment was not only religious. The problems of pagan Platonism were in the first place theological, and only secondarily and consequentially problems of religious practice. As Stephen Menn remarks, 'it is a very delicate question how far Augustine believes that Christianity exceeds Platonism in intellectual content'.[54] It is certain, however, that for him, the reform of religion depended ultimately upon knowing the true mediator, and knowing the truth of that mediator depended upon knowing the truth of the trinitarian unity of God. Only on the basis of a very fundamental conversion of doctrine could pagan Platonists move beyond the idolatry of theurgy and follow the true '*via ad patriam*'. '*Paucis mutatis verbis*': only a few words needed to be changed, but they were crucial words.[55]

Finally, as John O'Meara remarks, 'there is no simple statement to describe Augustine's use of the Neoplatonists'.[56] Perhaps even the word 'use' is misleading, if it suggests only an external, instrumental relation. John Rist gives us the striking phrase, 'ancient thought baptized', but it is a phrase which calls for explication of the form and effects of that baptism.[57] Augustine was a Platonist, giving Platonism a creative Christian interpretation.[58] He lead it beyond Plotinus and Porphyry in a direction of development in some ways parallel to its development in the history of pagan Platonism from Iamblichus to Proclus, in some ways decisively different by virtue of the illumination of Christian doctrine.[59]

In a recent essay on pseudo-Dionysius and Thomas Aquinas, Wayne Hankey proposes that 'we try to recuperate them as moments in a continuous Neoplatonic tradition beginning with the pagans'. He justly represents the thought of Denys as 'a transforming moment in the great change from pagan to Christian', and remarks that 'Christianising that theology requires transformations of it. These Denys begins. Aquinas pushes them further'.[60] However, Denys does not really 'begin' the transformations: they begin in that long Greek patristic tradition to which he belongs; and the Latin West also has its crucial moments of transformation, most decisively in the trinitarian theology of Augustine, to which the Dionysian doctrine is accommodated in early medieval theology.[61] If Aquinas pushes further the Dionysian transformations, it is really on the basis of the Augustinian transformations that he does so.[62] Augustine, also, must be understood within that 'continuous Neoplatonic tradition'; not simply as using Plotinus or Porphyry, but as effecting a profound conversion of Platonic theology.

To work out the details of that conversion, and thus to define precisely the character of that post-Nicene, post-Plotinian Augustinian Platonism and its historical significance is a monumental task.[63] It is one in which a century of critical scholarship has hardly made a beginning, and to which 'the postmodern retrieval of Christian Neoplatonism' has so far contributed little.[64] As Giovanni Reale remarks, *'proprio sul Platonismo di Agostino resta moltissimo da fare, o da rifare'*.[65]

Notes

1 See Augustine, *ep.* 6; CSEL 34/1.12. Of the correspondence between Augustine and Nebridius, twelve letters survive: *ep.* 3–14. *Ep.* 6 belongs to AD 389. On Nebridius, see A. Mandouze, *Prosopographie chrétienne du Bas-Empire*, vol. 1, Paris, Etudes augustiniennes, 1982, pp. 774–6.

2 See C. Starnes, *Augustine's Confessions*, Waterloo, Ontario, Wilfrid Laurier University Press, 1990, pp. 182–3, 202–5; P. Beatrice, 'Quosdam Platonicorum Libros. The Platonic readings of Augustine in Milan', *Vigiliae Christianae* 43 (1989), pp. 248–81; *Sant'Agostino, Confessioni, III (Libri VII–IX)*, ed. M. Simonetti, G. Madec and L. Pizzolato, Milan, Arnaldo Mondadori Editore, 1994, pp. 190–218.

3 A. Smith, 'Porphyrian Studies Since 1913', in *Aufstieg und Niedergang der römischen Welt*, II.36.2, Berlin/New York, Walter De Gruyter, 1987, pp. 717–73, at p. 770; to similar effect, G. Madec, *Saint Augustin et la philosophie. Notes critiques*, Paris, Etudes augustiniennes, 1996, p. 38.

4 *Ciu.*8.12; CSEL 40/1.374.

5 See M. Testard, *Saint Augustin et Cicéron*, 2 vols, Paris, Etudes augustiniennes, 1958; A. Solignac, 'Doxographies et manuels dans la formation philosophique de Saint Augustin', *Recherches augustiniennes* 1 (1958), pp. 113–48.

6 See R. Lorenz, 'Zwolf Jahre Augustinusforschung (1959–1970)', *Theologische Rundschau* 39 (1974), pp. 124–38: 'Augustins Kenntnis antiker und christlicher Autoren'. According to P. Courcelle, *Recherches sur les Confessions de Saint Augustin*, Paris, Etudes augustiniennes, 1950, Ambrose introduced Augustine at the same time to Christian spirituality and Platonic doctrines (pp. 138; 252–3); on Origen's Platonism, H. Crouzel, *Origène et Plotin: Comparisons doctrinales*, Paris, Téqui, 1992, and on Origen's influence, V. Grossi, 'La presenza di Origene nell'ultimo Agostino (426–430)', in *Origeniana Quinta*, ed. R. Daly, Leuven, Peeters, 1992, pp. 558–64, and R. Crouse, 'The Influence of Origen in the Philosophical Tradition of the Latin West: Augustine and Eriugena', also in Daly (ed.), op. cit., pp. 565–9.

7 G. Bonner, 'Augustinus (uita)', in *Augustinus Lexikon*, vol. 1, ed. C. Mayer, Basel, Schwabe & Co., 1986–94, cc. 519–50, at c. 529.

8 P. Alfaric, *L'évolution intellectuelle de saint Augustin*, vol. 1, Paris, E. Nourry, 1918, pp. 380–1; see P. Brown, *Augustine of Hippo. A Biography*, London, Faber & Faber, 1967, p. 104, n. 5: 'it is impossible to deny that he passed through a phase of "autonomous" Platonism, whose exponents regarded themselves as superior to Christianity'.

9 See, for example, G. Bonner, *St Augustine of Hippo. Life and Controversies*, London, SPCK, 1963, p. 86; for the term '*Denkmittel*', M. Schmaus, *Die psychologische Trinitätslehre des heiligen Augustinus*, 'Nachwort' in the reprint edition, Münster, Aschendorffsche Verlagsbuchhandlung, 1969, p. xv.

10 See C. de Vogel, 'Platonism and Christianity: A Mere Antagonism or a Profound Common Ground?' *Vigiliae Christianae* 39 (1985), pp. 1–62.

11 G. Madec offers the alternatives of influence, synthesis, discernment: 'Le néoplatonisme dans la conversion d'Augustin. Etat d'une question centenaire (depuis Harnack et Boissier, 1888)', in C. Mayer and K.-H. Chelius (eds), *Internationales Symposion über den Stand des Augustinus-Forschung*, Würzburg, Augustinus-Verlag, 1989, pp. 9–25; similarly, J. McEvoy, 'Neoplatonism and Christianity: Influence, Syncretism, or Discernment?', in T. Finan and V. Twomey (eds), *The Relationship between Neoplatonism and Christianity*, Dublin, Four Courts Press, 1992, pp. 155–70.

12 A. Trapè, 'Escatologia e antiplatonismo di sant'Agostino', *Augustinianum* 18 (1978), pp. 237–44. Trapè has in mind particularly Augustine's anthropology and conception of history.

13 R. Crouse, '*In Aenigmate Trinitas* (*Confessions*, XIII, 5, 6): The Conversion of Philosophy in St Augustine's *Confessions*', *Dionysius* 11 (1987), pp. 53–62; L. Obertello, 'Creazione e redenzione nel pensiero di Agostino', in *Boezio e dintorni*, Florence, Nardini, 1989, pp. 13–39, especially p. 28; see also M. Sciacca, *Sant'Agostino*, Palermo, L'Epos, 1991, p. 127: 'È Plotino . . . che diventa cristiano e non Agostino che si fa neoplatonica' ('It is Plotinus who becomes Christian and not Augustine who becomes Neoplatonic').

14 See G. Madec, 'Augustin et Porphyry. Ébauche d'un bilan des recherches et des conjectures', in M.-O. Goulet-Cazé, G. Madec and D. O'Brien (eds), *Sophies*

maietores. '*Chercheurs de sagesse*'. Hommage à Jean Pépin, Paris, Etudes augustiniennes, 1992, pp. 367–82, at p. 374.

15 E. König, *Augustinus Philosophus. Christlicher Glaube und philosophisches Denken in den Frühschriften Augustins*, Munich, W. Fink, 1970, p. 13.

16 See M. Lutz-Bachmann, 'Hellenisierung des Christentums?' in C. Colpe, L. Honnefelder and M. Lutz-Bachmann, *Spätantike und Christentum*, Berlin, Akademie-Verlag, 1992, pp. 77–98; W. Pannenberg, 'Christentum und Platonismus. Die kritische Platonrezeption Augustins in ihrer Bedeutung für das gegenwärtige christliche Denken', in *Ebraismo, Ellenismo, Christianismo, Archivio di Filosofia* 53 (1985), pp. 309–25; M. Bartolomei, *Ellenizzazione del cristianesimo*, L'Aquila / Rome, L. U. Japadre, 1984, provides a thorough account of the history, with a very full bibliography.

17 J. Hessen, *Geschichte oder biblische Theologie. Das Problem der Hellenisierung des Christentums in neuer Beleuchtung*, Munich / Basel, Reinhart Verlag, ²1962, p. 5; see also B. Lonergan, 'The Dehellenization of Dogma' (review of L. Dewart, *The Future of Belief*, New York, Herder and Herder, 1966), *Theological Studies* 28 (1967), pp. 336–51.

18 A good example of the genre is T. Boman, *Das hebräische Denken im Vergleich mit dem griechischen*, Göttingen, Vandenhoeck & Ruprecht, 1952.

19 On the unity of philosophy and theology in Augustine, see R. Crouse, 'St Augustine's *De trinitate*: Philosophical method', in *Studia Patristica*. Papers presented to the Seventh International Conference on Patristic Studies held at Oxford 1975, vol. 16, ed. E. Livingstone, Berlin, Akademie-Verlag, 1985, pp. 501–10.

20 A. Nygren, *Eros und Agape. Gestaltwandlungen der christlichen Liebe*, tr. I. Nygren, Gütersloh, C. Bertelmann Verlag, 1930; on the '*caritas* synthesis', pp. 351–443. On the work as 'always an indispensable point of reference', G. Reale, *Agostino. Amore Assoluto e 'terza navigazione'*, Milan, Vita e pensiero, 1994, p. 63.

21 See Nygren, op. cit., p. 393. He associates the predominance of *eros* specifically with Augustine's Neoplatonism, 'never for Augustine a phase which is eventually overcome', p. 359. On the doctrine of *eros* in Plotinus, see J. Lacrosse, *L'amour chez Plotin*. Brussels, Editions Ousia, 1994.

22 V. Capánaga, 'Interpretacíon agustiniana del amor. Eros y Agape', *Augustinus* 18 (1973), pp. 213–278, is a very thorough criticism of Nygren's thesis. For more recent discussions, see D. Dideberg, 'Caritas. Prolégomènes à une étude de la théologie augustinienne de la charité', in *Signum Pietatis. Festschrift für Cornelius Petrus Mayer OSA zum 60. Geburtstag*, ed. A. Zumkeller, Würzburg, Augustinus-Verlag, 1989, pp. 369–81; J. Pieper, *Faith, Hope, Love*, San Francisco, Ignatius Press, 1997, pp. 211–22, discusses the problem with reference to Nygren and to Karl Barth.

23 J. Burnaby, *Amor Dei. A Study of the Religion of St Augustine*, London, Hodder and Stoughton, 1938, reprinted Norwich, Canterbury Press, 1991, especially pp. 15–21; *The Philosophy and Theology of Anders Nygren*, ed. C. W. Kegley, Carbondale Ill., Southern Illinois University Press, 1970, brings together Burnaby's criticism, 'Amor in St. Augustine' (pp. 174–86), and Nygren's 'Reply to Interpreters and Critics' (pp. 362–4).

24 See L. Pizzolato, *L'idea di amicizia nel mondo antico classico e cristiano*, Turin, Einaudi, 1993, p. 316.

25 *S. Denis* 14, in MiAg 1.66–7; see A. Solignac, 'La conception augustinienne de
l'amour', in *Oeuvres de Saint Augustin, Les Confessions* (= BA 14), Paris, Desclée
De Brouwer, 1962, pp. 617–22.

26 *S.* 344.1; PL38.1512.

27 *Doctr. chr.* 1.27.28; CSEL 80.23; *Ciu.* 15.22; CSEL 40/2.109.

28 J. J. O'Donnell, *Augustine, Confessions, I, Introduction and Text*, Oxford, Clarendon
Press, 1992, p. xxiv.

29 R. J. O'Connell, *St Augustine's Platonism*, Villanova, Penn., Villanova University
Press, 1984, pp. 24–5, with reference to O. Du Roy, *L'intelligence de la foi en la
trinité selon saint Augustin*, Paris, Etudes augustiniennes, 1966, and A.
Mandouze, *Saint Augustin. L'aventure de la raison et de la grâce*, Paris, Etudes
augustiniennes, 1968. To similar effect, Du Roy's article, 'Augustine, St', in the
New Catholic Encyclopedia, vol. 1, New York, McGraw-Hill, 1967, pp. 1041–58,
especially pp. 1053, 1057.

30 O'Connell, op. cit., p. 25; see also p. 26: 'the years convince me more and more
strongly that Neoplatonism was scarcely geared to deal sympathetically with
the refractory stuff of the incarnate human condition'. A. H. Armstrong, in an
earlier Augustine lecture on the same theme, *St Augustine and Christian
Platonism*, Villanova, Penn., Villanova University Press, 1967, saw more promise
in the Platonic aspects of Augustine's Christianity.

31 H. Dörrie, 'Was ist spätantiker Platonismus?' *Theologische Rundschau* 36 (1971),
pp. 285–502; ibid., 'Die andere Theologie', *Theologie und Philosophie* 56 (1981),
pp. 1–46; see also E. Paroli, 'Il conflitto fra Platonismo e Christianesimo nell'interpretazione di Heinrich Dörrie', in C. de Vogel, *Platonismo e cristianesimo*,
Milan, Vita e pensiero, 1993, pp. 107–38. On Augustine's Platonism as
'apologetic fiction', see Dörrie, 'Die andere Theologie', op. cit., pp. 40–2.

32 P. Aubin, *Plotin et la christianisme. Triade plotinienne et trinité chrétienne*, Paris,
Beauchesne, 1992, p. 228; see also pp. 90–1. However, as G. Madec remarks in
his review [*Revue des Études Augustiniennes* 39 (1993), p. 526], 'Malgré sa réserve
concernant *Enn.* V, 1, l'intention d'Augustin est bien aussi de souligner l'affinité
entre doctrines platoniciennes et chrétienne sur la Trinité' ('In spite of his
reservations concerning *Enneads* 5.1, Augustine's intention was always to
underscore the affinity between Platonic and Christian doctrines on the
Trinity'). See also, U. Pérez Paoli, *Der plotinische Begriff von Hypostasis und die
augustinische Bestimmung Gottes als Subiectum*, Würzburg, Augustinus-Verlag,
1990, especially. p. 87.

33 É. Gilson, *The Christian Philosophy of St Augustine*, tr. L. Lynch, New York,
Random House, 1960, p. 105.

34 Ibid., p. 108.

35 'Contrary to broadly held prejudices, neither the identification nor the complete
opposition [of the two concepts] will stand up to examination'. Translation by
editors. See J. Trouillard, 'Procession néoplatonicienne et création
Judeo–chrétienne', in *Mélanges offerts à Jean Trouillard = Les Cahiers de Fontenay*
(1981), pp. 1–30, at p. 1. See the comment of W. Beierwaltes:

> In via generale possiamo affermare a proposito della dottrina
> agostiniana della *creatio* che la concezione biblica del Dio creatore è
> stata unita alla concezione filosofica di un principio (il *nous*, pensiero,

spirito) che è causa degli esseri, dando origine così a una nuova dottrina.

(In general we can say with regard to the Augustinian doctrine of creation that the biblical conception of God the Creator has been united with the philosophical concept of a principle, the *nous*, thought, spirit, which is the cause of beings, and in this way he initiates a new doctrine.)

(Agostino e il neoplatonismo cristiano, Milan, Vita e pensiero, 1995, p. 128)

See also A. Manno, 'Pensiero Greco e creazionesmo cristiano', *Sapienza* 50 (1997), pp. 285–315.

36 K. Flasch, *Augustin. Einführung in sein Denken*, Stuttgart, Philipp Reclam jun., 1980, p. 403. See G. Madec's review, 'Sur une nouvelle introduction à la pensée d'Augustin', *Revue des études augustiniennes* 28 (1982), pp. 100–11.

37 Flasch, op. cit., p. 8. On diverse starting-points in Augustine, see also A. Solignac, 'La double tradition augustinienne: Anthropologie et humanisme', *Les Cahiers de Fontenay* (1985), pp. 67–77.

38 Flasch, op. cit., pp.187–91.

39 Ibid., p. 403. The same argument appears in summary form in Flasch's *Das philosophische Denken im Mittelalter*, Stuttgart, Philipp Reclam jun., 1988, pp. 36–40, and in the long introduction to his edition of *Simpl., Logik des Schreckens*, Mainz, Dieterich, 1990, pp. 19–138.

40 See T. G. Ring, 'Bruch oder Entwicklung im Gnadenbegriff Augustins? Kritische Ammerkungen zu K. Flasch, Logik des Schreckens. Augustinus von Hippo. Die Gnadenlehre von 397', *Augustiniana* 44 (1994), pp. 31–113; G. Madec's review of *Logik des Schreckens*, in *Revue des études augustiniennes* 37 (1991), pp. 387–90.

41 Flasch, op. cit., pp. 403–7.

42 On the Platonism of Augustine's time as Hellenised, Orientalised and Christianised, see Martin Heidegger, 'Augustinus und der Neuplatonismus', *Phänomenologie des religiösen Lebens. Gesamtausgabe*, II, 60, Frankfurt am Main, Klostermann, 1995, pp. 160–299, at p. 171.

43 G. Reale remarks in the preface to his edition of *Aurelio Agostino. Natura del Bene*, Milan, Vita e pensiero, 1995, p. 10, that without Platonism, it is impossible to understand Augustine (or, better, it is impossible to understand his stature as a thinker). On the progress of Platonic studies, see K. Corrigan and P. O'Cleirigh, 'The Course of Plotinian Scholarship from 1971–86', in *Aufstieg und Niedergang der römischen Welt*, II.36.1, Berlin/New York, Walter De Gruyter, 1987, pp. 571–623; A. Smith, op. cit.; G. Girgenti, *Porfirio negli ultimi cinquant'anni*, Milan, Vita e pensiero, 1994; G. Reale (ed.), *Verso una nuova immagine di Platone*, Milan, Vita e pensiero, ²1994, especially the essay by W. Beierwaltes, 'Il paradigma neoplatonica nell'interpretazione di Platone', pp. 43–69.

44 G. Reale, Introduction to C. Faraggiana di Sarzana, tr., *Proclo. I Manuali*, Milan, Vita e pensiero, 1985, p. ccxx; also G. Reale, *Per una nuova interpretazione di Platone*, Milan, Vita e pensiero, 1987, pp. 66, 70.

45 J. Dillon (ed.), *Iamblichi Chalcidensis in Platonis dialogos commentariorum fragmenta*, Leiden, E. J. Brill, 1973, pp. 412–16: Appendix B, 'Iamblichus and the Origin

of the Doctrine of Henads' = *Phronesis* 17 (1972), pp. 102–6; see also A. Smith, 'Iamblichus' Views on the Relationship of Philosophy to Religion in *De mysteriis*', in H. Blumenthal and E. Clark (eds), *The Divine Iamblichus. Philosopher and Man of Gods*, London, Bristol Classics Press, 1993, pp. 74–86.

46 See Iamblichus, *De mysteriis* 2.11 (ed. É. des Places, *Jamblique. Les mystères d'Égypte*, Paris, Les Belles Lettres, 1966, p. 96):

> et ce n'est pas non plus l'acte de penser qui unit aux dieux les théurges; car alors qu'est-ce qui empêcherait ceux qui philosophent théoriquement d'arriver à l'union théurgique avec les dieux? Mais la verité est toute autre: c'est l'accomplissement religieux des actions ineffables dont les effets dépassent toute intellection . . . qui opèrent l'union théurgique.

> (and it is no longer the act of thinking which unites the theurgists to the gods; otherwise who would impede those who philosophise contemplatively [*théoriquement*] from attaining theurgical union with the gods? The truth is altogether different: it is the religious accomplishment of ineffable acts, the effects of which surpass all intellection . . . which is at work in theurgical union.)

47 As Beierwaltes, *Agostino*, op. cit., p. 105, remarks, Porphyry 'interpreted the Aristotelian god . . . into the Neoplatonic horizon of a theological *henology*'. And thus, according to G. Reale, Introduction to G. Girgenti, *Il pensiero forte di Porfirio*, Milan, Vita e pensiero, 1996, p. 28: 'it appears clearly that the metaphysics of Porphyry is organised as an *onto-henology* or a highly personalised attempt at synthesis between *ontology* and *henology*'. See also K. Corrigan, 'Amelius, Plotinus and Porphyry on Being, Intellect and the One. A Reappraisal', in *Aufstieg und Niedergang der römischen Welt*, II.36.2, Berlin/New York, Walter De Gruyter, 1987, pp. 974–93.

48 See the discussion by Beierwaltes, *Agostino*, op. cit., pp. 135–8: 'La tesi di Agostino: funzione fondativa del pensiero di Dio'.

49 On the supra-rational faculty of the soul (*anthos nou*), see H. Lewy, *Chaldaean Oracles and Theurgy. Mysticism, Magic and Platonism in the Later Roman Empire*, ed. M. Tardieu, Paris, Etudes augustiniennes, ²1978, p. 168 and n. 383; Reale, Introduction to *Proclo*, op. cit., p. clxxviii. For Augustine's assessment of the problems of theurgy and mediation, see *ciu.* 10.27, with reference to Porphyry; his correspondence with Longinianus, *ep.* 233–5, and *s. Dolbeau* 26 = F. Dolbeau, *Augustin d'Hippone. Vingt-six sermons au peuple d'Afrique*, Paris, Etudes augustiniennes, 1996, pp. 345–417. Dolbeau comments (p. 345): 'Ce *Contra paganos* est en fait un *Contra sacrilegas purgationes philosophorum*, visant les néoplatoniciens, avant de culminer sur le plus bel exposé pastoral qui nous soit parvenu *De uero mediatore Christo*' ('This *Contra paganos* is in fact a *Contra sacrilegas purgationes philosophorum* – aimed at Neoplatonists – before it culminates in his most beautiful pastoral exposition *De vero mediatore Christo* to have come down to us').

50 'Circolo ermeneutico' is G. Reale's phrase for the dialectical relation between faith and reason. See Reale, *Agostino. Amore Assoluto*, op. cit., p. 62.

51 On the importance of this point for the history of mysticism, see R. Crouse,

'What is Augustinian in Twelfth-Century Mysticism?' in F. van Fleteren, J. Schnaubelt and J. Reino (eds), *Collectanea Augustiniana. Augustine. Mystic and Mystagogue*, Frankfurt am Main / New York, Peter Lang, 1994, pp. 401–414.

52 G. Madec, 'Si Plato viveret . . . (Augustin De vera religione 3.3)', in *Neoplatonisme, Mélanges offerts à Jean Trouillard = Les cahiers de Fontenay* (1981), pp. 231–47; see also Adolf Harnack, *Lehrbuch der Dogmengeschichte*, vol. 3, Freiburg, J. C. B. Mohr, 1890, p. 95: 'Augustin hat die Entwickelung der antike Philosophie zu Ende geführt . . . was längst gesucht wurde – das Innenleben zum Ausgangspunkt des Denkens über die Welt zu machen – das hat er getan.' ('Augustine led the development of ancient philosophy to its end . . . what was sought for so long – to make the inner life the point of departure for thinking about the world – that is what he has done.')

53 G. Madec, *Saint Augustin et la philosophie*, op. cit., p. 20.

54 S. Menn, *Descartes and Augustine*, Cambridge, Cambridge University Press, 1998, p. 195. Contrary to Menn (p. 200), Augustine does not think 'the Platonists had the orthodox doctrine of the Trinity', but only a vague intimation, at best approximating a kind of Arianism. See Crouse, '*In Aenigmate Trinitas*', op. cit., pp. 59, 60.

55 *Uera rel.* 4.7; CCL 32.192: 'et paucis mutatis verbis atque sententiis Christiani fierent'.

56 J. J. O'Meara, 'The Neoplatonism of St Augustine', in D. J. O'Meara (ed), *Neoplatonism and Christian Thought*, Norfolk Va., International Society for Neoplatonic Studies, 1982, pp. 34–44.

57 J. Rist, *Augustine. Ancient Thought Baptized*, Cambridge, Cambridge University Press, 1994.

58 On Augustine as 'more a creative interpreter than a passive recipient of Greek philosophy', see N. Blázquez, 'San Agustín, intérprete de la filosofía griega', *Augustinus* 30 (1985), pp. 315–39.

59 See R. Crouse, '*Primordiales Causae* in Eriugena's Interpretation of Genesis: Sources and Significance', in G. Van Riel, C. Steel and J. McEvoy (eds), *Iohannes Scottus Eriugena. The Bible and Hermeneutics*, Leuven, Peeters, 1996, pp. 209–20, at p. 216. As Beierwaltes, *Agostino*, op. cit., p. 157, suggests, Augustine's Christian doctrine involves an essential transformation of the philosophical element, a new form of thought, and is unthinkable without it.

60 W. Hankey, 'Denys and Aquinas. Antimodern Cold and Postmodern Hot', in L. Ayres and G. Jones (eds), *Christian Origins. Theology, Rhetoric and Community*, London/New York, Routledge, 1998, pp. 139–84, at p. 173.

61 See S. Lilla, 'The Neoplatonic Hypostases and the Christian Trinity', in M. Joyal (ed), *Studies in Plato and the Platonic Tradition. Essays Presented to John Whittaker*, Aldershot, Ashgate, 1997, pp. 127–89.

62 See W. Hankey, 'Dionysian Hierarchy in Thomas Aquinas: Tradition and Transformation', in Y. de Andia (ed), *Denys l'Aréopagite et sa postérité en orient et en occident*, Paris, Etudes augustiniennes, 1997, pp. 405–38: 'What is given a Procline or Dionysian hierarchical order is a typically Augustinian consideration of the divine essence' (p. 436).

63 On Nicaea as a turning-point for Christian Platonism, see F. Ricken, 'Nikaia als Krisis der altchristlichen Platonismus', *Theologie und Philosophie* 44 (1969), pp. 321–41.

64 The phrase is from Hankey, 'Denys and Aquinas', op. cit., p. 139.
65 'Precisely with regard to the Platonism of Augustine there is so much to do, or to re-do'. See G. Reale, 'La recezione del platonismo nel "de ordine" di Agostino', in F. Conca, I. Gualandri and G. Lozza, *Politica, cultura e religione nell'impero romano (secoli IV–VI) tra oriente e occidente*, Naples, M. D'Auria, 1993, pp. 89–109, at p. 90; see also J. J. O'Donnell, 'To Make an End is to Make a Beginning', *Augustinian Studies* 25 (1994), pp. 231–6, at p. 234:

> The place of 'Platonism' in Augustine has been looming larger for forty-odd years, since Courcelle's first book at least. There is no comprehensive reassessment of the debate and of the underlying material . . . There is opportunity for a fresh approach, one I am not entirely confident I can adumbrate.

5

THE FUNDAMENTAL GRAMMAR OF AUGUSTINE'S TRINITARIAN THEOLOGY

Lewis Ayres

In much modern appropriation, Augustine is often treated as the source and exemplar of a distinctively western style of trinitarian theology.[1] This division of trinitarian theologies into 'eastern' and 'western' began, in its modern scholarly form, as a way of indicating the superiority of the 'western' and primarily medieval variety.[2] Ironically, in recent writing, the same division has been used in order to highlight the supposed deficiencies of the West. However, this irony aside, one unfortunate consequence of making Augustine so central to this grand historical narrative of trinitarian theology has been that the unsympathetic reading of his thought commonly found among modern theologians tends to foist onto him all the evils that are supposedly characteristic of later western tradition. Because the overall narrative is accepted as a scholarly given, Augustine is 'read' to fit the place the narrative accords him.

At this point, another irony appears: the modern denigration of this area of Augustine's thought has occurred just as Augustinian scholars have begun to criticise and radically revise the accounts of his trinitarian theology that have been standard since the early years of this century.[3] Unfortunately, the critiques of Augustine's trinitarianism found in much modern theological writing do not occur actively *against* this recent trend in Augustinian scholarship – engaging directly and in detail with original texts and attempting to refute these new scholarly arguments – but largely in *ignorance* of it.[4] To put matters starkly, the account of Augustine's trinitarianism found in modern theological writing is often just the re-presentation of no longer tenable scholarly arguments as if they were simply given: thus, Augustine is also 'read' into the story, largely without much attention to his texts. Given these problems, the greatest difficulty in attempting to shape debate over Augustine's trinitarian theology is to encourage modern writers (and some patristic scholars) to turn in detail to Augustine's texts in their immediate historical context, and to suspend comments about the wider course of theological history. Only through such careful reading can we hope to discuss these texts fruitfully, and slowly begin to assess the wider story that has remained untested for the last few decades.

There are, of course, a number of different charges made against Augustine. Some writers, especially in the English-speaking world, have claimed that Augustine's trinitarian theology is insufficiently trinitarian, that it is overly focused on the unity of God and that it relies upon an alien 'Platonic' metaphysics that serves to prevent a fully trinitarian theology.[5] For example, Cornelius Platinga sees two forces at work in Augustine's trinitarianism: on the one hand, his attention to biblical material draws him towards a pluralistic 'social' trinitarianism while, on the other hand, his commitment to a 'Platonic' doctrine of God's unity and simplicity draws him to corrupt the biblical account in the direction of the focus on God's unity that has been so consistently a mark of western theology.[6]

One related charge, that has come especially from Orthodox theologians, is that Augustine's theology is insufficiently 'personal'. This critique alleges that, because Augustine concentrates so strongly on the unity of God, and on describing this unity through focusing on the shared divine 'essence', he fails to be attentive to the Father's *monarchia* and to the personal foundation of the divine communion. In the strongest of these critiques, Augustine's doctrine of *filioque* stands as proof that he saw the Trinity founded in the unitary divine essence.[7] Although there are other charges made against Augustine, these are in many ways central, because they attack Augustine's ability to set out an appropriate account of the relations between the three persons and the one nature. It is these charges I shall be particularly concerned with in this essay.

My aim here is to offer an account of the most fundamental 'grammar' of persons and essence in Augustine's trinitarian theology. By 'grammar', I refer to the matrix of principles and rules for theological discourse that Augustine inherited and developed. Thus, in asking about the 'grammar' that Augustine developed, I am seeking an answer to the question 'of what Augustine thought were the most fundamental rules for speech about God, if we are to speak appropriately and run as little risk of speaking unworthily as possible.' These rules or principles provided the basis for both the reading of Scripture and for articulating more detailed presentations of the doctrine (in part through the use of likenesses or 'analogies'), and in part they must be reconstructed by seeing how they are used in those situations.[8] Using the term 'grammar' in this context is particularly warranted because of Augustine's insistence that God is ultimately incomprehensible: the task for Christians attempting to set out appropriate terms in which to talk of God is not best described as one of learning how to describe God's nature, but as one of learning how to articulate appropriate rules for human talk of God. Those rules are formed through attention to Scripture and through learning how the practices of Christianity shape certain strategies in theological language rather than others. Creation and God's redemptive action are such that we may talk of God more or less appropriately, using a more or less appropriate grammar, but God is of such a nature that we cannot directly comprehend or describe God.[9]

This essay is divided into three sections. The first section discusses some of the key principles apparent in Augustine's early trinitarian theology and his debt to Platonic themes. If we are to understand the grammar of Augustine's mature trinitarianism, we will need to see something of the sources and concerns that stimulated that development. The second section attempts to show how Augustine came to articulate his mature trinitarian theology through deploying a notion of divine simplicity to develop his inherited Nicene trinitarianism. The concluding section reflects on the relationship between the themes considered in this essay and some of the other charges made against Augustine.

The early Augustine

When the origin of Augustine's trinitarian theology is mentioned in critiques of his thought, two interrelated strategies are frequently found. On the one hand, Augustine's earliest writings are often considered only against the background of Neoplatonic writing, and, on the other, Augustine is usually considered without reference to his immediate theological forebears, the Latin theological tradition of the fourth century. In this attitude, we see echoes of the thesis that Augustine 'converted' first to 'Neoplatonism' and only then truly to Christianity. However, this thesis is rejected by the vast majority of modern Augustinian scholars as being far too simplistic, and its vestiges need to be expunged from treatments of his trinitarian theology. Nevertheless, despite the highly problematic nature of this discredited thesis, some Platonic themes were central to the development of Augustine's trinitarian theology. Hence, we need to begin by thinking about both the character of this Platonism, and, subsequently, the sources for his earliest assumptions in trinitarian theology.

In Book 7 of the *Confessions*, Augustine sets out for us what was perhaps the most important shift in his understanding of God, a shift to a position that basically remained with him until his death.[10] He tells us that he had originally conceived of God as an extended, and perhaps infinitely diffused, material substance. Augustine tells us that the most fundamental problem he saw with this account was that God's materiality must imply God's divisibility (*conf.* 7.1; cf. 7.5). However, through reading some 'books of the Platonists' at the same time as he was returning to his Christianity, Augustine came to a new account of God. This account involved five interrelated and, for Augustine, inseparable elements.

These elements are described at *Confessions* 7.10.16 ff. First, Augustine realised that God was the 'light' of 'Truth itself': immaterial, eternal and everywhere and indivisibly present. God was the immaterial source of all perfections and of all Truth. Second, Augustine understood that God was distinct from all, and yet calling to and drawing all things towards Truth through a benevolent providence. Third, Augustine saw that God was Being itself. 'Truth itself' was identical with the real source of all existence, and thus the incorporeality and infinity of Truth itself did not mean that God was literally nothing (*nihil*). Fourth, Augustine reasoned that all things that are not Being itself exist only by participation in God and through the gift of Being from God. Thus, he could say of himself, 'unless my being remains in Him, it cannot remain in me' (*conf.* 7.11.17). Fifth, Augustine discovered a paradoxical relationship between the soul and God. On the one hand, the soul was immaterial and 'above' the material reality of the body, and when discovered to be such served as a pointer to the nature of God. On the other hand, the soul was still mutable and served only to reveal the incomparable and infinitely surpassing reality and 'light' of the divine.

If we were to add one more point to this list, but a point that does not appear at *Confessions* 7.10.16, it would be that God was 'simple'. At *Confessions* 4.16.28 Augustine describes God as 'marvellously simple and unchangeable' (*mirabiliter simplex atque incommutabilis*). This is taken to imply the foolishness of trying to think of God as subject to accidental predication: imagining God as 'having' greatness or beauty as qualities of a divine 'nature' or 'substance'. Instead, God *is* inseparably and eternally greatness or beauty itself. There is no division possible between being and attributes in the God who 'simply' is those qualities that we want to predicate of God. Divine simplicity is treated as an essential corollary of Augustine's conception of God as immaterial, unchangeable and as Truth itself (although it is by no means simply a 'Neoplatonic' idea).

It is important to realise that Augustine does not offer the summary in *Confessions* 7.10.16 as a comprehensive account of what the Platonic texts said about God. This summary is, rather, an account of certain elements found in those texts that provided a great leap forward in his understanding of God and of reality. It is, therefore, a partial account of how some themes from those texts provided convincing answers to questions raised by his engagements with such movements as Manichaeism and Scepticism (to give just two examples). Indeed, the picture is further complicated when we see that Augustine's encounter with these texts occurred *during* his slow return to Christianity, and *after* his initial encounter with Ambrose of Milan and with Ambrose's spiritual exegesis of the Old Testament. Augustine's eclectic borrowings from Platonism thus took place in the context of an existing knowledge of, and some degree of commitment to (if not yet full faith in) Christian doctrine (cf. *conf.* 7.5.7). As this knowledge and commitment grew, Augustine encountered those texts, and they, in turn, provided a fundamental intellectual orientation which enabled him to articulate more coherently the doctrine that he had begun to treat as authoritative.[11] A final, but important complication to note is that as his theological knowledge grew, he encountered figures whose own theology was already marked by strong commitment to many of the very principles that he had learned from his Platonic reading (writers such as Hilary and Ambrose).[12]

As an important example of the eclectic character of these borrowings, we can note that at *Confessions* 7.9.13–14 Augustine describes his excitement at first reading these texts and seeing in them parallels (under different names) to the Father and Son and to their interrelationship. This passage is revealing because it shows that Augustine came to those texts with an existing knowledge of trinitarian theology, and, in particular, of a Nicene theology which insists on the Son's co-eternal divinity. When Augustine went on to describe what he took from those texts, it is notable that he mentioned, as we have seen, general conceptions of God's immateriality, God's creative providential ordering and the participation of all reality in Being itself, but he did not describe himself as taking any specific details of the ways in which the three Neoplatonic hypostases related together. Although some scholars have attempted the task, it is extremely difficult to make any direct and certain equations between Neoplatonic characterisations of the three hypostases and Augustine's earliest allusions to the trinitarian persons. Recent work by Nello Cipriani, in particular, has shown that such allusions as there may be in Augustine's earliest texts probably demonstrate engagement with Ambrose, and especially with Victorinus, and that it is *their* engagement with Neoplatonic texts which may be reflected in Augustine.[13] Hence, we must look elsewhere for evidence of the most fundamental principles of Augustine's early trinitarianism.

We might begin this task by noting the significance of a text that has been greatly neglected in the study of Augustine's trinitarian theology, his *Letter* 11. The letter was written in AD 389, only three years after his conversion, and contains one of the very earliest direct discussions of trinitarian theology.[14] Augustine presents a key principle thus:

> For, according to the Catholic faith, the Trinity is proposed to our belief and believed – and even understood by a few saints and holy persons – as so inseparable that whatever action is performed by it must be thought to be performed at the same time by the Father and by the Son and by the Holy Spirit . . . the Son does not do anything which the Father and the Holy Spirit do not also do.
>
> (*ep.* 11.2)

Here, Augustine takes as a fundamental axiom of trinitarian theology the doctrine that the three persons work inseparably. Augustine does not argue for this point, but, rather, states it as an inherited part of tradition, and thus provides us with a key indicator of the specific tradition in which his early trinitarian theology should be located.

It is not surprising that he would see this principle as fundamental to orthodox trinitarian theology, given its centrality to the previous generation of Latin anti-'Arian', or more accurately anti-'Homoian' theologians.[15] The works of some of those theologians Augustine knew well and, indeed, his own catechesis occurred within that tradition.[16] For example, in his *De Spiritu Sancto* (c. AD 387–90) Ambrose writes:

> If then the peace of the Father, the Son and the Holy Spirit is one, the grace one, the love one and the communion one, the working is certainly one, and where the working is one, certainly the power cannot be divided nor the substance separated . . . And not only is the operation of the Father, Son and Spirit everywhere one but also there is one and the same will, calling and giving of commands.[17]

In this text, we see the doctrine's polemical origins. Many non-Nicene theologians argued that the divided activity of the persons indicated that the Father and Son were separate beings and that only the Father was truly God. For example, the fact that only the Son became incarnate and visible, or that the Spirit is spoken of as being sent only *after* the ascension, seemed to indicate that 1 Tim 6:16 was right to insist that only the Father 'has immortality and dwells in unapproachable light'. Against such theologies, pro-Nicene writers argued that as the activity of the three is seen to be one, so must their nature be one. Much exegetical effort is expended by such figures as Ambrose and Hilary to show that the activities of creation, redemption and sanctification are described in such a way that it is clear that *all* three persons are equally involved. The doctrine of inseparable operation also implies that whatever the three trinitarian persons possess by virtue of being, God may be spoken of in the singular: God is, to amalgamate some of the terms used, one power, one nature, one virtue, one goodness. Although this doctrine is fundamental to late fourth-century, orthodox, Latin theology, it is important that we do not think of 'inseparable operation' as a peculiarly Latin phenomena. The inseparable operation of the three irreducible persons is a fundamental axiom of those theologies which provide the context for the Council of Constantinople in AD 381 and for the reinterpretation of Nicaea, which came to be the foundation of orthodox or catholic theology at the end of the fourth century. It is a principle found in all the major orthodox Greek theologians of the later fourth and fifth centuries, and enters later Orthodox tradition through such figures as John of Damascus in the eighth century.[18]

Thus, *Letter* 11 enables us to observe that Augustine's earliest understanding of the trinitarian persons sits within the traditions of late fourth-century (Latin), pro-Nicene theology. *Letter* 11 offers some account of the relations between the persons, but a more extended account of Augustine's early understanding of the roles and nature of the three persons is seen particularly clearly in the short *De fide et symbolo* of AD 393, a brief commentary on the creed read to African bishops assembled in Hippo. Here, we read that the Word was not made out of either nothing or pre-existing matter but 'from [the Father's] eternal substance'. The existence and consubstantiality of the Word demonstrates that, unlike any human speaker, the Father has the power to reveal himself perfectly (*f. et symb.* 3.4–4.5). The Father is also the personal source of the Son's co-equal nature: 'The Son as Son has received existence from the Father . . . the Son owes the Father his existence, but also owes him his equality with the Father' (*f. et symb.* 6.18). At the same time, although we can make such statements, we cannot claim comprehension of the ineffable God: no corporeal analogy can reveal to us the workings of the divine nature of 'He who is'. Augustine's concerns here again reflect those of immediately preceding tradition. One of his central concerns in the christological sections of this text is to show the equality of Father and Son who are of 'one substance'. He makes use of a key anti-'Homoian' verse, in claiming that the Father does all things through the Word who is 'the Power and Wisdom of God' (1 Cor 1:24), and he shows himself well aware of other key texts in dispute, such as Prov 8:22 and those texts that seem to point to the Son's subordination. We should also notice the emphasis he places on the Father and Son being of one substance, and how he assumed that this theology enables us to talk of a true revelation of the Father through the Son.

Augustine then comes to the Spirit, and the question of origin becomes more complex. He lists two basic principles: the Spirit is not begotten like the Son; the Father is the ultimate source of the Spirit (and, thus, the Spirit is not begotten by the Son at one remove from the Father). Further progress in describing the nature of the Spirit's procession (beyond simply saying that it is 'different' from that of the Son) can only be made by describing the place of the Spirit within the Trinity. In an attempt to make progress, Augustine turns to an argument he describes as that of others: 'some have even dared to believe that the Holy Spirit is the communion (*communio*) or deity so to speak of the Father and Son' (*f. et symb.* 9.19).[19] Expanding on this, Augustine says that the Spirit is the love between Father and Son and is thus 'the love of God'. The Spirit is also called the 'love of God' with reference to humanity, because it is by the Spirit that we are enabled to follow Christ. Although Augustine has previously described the Spirit as the gift of God, as the finger of God and as the love of God, this is the first attempt he makes to describe the Spirit as the communion of Father and Son. The attempt does not occupy much text and is rather clumsy. Nevertheless, this passage does show evidence of engagement with his predecessors: allusion to Marius Victorinus is possibly to be found in the idea of the Spirit as the communion of Father and Son, while allusion to Ambrose and to Jerome's translation of Didymus the Blind's *De Spiritu Sancto* stands conceivably behind the odd (and not repeated) equation of communion and 'deity'.[20]

Interestingly, especially in view of the next section of this essay, Augustine admits that 'others' have refused to see that such a theology does not accord the Spirit truly substantial existence, because the joint between two bodies is not itself a body.[21] To defend the idea of the Spirit as communion, we see Augustine making subtle, if highly condensed and suggestive, use of his 'Platonic' resources. In a few short sentences, he argues that the Spirit is only thought to be 'in-substantial' by those who (perhaps inadvertently) conceive of the joining (*copulatio*) between Father and Son as the joining of two material bodies, and therefore think that when the two joined bodies are separated the 'joint' does not remain. However, Augustine argues, once we realise that God is immaterial and simple, then we shall see that the analogy between the joining of two material bodies and the joining of Father and Son is mistaken. In God, there are no relationships that are not eternal and essential to God, there is nothing in God that is not eternally part of what it is to be God. Hence, it is not the case that the love between Father and Son is only a temporary aspect of Father and Son. That love is inseparable from the reality, being or substance of both, and, thus, the Spirit may be conceived as love *and* as a divine and 'substantial' person.[22]

I will not discuss the development of Augustine's view of the Spirit's procession in any detail in this essay, except to indicate briefly during the next part of the argument that his view of the Spirit as communion does not indicate that the Spirit's procession stems from some sort of 'shared' divine essence, rather than from the personal work of Father and Son.[23] For my argument here, the significance of the pneumatological reasoning we have just followed in *De fide et symbolo* is that Augustine again attempts to advance on his sources through applying the explanatory resources of his 'Platonic' account of God's nature to deal with an inherited problem. In the case of Father and Son, he has insisted – in a way that would have made Ambrose or Hilary proud – that the generation of the Word by the Father does not imply subordination, because the generation and its product are subject to the rules of God's immaterial and ineffable nature. Now we see him applying the same methodology to pneumatology.

After offering this exploratory account of the Spirit, Augustine admits that there is an important distinction between believing rightly about the Trinity and grasping the significance of that belief or growing in understanding of it. The distinction is one we find throughout Augustine's career: appropriate belief should form a basis and focal point for a continuing struggle to articulate a reasoned account of the propositions that are believed. Augustine insists that we should begin by *believing* that:

> the Father is God and the Son is God and the Holy Spirit is God; that there are not three Gods, but that the Trinity is one God; that the persons are not diverse in nature but are of the same substance; that the Father is always the Father and the Son always the Son and the Holy Spirit always the Holy Spirit.
>
> (*f. et symb.* 9.20)

The last clause is aimed against any trinitarian analogy which speaks of a shared substance that may 'move' from person to person and, in particular, suggests a formula by which the early Augustine attempts to exclude Sabellian belief. To this expression of the most basic trinitarian grammar, we might add the following complementary statement from a little earlier in the text:

> [we must believe] that Trinity is one God. Not that Father, Son and Spirit are identically the same. But Father is Father, the Son is Son and the Holy Spirit is Holy Spirit, and this Trinity is one God, as it is written 'Hear O Israel, the Lord thy God is one God.
>
> (*f. et symb.* 9.6)

From the texts I have examined in this section of the essay, we can see some of Augustine's most fundamental trinitarian principles and we can see the task that Augustine has inherited from tradition, and from his personal development, in attempting to articulate an account of Christian belief about the relationship between the three persons and the one substance. The two quotations in the previous paragraph set out perhaps the most fundamental grammar of the relations between persons and essence: the persons are irreducible, and yet God is one. This basic grammar, which I take to be pro-Nicene and spanning the Greek–Latin divide, is taken by Augustine to form the basis for our articulations of the generation and action of the three persons. The principles of that generation and conjoint activity constitute themselves a level of trinitarian grammar inherited from previous Nicene exegesis. In the attempt to show how we may deploy these principles in the task of articulating our beliefs, we have seen Augustine turning to what we might term his complementary grammar of divine simplicity as identified in *Confessions* 7. Our task now is to examine how Augustine maintained his Nicene principles, but came to articulate them in increasingly sophisticated ways using this grammar of divine simplicity.

The mature Augustine

The basic principles of Augustine's trinitarian grammar remained with him in subsequent decades and, indeed, their insistence on the irreducibility of the divine persons was considerably strengthened. To show that this is so, we can turn to his *Sermon* 52 (c. AD 410). This sermon, which relates the narrative of Christ's baptism in the Jordan at Mt. 3:13ff, furnishes a fascinating document which anticipates some key aspects of the latter half of the *De trinitate*. In the descent of the dove over the head of Jesus, and the sounding of the voice from heaven acclaiming Christ (Mt 3:16–17), we are presented, says Augustine, with 'a sort of separated Trinity': each of the three persons seems to be accorded a different activity.

Augustine had no sooner pointed towards this seeming separation of the persons and their activities, when he imagines himself open to a charge from an imaginary interlocutor, 'But one may say to me: "Show the Trinity to be inseparable: remember that you are Catholic and that it is to Catholics that you are speaking"' (*s.* 52.2).

Once again, the doctrine of inseparable operation is taken as a well-known and fundamental doctrinal rule. The doctrine is then given a gloss that shows how clearly this is a doctrine about the unity of three irreducible persons:

> the Father, Son and Holy Spirit are a Trinity inseparable; one God not three Gods. But yet so one God, as that the Son is not the Father, and the Father is not the Son, and the Holy Spirit is neither the Father nor the Son, but the Spirit of the Father and of the Son. This ineffable Divinity, abiding ever in itself, making all things new, creating, creating anew, sending, recalling, judging, delivering, this Trinity, I say, we know to be at once ineffable and inseparable.
>
> (*s.* 52.2)[24]

Augustine now asks how it is that such a faith may be seen as consonant with the separation between the persons seemingly apparent at Mt 3:13ff (*s.* 52.4). Against the seemingly obvious separations of Mt 3:13ff, and the conflict between Scripture and traditional confession that seems now to have become apparent, Augustine says that he will first consider the relationship of Father and Son. To do so, he brings forward John 1 and Wisdom 8:1, which, taken together, are read as indicating that the creating and the ordering of the world are jointly the work of the Father and the Son (*s.* 52.5). Having made his way via Scripture back towards the doctrine of inseparable operation, which had seemed initially against Scripture, Augustine restates the paradox caused by inseparable operation as a doctrine, even when it is seen (truly) as a doctrine of Scripture.

He does so by drawing attention to a basic problem of such a trinitarian grammar: should we say that the Father was also born of the Virgin? 'God forbid', he says, 'we do not say this, because we do not believe it' (*s.* 52.6). Indeed, he continues, the creed seems to make it clear that the Father was not born of a virgin, did not suffer and did not rise again: these are, the creed teaches us, the works of the Son. Thus, Augustine's tactic in this restatement of the problem is to draw attention to the problems of a 'Patripassian' reading: a reading which would *over-*, or wrongly, emphasise the inseparability to the extent of contradicting the creed. However, this argument has so far only brought us back to our starting point: if the creed is right, then we seem to have a clear example of the Son doing something that the Father does not. Augustine moves us forward by first stating the answer he thinks necessary in his own words and then by demanding that it be proved by the Scriptures. The answer, in sum, is that:

The Son indeed and not the Father was born of the Virgin Mary; but this very birth of the Son, not of the Father, was the work both of the Father and the Son. The Father indeed suffered not, but the Son, yet the suffering of the Son was the work of the Father and the Son.

(s. 52.8)

The sections that follow list scriptural testimony to demonstrate the appropriateness of this formula for describing the scriptural accounts of the Son's birth, death and resurrection. At the end of this demonstration, Augustine leaves us with a general principle, 'You have then the distinction of persons, and the inseparableness of operation' (s. 52.14).

This extended discussion repeats all the basic elements of the rules for trinitarian discourse that we saw in *Letter* 11 and *De fide et symbolo*. Augustine sets out his principles in formulae that advance on the early formulations, but which are in clear continuity with them. For example, the virtue of the formula in the last paragraph is that it enables us to insist clearly that the Son alone becomes incarnate, and that the union of divine and human natures that constitutes the Incarnation involves the second person of the Trinity in a way that it does not involve the other divine persons. Nevertheless, such formulae insist that we must still speak of the Incarnation as being the work of the undivided Godhead: all three persons enable this to happen. At the same time, this formula is compatible with the insistence that, through that union, Christ's human nature (and the rest of humanity) is united with the Trinity as a whole.[25] Although Augustine does not possess the complex christological language of later generations for talking about the particular activity of the Incarnate Word in a trinitarian context, his principles are compatible with forming the basis for those later developments (a statement also true of the Cappadocians).

The formulae we have seen in *Sermon* 52 are austere: they are an attempt to set out appropriate rules for an orthodox reading of Scripture and for orthodox talk of God. To use a description I outlined earlier, they are an attempt to set out what we must *believe* rather than a detailed *articulation* of trinitarian belief. However, it is important to note that in these statements of belief, which are intended as the foundation for more complex articulation, we have not as yet seen any evidence to sustain the charge that Augustine 'begins' with the unity of God in a way that promotes the divine essence as prior to the persons. I wish now to turn to those mature texts in which he does attempt to offer a more nuanced articulation of what it means to say that there are three persons and one God. In particular, I am concerned to offer an interpretation of how *De trinitate* 7 makes use of an understanding of God's simplicity, to develop our understanding of the unity of the three persons without sacrificing the principles that the persons are irreducible and that the Son is generated eternally out of the Father's 'substance'.

As is well known, Augustine consistently argues that fallen humanity has a tendency to avoid thinking with sufficient rigour through the consequences of God's being an immaterial reality: we are consistently drawn to imagining God according to the characteristics of material objects. We might say that the (often unconscious) tendency of fallen humanity is to apply to God the rules we use for *the grammar of* material objects.[26] Within this general critique of fallen humanity's discourse about God, Augustine diagnoses, as a particular problem, our tendency to separate persons from essence, to treat the essence as something 'behind' the persons. In his *Letter* 120 (c. AD 410) Augustine argues that we must not conceive of the relationships between the persons according to material analogies. The three should not be imagined as three large objects spatially bounded, nor as touching, nor as extended in any shape, such as a triangle (*in modum trigoni*). Augustine goes on to argue, on the one hand, against any attempt to conceive of the persons as somehow limited, and the divinity as infinite and, on the other hand, against any assertion that the substance of the Trinity is different from the Father, the Son and the Spirit. Augustine says:

> the Father, the Son and the Holy Spirit are the Trinity, but they are only one God; not that the divinity, which they have in common, is a sort of fourth person, but that the Godhead is ineffably and inseparably a Trinity.
>
> (*ep.* 120.3.13)

> You know that in the Catholic faith it is the true and firm belief that the Father and the Son and the Holy Spirit are one God, while remaining a Trinity . . . the Trinity is of one substance and {the} *essence is nothing else than the Trinity itself.*
>
> (*ep.* 120.3.17, emphasis added)

Augustine then says that the word 'substance' is confusing here because it makes us think of a unitary 'reality' apart from the three persons. Augustine suggests that 'divinity' is a better term or 'essence', which he takes here to be closer to Greek *ousia* and to remind us of God's status as Being itself. Thus, we again find a hint that the best way, according to Augustine, that we can successfully articulate what we mean by the unity of God and the irreducibility of the persons, is by attention to the grammar of divine simplicity rather than the grammar of materiality. To appreciate such an articulation contextually and more extensively, we can turn to *De trinitate* 7, although we must first, briefly place that book in the context of Books 5 and 6.

At the beginning of *De trinitate* 5, Augustine describes what it means for God to be one essence, or *ousia*, by reference to God as Being itself, the only being that is unchangeable and hence not capable of possessing accidents (*trin.* 5.2.3–3.4). His summary of God's attributes here reiterates the same themes we saw at *Confessions* 7.10.16, and enables Augustine to insist that we must continually guard our speech so that God is not described as a reality like other realities. Augustine then begins to consider whether words used of God always describe God's essence, or whether they sometimes describe things 'accidental' to God. He does so in response to some Homoian theologies which claim that all terms used of God describe God's substance, thus that 'unbegotten' describes the substance of the Father while 'begotten' describes the substance of the Son. Augustine first argues that the Homoians are right to say that nothing accidental may be predicated of God. Following an argument with which we are now familiar, Augustine says that God is simple, that is, in God all qualities are identical with God's essence : to be is the same as to be wise, to use a key Augustinian example. Nevertheless, Augustine continues, not all things are said of God directly about God's substance. Such an assumption would imply a series of basic contradictions or incoherencies in Scripture. We can see one of these immediately in the 'Arian' suggestion that both 'begotten' and 'unbegotten' are spoken according to substance. If these two terms are understood to be predicated directly about God's substance, they indicate a distinction between Father and Son such that the two cannot be 'of one substance'. However, argues Augustine, by applying the same rules, Jn 10:30's 'I and the Father are one' would then also have to be applied to God's substance and would indicate that there was no such distinction! The Homoian suggestion seems initially attractive, but it yields a basic incoherence (*trin.* 5.3.4).

Augustine's famous solution to this problem is that the only category we may discern in our talk of God, other than language about essence or substance, is language in terms of relation (*trin.* 5.5.6–5.7).[27] We may summarise his twofold solution in these terms: we can, on the one hand, say that God 'is' something. By so doing, we mean that this quality or term is essential to God, it is essential to what Father, Son and Spirit are. In any such case, we are not to think that there is more essence in two or three than in one divine person, or that the essence is something from which the three persons stem. On the other hand, we can talk of Father, Son and Spirit in so far as they are related to each other. In this case, to give an example, we may say that the Father is eternally Father and the Son is eternally Son without meaning that they are distinct substances or that the Son is only 'accidental', separable from what it is to be God. In such a case we are saying that 'Father' and 'Son' are terms which indicate relationships, but that those relationships are essential to being God.

In this way, we have established a coherent language for talking about the unity of God's being (according to substance), *and* we have ascertained a way to talk about the distinctions between the persons without simply contradicting what we say about God's unity (according to relation). This twofold language also enables us to speak of God's unity, and of the distinct persons, without implying that the distinctions are somehow secondary to the shared substance : terms that are used 'according to relation' designate relations that are eternally so. Augustine's primary concern throughout this argument is to demonstrate the appropriate structure of a coherent language in trinitarian theology: we can now understand more clearly how to talk about the Trinity, and how to interpret scriptural texts about God, without falling into the most irreducible incoherence, all the while preserving the principles of the unity and distinctness of the persons. Thus far, the argument is relatively well known and it is probably clear by now that one of the key points of departure for this argument is the idea of God's simplicity. However, there are other dimensions to the argument that have not yet been considered, and they are essential if we are to grasp the full significance of how the grammar of simplicity helps Augustine to articulate his Nicene trinitarian theology. Augustine's insistence that God is immaterial, and that the essence is not prior to the persons, should begin to help us realise that he does not want us to take his division of trinitarian language into essential and relational, as indicating that God is one thing or substance with secondary internal divisions. Nevertheless, he has further to go in explaining how badly to do so would mistake his intentions.

The further dimensions to Augustine's above-mentioned argument are particularly drawn out in the first half of Book 7. Here, the question Augustine poses is whether each of the persons may be called God singly, or whether the term is only appropriate when used of the three together. Augustine begins by offering a *reductio ad absurdum* argument demonstrating the dire consequences of saying that the Father is wise 'in the same way that he speaks' (*trin*. 7.1.1). The Father speaks *through* the Word: is he then wise '*through* his Wisdom'? The argument that follows has an important exegetical context (although that will not concern us directly). Much of Book 6 was aimed at refuting non-Nicene (and earlier Nicene) exegesis of 1 Cor 1:24. That argument is now being invoked as a preliminary to Book 7. Augustine is unhappy with the idea that the Father is wise *through* the eternal presence of his Wisdom in the form of the co-eternal Word. The reasons for his unhappiness stem from his understanding of God's simplicity, and this will require further clarification.

If we were to say, as some Nicene exegetes had done (see *trin*. 6.1.1), that the Father was wise *through* the eternal presence of the Father's Wisdom, then the same argument would pertain about Power (because the two terms are joined in 1 Cor 1:24): the Father would be, or would have, Power only through the presence of his Power to him. Now, unless we were to allow that the Father was wise by virtue of one thing and powerful by virtue of another, the logical consequences of this move would be that the Father was only God because of the Son's presence: at its most absurd, the Son would be the deity of the Father! For Augustine, this leap may be made because the Father's 'power' must be essential to, and expressive of, the Father's divinity. Obviously enough, it makes no sense to think of the Father as being wise – let alone being God – by participation in something else. To assert this of

God would ultimately mean that the Father simply was not God 'in himself'.[28] To understand Augustine's alternative account of how the Son may be the Wisdom of God while the Father is still wise 'in himself', it may be helpful to follow his argument in three steps.

1   Augustine first insists that 'every essence which is spoken of relatively is something apart from that relative predication'.[29] Note that, at this stage in the argument, Augustine does not speak of divine essence with reference to the Trinity as a whole; he is talking of the Father only, while insisting that the persons are not limited as relations. The Father is something 'in himself' and only *because* the Father is such an essence can the Father be spoken of in relation. In fact, this point follows from both Augustine's insistence that to be in relation implies the existence of something which may be in relation, and from the argument that because the Father is God and God is simple, therefore the Father must be wise 'in Himself', in his essence. To call the Father God implies that the Father is 'in Himself' Wisdom itself, Being itself. The individual reality of the Father is thus affirmed.

2   The Father generates the Son. More precisely, we may say that the Father generates the Son's essence: what the Son *is* has been generated by the Father. The Father is the source of the Son's existence. Just as the Son is light from light, Augustine says, so too the Son is Wisdom generated from Wisdom and even *essentia de essentia* (*trin.* 7.2.3). However, this does not mean that the Son is only a part of the Father, or not truly a person 'in himself'. To explain why, and thus to explain the full nature of the generation of the Son, Augustine turns again to the grammar of divine simplicity. If the Son is Wisdom (as 1 Cor 1:24 tells us) and if the Son is God (as the creed tells us), then the Son must 'be wise,' he must be 'Wisdom itself'. In other words, given the identity of 'to be' and 'to be wise' in God, if the Son is truly divine then he must be 'Wisdom itself'.

We may repeat the argument in other terms that bring out another key aspect. To use the term 'God' of the Son must mean that as 'Wisdom itself' the Son is not wise, or powerful, or good, or God by participation in anything else: calling the Son 'God' means that *all* the arguments Augustine has applied to the Father must now be applied to the Son. The grammar of simplicity means that we must say that for God the Father to generate another, a 'Son', both the generator and the generated must be Wisdom and God 'in themselves': the grammar of simplicity allows us to say truly that 'the Father has given the Son to have life in himself' (Jn 5:26). Thus, Augustine is using simplicity as a tool for exploring the unity and multiplicity that the principles of Nicene trinitarian belief commend, and by this we see that a simple being may generate another who is also co-equal and simple.

3   However, the language of divine simplicity goes still further. If the Son

is Wisdom itself and the Father is Wisdom itself, we can continue to say that the Son's essence must be identical with the Father's essence. Obviously, there cannot be two instances of 'Wisdom itself'. Note, however, that this unity does not result from the fact that our grammar forces us to speak of an underlying or shared substance proper to the three persons, as would many material analogies. In other words, a 'material' grammar would only permit us to imagine the unity of the three by drawing an analogy with a material substance shared within three objects, a material substance that would be the ground of or basis for their unity. (One might say, of course, that the example of three people provides a material example, but one which escapes this trap. For Augustine, as for Gregory of Nyssa, such an example fails because it cannot provide an adequate analogy to the inseparable and consubstantial unity of the three divine persons.) However, the grammar of simplicity provides very different linguistic resources for our imagining the unity of the three. When we apply this grammar to the principles of trinitarian theology, we discover, first, that we have found a language in which to speak of the generation of Son from Father as the begetting of one who is truly consubstantial, one who is truly also wisdom and life 'in himself'. But, if we consistently apply this grammar to the principles of trinitarian theology, then the natural conclusion of this generation is that the three persons must be both distinct and also one in the unity of existence and wisdom itself. Although the unity and multiplicity of the triune communion stills remains beyond our intellectual grasp, this language may help to shape our imagination beyond the possibilities that a purely material grammar provides. Such language draws us to the individual reality of the persons and then *immediately* to their unity, without the need to imagine a substance or something which provides that linkage.

In summing up the result of these three steps, we can say that the Father generates the Son who is light from light, wisdom from wisdom and essence from essence. The Son is an essence in Himself, not just a relationship: to speak of the person of the Son is to speak of the Son's essence. And yet, because the Father's and the Son's essence are truly simple, they are of one essence. Because the principles of his trinitarian faith tell him that the Spirit is also God and is a distinct person, the same arguments apply to all three persons. Thus, in using the grammar of simplicity to articulate a concept of Father, Son and Spirit as each God and as the one God, we find that the more we grasp the full reality of each person – the full depth of the being that they have from the Father – the more we are also forced to recognise the unity of their being. We do not identify the unity by focusing on something other than the persons: it is focusing on the persons' possession of wisdom and being 'in themselves' that draws us to recognise their unity. The triune communion *is* a consubstantial and eternal unity ; but there *is* nothing but the persons.

Of course, Augustine's attempt to work *towards* a concept of the unity of God's essence is not intended as a proof: Augustine takes the unity of God's essence to be a truth of the faith. It is, perhaps, better to say that Augustine is making use of the grammar of simplicity to articulate a reasoned presentation of the fundamental principles of trinitarian faith, as we have seen them set out consistently in *De fide et symbolo* and *Sermon* 52.[30] It is also important to reiterate my earlier point that Augustine does not think we can thus comprehend the divine essence: all we have done is to show how our language of God may be given some coherent structure without slipping from the bedrock of right belief.

Much of this sophisticated argument is repeated at *De civitate Dei* 11.10, and it may help to follow through that argument also. Here, Augustine again discusses the nature of God's simplicity, but with special reference to those who might see God's triune nature and God's simplicity as incompatible. Augustine argues directly that to say God is simple is not to say that God consists solely of Father, Son or Spirit (as might be the case for a non-Nicene theologian who concludes, on the basis of 1 Tim 6:16, that only the Father is immortal). Nor is it to say that there is really only a 'nominal Trinity' without really 'subsisting persons' (as Sabellians might argue). Rather, Augustine says, repeating his by now standard definition, to call something simple is to say that its being is identical with its attributes: 'it "is" what it is said to "have"'.

Augustine offers two arguments for why God must be simple. First, things that are not simple are corruptible and changeable because qualities are susceptible to loss: God is not so. Second, things that are not simple possess their qualities through participation: but God possesses, or better, *is* nothing through participation, and thus God can most fittingly be described as simple. We have seen these arguments before. Hence, Augustine insists, we must speak about the generation *and* relation of the divine persons in the context of God's simplicity. That which the simple God 'begets' will be equally simple. The begetter and the begotten we call Father and Son: the simple Father begets a Son who is equally simple. Once again, the Father is the source of the divine essence and simplicity. Each of these divine persons, 'in Himself', has a being in which being and qualities are identical, and each may be said not only to be living (to have life), but to be *life itself* (Jn 5:26). Thus, the being of these two is also the same: they are of one being or substance. As I explained earlier, I have not been concerned in this essay to defend or even to describe Augustine's account of the Spirit's generation: that is a different matter. However, from what we have seen so far, I think it is fair to draw the conclusion that there is no intrinsic connection between Augustine's assertions that the Spirit is the communion of Father and Son as a 'substantial' person, or that the Spirit proceeds from Father and Son (through the Father's act of *principium*), and some sort of tendency towards the primacy of a divine substance.[31]

Before moving on, we should note finally that Book 7 of *De trinitate* also hints at an important argument we find in full form in Book 15. At *trin.* 15.6.10, Augustine offers a short résumé of the argumentation which led to the discussion of the conjoint action of *memoria*, *intellegentia* and *voluntas* when focused on God as an imperfect analogy for the trinitarian communion. Augustine ends this résumé with two criticisms of his analogy. First, this triad is found *in* the human being but it is not identical *with* the human being: the Trinity itself is identical with God, not with something *in* God (*trin.* 15.7.11). Second, none of the three terms of Augustine's final analogy should be taken as equivalent to a person of the Trinity: the Father is not somehow equivalent to memory, the Son to intelligence and the Spirit to will. Importantly, Augustine argues that this cannot be so, by directly drawing a parallel with the argument in Book 7 that the Father is not wise because the Son is continually present, but because Father and Son share the one wisdom that is identical with God's simple essence (*trin.* 15.7.11). If God is a simple essence and yet irreducibly trinitarian, then each of the three persons must possess their *own* memory, intelligence and will. Later, in Book, 15 he writes: 'all together possess and each one possesses all three of these in their own nature'.[32] None of the persons is dependent on the others for anything that is essential to God, although the essence of the three persons is one. Thus, not only does the doctrine of divine simplicity provide a grammar for asserting the generation of the persons from the Father, but it also provides a grammar for ensuring the irreducibility of the persons in our trinitarian language.

Conclusion

The charge that Augustine's theology describes the divine essence as prior to the divine persons, or as the source of the persons, is unwarranted. In fact, he consistently and specifically rules out any such account of the divine essence. He also clearly maintains the Father as the personal source of the divine simplicity and essence. Using the grammar of simplicity, Augustine argues that we should beware of speaking about a substance in which the three persons are 'contained': there is *nothing but* the three co-eternal and consubstantial persons. Thus, one of the most fascinating things about Augustine's mature trinitarian theology is that it is the 'grammar of divine simplicity' that enables further development of such a sophisticated Nicene theology.

One of the great virtues of David Burrell's remarkable book, *Knowing the Unknowable God*, is that it shows so succinctly how the medieval distinction between essence and existence enabled theologians to talk about the distinction between God and the world in a meaningful way.[33] By reflecting on the idea of existence as essential to all things, and yet not as a predicate of them,

God could be coherently described as the source of all existence, without implying in any simple fashion that God could be comprehended by the intellect, and without subjecting God to the grammar of material objects. The distinction itself occurred within the created order, and yet provided the grammar for a discussion of what lay beyond it. In Augustine's thought, I suggest, the grammar of simplicity plays a similar role.

Christians are continually faced with the task of talking coherently about a God who is distinctly Father, Son and Spirit, and yet who is also the one God of Israel. We cannot fully comprehend this mixture of unity and distinctness according to *any* earthly analogy,[34] and, indeed, Augustine sees what he thinks of as the two main trinitarian heresies to be the product of too easy an application of material analogies to the Creator. However, if this is so, then we must search to see if there is any language that will provide us with terms for articulating the structure of our belief beyond just re-stating its most fundamental principles. For Augustine, the grammar of simplicity is directed to just that task. Thus, this language or grammar does not function as a sufficient description of God, but rather as a tool for articulating the basic statements of trinitarian belief that Augustine takes to be a matter of revelation.

Although it is foolish to attempt to rule out Platonic influence on Augustine's trinitarianism, there is yet another irony in the fact that the key role 'Platonism' plays in Augustine's doctrine of God is virtually the opposite of that which it is taken to play by those who commonly criticise the 'Platonism' in his theology.[35] The grammar of God's simplicity (which Augustine closely links with his Platonic readings) serves not to make God a unitary essence, or to replace biblical exegesis with discussion of the three Neoplatonic hypostases. Rather, that grammar serves to enhance the explanatory power of a fully Nicene trinitarianism, in which the order of trinitarian generation is preserved, and in which Father, Son and Spirit are equally bound by the terms of divinity without ceasing to be 'other' to each other. Thus, we see how well the sources of Augustine's doctrine of God came to meld: Latin pro-Nicene theology (already partly 'Platonic' in character), and some themes derived from a Platonic cosmology, formed the basis for what we should recognise as a key statement of Nicene trinitarian theology.

This essay has not set out to refute all the chief criticisms directed towards Augustine's trinitarian theology. However, if my approach to this one key aspect of those erroneous interpretations is correct, then I would also wish to argue that the groundwork has been laid for a more comprehensive refutation of many other criticisms frequently levelled against Augustine's trinitarianism. The lines of such a refutation can be seen by noting the importance Augustine places, first, on the incomprehensibility of the divine nature to human (and especially fallen) intelligences, and, second, on the need for Christians to struggle to grow in the ability to imagine the divine through the cultivation of appropriate faith and practice. The development and purification of the Christian intellect occurs within an *askesis* of the Christian as unified body and soul, as an embodied rational being living within the Christian sacramental community. From the period before writing the *Confessions* until his death, Augustine articulated this process of purification within a christological perspective.[36] Within this christology, one of the functions of the incarnate and resurrected Christ is to lead our intelligence beyond an obsession with the material, to imagine the immaterial reality of the divine as the source of our material world.

Thus, all Christian talk of God finds itself located *within* this reformation and reorientation of the Christian: indeed, we may see that Augustine locates the enterprise of theological reflection within the economy of redemption in three key ways. First, we can only understand the task the theologian faces by grasping something of the nature and purpose of the redemptive drama as a whole. Only when we see how that drama represents God's speaking in the world, so that we may no longer be subject to it and to its powers, can we grasp the full task of attempting to talk of God. Second, Augustine's conception of theological reflection is, more particularly, part of the Christian's participation in the mystery of dying, rising and ascending with Christ: only *within* this movement may both the inner and outer person be restored and the mind come to imagine God, as far as it may, without delusion or self-deceit. Third, the exegesis of Scripture provides the point of departure for the enterprise of trinitarian theology and for the conjoint exercise of the rational powers that is central to that enterprise: but we can only come to see what is involved in reading this Scripture by seeing how a particular text fits within God's overall redemptive economy. Only then may we grasp how the materialism of scriptural texts about the divine challenges us to move beyond the material, and to begin to develop a grammar of divine distinction from the world – in Augustine's case to begin to develop a grammar of divine simplicity – in order to secure God's fully trinitarian nature. Thus, struggling to apply the grammar of simplicity to the triune God plays, for Augustine, a small part in the movement of the human being, in Christ, towards God as the creator and source of all wisdom and power and truth.

Notes

1 I would like to express my gratitude to the editors for comments on an earlier draft, and to Michel Barnes for the continuing conversation on the subject of this paper which is a fundamental part of my research. Some aspects of the first half of this article are set out in a more detailed form in my '"Remember that you are Catholic" (*serm.* 52,2): Augustine on the Unity of the Triune God', *Journal of Early Christian Studies* 7 (1999). M. R. Barnes, 'Re-reading Augustine's Theology of the Trinity', in S. T. Davis, D. Kendall and G. O'Collins (eds), *The Trinity: An Interdisciplinary Symposium on the Doctrine of the Trinity*, Oxford / New York, Oxford University Press, 1999, presents a complementary perspective to that essay. Other than the material listed below in n. 3,

the best extended introductory treatment of Augustine's doctrine of God currently available in English is B. Studer, *The Grace of Christ and the Grace of God in Augustine of Hippo: Christocentrism or Theocentrism?*, tr. M. J. O'Connell, Collegeville Minn., Liturgical Press, 1997.

2 See M. R. Barnes, 'De Régnon Reconsidered', *Augustinian Studies* 26 (1995), pp. 51–79; idem, 'Augustine in Contemporary Trinitarian Theology', *Theological Studies* 56 (1995), pp. 237–50.

3 Other than the articles of M. R. Barnes and my own articles cited in these notes, I think especially of F. Bourassa, 'Théologie trinitaire chez s. Augustin', *Gregorianum* 58 (1977), pp. 675–725; idem, 'L'intelligence de la foi', *Gregorianum* 59 (1978), pp. 375–432; J. Arnold, 'Begriff und heilsökonomische Bedeutung der göttlichen Sendungen in Augustinus *De trinitate*', *Recherches augustiniennes* 25 (1991), pp. 3–69; B. Studer, 'La teologia trinitaria in Agostino d'Ippona: continuità della tradizione occidentale?', in *Cristianesimo e specifità regionali nel mediterraneo Latino (sec. IV–VI)*, Rome, Institutum Patristicum «Augustinianum», 1994, pp. 161–77; idem, 'History and Faith in Augustine's *De trinitate*', *Augustinian Studies* 28 (1997), pp. 7–50 (the notes of this article list much other relevant work by Studer); M. Löhrer, 'Glaube und Heilsgeschichte in *De trinitate* Augustins', *Freiburger Zeitschrift für Philosophie und Theologie* 4 (1957), pp. 385–419; R. Williams, '*Sapientia* and the Trinity: Reflections on the *De trinitate*,' in *Collectanea Augustiniana: Mélanges T. J. Van Bavel*, ed. B. Bruning, M. Lamberigts and J. Van Houtem, vol. 1, Leuven: Augustinian Historical Institute [= *Augustiniana* 40:1–4], 1990, pp. 317–32; J. Milbank, 'Sacred Triads: Augustine and the Indo–European Soul', published elsewhere in this volume; T. J. van Bavel, 'God in Between Affirmation and Negation According to Augustine', in *Collectanea Augustiniana: Augustine, Presbyter Factus Sum*, ed. J. Lienhard, E. Muller and R. Teske, New York, Peter Lang, 1993, pp. 73–97.

4 A simple and easily administered test would be to consider how many of the recent presentations of Augustine's trinitarian theology make any attempt to engage with the arguments present in the scholarship listed above at n. 3.

5 For example, C. LaCugna writes: 'Augustine's point of departure in *De trinitate* was the unity of the divine essence shared by the three divine persons': C. M. LaCugna, *God For Us: The Trinity and Chistian Life*, San Francisco, Cal., HarperCollins, 1991, p. 214. On p. 10, she nicely shows how this account of Augustine is taken as the first step in a story of western failure at trinitarian theology.

6 See C. Plantinga Jr., 'Social Trinity and Tritheism', in. R. J. Feenstra and C. Plantinga Jr. (eds), *Trinity, Incarnation and Atonement: Philosophical and Theological Essays*, Notre Dame, University of Notre Dame Press, 1989, pp. 21–47. The assumption that biblical material necessarily and obviously results in a 'social' trinitarianism is itself a questionable, if not somewhat naïve, assumption given the length and sophistication of the exegetical debates in this history of trinitarian theology, and the peculiarly modern charcater of 'social trinitarianism' as Plantinga defines it.

7 V. Lossky, *The Mystical Theology of the Eastern Church*, Cambridge, James Clarke, 1957, p. 57, writes of filioquist theologies:

> The relationships of origin which do not bring the Son and the Spirit back directly to the unique source, to the Father – the one as begotten,

the other as proceeding – become a system of relationships with the one essence: something logically posterior to the one essence.

Of course this *may* occur, but whether it *necessarily* occurs is a very different question. My suggestion is that there is no indication that Augustine's pneumatology does not entirely satisfy Lossky's own description, as given on pp. 56–7, that '[t]he nature is inconceivable apart from the persons or as anterior to the three persons, even in the logical order'. This critique finds one of its loudest advocates in J. Zizioulas, who places much emphasis on a supposed reorientation of ontology towards a basis in the person by the Cappadocians. For example, see his account of the 'betrayal' of Cappadocian theology by later western tradition in J. Zizoulas, *Being as Communion*, Crestwood, N.Y., SVS Press, 1985, p. 88:

> By usurping the ontological character of *ousia*, the word *person/hypostasis* became capable of signifying God's being *in an ultimate sense*. The subsequent developments of trinitarian theology, especially in the West with Augustine and the scholastics, have led us to see the term *ousia*, not *hypostasis*, as the expression of the ultimate character and the causal principle (*arche*) in God's being.

I will argue here that, for Augustine, neither *person* nor *ousia* can express either the 'ultimate character' of God's being (I suspect Lossky would have argued against Zizioulas's extravangant claim here), or the causal principle in God. The 'causal principle' is ultimately the Father.

8 I have argued that Augustine specifically rules out the possibility of any technical analogy of proportion between God and the creation in my article 'Remember', op. cit. Rather, Augustine prefers the fluid terminology of *similitudo* ('likeness') to describe those resemblances he offers that we too easily term 'analogies'. Analogies of proportion are impossible because of our inability to comprehend the degree to which God surpasses or differs from any 'likeness' that we may offer.

9 My use of the term 'grammar' is related to George Lindbeck's famous use in *The Nature of Doctrine: Religion and Theology in a Postliberal Age*, Philadelphia, Pa., Westminster Press, 1984. The term has recently been applied elsewhere in Augustinian studies by Gerald Schlabach in his fine essay, '"Love is the Hand of the Soul": The Grammar of Continence in Augustine's Doctrine of Christian Love', *Journal of Early Christian Studies* 6 (1998), pp. 59–92. However, my own usage is a little more specific than Schlabach's: I use the term in a situation directly analogous to Lindbeck's distinction between a grammatical view of theological language and a propositional or experiential/expressivist view. In those areas of Augustine's trinitarian theology under consideration here, the appropriate grammar of trinitarian theological language is under discussion, rather than simple questions of description.

10 The argument of the next few paragraphs is related to that of L. Ayres and M. R. Barnes, 'God', in *Augustine Through the Ages: An Encyclopedia*, ed. A. Fitzgerald, Grand Rapids, Minn., Eerdmans, 1999. In this encyclopedia the articles on 'Trinity' and 'Being' are also of relevance to this section of this paper.

11 The historicity of the *Confessions* account on these points seems to be borne out in texts written soon after his conversion. For example, the complex character of

his debt to 'Platonism' is nicely highlighted by a discussion at the end of Book 3 of his *De Academicis* (AD 387). At *Acad.* 3.17.37ff. Augustine describes himself as becoming a member of the 'Platonic' school to combat the scepticism of the 'academic' philosophers who doubted the possibility of reliable knowledge. However, the description of the Platonic 'school', with which he decides to identify himself, is extremely wide. Following Cicero's own questionable account, the 'Platonic' school is presented as the underlying movement of all classical philosophy except for the Epicureans and Sceptics. Thus, for example, Augustine can confess membership of this 'school' while holding in the same work to a theory of cognition and of the unity of the soul that owes most to ancient Stoicism, and which many strict 'Platonists' would have thought mistaken. *De Academicis* itself may indeed quote or refer to some Plotinian texts directly, but in terms of philosophical doctrine, little or nothing is confessed as central that could not have been found at the time of Cicero (who died c. 230 years before the birth of Plotinus) save the name of Plotinus! In short, belonging to this school involves acceptance of the immateriality and reality of Truth and the soul, of the participation of beings in Being and of the possibility of reliable knowledge (*Acad.* 3.17.37): it does not seem to involve any more detailed an acceptance of the particular identifying doctrines of Plotinus or Porphyry. 'Belonging to this school' may be characterised a little further by noting that Augustine sees the ultimate authority as Christ: his 'membership' in the Platonic 'school' involves a belief that it is this school that will invariably provide the resources for articulating philosophical solutions to problems raised by Christian doctrine.

12 As I have argued above at n. 11, the idea that Augustine's sources for his account of God as immaterial, simple and as Being itself were, at least initially, texts that modern scholars term 'Neoplatonic' is open to little doubt. Yet, whether the ideas he took from them were uniquely Neoplatonic is another question entirely. In my article 'Remember', op. cit., I have explored how little his belief in these characterisations of God distinguishes him from predecessors such as Hilary or Basil, both of whom could articulate very similar principles without ('probably without', in the case of Basil) knowledge of strictly *Neo*-platonic texts.

13 See N. Cipriani, 'Le fonti cristiane della dottrina trinitaria nei primi Dialoghi di S. Agostino', *Augustinianum* 34 (1994), pp. 253–312.

14 Other key discussions before AD 389 are to be found at *ord.* 2.5.16; *b. uita* 4.34–5; *sol.* 1.2–4; *mor.* 1.16.26–9.

15 In which group I include such figures as Hilary, Ambrose, Gregory of Elvira, Phoebadius of Agen, Eusebius of Vercelli, and Rufinus. On the course of Augustine's developing engagement with Homoian exegesis, see M. R. Barnes, 'The Arians of Book V, and the Genre of *De trinitate*,' *Journal of Theological Studies*, new series, 44 (1993), pp. 185–95; idem, 'Exegesis and Polemic in *De trinitate* I,' *Augustinian Studies* 30 (1999), pp. 43–59. For introductions to Homoian theology, see R. P. C. Hanson, *The Search for the Christian Doctrine of God*, Edinburgh, T. & T. Clark, 1988, Ch. 18 (although Hanson's usefulness is limited because he does not clearly distinguish between Latin and Greek Homoians); the long introduction to R. Gryson, *Scolies Ariennes sur le Concile d'Aquilée*, Sources Chrétiennes 267, Paris, Cerf, 1980; M. Meslin, *Les Ariens d'Occident* 335–430, Paris, Seuil, 1967. D. H. Williams, *Ambrose of Milan and the*

End of the Arian–Nicene Conflicts, Oxford, Clarendon Press, 1995, p. 243, provides a useful list of Homoian credal documents.

16 That contemporary catechesis was shaped by immediate polemical needs, while still being focused around traditional baptismal creeds, is demonstrated with particular reference to Ambrose by D. H. Williams, 'Constantine and the "Fall" of the Church', in L. Ayres and G. Jones (eds), *Christian Origins: Theology, Rhetoric and Community*, London, Routledge, 1998, p. 127 ff.

17 Ambrose, *De Spiritu Sancto* 1.12.131; 2.10.101. Barnes, 'Re-reading', op. cit., makes the same point through reference to Hilary, *De trinitate* 7.17–18:

> what he had done was to be regarded as the work of His Father, because the latter Himself was working in whatever He did . . . all the things that the Father does the Son does in a like manner. This is the understanding of the true birth and the most complete mystery of our faith.

18 See Gregory of Nyssa, *On the Holy Trinity*:

> If . . . we understand that the operation of the Father, the Son and the Holy Spirit is one, differing or varying in nothing, the oneness of their nature must necessarily be inferred from the identity of their operation. The Father, the Son and the Holy Spirit alike give sanctification, and life, and light, and comfort, and all similar graces. And let no one attribute the power of sanctification in a particular sense to the Spirit, when he hears the saviour in the Gospel saying to the Father concerning his disciples, 'Father, sanctify them in thy name' . . . As we say that the operation of the Father, and of the Son, and the Holy Spirit is one, so we say that the Godhead is one.

The fundamental significance of this principle for later Orthodox thought is perhaps evident from its significance in John Damascene's *De fide orthodoxa*, 1.8: 'For there is one essence, one goodness, one virtue, one intent, one operation, one power . . . '. See also Lossky, op. cit., p. 53–4. Here, Lossky quotes this passage of Damascene to make this very point. One later point of discussion, and a possible distinction between many eastern and western theologians in later centuries, concerns the possibility. However, too much work remains to be done here. These latter observations also apply to remarks made by La Cugna, *God*, op. cit., pp. 97–9.

19 This use of *deitas* is odd and rather ill-conceived but, note nevertheless, that in context the phrasing in no way indicates that this *deitas* is any sort of divinity prior to the persons and their relations of origin. This *deitas* clearly originates with the Father. See the text of *f. et symb.* 9.19; BA 9.56: 'ut, quoniam Pater Deus et Filius Deus, ipsa deitas, qua sibi copulantur et ille gignendo Filium et ille Patri cohaerendo, ei a quo est genitus aequetur'. In other words: that which joins Father and Son is counted as equal with the one who generates the Son.

20 The links to these figures are not clear but, given Augustine's insistence throughout this text that his opinions are built on those of predecessors, we can point to some possible parallels (these are intended only as examples, not as an extended discussion of this complex question). Marius Victorinus, *Hymnus primus*, at line 3, describes the Spirit as the *copula* of the Father and Son. Ambrose, *De Spiritu Sancto* 3.10.59, uses the term *theotes* and links it with Jn 3:6.

A bad interpretation of these texts, in conjunction with an assumption that the Spirit is being spoken of as the *copula* or *communio* of the Father and Son, could well have contributed to Augustine's account. Didymus' contribution is less obvious (and more problematic: Jerome's translation was probably finished only in AD 390. If we could establish a clear link to Augustine, it would demonstrate the degree to which he was keeping up with the latest literature): *De Spiritu Sancto* makes frequent appeal to the discussion of the Spirit at Rom 5:5 in ways that closely accord with Augustine's usage of this Pauline text (a usage which is significantly more frequent after AD 393). It seems unlikely that Augustine's claim throughout *De fide et symbolo* that he is interacting with his predecessors is entirely a literary device (especially before an audience of bishops), and elsewhere in the text the debts to his predecessors can be established with greater certainty.

21 This comment of Augustine's indicates the problems we still face in tracing the sources for his argument here. We cannot identify with any clarity yet the 'others' to whom he refers.

22 This argument seems a hesitant one, but should not be misunderstood. Augustine does not appear to use it as a proof for the Spirit's nature as a consubstantial divine person. Rather, the argument seems to assume that the Spirit is such and seeks only to indicate that an account of the Spirit as *copula* or *communion* does not, if God is simple, undermine that belief.

23 For reasonably sympathetic accounts of Augustine's pneumatology see B. de Margerie, 'La doctrine de saint Augustin sur l'Esprit-Saint comme communion et source de communion', *Augustinianum* 12 (1972), pp. 107–19 and the comments of R. Williams, '*Sapientia*', op. cit.

24 Only slightly mischeviously, I would suggest that Lossky's stress on the 'apophatic' character of a very similar formula, while also stressing its basic rule-providing character (op. cit., p. 54), nicely mirrors Augustine's own intention.

25 For a brief account of the importance of this theme in Augustine and further bibliography see my 'The Christological Context of *De trinitate* XIII: Towards Relocating Books VIII–XV', *Augustinian Studies* 29 (1998), pp. 111–39.

26 Excellent, extended examples of this extremely common theme are to be found at *Io. eu. tr.* 1; *s.* 117 and *s.* 53 against 'anthropomorphites'.

27 One of the classic studies of this theme in *De trinitate*, 1, Chevalier's *Saint Augustin et la pensée grecque. Les relations trinitaires*, Fribourg, Librairie de l'Université, 1940, argued that Augustine's account of relation owed much to Gregory Nazianzen's use of *schesis*. Although this thesis is sometimes repeated in modern appropriation, it has not received extensive defence in recent Augustinian scholarship, nor is it likely to do so.

28 In what follows I have used the terms 'him' and 'himself' when talking specifically of Father and Son. By this use, I do not intend to claim anything about the 'gender' of God, simply to distinguish discussion of the Father as a particular person from discussion of God in 'Godself'. In neither case do I intend to imply that God has one or three 'selves' in modern terms.

29 See *trin.* 7.1.2; CCL 50.247: 'omnis essentia quae relative dicitur est etiam aliquid excepto relativo'. In a later critique of the inadequacies of both Greek and Latin trinitarian terminology, Augustine argues that to talk of a divine person is necessarily also to talk of a divine person's essence (*trin.* 7.6.11).

Comment is sometimes made on his remark as if it had given birth to a trend which led to the widespread, modern conception of a person as being identical with their 'innermost self'. In its context, Augustine's comment is intended only to indicate the impossibility of separating the divine persons from the essence. The question of Augustine's legacy to western conceptions of selfhood is another, far more complicated matter.

30 We can also say that the analogies proposed in the course of *trin.* 8–14 arise because of the impossibility of grasping the unity and multiplicity of God directly through the grammar of simplicity. Augustine offers the account we have seen here in Books 5–7 and then slowly moves towards the same argument from a different analogical base in Books 8–14, focusing much more directly on why we find it so hard to grasp the argument, and on how we must be reformed so as to grow in knowledge and love of God.

31 One would have to take this question further by consideration of *trin.* 15.17.27ff. There, Augustine repeatedly insists that the Spirit proceeds from the Father principally (*principaliter*) in the sense that the Spirit proceeds also from the Son, because the Father gives the Spirit to the Son so that the Spirit proceeds as joint communion. Of course, there are many further issues about this theology to discuss; however, it should be clear that Augustine clearly sees the Father as the personal source of both Son and Spirit. He also insists (*trin.* 15.17.29) that we should not imagine a temporal sequence of procession, the Spirit proceeding first from the Father to the Son and *then* from both Father and Son. Our temporal language of procession points to an eternal procession of the persons.

32 *Trin.* 15.17.28; CCL 50A.503: 'ut omnia tria et omnes et singuli habeant in sua quisque natura'.

33 D. Burrell, *Knowing the Unknowable God: Ibn-Sina, Maimonides, Aquinas*, Notre Dame, Ind., Notre Dame University Press, 1986, especially Chs 2 and 3.

34 See above, n. 8.

35 In any case, such an attempt probably owes more to the widespread modern theological fear of a generic 'Platonism', often if not usually expressed without any detailed or particular attempt at refutation.

36 See my 'The Christological Context of *De trinitate* XIII' op. cit.; idem, 'The Discipline of Self-Knowledge in Augustine's *De trinitate* Book X', in L. Ayres (ed.), *The Passionate Intellect: Essays on the Transformation of Classical Traditions Presented to Professor Ian Kidd*, Brunswick N.J.: Transaction, 1995, pp. 261–96.

6

SACRED TRIADS

Augustine and the Indo-European Soul

John Milbank

Introduction

In this esaay, I shall endeavour to bring together discussions of Georges
Dumézil's thesis concerning the tripartite structure of Indo-European
mythology, with discussions of trinitarian theology. My claim will be, first of
all, that the mythology led to an intrinsically aporetic characterisation of the
soul as a sphere of 'self-government in space'. Second, that Plato, initially,
and then much more emphatically Augustine, dissolved this construction
and resolved its *aporias* by substituting an alternative construction in terms
of 'government by the other through time'.

Dumézil's thesis

The French historian of religions, Georges Dumézil, who traced his intellectual lineage from the Durkheimian school of sociology, is famous for his
thesis concerning the prevalence of a specific sort of tripartite system of classification common to all ancient Indo-European cultures, and presumed to
trace back to a common ethnic–cultural–linguistic stock. According to
Dumézil's first formulation, the classification was derived from the division
of the lost original culture into three estates or social groupings, the first concerned with modes of legal, magical or religious ruling, the second with
defending and policing society by force of arms, the third with provision of
food and other material needs or luxuries.[1] This formal hierarchy was
assumed to bind together an *urstaat*, not a series of small localised societies,
which, one may note, are more marked by egalitarianism and a less alienated
mode of bonding that consists in the preservation of the same identical marks
on persons and things.[2] In Durkheimian fashion, Dumézil considered that
the characteristic representation of the sacred within Indo-European society
was a projection of the social order into the heavens, thus he claimed that the
gods also were divided into three estates, in so far as they were patrons of, or
themselves enacted, the function of ruling, warfare and cultivation (the latter

being taken to include sexuality). These three divine functions were assigned by Dumézil for convenience the names of three Roman deities: Jupiter (king of the gods), Mars (god of war), and Quirinus (god of agriculture).

Later in his career, however, Dumézil became much more cautious about the socially determinative aspect of his thesis, and indeed about how far such a symbolic order was really socially instantiated. He often seemed now to claim no more than the presence of an ideology floating free of the social facts, a circumstance which some commentators have found somewhat implausible, and yet should not be too quickly dismissed.[3] Such an ideology might arise, for example, from the *aspirations* of a ruling/fighting caste, especially if the agricultural and labouring classes were an alien, conquered or semi-conquered people. Or again, there may have persisted memories of much earlier, Mesolithic sacral *urstaaten*, evidenced by the megalithic monuments of the European Northwest. Whatever one's judgement here, it is clear that the later Dumézil made only the minimal claim for a common fundamental tripartite ideology, no longer regarded as a projection from preceding social facts, and with an often unknown degree of instantiation in those facts.

Dumézil also appeared to think that the most ancient mythic manifestations of this tripartite division were socio-spatial and cosmic-transcendent in character. The threefold order of society is taken as reflecting a threefold order in nature. However, he also claimed that, at a later stage, the soul–body compound in the individual, and then the soul taken alone, receive the same triadic imprint: the head or reason is seen as ruling the stomach or bowels, seat of the passions, with the auxiliary help of the heart, seat of human power and strength (and sense of self-importance, honour, and the claim to *recognition*).[4] Again, at a later stage, time is pressed within a fundamentally spatial matrix, so that theories of the stages of human life start to emerge: childhood governed by the emotions, youth by force and strength, old age by wisdom. This sort of notion has been most fully developed on the Indian subcontinent, where these three stages correspond respectively to the caste functions of *Vaisya-Sudra* (traders/cultivators) *Kshattriya* (warriors) and *Brahmana* (rulers). Even the course of collective history can be constrained within this scheme, and, indeed, this is what engenders the *cyclic* character of the Platonic account of historical time; over the ages democratic, oligarchic and aristocratic/monarchic regimes succeed each other, respectively dominated by emotion, force (*thumos*) and reason.[5] However, as reason is the *true* governing factor, democratic and oligarchic regimes are doomed to find themselves lacking in rule and so collapse. However, even a properly governed, aristocratic polity, where reason dominates, cannot last forever, because the extent of reason's power over force and the passions is inherently limited, in so far as they are inferior spheres, subordinate to reason, they are, just for this reason, extra-rational and irrepressibly insubordinate. The 'paradox of hierarchy', according to which the lower stages of a hierarchical structure must contain a mirroring inversion of the overall hierarchical order – so that in this case, in the lower region, passion dominates reason – is here in full force.[6] It is his sense of this paradox which causes Plato to discuss in the *Republic* the way in which governing rule, with fatal necessity over time, is contaminated and compromised by what it seeks to govern. In doing so, he brings to light (if we are to follow Dumézil's thesis) both the Indo-European recommendation of order, and the Indo-European paranoia concerning disorder which follows from the very mode of this recommendation.

Objections to Dumézil

However, there are three main possible objections that may be brought against Dumézil. The first is that the evidence for an all-embracing tripartite ideology outside the case of India is incomplete and often scanty. For example, while there are a few indications that the Norse gods were once divided into three, the evidence is much less conclusive than Dumézil claimed.[7] Yet, as against Dumézil's over-zealous critics, it must be insisted that where traces of tripartite ideology do occur, they are often very marked and unambiguous. Not only do we have, for example, Caesar's remarks that Gallo–Celtic society was divided into druids, warriors and farmers, but also threefold classifications of medical cures and categories of wrong-doing.[8] The latter two instances, especially, suggest that tripartition is more than a 'natural' division for society or the self, but in the Indo-European case was consciously encouraged and applied systematically to every field of endeavour. Nevertheless, the question of whether tripartition was the dominant or sole ideology in all Indo-European cultures, or even for a mooted original Indo-European 'homeland', has to remain far more open than Dumézil was prepared to admit.

The second objection, voiced mainly by English anthropologists, concerns just that claim already alluded to; namely that Dumézil's triads are so natural and obvious as to be well-nigh universal rather than culture-specific. All societies have to work, to defend and police themselves, and rule themselves by legal decree or magical superstition in addition to naked force. Likewise, every human individual experiences himself or herself in terms of his or her desires, needs and passions as well as the disciplinary power he or she can exert over others and himself or herself, and finally, of intellect which imposes pattern and order upon his or her experience. To back up this claim that tripartition is but truism and banality, counter-examples were cited against Dumézil. For example, in a famous BBC Third Programme broadcast on the radio in 1953, John Brough pointed out that the Old Testament God is described as 'enlightening, strengthening and consoling', thereby exhibiting precisely Dumézil's three categories, despite the fact that the Hebrews do not (or, at least, do not fully) belong to the Indo-European linguistic (and on Dumézil's view linguistic–cultural) family.[9] However, Dumézil fairly claimed in reply to Brough that the Old Testament does not contain – for example in its laws – any conscious reflection on such a threefold classification of the kind one finds in Plato's *Republic* or in Hindu law-codes. More crucially, it exhibits no *hierarchical* exemplification of the scheme, and certainly no ontologised social stratification of the kind found in India. Dumézil's counter-blast was further buttressed by others indicating, for example, that North American Indian mythology and social organisation is governed by a quite different fourfold pattern of classification.[10] (It should be noted here that, as in the case of the Indian caste system, a fourth category can sometimes be detected in the Indo-European scheme – partially integrated with the third, like the Indian *Sudra* – but it designates the outsider or semi-outsider, the lowest of the low, beneath the exercise of a regular 'function'; or else a joker–trickster role).[11]

Despite the suspicions of Brough and others, it can fairly be claimed that Indo-European societies often seem to have foregrounded a tripartite division, reflected upon it, sometimes (as in the case of India) rigidly enforced it, and, in particular, to have created strict parallels between a threefold cosmos, society and individual soul/body. In addition, they seem commonly to have construed the division as a hierarchical ordering of space: reason being placed above the passions, but governing them with the help of an auxiliary which is force or power, an agent whose ambiguously mercenary character in both person and state has always to be reckoned with. Nonetheless, it should be noted that, within this consensus, the character of the topmost function of 'ruling' has been construed very differently in East and West. In the East, where kingship and the 'Asiatic mode of production' has dominated, and gurus have always been equated with kings, the highest rule has been seen as *logos* and more as a sort of impersonal super-power which enables one to be indifferent to all pain and passion, and also *magically* to control and transform things.[12] Here also, the highest stage of life raises the individual beyond the political into a sphere of private self-sufficient contemplation which is equated with a maximum degree of power and freedom. In the West, by contrast, where more or less independent cities have flourished and decisively influenced all of western culture, 'rule' has involved either aristocratic or democratic modes of participated power among equals, such that, in consequence, that topmost function has been construed as *dikaiosune*, a 'just positioning', not rule by a higher force, but rule through discrimination, or allocation of things to their 'proper' places.

This trust in *logos*, then, renders possible the universality of both 'philosophy' in general, and 'ethics' in particular. Correspondingly, such universality does not, as in India, break with the political/social sphere, and political practice remains an aspect of the highest human life. (Hence, those like the Pythagoreans–Platonists advocating some withdrawal from the *polis* were nonconformists, not standing, like gurus, in a position beyond the social order which is nonetheless at its apex; moreover, their philosophic community itself was a kind of counter-*polis*).[13]

The third objection takes us back to the question of the plausibility of a free-floating ideology. Colin Renfrew, among others, has argued for a far older root for Indo-European culture, a claim which is not implausible since evidence from elsewhere (for example Africa) shows that oral cultures tend to be *more* preservative of existing linguistic norms, precisely because they have to expend so much effort in the task of preservation through memory.[14] Hence the persistence of striking linguistic similarities over long ages and long distances is only implausible when measured by the norms of linguistic change for post-literate societies. However, if Renfrew is right, and Indo-European dispersal was coincident with the spread of farming in the Neolithic age, then it would seem that we are dealing with relatively pacific, egalitarian communities without even chieftains, to whom surely even a mere ideology of tripartite hierarchy would be alien. This is Renfrew's conclusion against Dumézil, but two counter-objections can also be raised. First, the early date for dispersal remains conjecture, and lack of archaeological evidence or known reasons for later migrations of armed warriors on horseback (the traditional model for Indo-European dispersion) does not at all render them entirely implausible (there is also no archaeological evidence for some migrations that we know of from written survivals). Second, Renfrew's characterisation of the first agriculturists is not clearly established: did the displacement of the Mesolithic practices of some by others not involve much conflict, accompanied by organisation and hierarchy?[15] A denial of some form of emerging chieftainship to this seems unwarrantedly dogmatic. Were such a thing in place, could not the 'Neolithic incursors' already have been acquainted with, and envied, a hierarchical structure, and perhaps also have borrowed some of its features? It is not implausible to imagine some sort of dialectical interplay between settled sacral–legal power (Dumézil's first function) and a more mobile and aggressive and technically skilled power (Dumézil's second and third functions) at the cusp of transition to the Neolithic age, as well as at a later stage of incursions by armed warriors.[16]

For our purposes here, only the negative conclusions matter; later dispersal cannot be entirely ruled out, and perhaps not even the 'interactive' rather than dispersive explanation for Indo-European commonality. If dispersal was earlier, then it does not disprove the possibility of an equally early source for the ideology of tripartition. Notably, linguistic experts seem unconvinced by Renfrew's 'weak' construal of the ancient common Indo-European participle *re*, it does indeed seem always to convey strong connotations of a sovereign rule.[17]

Dumézil's thesis and psychology

As has been mentioned, Dumézil and others have tended to see the application of tripartition to the psychic sphere as a later and secondary matter. Perhaps, however, this can be called into question. The Celtic lists of vices which cite jealousy, fear and avarice (respectively vices of cognitive representation, courage and desire) are believed to record a very ancient division, and I have already alluded to the presence of similar schemes in the threefold sins attributed to Heracles, Jason and the Scandinavian (anti)hero Starkadr, in myths with presumably equally ancient roots.[18] This might lead one to ask whether it is not just as likely that primitive peoples would impose the form of psychically experienced human body – in terms of head, chest and belly or other variants – upon society, as that they would construe psychosomatic life in terms of social class structure and class struggle. One example may help to support such a contention. In Indian tradition, the three psychological variants – *dharma* (law), *karma* (passion) and *artha* (interest) – or the three 'qualities' or *guna*, namely *sattva* ('goodness'), *rajas* (passion) and *tamas* (obscurity) are usually seen by commentators as later applications of cosmic–social principles in which *sattva* means sky and government, *rajas* means the dim horizon of desire, which fuses Dumézil's second and third function, while *tamas* means the obscurity of the earth, corresponding to the hidden dividend of economic interest (belonging to a shadowy fourth function).[19] However, if we explore the mythic context a little more, we discover that these three cosmic principles are, for Hindu myth, derived from the divisions of a first sacrificed cosmic *man* (*Purusa*): this suggests, therefore, that divisions of the self are co-archetypal with those of society and cosmos and not in any way secondary or evolutionarily later. Such an argument can also be supported by the fact that sometimes the ruling god himself contains the subordinate functions. Hence, in the *Anabasis* we read that away from home Xenophon omitted to sacrifice to *Zeus Meilichios*, protector of finances, and in consequence found himself short of money, despite being successful in war and command, having remembered to sacrifice to Zeus-King and Zeus-Saviour.

Moreover, there is a further point here to be taken into account; namely that the threefold order is often located not merely *within* the respective spaces of the heavens, society and the soul–body complex, but also as an order which *links* all three. Here, the heavens fulfil the ruling function, society, that of the lower passions, and the soul the ambiguous, mediating function of force. Hence, perhaps, one may legitimately speculate, the importance in many Indo-European societies of shamanistic figures and sacred kings, often highly ambiguous figures, regarded as capable of malice as well as of magical benefit. At least these *privileged* souls, therefore, seem always to have held a crucial place within the tripartite fantasy.[20]

Since Dumézil himself appears to have abandoned any strictly sociological notion concerning the primacy of the organisation of the social whole for the development of religious notions, one may assume that the same may apply for conceptions of the inner life and the organisation of the soul. Such a supposition would, in turn, suggest that the macro–microcosmic patterns of analogy between cosmos, society and human individual, operated as a kind of mutually confirming relay system, for which each site was used to illuminate the other two, and the supposed likeness of all three to each other helped to confirm that each site was indeed internally composed of a hierarchical threefold order.

Platonic philosophy and the Indo-European myth

The last consideration may help to illuminate certain tensions within Platonic philosophy. According to Dumézil himself, Indo-European cultural patterns, including tripartition, are much less marked in the case of Greece than in those of Rome, Scandinavia and India, a circumstance perhaps due to the strong influence of pre-Indo-European elements within the Aegean era and equally to the democratic/military tradition of formal equality or *isonomia* (though the latter constitutes a reduction to bipartition, force over passion).[21] While this is probably the case, researchers since Dumézil have none the less pointed to several elements of tripartition in Greece that he did not allude to, notably in the case of Hesiod's myth of successive human eras as analysed by Jean-Pierre Vernant.[22] Also, less certainly, but quite plausibly, are the three phases of the *Iliad* according to Julian Baldick, which he claims move from an exposition of Agamemnon's sovereignty, through an account of Hector's battles, to the eventual submission of the mercenary Achilles to Agamemnon's rule.[23] Thus, the epic recounts both the internal and external subordination of the third function with the help of the second, since just as Achilles sulks because of the loss of the booty of women (whose fertility belongs with the third function), so also Troy is fighting not on behalf of sovereign rule, but of Paris's adulterous capture of Helen.

However, while the above may be an accurate diagnosis, there is here no explicit and manifest espousal of either political or psychic tripartition, of the kind evidently present in Plato's *Republic*. Here, uniquely for the West, we have a systematic exposition of tripartition and exploration of its *aporias*. Included among the latter is the possibile vicious circularity of what I have called the mutually confirming relay-system, which extrudes in Plato's text as a hesitation between soul and city as alternative starting points. However, this hesitation can itself be read as but one example of an irresolvable yet necessary oscillation in Greek philosophy between 'the near to us', which may include *both* the soul and a little further off the city, and the 'the distant', which may mean the city, but is more fundamentally the cosmos.

Philosophic knowledge must be both *manifest* and *complete*, yet only the near is fully manifest, while only the distant is fully complete. Hence, pre-Socratic beginnings with the 'distance' of the natural cosmos, were quickly succeeded by the Socratic recommencement with what is near, with psychology and politics. Within this recommencement, however, the same aporetic hesitation is doomed to reappear as one between the soul and the city. Perhaps an unambiguous choice for the first foundation awaits Descartes, who in the *Discours* explains that an ideal city is the work of one consciousness, not on account of the *truth* of this consciousness, but, rather, on account of its greater probable *formal self-consistency* as compared with a work of mutual collaboration.[24]

Plato's Socrates, however, did not yet take this course. Instead, he in advance invented and subverted the Cartesian view of near and far, by making *the city* the near – comparing it to larger, visible letters of the alphabet – and *the soul* the remote, comparing it to small letters scarcely legible.[25] This is in keeping, however, with *one* view of the soul as that which mediates the cosmic and political, traceable through Pythagorean tradition, a view which is perhaps *more* ancient and more Indo-European than the naturalistic accounts of the soul as found in Homer.[26] In Plato's case, however, the soul to whom the cosmos is somewhat obscure, can nonetheless clarify the cosmic through its access to the supra-cosmic, or realm of the forms. This circumstance tends to make Plato's resolution of the *aporia* between soul and city on the side of the soul – unlike that of Descartes – somewhat disruptive of the Indo-European legacy. For the soul is *not* preferred because of closeness and clarity, but rather on account of the opening upon distance, yet not a simply *palpable* distance; rather a distance only given in the light of the good, or in the words according to the ideal *excellence* of the forms, rather than simply their factuality. Inevitably, therefore, Plato is led in the *Republic,* and still more in later dialogues, to explain how there is a component of higher desiring, of *eros*, in our cognition of the supra-cosmic realm. Hence, with the ideas of both the invisible sun of the good, and of the higher *eros*, Plato has disturbed the sovereign priority of rational rule over all passion, together with the essential *immanentism* of this notion, namely, that it is a paradigm of self-government, or rule of the whole by higher parts of the whole over lesser, which in the case of the soul can only be taken to echo the self-rule of the cosmos. Instead, Plato intimates a kind of rule through *ecstasis*, or, more precisely, an ecstatic tending towards that which calls things to be by virtue of, and in various degrees of, intrinsic excellence, and *not* towards a mere higher element within the *same* cosmos or totality as oneself, which commands merely through subordination, and not exemplarity.

However, the Platonic subversion of Indo-European ideology is not truly carried through to the end. This is because Plato fails to allow the notion of 'the good' altogether to cancel the notion of 'justice'. It is clear that, in the *Republic*, the two themes are in tension, since justice is defined purely immanently as the division of labour, or what pertains when every function, whether psychic or political, sticks to its own appointed role.[27] The problem here is that, since the topmost function of 'ruling' holds its place merely in terms of keeping the other two functions in *their* places, ruling appears to be without a quality of its own, and to take on the character, as Socrates' sophistic opponents insinuate, of a mere manipulative oratorical power, more forceful than force itself which is *thumos* (Dumézil's second function).[28] It is the notion of the contemplation by the *logos* of the forms in the light of the good that succeeds in breaking this *impasse*, yet only by insisting that to be ethical is prior to doing justice, since it consists in the contemplation of the eternal forms without fear or possibility of violation (according to the *Phaedo*), while justice is always a *reaction* to the fear of displacement within the psychic or social order.[29] Hence, the government of the city or the soul by the vision of the good lies in excess of justice as division of labour, and rather, as recent commentaries following Gadamer have argued, in the exercise of *phronesis*, or the constant improvisation through time of newly appropriate and harmonious actions beyond any a priori specifications.[30] Nevertheless, for all this, Plato is not able to allow the notion of the good, as something manifest in time through the arrival of ever-new participations in its excellence, altogether to displace the notion of justice, which is comparatively static and spatial, and *just for this reason* requires no transcendent referral. (It will be noted that I am here insinuating, against the entire post-Heidegger legacy, that it is autonomous immanentism which points to a false 'metaphysical' suppression of temporality, and *not at all* transcendence and the vision of the good.) Thus, he fully retains, as one aspect of ideality, the subordination of passion and power to reason, and of aggressive, erotic and labouring modes of sociality to that of discursive political rule. However, to do so is to fail to overcome Indo-European tripartite ideology in three crucial aspects, namely its advocacy of self-government, the aporetic impossibility of this programme, and its construction of an illusory realm of interiority. I shall now more fully characterise these three dimensions.

First of all, self-government. It is paradigm that defines from the outset both western knowledge and western science. For rule here always operates within a definite whole or totality, whether this be cosmos, city or soul. According to this scheme, a single person is not fundamentally governed by an other or by his love for another, which other person might be equal to him but different; and what is perhaps most crucial here is that men should not be governed by their love for women. On the contrary, a person can only be legitimately influenced from outside himself, in the Indo-European view, if this outside is, in fact, the controlling part of a whole within which he is also included. As a *subject* of government, he ceases to be a person in relation, and is reduced to the level of subordinate part which serves the whole. Moreover, this authority can be internalised so that the subject can also treat himself as an unfractured spatial whole, hierarchically arranged. Because my soul is a microcosm of the social macrocosm, I can become self-governing; hence, Greek ethics ultimately concerns an economy of self-control within a totality which keeps the passions within bounds and in their right places. Since passion is characteristically encoded as 'female', and reason as 'male', this same scheme neutralises sexual difference by reducing it to a subordinate aspect of a single essential human subjectivity.[31] The alternative that is foreclosed by this scheme is the priority of *relation*, which at once establishes the priority of *community*, yet also indicates that one only has community with a genuine other, who is always arriving and is never circumscribable.[32] Within the priority of relations, both the political and the psychic whole are dissipated, since relating in a series continues for ever and is never foreclosed. Again, within this priority, a person's true identity ceases to be defined in terms of the rule of reason over the passions, but consists in the open series of events of signifying and desiring reference to other things and persons. *Both* soul and city in this perspective vanish, since they are only sustained by the vicious mutually supporting relay-system of analogy between them: their apparent founding of each other in the principle of 'self-government'.

Second, the *aporia* of this principle of self-government. This is none other than the 'paradox of hierarchy' already alluded to. If force and passion require to be governed by reason, then reason is not co-terminous with reality, and cannot even reflect all of reality, since something will remain opaque; in the lower reaches of the hierarchy, everything is reversed. Hence, in Plato's *Republic* a chaotic realm will, in time, always contaminate both *logos* and political control. Those who should rule – the philosophers – will not wish to rule, for fear of this contamination.[33] However, such fear is, in effect, a recognition that philosophy's ambition to be a total discourse must remain forever thwarted, its theoretical identification of essential sites of identity will always have to be supplemented by the mere *narration* of the vagaries of force and passion which disturb these sites, rendering 'error' not just a cognitive mistake, but a real and ineliminable *event*. Thus, the city that must be ruled by self-governing law is a city that cannot, for long, be ruled, and the soul that must be healed by self-governing reason is a soul whose mortal sickness can be but briefly allayed.

The third point concerns the construction of an illusory *interiority*. The identification of a vicious relay-system between soul, city and cosmos (indicated more sharply when the cosmos is represented as a single man) has revealed that individualism is not a modern deviation, but was on the Indo-European agenda, and perhaps other cultural agendas, from the outset, at least in a latent mode. For as Jean-Luc Nancy has pointed out, one and the same metaphysic of self-government upholds *either* an organic pseudo-community, in which persons are reduced to parts, and there is no openness to new arrivals, or *else* the autonomous liberal subject.[34] The two emphases are, in fact, reverse ways of solving a second *aporia* of self-government, namely, as to whether one stresses the far-off totality which is yet somewhat obscure – strong on government, weak on self – or the seemingly present totality, whose workings are manifest, yet is only problematically all inclusive: strong on self, weak on government. By the same token, philosophy also, if it is taken in its pre-Socratic immanentism impulse to reflect the cosmos without reference to the sacred (since it is actually, against Heidegger, the Socratic reinvocation of the sacred which disturbs this proto-ontological project), is, from the outset, latently epistemological and subjectivist, since it is also enabled by the myth of self-government which includes a moment of perfect self-reflection. This is despite the fact that this myth cannot be philosophically established, and includes reason within a *mythos* or narrative that reason can never perfectly master.

These sorts of consideration tend to lend support to the idea that in Indian visions of an original cosmic man, or *purusa*, and likewise, as Louis Dumont argues, in the aspirations of the guru to total liberation, one has a kind of 'other worldly' individualism that is one source for our contemporary 'this worldly' variant.[35] Furthermore, in both the Indian and the Platonic instance, notions of interiority can be interpreted as effects of Indo-European tripartition (while the hero enacts a kind of decapitated 'bipartition').[36] For two things in combination contrive to establish a supposed inviolable interiority. They are hierarchy and heterogeneity. Properly speaking, there are no internal spaces; an internal space is only a fold which can be unfolded and so re-externalised. Every inside can be penetrated because we really remain always on the outside, we go inside a house, because the outer walls fold inwards, while remaining, strictly speaking, exterior. However, notions of hierarchy and heterogeneity help to obfuscate this condition. Applied to the soul by Plato, hierarchy suggests that *one* part of the soul, the *nous*, touches the transcendent ideas, while inversely, only the passions touch the subterranean depths of chaos. Hence *force* or *thumos* in the middle is hermetically sealed; it enjoys no unmediated access to the external world, while equally, passion has no unmediated access to the above, and reason no unmediated access to the below. This hermetic sealing requires *also* the notion of heterogeneity, or the idea that the three functions of the soul are so generically different that there is no common medium between the three. However, this, of course, renders the *modes* of rational control over force, and of forceful control over desire, entirely invisible and esoteric, fostering in consequence the sophistic suspicion that there only exists the visibility of the more subtle force of trickery, or of a lust for power masquerading as law. (However, it can also be claimed that democratic 'decapitated bipartition', or twofold hierarchy, and even a heterogeneity of two equal powers – Dumézil's 'priestly' and 'kingly' aspects of sovereignty – suffice to generate interiority).[37]

I have defined the Indo-European soul, therefore, in terms of an entire concealed mythic apparatus whose components are:

1   self-government
2   the *aporia* or paradox of hierarchy
3   the *aporia* of near or distant
4   the vicious relay-system between soul, city and cosmic
5   the constitution of interiority by hierarchy and heterogeneity.

Many movements in philosophy, in Plato himself, Aristotle, the Stoics and Plotinus, have helped to qualify or disturb this apparatus, without entirely displacing it. I now wish to show how the terms for its displacement have already, once and for all and comprehensively, been long ago set out.

Indo-European triapartition and the theology of the Trinity

Scholars have traced the impact of Indo-European tripartition into the Christian era, for example, in the doctrine of three estates – clerical, military and agricultural – which survived beyond the Middle Ages.[38] However, the obvious question of the possible relation of this scheme to that other triad, the Christian Trinity, seems, oddly, never to have been posed.

In its origins, clearly, the doctrine of the Trinity has nothing to do with Dumézil's triad, nor does the latter affect the course of trinitarian speculation. The interesting possibility is, rather, the reverse, namely that trinitarian theology is an implicit disruption and subversion of Indo-European ideology. This is what I now wish to claim, with reference to Augustine and his treatment of the soul in *De trinitate*.

First of all, one can observe that Augustine's characterisation of the three divine persons (or 'somethings' as he says) does loosely approximate to the three sites of Indo-European tradition, but not in the expected order.[39] It is God the Father whom Augustine frequently identifies with capacity, the power to create, and the weight of existence.[40] God the Son he identifies with *logos* or rational government, and God the Holy Spirit with will or a probing and delighting desire (*dilectio*).[41] Despite this approximation, Augustine's construal of these three sites is entirely novel and disruptive in relation to pre-Christian tradition; first, as is already apparent, because he places power before reason, and second and third, because he abolishes both hierarchy and heterogeneity, which means that, in turn, the ground of interiority is dissolved, the *aporias* of self-government vanish, and there is no longer any need for a relay-system of mutually confirming analogy, since neither soul, city nor cosmos in their discrete forms can survive this abolition.

Let me take these three points in turn. First, reason no longer controls power, but is itself the infinite manifestation of power. Therefore, it no longer needs supplementation by power to reinforce its decrees over desire. In a *sense*, the philosophic *logos* is here purified and *saved* from its subordination to a mythic discourse which narrates the history of its dealings with force and passion, since reason now rules by its own inherent means of peaceful persuasion. The latter is a key term, since Augustine only in this fashion 'saves' philosophy by characterising reason more as internal speech, something produced in time by power and therefore more akin to a rhetorical *logos*.[42] Also, he does, indeed, associate the trinitarian positions with those of *inventio*, *dispositio* and *elocutio* in oratory[43]. Reason, as rooted in an inaccessible divine infinite reason, has now become much more a word that we must first hear, and feel compelled by, before enunciating it in our fashion.[44] In consequence, sophistic suspicion is no longer held at bay by the problematic doctrine of the esoteric compulsion of force by reason, but instead by Augustine's radical liberation of power from the taint of violence, since, for him, unruly force involves conflict, and every conflict some mode of weakening. A harmonious peaceful order is always stronger, and to submit to the powerful word is to receive the gift of reason.[45] Hence, while power and reason are not exactly to be identified, reason as infinite is no longer delimited, and concomitantly the field of power is not a literal region or substance outside the sway of reason. Instead, force *exhaustively* manifests itself as order, even though order as infinite is never foreclosed, or once and for all graspable.

Second, there is no more hierarchy. The Father is not superior in the Godhead to the Son, nor the Son to the Spirit. Thus, if paternal is manifest in filial order, this order is nonetheless nothing but an infinite effectivity, or something *creative of being as such*, it is that which establishes, ever anew. Likewise, reason is not 'in control' of love which for Augustine is a passion, albeit a higher one. In a radicalisation of the Platonic subversion and refounding of philosophy through a doctrine of *eros*, Augustine renders love (which he construes as both donating and desiring, both agapeic and erotic) as the *measure* of reason itself.[46] To this aim, he cites St Paul's attack on the Greek logos, 'If anyone thinks that he knows anything, he does not know as he ought to know. But if anyone loves God, the same is known by him' (1 Cor 8:2–3). For Augustine, the objectifying gaze of philosophy without love produces no truth, but merely satisfies a perverse voyeuristic desire, or *curiositas*.[48] By contrast, only when something is genuinely loved for its goodness, and to an appropriate degree given or allowed to be by us in its goodness, is it truly seen, although this implies inversely that we should love the thing in the light of how we judge it should be. Judgement is something which, as Augustine makes clear in Books 8 and 9 of *De trinitate*, arrives afresh with each new circumstance and is not the implementation of a priori standards but the active application of the concrete standard which is Christ-justice incarnate. Indeed, its implication with desire shows that to judge truly is nothing but the *aspiration* to judge with infinite, divine exactitude. Desire and Vision have become inseparable, supplying each other.

Third, there is no more heterogeneity. Father, Son and Spirit are not substances, nor qualities, nor accidents, nor aspects of a single substance, into which category Augustine refuses to place God. Instead, they are, in terms of essence – meaning both Being itself and Unity itself – identical, and only distinguished by their relations, which, in a fashion impossible for any ontic reality, and therefore impossible for us to conceive, exhaustively characterises them.[49] The Father *is* without remainder Fatherhood, or the giving of birth to the Son. The Son *is* without remainder the offering of all back to the Father. The Father and Son together *are* the manifestation of love that does not exist before *mutuality*, and yet in this mutuality gives itself outside the original dyad as this new possibility of love. Finally, the Holy Spirit *is* this emanating mutuality that only persists in constantly receiving itself from the mutual love of Father and Son.[50] Such a doctrine of substantive rationality, which Augustine first perfected, allows one to construe diversity as a kind of absolute incommunicability – the Father is never in the place of the Son, and so forth – and yet not as a diversity of substance, kind or essence. Hence, heterogeneity is here abolished, and the categories of same and different, and of 'internal to' over against 'external to', are dramatically transgressed.

This reconception of tripartite division in the case of the absolute, or God, is carried over by Augustine into the psychological realm. Famously, Augustine sought to clarify the Trinity by appeal to psychic analogues. However, as Rowan Williams and Lewis Ayres have explained, this attempt has been badly understood and criticised only under misapprehensions.[51] It is not the case that Augustine subordinates our access to the immanent or eternal Trinity via the manifestation of this Trinity in the historical economy – that is to say, the Incarnation of the Son, and the giving of the Spirit to the Church – in favour of pseudo-ontological speculation about the soul. On the contrary, Augustine begins by *radicalising* a stress that we only have participatory access to the eternal by *remaining within* the structures of space, time and human language.[52] The Trinity is first disclosed to us in these structures, and salvation for Augustine is the event of the disclosure at *one time*, in *particular* relations and *specific* words of how *all* time, relating and speech should *properly* occur. Hence, the supposed 'psychological' terms of Augustine's reflections on the Trinity are, first of all, the metaphors for memory, language and desire ('voice', 'image', 'word', 'food', 'gift', 'flame', etc.), which the New Testament *itself* uses, and by interrogating these three phenomena, Augustine is at once seeking to clarify the metaphors *and* – more crucially – seeking to purify the phenomena, in the light of the given metaphorical pattern.

For Augustine, the first key analogical term is not the soul at all, but love. God has been revealed as love, and, therefore, one must ask, is love itself triune? Augustine finds that it is, and consists of lover, beloved and the love that flows between them.[53] Thus the prime analogue for the Trinity is relational, which is to say, *neither* psychic nor political. However, Augustine proceeds none the less to involve a psychic analogy because, first, the soul is relatively self-sufficient and unified, and so, in this respect *alone*, more like God, and second, because the beloved is not generated by the lover, like the Son by the Father, while the image or word which *intends* the beloved *is* generated in the soul of the lover by memory, which is Augustine's psychic analogue for the Father.[53] However, the fact that, according to Augustine's innovative gnoseology, the inner word is generated as ecstatic knowledge of something outside the soul (such that it is through and through 'intentional') still preserves the social relations and desiring content. His final analogue of memory, understanding and will means that knowledge of the other is born in recall of the other in the past, and driven by desire of the other in the future.[55] This may seem to be confuted by the fact that Augustine eventually talks of the soul which simply remembers, knows and loves itself as the most exact image of God.[56] Surely we have here the perfecting of a solipsistic interiority? Yet, in truth, the reverse is the case, because, for Augustine, to know oneself *genuinely* means to know oneself as loving what one should love namely God and one's neighbour as oneself.[57] Hence, not interiority but radical *exteriorisation* is implied, and Augustine, therefore, uses paradoxical formulations which imply that the soul cannot contain itself.[58] As the soul is memory, and this is always memory of the other, and as, likewise, it is inner word, which as a signifier is only in referral to something else, and as, finally, it is love, which is a passion *only* through ecstatic referral, it follows that the soul which recollects knows and loves itself, only loves itself as God and everything else. The true, imaging soul is a soul crossed out.

Such a radical critique of interiority is what one might expect if Augustine applies to the soul his obliteration of hierarchy and heterogeneity. However, it appears drastically at variance with received pictures of Augustine as discoverer and virtuoso of the interior sphere. How can my account really be true? What must be argued here, against Charles Taylor and others, is that Augustine's use of the vocabulary of 'inwardness' is not at all a deepening of Platonic interiority, but something much more like its subversion.[59] An examination of Augustine's texts (especially the *Confessions*) suggests, first, that inwardness for Augustine involves remaining within our *createdness* and not imagining that some psychic aspect of ourselves is really part of an eternal substance. (Here it is relevant that there are hints in Augustine of a monistic ontology underlying his apparent dualism, for which soul and body are both 'numbers' representing different degrees of *tonos* or tension.)[60] Second, and in consequence, it means remaining within time and travelling to God by gathering ourselves again through memory, through a tearful *shedding* of ourselves and an expectation governed by right desire. (This 'descent' into a interior which is really our past is itself only a non-identical repetition of the *divine* descent into the darkness of sin in the Incarnation; a descent possible initially only for God, precisely because he alone is entirely *exterior* to sin.) In both cases, an exteriorisation that turns the soul inside out is involved, because the conditions for autonomous interiority – hierarchy and heterogeneity – have been removed. For Augustine, in the case of the higher *eros*, reason no longer governs passion through the wielding of power in space, but instead the power of memory, the trace of particular events, precedes reason which is, in turn, overtaken by a future-orientated desire. There is a sequence of before, between and after here, and yet each element is ecstatically implicated in the other two without any hierarchical priority or heterogeneous difference of isolatable quality or occurrence.[61] For Augustine's strongest insight is not at all that a hermetically sealed soul is most like the Trinity, but, rather, that the nearest analogue to trinitarian substantive relations lies not in any spatial entity, but in the lack of punctuality and the occurrence of aporetic ecstatic inter-involvement between past, present and future, which he was, of course, the first person to explicate fully. Paradigmatically, for Augustine, it is time itself that is most like that which does not change, and the trick is to realise that if the eternal has been given to us as a *gift*, and, therefore, as that which constantly passes and cannot be held on to, this may reveal that the eternal is in *itself* gift; for Augustine, the name of the Holy Spirit, which is the upshot and renewal of reciprocity.[62]

One might, indeed, argue that it is not, as so often claimed, that Augustine discovers the essence of time to be psychic (a claim obviously incompatible with his clear belief in real, literal created time), but rather that he sees the ecstatic, folded back upon itself, tracing and projecting character of time, as the condition for psychic life, which is time as aware of itself.[63] It is this radical temporalisation of the soul that ensures that it is the *whole soul* which touches God, no part of the soul being hermetically sealed under a mode of spatial government. Indeed, it is just because there is *no longer* any interiority in this spatial sense, that Augustine does speak of our touching God from within, for if every part of the soul is as near the surface as any other part – memory and desire as much as reason – then, conversely, this transcendent surface which is God can permeate equally every part of the soul. Just because there is no ontologically sealed inner space, we are more likely to experience God as a welling up from within, or as an invasion and bursting apart of our bounds. Thus, in the *Confessions*, Augustine supplements metaphors of 'looking' at God, which tends to preserve boundaries with (neoplatonically and eucharistically observed) metaphors of *eating*, where the most external becomes the most internal, and of *weeping*, where an accumulation of egoistic 'blocked' interiority surfaces and is 'shed'.

For this reason, it becomes inadequate to speak simply of the absence or presence of metaphors of interiority. What we need instead is a comparison of different *economies* of interior in relation to exterior. In the Platonic economy, there is a travellable distance from an inviolable interior to the exterior, but in the Augustinian economy there is no distance to travel, because the most exterior is, by virtue of that very exteriority, also the most interior to us, far from being inviolable, our innermost heart ceases to be *us* at all.[64] This alternative economy depends entirely on the fact that 'the external' is now no longer the highest level of a cosmic whole within which we are also included, but is a genuine transcendent outside any whole, and, therefore, not hierarchically over-against us, but the giving source by which alone we are at all. Hence, cosmos, also, along with soul and city, is finally crossed out. Furthermore, since the transcendent is the maximally external which is also the maximally internal, the Indo-European hesitation between near and far is also overcome. Neither completeness *nor* clarity are available, but instead the infinite is given to us as most near in its very distance, and, therefore, *a fortiori* there is no more vicious relay-system between the three.

It is more complete overcoming of immanence that permits Augustine to also dispense with Plato's preservation of justice as non-negotiable division of labour, and instead to focus more consistently upon the good as something ceaselessly mediated to us in time. Here, the critique of heterogeneity is crucial; there is, for Augustine, no real external operation of power on reason or reason on desire, since we can also envisage these operations entirely as the mutations of power itself, of signification itself, or else of desire itself. In consequence, these operations have become more esoteric and surveyable, and involve no longer a bizarre and finally arbitrary mediation between absolutely diverse qualities.

This same lack of heterogeneity means that the paradox of hierarchy is removed. For now, force and passion no longer escape the rule of reason by exercising a pseudo-sovereignty in the lower realms. The aspiration to completeness of the philosophic *logos* is at last, therefore, fulfillable, and yet this is at the cost of a *merely* philosophical *logos*. This new *logos* only orders or mirrors in so far as it is *also* powerful and effective, and also rightfully desiring of the other. Since reason is for it that which effects or creates, reason can no longer itself guarantee this effectivity, which must rather be a matter of hope. Furthermore, since reason is also for it that which rightfully desires, there must be faith in, and love for, an ultimate reality which is rightfully desirable.

Hence, the new *theological logos* only achieves rule as also a hopeful pragmatics and a trusting erotics (a theme which, in her later works, Gillian Rose enunciated in a newly seminal fashion).[65] None the less, this *logos* which does not seek only to rule, nor to subordinate force and passion to rule, can alone fully rule and indeed *does* rule (unlike modern western states and economies), whether we observe this rule or not. It alone can fully rule and fully heal, but not rule the city nor cosmos, nor heal the soul, for all three have been exposed as illusory spheres of self-government, founded in the echo-chamber of myth, and subject to irresolvable *aporias*. Instead of the tale of this *logos*, one can, at least, be open to receiving the story of another one, a story indeed not foundable by reason, and yet one which narrates a reconceived reason as co-terminous with the force and longing of narrative itself. Furthermore, this *logos* of government-by-the-other is, I submit, though not demonstrable, at least not subject to the dissolving antinomies of the older one and indeed – albeit through the course of more than a mere immanent development – it resolves these antinomies. (To this degree, I am prepared to be Hegelian.)

No ruling or healing, then, of city, soul or cosmos, but instead a simultaneous ruling–healing - and so we need a different word – of relations. Augustine cites the classic definition of the just soul, 'it gives all their due', that is to say, according to its own measures and that of the city, it gives what is 'proper' to others and retains what is 'proper' for itself.[66] But in order to refuse 'justice', and embrace the good as an exercise of judgement only with and through 'right desire' (Augustine cites Paul's *Epistle to the Romans* 13:8, 'owe no man anything except to love one another'). The soul is, therefore,

only its proper self in the infinite return of a debt to others, a debt perpetu-
ally renewed in every repayment, and owed only *because* freely given.

So no debt at all, but delirium of arrival.

Notes

1 G. Dumézil, *Jupiter, Mars, Quirinus*, Paris, Gallimard, 1941; idem, *Mitra-Varuna*, Paris, PUF, 1949; idem, *Les dieux des indo-europées*, Paris, PUF, 1952; J.-P. Verchant, *Myth and Society in Ancient Greece*, tr. J. Lloyd, Brighton, Harvester, 1980; C. S. Littleton, *The New Comparative Mythology*, Berkeley, University of California Press, 1966.

2 See P. Clastres, *Society Against the State*, tr. R. Hurley, Oxford, Blackwell, 1977; and G. Deleuze and F. Guattari, *A Thousand Plateaux*, tr. B. Massumi, London, Athlone, 1987, pp. 242ff, 351, 424ff.

3 See W. W. Belier, *Decayed Gods, Origin and Development of Georges Dumézil's 'Idéologie tripartie'*, Leiden, E. J. Brill, 1991. Belier notes that Dumézil originally used the evidence of Propertius, *Elegy* IV, I, 9–32, that there were three Roman tribes – *Ramnes, Tities, Luceres* – to support the thesis that this reflects a tripartite hierarchic structure in practice, but later suggested this was only an ideal requirement. However, Belier's claim that the equal size of these three 'tribes' belies reference to a class division scarcely seems convincing. For further scepticism, see C. Renfrew, *Archaeology and Language, The Puzzle of Indo-European Origins*, London, Penguin, 1989, pp. 251–9.

4 See Dumézil, op. cit., pp. 63–8; E. Senart 'Rajas et la théorie l'indienne des trois gunas', *Journal Asiatique* 2 (1915), pp. 151ff.

5 Plato, *Republic* Books 8 and 9; idem, *The Statesman*.

6 See L. Dumont, *Homo Hierarchicus*, tr. M. Sainsbury, Chicago, University of Chicago Press, 1970; S. Tcherkezoff, *Dual Classification Reconsidered*, tr. M. Thom, Cambridge, Cambridge University Press, 1983.

7 R. I. Page, 'Dumézil Revisited', *Saga-Book* 20:1–2 (1978–9), pp. 49–69; G. Dumézil, *Gods of the Ancient Northmen*, Berkeley, University of California Press, 1973.

8 Julius Caesar, *Gallic Wars* 6.13. There are *duo genera hominum*, *druides* and *equites*, while the rest of society, ruined by debts, is forced to solicit slavery.

9 J. Brough, 'The Tripartite Ideology of the Indo-Europeans, an Experiment in Method', *Bulletin of the School of Oriental and African Studies* 22 (1957), pp. 68–86. G. Dumézil, 'L'ideologie tripartie des indo-européens et la bible', *Kratylos* 4 (1958).

10 See Littleton, op. cit., pp. 196, 202, 209.

11 J. P. Mallory, *In Search of the Indo-Europeans*, London, Thames and Hudson, 1989, p. 271; Dumézil, *Jupiter*, op. cit., p. 41.

12 See N. C. Chaudhuri, *Hinduism*, London, Chatto and Windus, 1979; K. H. Potter, *Presuppositions of India's Philosophies*, Westport, Greenwood, 1963, pp. 3–15; J. Milbank, 'The End of Dialogue' in *Christian Uniqueness Reconsidered*, ed. G. d'Costa, New York, Orbis, 1990, pp. 174–92.

13 See M. Detienne, *Daimon. De la pensée religieuse à philosophique, la notion de daimon dans le pythagorisme ancien*, Paris, Société d'Edition «Les Belles Lettres», 1963;

J.-P. Vernant, 'The Individual within the City–State', in *Mortals and Immortals*, ed. F. I. Zeitlin, Princeton, Princeton University Press, 1991, pp. 318–35. One should also note that, according to Dumézil, the first function was divided into a kingly and a priestly role, with significant variations between different Indo-European cultures. In India, the priestly (Brahmanic) function was supreme; in Greece it was relatively independent and sometimes marginalized, hence the Pythagoreans; in Celtic lands, the Druids possessed a guild solidarity surpassing their fealty to kings; while in Rome, the *flamen dialis* was taken captive by the political power. It was *this* circumstance, Dumézil claimed, that permitted Rome to be uniquely disciplined and all-conquering. See Dumézil, *Jupiter*, op. cit., pp. 123–5; idem, *Mitra-Varuna*, op. cit.

14 See Renfrew, op. cit.

15 See C. Renfrew, *The Megalithic Monuments of Western Europe*, London, Thames and Hudson, 1983; idem, *Before Civilization*, London, Penguin, 1990, pp. 235–72.

16 See Deleuze and Guattari, op. cit.; Mallory, op. cit., pp. 111, 135, 166ff.

17 See M. Detienne, *Les maîtres de verité dans la grèce archaique*, Paris, Maspero, 1967, pp. 1–8.

18 See J. Baldick, *Homer and the Indo-Europeans, Comparing Mythologies*, London, I. C. Taurus, 1994, pp. 25–7. In ancient Ireland, Queen Medb wanted a husband without jealousy (of another ruler), fear or avarice. See also Dumézil, *Jupiter*, op. cit., p. 115; and 'the three oppressions of the Isle of Britain' concern *government* (the race of men who hear every word spoken in the island), *war* (the two dragons who fight and paralyse all life) and *food* (the magician who steals in the night the provisions of the magic cauldron stored in the palace). See Dumézil, *'L'ideologie tripartie'*, op. cit., p. 20.

19 For the Indian material, see Senart, op. cit.; D. Pralon, 'Le modèle tripartie dans la philosophie du IVe siècle BC', in *Georges Dumézil*, Paris, Pandora, 1981, pp. 121–36; Dumézil, *Jupiter*, op. cit., pp. 63–7, 195–7, 257–60. Dumézil notes equivalent Roman cosmic divisions into *numina caelestia, media* and *terrestria*, citing Servius's *Commentary on Hesiod* III, 134 and VIII. See also *Rig Veda* X, 90. After the dismembering of the primordial human victim of the first sacrifice, the Brahmans emerged from his mouth, the warriors from his arms, and the farmers from his thighs; at the same time the cosmic sky from his head, the local atmosphere from his navel and the earth from his feet. For Xenophon, see *Anabasis* III, I, 6–12; VI, I, 22; VII, 8, 107, and J.-P. Vernant, 'Aspects de la personne dans la religion grecque' in *Mythe et pensée chez les grecs, Études de psychologie historique*, Paris, Maspero, 1966, pp. 267–82.

20 See Senart, op. cit., and Dumézil, *Jupiter*, op. cit., pp. 64–7, 94–9; Detienne, *Les maîtres*, op. cit., pp. 1–8, 16ff; A. Yoshida, 'Survivances de la tripartition fonctionelle en Grèce', *Revue de l'histoire de religion* 181 (1964), pp. 21–38; J.-P. Vernant, *Les origines de la pensée grecque*, Paris, PUF, 1962, pp. 110–1.

21 Dumézil, *Jupiter*, op. cit., p. 17.

22 J.-P. Vernant, 'Le mythe hésiodique des races', in *Mythe et pensée chez les grecs*, Paris, Maspero, 1978, pp. 13–80; idem, 'Oedipus without the Complex', in J.-P. Vernant and P. Videl-Naqut, *Myth and Tragedy in Ancient Greece*, New York, Zone, 1990, pp. 97–8.

23 Baldick, op. cit., and see also Pralon, 'Le modèle tripartie', op. cit. Pralon suggests plausibly that the pre-Socratic democratic/military paradigm in

Greece, concentrated around *isonomia*, was alien to the tripartite model, which surfaces only with philosophy. On the other hand, one should take seriously Detienne's argument in *Daimon*, op. cit., that the Pythagorean/Philolaen tradition may preserve traces of much older tradition from a common Indo-European stock. Pralon lists the apparent traces of tripartition in Aristotle's *Politics* as well as in Plato's *Republic*. Adding to Pralon, one can list these as:

1   Hippodanus of Miletus divided the city into three parts: sacred, public, private servicing, repectively, worship, war and agriculture (*Politics* II, 8)
2   [not in Pralon] There are three different motives for stealing to enjoy without pain, its remedy is philosophy; so one has a perversion of 'first function' virtue, covetousness (related to the second function 'spiritedness') and sheer need (the third function) (*Politics* II, 7)
3   Aristotle himself recommends a threefold division of the land of the city into public for gods, public for communal feeding (especially related to war) and private (*Politics* VII, 10)
4   There are three ingredients of excellence: intellectual and moral, bodily ('spiritedness' athleticism, health), and external needs (*Politics* VII, I)
5   One needs wealth to support religion, war and material needs (*Politics* VII, 9) and this gives rise to a division of social order into priest, judges and councillors (as with Plato, and for Greece in general, the military and the ruling functions are intimately linked) and farmers and artisans. For Aristotle, only the military and deliberating classes contain full citizens, thus he upholds also the hierarchic aspect of Indo-European tripartition. Pralon also discusses tripartition in Pindar and other writers.

24 R. Descartes, *Discourse on the Method*, tr. J. Cottingham, R. Stoothoff, D. Murdoch and A. Kenny, in *The Philosophical Writings of Descartes*, vol. 1, Cambridge, Cambridge University Press, 1985. See Part Two, VI, 11. See also C. Pickstock, *After Writing: On the Liturgical Consummation of Philosophy*, Oxford, Blackwell, 1998, pp. 57–61: 'The Cartesian City'.
25 Plato, *Republic* 368.
26 See Detienne, *Daimon*, op. cit., pp. 23–4.
27 *Republic* 433–4.
28 See A. Ophir, *Plato's Invisible Cities, Discourse and Power in the Republic*, London, Routledge, 1991.
29 *Phaedo* 68c–69e.
30 *Republic* 505a; 521a: 'good and prudent life'; 582a: 'By what must things that are going to be judged be judged? Isn't it by experience, prudence and argument?'
31 See L. Irigaray, *Speculum of the Other Woman*, Cornell, Cornell University Press, 1985.
32 See J.-L. Nancy, *The Inoperative Community*, ed. P. Connor, tr. P. Connor, L. Garbus, M. Holland and S. Sawhney, Minneapolis, University of Minnesota Press, 1991, especially pp. 1–43.
33 *Republic* 488–5012.
34 See Nancy, op. cit.
35 L. Dumont, 'De l'individu hors du monde à l'individu dans le monde' in L. Dumont (ed.), *Essais sur l'individualisme*, Paris, Seuil, 1983, pp. 33–67;

J.-P. Vernant, 'The Individual', op. cit. Vernant points out that the Pythagoreans and their heirs were 'dissenters', unlike the gurus, and argues that Greek military *isonomia* engendered a much more egalitarian mode of individualism. However, the role of 'hero' also traces from that of an *outsider*, from the one who first *escapes* the fixed cosmos of sacral kingship, as even in the case of the epic of Gilgamesh: 'Unlike the Omnipotent pharoah, a deity incarnate from whom flowed the sustenance of nature and society, the hero of the epic, the prototype of the King, was cast against an alien world from which he attempted to wrest order'. See J. G. Gunnell, *Political Philosophy and Time, Plato and the Origins of Political Vision*, Chicago, University of Chicago Press, 1987, p. 40. See also the account of Odysseus in T. Arno and M. Horkheimer, *Dialectic of Enlightenment*, tr. J. Cumming, London, Verso, 1992, pp. 43–81. This hero figure is also moved by an ideal of ascetic 'self-government' that concerns the regulation of the passions, though here for a more functional end. In a sense, *isonomia* is like decapitated tripartition, and, in this respect, also proto-Cartesian. While I argue in the main text below, that the hierarchic 'entrapment' of *thumus* between above and below helps to create a notion of 'the interior', a mere hierarchy of two plus heterogeneity is *also* sufficient to generate the notion of an inner unspecified 'middle' between two poles. And, indeed, heterogeneity *alone* can generate interiority. This is the case for the relation of Dumézil's kingly and priestly aspects of the highest function in *Mitra-Varuna*. As Detienne and Guattari, op. cit., p. 351, remark, this 'forms a *milieu* of interiority'.

36 Ibid.

37 Ibid.

38 See G. Duby, *The Three Orders. Feudal Society Imagined*, tr. A. Goldhammer, Chicago, University of Chicago Press, 1980, pp. 6, 45, 113–18. Duby discusses the way in which the threefold feudal scheme (hierachical and heterogeneous) was in tension with a hierarchy inherited from Dionysius the Areopagite (with an ultimately trinitarian basis); of divine signs/initiating/initiated. Here, first of all, the topmost authority is not personified except in God, and hence the 'top' is truly transcendent and ineffable in character, not the upper part of a single whole, but the *source of meaning of the whole*. Second, there is no heterogeneity, since one can be initiated upwards. Such a hierarchy is used as the basis for his conciliarist ecclesiology by Nicholas of Cusa in *The Catholic Concordance*, tr. P. E. Sigmund, Cambridge, Cambridge University Press, 1991, Book 1. However, by the end of the Middle Ages it had become rare, and ecclesiastical hierarchy was being conceived in more 'physical' terms with personified authority on top, instead of the mysterious symbolic presence of an ineffable deity giving itself eucharistically through time. See H. de Lubac, *Corpus Mysticum*, Paris, Aubier-Montaigne, 1949. This later development owes something to the increasing intrusion of 'Indo-European' tripartite ideology: as Duby records (op. cit., pp. 45, 115), Adalbert already found the Dionysian scheme too 'mystical', and rejected also the Gelasian scheme of two 'powers' (ecclesiastical and lay, with the latter subordinate) in favour of a threefold hierarchy of *oratores, bellatores* and *laboratores* which a) gave the feudal classes constitutional power, and b) reduced ecclesiastical power to a more legalistic kind of entitlement.

39 See *trin.* 7.9.

40 *Civ.* 11.24–7: '[The City of God] is strong with God's eternity; it shines with

God's truth; it rejoices in God's goodness' (*ciu.* 11.24); [all philosophers agree that] 'there is some cause underlying nature, some form of knowledge, some supreme principle in life. There are also three things looked for in any artist, natural ability, training and the use to which he puts them. Those are needed for any real achievement; and his ability is judged by his talent, his training by his knowledge, his use of them by the enjoyment of the fruits of his labour' (*ciu.* 11.25); 'we resemble the divine Trinity in that we exist; we know that we exist, and we are glad of this existence and this knowledge' (*ciu.* 11.26).

41 *Ciu.* 11.25–7; *mus.* 6.11.1: 'delight (*delectatio*) is a kind of weight in the soul'; *trin.* 9.12.17.

42 *Ciu.* 9.9–16.

43 *Trin.* 15.10.17. The triad of 'talent, learning and use' appears related to the rhetorical triad.

44 *Conf.* 1.1.

45 *Ciu.* 15.5. See J. Milbank, *Theology and Social Theory, Beyond Secular Reason*, Oxford, Blackwell, 1990, pp. 380–438.

46 See C. Osborne, *Eros Unveiled, Plato and the God of Love*, Oxford, Clarendon Press, 1994, pp. 201–19.

47 *Trin.* 9.1.

48 *Conf.* 3.2; 10.35; *ciu.* 10.3.4.

49 See D. Dubarle, 'Essai sur l'ontologie théologale de st Augustin' in *Dieu avec l'être*, Paris, Beauchesne, 1986, pp. 167–258. One should also note that, unlike Aquinas, Augustine makes *no* absolute distinction of 'one essence' versus 'three persons', and is quite prepared to elide person/essence, (*trin.* 7.4). It is somehow possible for him that there is a single *essentia/persona* necessarily repeated twice: once as a relation, and second as a relation to this relation. This scheme makes it absolutely clear that there is in God no phantom *genus* divisible into species: it is not, as Augustine says, as if the essence were like gold formable into three different statues (*trin.* 7.11).

50 *Trin.* 1.22–31; and Book 5.

51 See R. Williams, The Paradoxes of Self-Knowledge in the *De trinitate* ', in *Augustine. Presbyter Factus Sum*, ed. J. T. Lienhard, E. C. Muller and R. J. Teske, New York, Peter Lang, 1993, pp. 121–34; idem, 'Sapientia and the Trinity, Reflections on the *De trinitate*', in *Collectanea Augustiniana. Mélanges T. J. van Bavel*, ed. B. Bruning, M. Lamberigts and J. Van Houtem, vol. 1, Leuven: Augustinian Historical Institute [= *Augustiniana* 40:1–4], 1990, pp. 317–32; L. Ayres *The Beautiful and the Absent. Anthropology and Ontology in Augustine's* De trinitate, unpublished dissertation, Oxford University, 1994.

52 *Trin.* 1. And there is a primacy here of time and language over space. For, in Book 2 of this work, Augustine explains that the 'way of faith' does not speak of ideas *either* in purely corporeal terms, *nor* in purely psychic terms, nor in purely *ineffable* terms. This appears to exclude all possibilities, yet Augustine explains that the way of faith, exemplified in the discourse of sacred scripture, draws from *both* bodily and psychic images, and then *rises gradually* to the ineffable, 'sublime and sacred things'. The point here, then, is *first* that the way of faith is 'analogical', but, second, that analogy *takes time*, 'one rises gradually'. Thus, it is remaining in time that pays tribute to both the ineffability and yet plenitude of eternity; while this tribute cannot be paid by merely static, 'spatial' representations.

Augustine also stresses that the Father and the Holy Spirit must manifest themselves just as much within finite structures as the Son, albeit not in the mode of 'incarnation', thus the Father is manifest as a calling 'voice' (*trin.* 6.4), the Spirit as a *hovering* dove and flames and as *our* gift as well. Hence, there is absolutely *no* truth in Karl Rahner's allegation (*The Trinity*, tr. J. Donceel, London, Sheed and Ward, 1970) that Augustine fails to have an adequate economic analogue for the presence of the Holy Spirit in the Church, equivalent to the incarnational presence of the Son, thereby opening the way from a supposed shift from a concern with the historical economy as a necessary mode of access to knowledge of the Trinity in favour of an ontological speculation ungrounded in revelation. In fact, on the contrary, Augustine stresses still more than Rahner a mediation of trinitarian presence only via finite image.

First, Augustine strongly insists that the 'substance' of the hypostasis of a trinitarian person never actually 'appears' in its finite manifestation, *even* in the case of the incarnation; its personhood is only apparent within a pattern of image and symbol: 'what appeared . . . was not the very substance of the Word of God in which he is equal to the Father and co-eternal, nor the very substance of the Spirit . . . but something created that could be formed and came into being in those ways' (*trin.* 2.27).

Second, the persons act unitedly *ad extra* for Augustine, precisely because their distinction *cannot* be disclosed in any idolatrous and fictional interlude 'between' Creator and created, but *only* as a 'trace' within the structures of creation itself. By contrast, any suggestion of some sort of recognizable distinction of the persons in their economic activity – one more creating, the other more saving, the third more perfecting, etc. – (as advocated by Yves Congar and others) does *not* do justice to the primacy of history, since it postulates events in a mythical 'not quite yet created' realm.

Where Rahner suggests the identity of the immanent with the economic Trinity, it is much more that for Augustine *there is no* economic Trinity, but, rather, the full subscription of one sequence of time into the immanent Trinity – a subsumption only disclosed to us through the usual means of finite disclosure – such that all time is re-disclosed as echoing the creator, the trinitarian God. And there is a further, and quite crucial irony here. Rahner and others imagine that Augustine is inaugurating a kind of 'decadence' that speculatively removes theology from the reading of Scripture. In reality, the refusal of the primacy of the Augustinian *vestigia* by Rahner, *precisely repeats just such a decadence.* For, as H. de Lubac pointed out (op. cit., p. 274), the crucial 'betrayal' in history of trinitarian doctrine occurred not with Augustine, but rather with Gilbert de la Porrée, who first deemed the reflections on the *vestigia* to be a mere optional extra – simple 'comparisons' – and not the prime site for theology itself. Gilbert could only make this claim because he had already reduced the revelation of the Trinity to a kind of *datum*, upon which a dialectical theology could surmount deductions, while the Augustinian reflections assume that what one starts with is rather symbols and images which need a complex decoding, involving first scriptural exegesis, and then a kind of 'phenomeno-logical' as well as logical reflection on the realities of remembering, speaking and aspiring to which these images allude. Hence, the Augustinian approach, for which the unravelling of *vestigia* is trinitarian theology, *conserves* the belonging together of *lectio* and *ratio* which Rahner purports to restore, and yet, in Gilbert's distant wake, still in fact deserts (for a positivism at once 'rationalistic' and 'mythological').

53 *Trin.* 8.10–14.

54 *Trin.* 9.2–8.

55 *Trin.* 10.17–19; 11.11–12.

56 *Trin.* 10.13.19; 8.12:

> For just as a word both indicates something and also indicates itself, it does not indicate itself as a word, unless it indicates that it is indicating something, so too does love indeed love itself, but unless it loves itself loving something, then it does not love itself as love. Who, therefore, does love, except that which we love with love?

For Augustine, *each* aspect of the soul: memory, understanding and love, is *radically intentional* and indeed, in the passage of *trin.* where he enunciates a *cogito* (*trin.* 10.5–15), Augustine denies that the soul is an 'essence' in the usual sense, and instead declares that which we cannot doubt is its relationality, the soul is knowledge, because it is knowledge *of* something (likewise memory and love of something). Hence, we should take relationality – intentional knowledge – as its essence. The difference from Descartes here concerns:

1   a more ecstatic intentionality which precludes any scepticism concerning the existence of the external world
2   a more emphatic incorporation of love and will into intentionality
3   an insistence that all knowledge is memory, such that if a knowing awareness is always a trace it cannot be primarily a supposed 'mirror' of an external world, but is constituted as a 'fold' of an extra-personal process.

At *trin.* 8.9, Augustine also insists that one can only love (and know oneself as one's true self) if one is *just* towards others.

57 *Trin.* 8.10; also 4.8.9. In these passages, the soul knows itself most of all, but its essence is justice, giving each thing its due, and *what* is due is love to God and neighbour. The point here is *not* that we most know ourselves by a kind of 'inner glance', but, rather, that the soul is not something that can be looked at as an 'example' or a genus; it is known *within intentional activity*. One may note here that, even with Descartes, the *cogito* involves as awareness of being the subject of the *passions* as well of cognition. This might seem to imply an ecstatic element, as with Augustine, although Descartes' functional and not gnoseological role for the passions seems to me finally to belie this, see M. Henry, 'The Critique of the Subject' in *Who Comes After the Subject?* ed. E. Cadava, New York, Routledge, 1991, pp. 157–66.

58 *Conf.* 10.8.15: 'Magna ista vis est memoriae, magna nimis, deus, penetrale amplum et infinitum, quis ad fundum eius pervenit? et vis est haec animi mei atque ad meam naturam pertinet, nec ego ipse capio totum quod sum.' See also *trin.* 15.42,

> to put in a nutshell we can say, 'It is I who remember, I who understand, I who love with all three of these things – I who am not either memory or understanding or love, but have them.'

> This indeed can be said by one person who has these things and is not himself these three things.

Augustine goes on to say that, by contrast, God *is* these three things; the implication of the above sentence, then, seems to be that what the mind is – a reflection of the Trinity as a memory, understanding and will – is also *not* itself, but more than itself, God. For while 'I' am not love and knowledge, they are still not *in* me (or in my mind) like qualities in a subject, for after all they *are* me (*trin.* 9.5).

59 C. Taylor, *Sources of the Self*, Cambridge, Cambridge University Press, 1989, p. 115–59.

60 *Mus.* 6.1; *imm. an.; conf.* 3.6: every *corpus* has a *vita* and an *anima*. See also E. Zum Brunn, *St Augustine, Being and Nothingness*, New York, Paragon, 1988, pp. 9–22; K. Flasch, *Augustinus, Einführung in Sein Denken*, Stuttgart, Philip Reclam jun., 1980. Zum Brunn discusses how, for Augustine, (a) *both* soul and body are mutable (*trin.* 3.8) while *both* also are indestructible although the body is divisible *ad infinitum*, and (b) how a body, like a soul, is more in being when better formed by beauty; the 'form' of a body is not identical with any of its parts, and only *these* are entirely destructible and purely nothing. What is *real* in a body, as in a soul, is participation in eternal being. Hence, there is something in Augustine highly analogous to the denial of any ontological status to materiality as pure receptivity, such as one finds with the Cappadocians. In both cases, creation *ex nihilo* seems to imply an ontological monism that almost obliterates the spirit/matter distinction. (The above perceptions also indicate for Zum Brunn just how essentially Augustinian *Eckhart* is.)

61 *Conf.* 10–11. As regards Augustine on time, my tentative reading can be summarized as follows.

1 Time is created by God, not by the soul as for Plotinus (see *Enneads* 3.7.71), so it is real and 'external'.

2 The past and future 'are not' and nor is the present, since it instantly vanishes.

3 Past and future 'are present' only in the soul, yet this does not cancel the *aporia*, for 'presence' is not either. What one 'measures' is not presence *to* the soul but *distensio animi*, the soul is 'scattered', 'dispersed' in time.

4 *De Musica* indicates that *every res* is composed of 'time spans' – tensional traces and foreshadowings – that have ontological priority over 'space spans'. This allows one to marry the creationist realism with 'the psychic essence' of time without attributing any idealism to Augustine (a hermeneutic assumption of coherence permits this invocation of the earlier text), and thereby to show that Augustine *fully anticipates* Heidegger, despite the latter's denial.

5 The *aporia* is not resolved, if time is psychic, *psyche* is also temporal and thereby itself enmeshed, 'lost' in the *aporias* of time. For that reason, we are to leave distention in time for the *intention* of God. We are to make the ecstatic leap into eternity.

6 Yet elsewhere, Augustine seems to insist on *remaining* in time to get to God. *Intention* and *distention* appear to be resolved *christologically*. One only intends God via Christ, thus if the answer to what is time is 'self', then the

101

answer to 'what is self' is not simply dispersal *or* intention, but, rather, the receiving back of our true self from Christ via the church. Hence, Christ restored the true process of time; Christ *is* time, and in receiving Christ we do not resolve the *aporia*, for only God in eternity outside time literally comprehends it, and time is, as it were, the evidence that finitude is *of itself* a void), but we discover that we are to 'comprehend' time as the mystery of the possibility of charity, of giving and of co-inherence. Hence, the only graspable meaning of time is an *ethical* one; time is the time of *cura* (care), as Heidegger will attempt to repeat.

62 *Trin.* 2.7.11; 5.16; 6.4. Augustine says here that the Holy Spirit as divine gift is as much ours (the recipient) as God's (the donor), *unlike* the Father and the Son (who is only 'equally human' with one man). Hence, it is clear that:

1   the Spirit includes us radically within the substantive relations of the Trinity
2   this inclusion amounts to a *radical reciprocity* in which we are elevated into a 'giving back of God to God' – although entirely within and by God – despite our constitutive nothingness
3   it also implies *some* kind of equivalent of the 'hypostatic union' between Jesus and the logos as occurring between *all* redeemed human beings and the Holy Spirit. This also makes *utter* nonsense of any idea that Augustine began to substitute a hypostatised notion of grace for salvation as the gift of the Holy Spirit.

63 This position is suggested generally at *conf.* 1.5–7, 9–12, especially 1.6.10, as well as *passim* in Books 3 and 4. See Zum Brunn, op. cit., pp. 9–22.
64 *Conf.* 3.6.11: God is *interior intimo meo et superior summo meo* ('deeper than my innermost being and higher than the heights which I attain').
65 See Gillian Rose, *Mourning Becomes the Law*, Cambridge, Cambridge University Press, 1996.
66 *Trin.* 8.9.

Part II

THE ORDER OF LOVE

(Augustine, *City of God* 15.22)

7

INSUBSTANTIAL EVIL

Rowan Williams

Mali enim nulla natura est; sed amissio boni mali nomen accepit.[1] Thus Augustine most epigrammatically sums up his view on what might best be called the 'grammar' of evil. Talking about evil is not like talking about things, about what makes the constituents of the world the sorts of things they are; it is talking about a *process*, about something that happens to the things that there are in the universe. Evil is not some kind of object – so we might render the phrase from the *City of God* – but we give the name of 'evil' to that process in which good is lost.

As all students of Augustine know, the formation of this principle is described in the *Confessions* as a crucial moment in Augustine's liberation from both Manichaeism and the kind of problems that had brought him into Manichaeism in the first place. It is not too much to say that the sorting out of the grammar of evil is an indispensable part of that sorting out of the grammar of 'God', which cleared the way for his return to Catholic Christianity. This also suggests two preliminary considerations for any discussion of the strengths and weaknesses of his theodicy (to use a word that is, in fact, misleading where Augustine, and most pre-modern theologians, are concerned).[2] First, we shall not understand Augustine on evil without some attention to Augustine on God, and, by obvious extension, Augustine on humanity and salvation. Second, if Augustine's account of evil is to be challenged or rejected, we have to ask what the implications might be for his doctrine of God; can the two grammatical concerns with which he wrestles, especially in *Confessions* 7, be sufficiently disentangled for his doctrine of God to emerge unscathed? Since Augustine is, by common consent, one of the formative influences on what has passed as the orthodox doctrine of God in western Catholicism, this is a serious consideration.

In what follows, I do not intend to offer a full summary of what he has to say about evil; there are several satisfactory accounts available.[3] I shall be taking up four specific points of criticism from modern discussion of the question, and attempting to assess their gravity. Three of these are given eloquent and clear statement in John Hick's near-classic survey of the history of theodicy, *Evil and the God of Love*.[4] The fourth, less easy to state, is sketched in a recent and very searching essay, *Escape from Paradise. Evil and Tragedy in Feminist Theology* by Kathleen Sands.[5] As the argument advances, it will, I think, become clear that all these criticisms in fact focus on a single issue which might be represented as the question of what it is to speak of 'a' world at all, with all that this implies about the universe's relation to a maker.

Existence and goodness

John Hick, in the work mentioned above, is careful to acquit Augustine of the charge of teaching that existence is a sort of variable property of things, a quality of which a particular existent may have more or less.[6] It may occasionally sound as though Augustine is confusing the 'axiological' sense of 'existence' – the degree of intensity or energy of being that might allow us to say that an artist, for example, lives more fully than another person – with the sense of existence as sheer thereness: a 'lower' form of existence is not less *existent*. However, Hick grants, this is not fair to Augustine, who does not have a concept of sheer thereness: to be at all is to have a particular place in the interlocking order of things, to be possessed of 'measure, form and order'.[7] That is to say, to exist is necessarily to exemplify certain 'goods', to be, in a certain way, actively exercising the ordered and interdependent life that belongs to the creatures of a good God. In this sense, to say that existence can be 'graded' is not to make any crass mistake about the possibility of different degrees of 'thereness', but simply to observe that the exercise of the goods that go with existing may be more or less constrained in its environment, more or less capable of modification of that environment; within the overall notion of interdependence, some realities are more dependent than others.

Nevertheless, this does not quite meet Hick's doubts. *Why*, he asks, should we assume that 'measure, form and order' are good? In any case, for whom are they good? For the particular realities in the world, or for God?[8] This is not a wholly clear challenge, but it seems to mean something like this: to say that ordered existence is good from the point of view of an individual being is to say that such a being would rightly and intelligibly desire the persistence of their life. However, not all beings in the universe are destined to live for ever: for the merely animate, as opposed to the spiritual, creature, continued existence is not properly desirable beyond their allotted span. In God's eyes, it is good that they perish when they do (whatever they might think about it or desire). Likewise, it is good that a spiritual creature, however depraved, should continue in being, so as to go on exhibiting the specific kind of good associated with spiritual existence. Hick characterises the whole of this scheme as 'aesthetic rather than ethical': God is perceived more as 'the Artist enjoying the products of his creative activity . . . than the Person seeking to bring about personal relations with created persons'.[9] The perspective offered by Augustinian theodicy is ultimately determined by metaphysical considerations, considerations – to use the language I employed earlier – about the grammar of 'essences and substances' in a created universe. This objection is, as we shall see, close to the others Hick advances: in so far as this is a theodicy governed by aesthetic criteria, it fails to do justice to the personal. The justification lies in the eye of the divine beholder, the one 'subject' to whom the whole system is present or visible.

I have argued elsewhere that a theodicy that privileges the observer's standpoint is theologically and spiritually vacuous; that an 'aesthetics' of evil is not, in any helpful sense, a properly theological response at all to the question.[10] Is this however, what Augustine is doing? Hick's stress on the problematic nature of whose 'point of view' is being invoked in the argument very definitely treats his scheme as one in which the resolution is achieved by an appeal to an intrinsically inaccessible standpoint, a non-human (and, therefore, strictly non-thematisable) perspective. I suspect, however, that this is to iron out some of the complexities of Augustine, even to impose an anachronistic interpretative grid upon him. The discussion of evil in *Confessions* 7 has quite a lot to say about points of view; but there is no appeal to a divine point of view, to an idea that existence is 'good' in the eyes of God, never mind the concrete perspective of actual existents.[11] Time and again, Augustine writes of learning to 'see' afresh; when, in 7.13, he acknowledges to God that *tibi omnino non est malum* – 'for you, evil is just not there at all' – he goes on at once to say that the same must be true of creation as a whole. There simply is not any such *thing* as evil; not just because it doesn't exist from 'God's point of view', but because it cannot exist, for all the reasons that Augustine is in process of elaborating. If there is no evil in the eyes of God, that is not because God is in a position to make a *judgement* for which we have insufficient grounds; it is because that which is evil is not a subject to which qualities can be ascribed, not a *substantia*. There is no thing for God to see. Of course, God is *aware* of the states of affairs we call evil; but, unlike us, God is not tempted to short-circuit the argument and ascribe to evil a substantive life it does not and cannot have.

The point is not therefore an aesthetic one, in Hick's sense: God looks at the whole of creation and approves of the value or goods it exemplifies as a whole, irrespective of the standpoint of particular existents. I can learn to 'see' exactly what God sees, in a rather simple way, by grasping the conceptual nonsense of thinking of evil as a sort of stuff. However, this is not really the most adequate response: the whole language of views and standpoints presupposes an observing subject, when what Augustine is talking about is the capacity simultaneously to grasp the nature of evil as the perversion of my own capacity to see or know, and to become open in love and knowledge to the reality of God. To see evil as privation is to see it as something that affects my own perception of what is good for me: if evil is the absence of good, it is precisely that misreading of the world which skews my desires; so that to read the world accurately (in its relation to God the creator) is also to repent. Furthermore, that accurate reading of the world arises from the renewal of my own creaturely relation to God, my own shift into a relation to God that worthily represents what God truly is, and that thus overcomes the evil which is constituted by imperfect, corrupt or nonsensical pictures of the divine.

There is, in other words, a tight connection between the adoption of a particular 'doctrine' of evil and the reordering of desire towards its proper end. Within the Augustinian frame of reference, it will not make sense to think of God and God's creatures as having comparable and potentially competing points of view: the point of view of a creature, considering itself *in* itself, is not a neutral *locus standi*, but is itself an illustration of what evil is; an account of the good of a creature abstracted from its place in the universe overall as ordered and loved by God.[12] And the 'point of view' of God, if one can even begin to use such language, is not a perspective alongside others, the divine 'interest' considered alongside other 'interests' to be satisfied. Augustine is clear in the *De doctrina christiana* that God's relation to creatures (unlike the mutual relations of creatures) cannot be strictly categorised either as 'use' or as 'enjoyment'.[13] 'Use' is any relation to another being that furthers the user's ends, that makes the item used an instrument for some further good, while 'enjoyment' is finding one's fulfilment in concentrating one's action, vision and energy on some reality outside oneself. God has no need of anything to further the divine purposes, since God does not act, as we do, by strategy and skill in deploying finite resources; nor can God find fulfilment in anything other than God, being wholly self-sufficient, necessarily and eternally possessed of bliss. The only sense, according to Augustine, in which God 'uses' creatures is so as to make them instrumental to their *own* fulfilment; as if we were to work on some portion of the world, treating it as deserving of an attention wholly independent of the possible benefit it could be to us.[14]

In the light of all this, it could never be said that God has a 'point of view' competing with ours or that of any creature, that God has a definition of the good relating to the divine perspective or concern (in terms of aesthetic satisfaction for God?) that takes no account of the creature's perspective. The creature's perspective simply *is* defined by God's creative purpose; but that divine purpose is to maximise all possible fulfilment for the creature, since the good, the joy, the flourishing of the creature could never be in any way a threat to the divine bliss.

To understand evil is not to look at detached phenomena and (by some curious mental gymnastics) arrive at the conclusion that the beauty of the whole outweighs the deficiencies of the parts, let alone rationalising such a conclusion by asserting that this is how God sees things. It is part of a many-layered spiritual reconstruction, the process traced in *Confessions* 7. At the beginning of the book, Augustine is still in thrall to a kind of sophisticated materialism.[15] What exists is a complex of extended realities, one of which

(God) is invulnerable to the erosion or invasion that diminishes and damages others. In such a universe, the question of where the erosion comes from might make sense: we could properly ask, if the 'territory' of one reality is being invaded, what force is it that takes up the space lost by the original entity. *Unde malum?* 'Whence is evil?' is an intelligible query. The break-through to a new frame of reference comes when Augustine reflects on the activity he is, in fact, engaged in: thinking itself. The mind does not take up space; there is a mode of presence in the world that is not an occupying of concrete territory, the possession of an exclusive and impenetrable block of the finite room there is in the world of material objects. If this way of being in the world that we call mind or thought is conceived as if it were a kind of material thing, the more free and flexible mode of presence is being subjected or reduced to the less, the 'higher' to the 'lower', the more active to the more passive. If we go on to ask how the mind evaluates and orders or unifies its environment, the question arises of whence the mind derives its standards, its sense of real and mutually relative (ordered) structures. The answer given to Augustine by the Platonist literature he is studying is that the mind is itself activated by a yet more free and active presence, the radiance of a truth that is not static or passive. It is at this point that he returns to the problem of the 'derivation' of evil, and finds the difficulty dissolved, or, at least, so redefined that the original question has to be discarded.[16]

The source of all things is the light and truth of the divine, that agency that is wholly unconstrained and, thus, immaterial and invulnerable (incapable of being modified by any other agent). As such, the divine is not ever on the same level as, or in competition with, finite agency, which is always in some measure constrained and vulnerable (were it otherwise, it would be indistinguishable from the divine). In what is not divine, there must be a plurality of agencies, and this means a variety in the level of freedom or self-determination realised by an agency. The world is, therefore, an interlocking system of action and passion. *Purely at the level of the natural order at large*, what may look to the unreflective observer like 'evil' – the aesthetically disagreeable, the contingently annoying – is no more than a particular arrangement of action and constraint, perhaps, specifically, a case of action more unstable or vulnerable or liable to variation as a result of circumstances than human action, and, above all, that distinctive action that is mental functioning.[17]

Likewise, at the level of my actual experience of the world, evil is a failure of the appropriate balance between action and constraint that ought to be operative in a specific interaction in the world: paradigmatically, it is the submission of the mentally active human subject to the dominance of selfish and materially defined goals, with all the consequences of such an imbalance in the wider human and non-human environment. The characteristic problem of the human agent is twofold: it is the subordination of spirit to trivial and finite desires; but at the same time, it is the confidence of created spirit that it is able by its own immanent action – self-knowledge and self-improvement – to free itself from this subordination. The solution lies only in the reconnecting of the finite mind with infinite agency, with the loving wisdom of God; and the opening of that connection depends on the initiative of God in Jesus Christ.[18]

I have laboured the argument of *Confessions* 7 in this way in the hope of demonstrating more clearly how inadequate it is to describe Augustine's concern as 'aesthetic', and how misleading it would be to think of Augustine as privileging a divine 'point of view'. The process being depicted in the book is highly complex: it makes no sense at all without the prior conviction that all finite agency considered simply *as* agency or free self-adaptability is animated by God, and directed by God (through its location in a certain place in the scheme of things) towards its fullest possible orderliness or balance, which for sentient creatures means its fullest possible joy. The positive point of the argument, as laid out in the text of the *Confessions,* is to rule out any statement of the cause or source of evil that treats it in a spatialised way; and it is essential to this goal that God and the created mind are simultaneously 'despatialised'. If God – the most fundamental form of activity that there is – cannot be properly thought of as occupying a territory, and if the human mind or spirit reflects this primary activity in its own non-territorial character, if, in short, the relation between God and the mind is rightly spoken of in terms of time, rather than space, evil, as that which interrupts the relation of creator and creature, belongs in the same frame of reference. Its origins are to be sought in the interactions of the world's history, not in a classification of substances within a single territory, a single medium of extension. Furthermore, if this is what Augustine is pursuing, the charge of teaching a resolution of the problem of evil in terms of 'essences' rather than 'personal relationships' is a caricature; and the aesthetics of Augustine's model cannot be reduced to the idea of a resolution by appeal to a divine perspective, a divine satisfaction with the cosmic picture, uncon-nected with the subjectivity of created beings.

Moral personality

The above attempt at clarification has a good deal of bearing upon the next major area of criticism articulated by Hick. He observes that there is, or should be, an important difference between 'metaphysical' and 'empirical' accounts of the reality of evil: whatever the accuracy of the metaphysical definition of evil as privation, it cannot be accurate to speak of evil *as experienced* in such terms. 'Empirically, it is not merely the absence of something else but a reality with its own distinctive and often terrifying quality and power'. An evil will is not automatically one that tends towards disinte-gration and final extinction: 'it may retain its degree of mental integration, stability, coherence, intelligence, lucidity, and effectiveness . . . one thinks, for example, of Milton's Satan or of Iago in fiction, and of such men as Goebbels in recent history'.[19] Evil activity has a power and 'integrity' of its own. Furthermore, if evil is to be described as the absence of good, does this not mean that, for example, pain has to be described as the absence of pleasure, which is a grossly inadequate account of something that manifestly *impresses* itself upon the subject?[20]

This is intuitively quite a powerful point; but it reveals a profound confusion. What the Augustinian argument claims is that the 'terrifying quality and power' of evil derives from those elements, in whatever reality we are talking about, that are most alive and active. Evil is dreadful and potent because of the kind of world this is, a world in which the active, joyful goodness of God is mirrored or shared by creatures. Because the 'underlay' of worldly reality, so to speak, is this intensity of action, the diversion or distortion of worldly reality is appalling. For evil to 'impress' in the way already touched upon, it has to employ the vehicle of action and, in the human sphere, intelligence. The corrupted will is certainly not, *ipso facto*, a weak or powerless will, so long as it shows the typical excellences of will: liberty, energy, persistence or whatever. What makes its evil terrible *are* those excellences; nothing else. What is distinctively *evil* in the evil will is simply not capable of being spoken of or understood in terms of liberty, energy and so on. It is true that the passionate desire for what is false ultimately leads the subject to destruction; but this does not mean that the quest for falsehood is automatically half-hearted or vague.

To say that a Goebbels — or a Radovan Karadzic or a Saddam Hussein — exemplifies lucidity, coherence, effectiveness and so on in his actions is certainly not to claim that his pursuit of his desires is a simple instance of homogeneous 'evil', exercising power and effectiveness. It is to recognize that, if evil itself is never a subject or substance, the only way in which it can be desired or sought is by the exercise of the goods of mental and affective life swung around by error to a vast misapprehension, a mistaking of the unreal and groundless for the real. The more such a pursuit continues, the more the desiring subject becomes imprisoned, enslaved, hemmed in; the more the typical excellences of will and intelligence are eroded. However, that does not mean that the effects of this nightmare error are lessened.

To put it more pictorially: the more power, dignity and liberty adhere naturally to a created being, the more energy there will be for the pursuit of false or destructive goals, illusory goods. The corruption of a human will is a more far-reaching disaster than the corruption of an animal will, because the latter has a severely limited range of possibilities for innovation on the basis of reflection. A wicked human is an immeasurably greater problem than a wicked hamster (if, indeed, we could give much content to such an idea); and Augustine and the majority of Christian theologians up to the Enlightenment would have added that a corrupted *angelic* will is an immeasurably greater problem than a corrupted human will, and that a fair number of our difficulties in this world derive from just this problem. The dispositions and habits of intelligent beings have a wide range of effects, because intelligences exist in conscious and creative interaction and interdependence: that is why they can do more damage; and it is one reason for the disproportion between the experience of evil and the level of moral culpability in any individual's life.

An Augustinian would have to say that this and this alone does proper justice to moral personality, however paradoxical that may sound. Consider the alternative. Evil possesses – as such – a power of initiative, a capacity to set intelligible goals and to advance those goals in a lastingly coherent manner. This implies that evil impinges on a finite agent in the way that another finite agent would, and that there is nothing absurd in proposing, or having proposed to one, a set of objectives specified as evil in themselves and claiming to be proper objects for rational pursuit. The first point pulls back towards Manichaeism: evil as an invasive 'other', struggling with the moral responsibility of the finite person, so that the victory of evil is the victory of a subject, or substance, distinct from the finite person. The second allows that what is good for one subject is not necessarily good for any other: that there is a plurality of intelligible goods, goals that may be pursued without absurdity by reasoning subjects.

This undercuts a fundamental aspect of Augustine's theology: that the good of all persons is both unified and interdependent (I can not specify what is good for me without including what is good for you in the same calculation), and that any alternative simply makes the entire process of human moral and spiritual reflection impossible.[21] As we might now put it, *discourse* itself fails if one party is allowed to talk about wanting the dissolution of its own mental or spiritual identity as a discussable option, or to claim to be pursuing goals that are incapable of being described to other agents as consonant with, or convergent with, their own purposive desires. Augustine's assumptions and arguments about the unreality of evil as an independent substance, cause or agency are bound up with a conviction about the location of evil in the malfunctioning of relations between subjects, not in the relation of this or that subject to some other *thing* called 'evil'. Any notion that the latter could be a possible grammar for talking of evil has to be recognised as subverting the very idea of intelligibility as something relating the individual's mental/verbal life to a system or order transcending the individual frame.

In other words, if the Good is in some sense one, evil cannot be allowed a place of its own, outside the system of balancing and interweaving relations that actualise the Good for particular beings, and which, in a contingent world, are vulnerable to malfunction and distortion. A discord on a musical instrument is not the result of the instrument being interfered with by an external agency *called* discord, it is a function of the workings of what is there, of what constitutes the instrument itself. Some years ago, Harold

Koren, the *New Yorker* cartoonist, depicted a garage mechanic explaining the situation to his customer: the car bonnet is open, revealing a fanged and hairy creature smiling a little sheepishly at the owner. 'Well', says the mechanic, 'there's your problem'. It is an admirable illustration of exactly what Augustine wants at all costs to avoid. So, far from undermining the idea of moral personality, this scheme in fact seeks to defend the integrity of personal agency from a mythological conception of something outside that agency displacing the person's own responsibility.

If it is argued that a person's agency can be powerfully motivated by evil desires, or that a person's intelligence can work strongly and consistently for evil ends, Augustine's reply would have to be along the lines sketched in Book 19 of the *City of God*. It is an *analytic* truth (as a modern person would say) that desire desires satisfaction, that the disequilibrium represented by the acknowledged lack that fuels desire seeks the restoration of equilibrium. All things seek 'peace'; even twisted and nightmarish desires are movements towards order, an order hideously misunderstood, it may be, but order or harmony, none the less. What is sought is sought *as* good; what is sought is a peaceful universe. The degree to which an agent's perception of peace is blinkered by their own self-concerned definition of the good is the degree to which their desire is destructive of their own ultimate reality, or integrity, and of whatever order or harmony there is immediately around.[22]

To return to Hick's original statement of his difficulty, what we experience and call evil is, indeed, not simply a void, a lack; but it is the effect of a lack, the displacement of true by untrue perception. A vacuum is a 'lack', an absence; but its effects within a system of forces may be powerful. The complaint that evil-as-privation does not do justice to the experienced reality of evil presupposes that the Augustinian account is a blend of 'metaphysical' and 'experiential', and that an adequate account should balance both. However, this is a misunderstanding. As any reader of Augustine will be aware, what he can say of specific *mala* in no way weakens their substantial and historical reality. An 'evil' is, by definition, a concrete state of affairs, and a great evil is a massively effective disruption of the world's order; evil perpetrated by an intelligent being is grave and terrible because of the power of intelligence in the order of things. How one describes *mala* is, in an important sense, irrelevant to the programmatic question of what evils should be ascribed to. Furthermore, to ascribe them to anything other than skewed, or damaged relations between agencies in the world is finally to threaten the entire possibility of intelligible talk.

The principle of plenitude

The last of Hick's objections I wish to examine has to do with the alleged involvement of Augustine's scheme with a Neoplatonic assumption that must be questionable for a modern reader.

'God acts deliberately to form a universe, and He acts in terms of the principle of plenitude, considering it better to produce all possible forms of being, lower as well as higher, poorer as well as richer, all contributing to a wonderful harmony and beauty in his sight, than to produce only a society of blessed archangels'.[23]

As becomes clear in the lines following, this is really another version of the objection to an allegedly 'aesthetic' emphasis, obscuring the priority of personal relationship in God's purposes. All that Augustine does to Christianise the Neoplatonic emanationism underlying the 'principle of plenitude' is to substitute God's creative will for the automatic 'radiating' of being from the One; but this, in fact, intensifies the difficulty. Why should God act according to any 'principle'? Once we have imagined that creation's form is in some sense dictated by a principle, we have lost sight of the all-importance of God's will to engage with finite persons whose freedom mirrors God's own. The love of God is being conceived in 'metaphysical rather than personal terms'.[24]

This is not all that easy to assess as an argument. Augustine certainly speaks in *Confessions* 7.13 of the totality of beings as better than the higher elements alone (*meliora omnia quam sola superiora*), and in *City of God* 11.22 of the principle that things must be unequal for there to be any particular things at all (*ad hoc inaequalia, ut essent omnia*). However, what he does *not* do is to advance a simple claim that God creates the maximum possible variety of creatures. His argument, where it occurs (and it is found less clearly elaborated in *De natura boni* and *De Genesi ad litteram*), turns on the appropriateness of there being diverse levels of being; not necessarily 'every conceivable kind of being'.[25]

Furthermore, the justification of variety or inequality that is offered takes us back to the point already variously articulated in these pages: the universe is a system of interdependent agencies; by the creator's providence, each thing is what it is in virtue of where it stands in the universal order. Thus, things further down the scale that contribute to the good of things higher up, find their *own* good in so doing. Without that use of the lower levels of creation, the higher elements would not be what they are, or flourish as they should. Thus, the principle Augustine is elaborating is not one of 'plenitude' in the sense of a realisation of absolutely all possibilities of being, or even of all 'compossible' outcomes, to use a modern logical term, but one of universal interdependence. Of course, it is expressed in a strongly hierarchical idiom that undoubtedly owes an uncomfortably heavy debt to Neoplatonism and falls harshly on the modern ear; but the fundamental point, that inequality in the sense of variegated levels of capacity or resource in the natural order is necessary in a world in which things become, in which things acquire their concrete identity through *processes*, is less obviously mortgaged to problematic patterns of thought.

Certainly, the aesthetic is a significant consideration: Augustine's remarks about the importance of the eyebrow to the well-proportioned face, or his confidence that a world containing sin can still as a whole be beautiful, as is a picture with dark patches, come close to the aestheticism Hick and others criticise so sharply.[26] The apparently unimportant detail (the eyebrow) is the object of God's care and craft for the sake of a larger picture. The darkness of sin in itself is terrible, but yet the entire universe does not, because of it, cease to reflect the order of God's wisdom; the implication is that the ultimate punishment of sin, in manifesting God's just laws, balances once again the order of the whole. However, this is not simply either a celebration of unstructured diversity, or a claim that sin would be less offensive if we somehow knew how to look at it. The 'unimportant' detail *serves* the proportion and beauty of a more complex reality; it is part of a system, but also part of a convention of seeing and valuing, the social practice of recognising and appreciating beauty. Furthermore, the manifestation of God's justice in the punishment of sin is something worked out in the passage of time: it is, once again, in the *process* of the world that order is shown, not in the perspective of a timeless observer. Sin is not in some way 'good', or even bearable, when seen against a sufficiently broad backdrop: what is good is the process of the universe which, in God's providence, includes in its final reckoning the manifestation of the gravity of sin and the triumph of God's healing and rectifying action.

The principle of plenitude, as articulated by Hick, sounds as though it is claiming that the world is simply an accumulation of as many different kinds of thing as possible, and that God has virtually no 'choice' but to create such a maximal diversity. What Augustine actually says is that, once God 'chooses' to make a world that is both temporal and interdependent, the logic of that free determination requires variety and the oscillation of circumstances as agents act upon each other, never at any one point attaining perfect balance within the world's history.

This is, I think, compatible with what Augustine says in *City of God* 11.23, that, without human sin, the world would have been full 'only with good natures'; there is a difference between the protracted mutual adjustment of natures that are imperfect (that is, temporal and contingent), but not corrupt, and the mutual erosion of natures that are corrupted, destructive of their own integrity and that of others. However, this is admittedly not something Augustine clarifies with any precision, here or elsewhere. What he is reasonably clear about is that the ascription of evil to 'lower' elements in creation is a mistake, a failure to see how they fit into the good of 'higher' levels of organisation, and so into the good of the whole. Their relative passivity, or even ugliness and imperfect or unpleasing forms, are not marks of an *eroded*, corrupted life, a life that is less than it *should* be, but are simply the signs of a particular place in the interweaving of finite agents, a place in which little transforming initiative can be taken. Without sin, the hierarchy of the universe would have been a steady flow of interaction in which what is conventionally called the 'corruption', the disintegration, of elements is only a moment in their proper temporal unfolding and mutation, which is, in itself, good. It is only with the corruption of will and intelligence that change and passivity become problematic, infecting the whole of the world's order. Hence, Augustine's conviction that the Fall has *physical* consequences (human death).[27]

Thus, it would be a mistake to read Augustine as subscribing to a simple belief that God 'had' to make the maximum possible variety of creatures. For the creation to be the kind of creation it is, there must be an *interlocking* variety of some kind, so that the 'goodness' of any one agent or agency in the world cannot be assessed in and for itself. The implication is also present, in this, as in other parts of Augustine's general argument, that for there to be *any* kind of creation, variety and interaction are inevitable. For the world is, by definition, not God; therefore, it is subject to change. The contents of the world are mutable and passible, and thus are bound to be acted upon by each other, and if the world as a whole is good, then its good must be realised through interactive processes; all things are good in virtue of where they stand in a system of acting upon and being acted upon. Thus, a creation of *any* kind entails variety, variety of freedoms and variety of dependencies. To see this only in terms of a 'principle of plenitude', or a primarily aesthetic understanding of the world's variety, is to miss Augustine's always crucial interest in time and change as, paradoxically, intrinsic to the good of finite things.

The possibility of the tragic

Kathleen Sands' essay on feminist theological perspectives in theodicy offers a clear, and rather novel, typology of theodicies, together with a nuanced appreciation of how her ideal types mingle, and even spill over into each other, in the work of particular theologians. Classically, she argues, Christian (or, at least, western Christian) thought deals with evil on either a 'rationalist' or a 'dualist' basis.[28] Rationalism designates a metaphysic that assumes that the universe is basically harmonious and intelligible; evil is the refusal of intelligibility, the refusal to occupy a rational place in the order of things. One implication of such a model is that there is no evil 'beyond comprehension or rehabilitation'; and this survives even in a secular culture, as the dominance of a rational order of discourse, an order without bias or interest, which must always work to assimilate and correct the rebellious discourses of those who refuse 'objectivity and universality'. Dualism understands evil as a real moral other, the object of an unconditional hostility and an unremitting struggle. In some sense, evil has its own ontological presence: there is no fore-ordained identity between the true and the good, or the real and the rational, so that this approach 'provides ideological frameworks for strategies of withdrawal, resistance, and destruction'.[29]

However, these are not simply two neatly defined alternatives: they tend to collapse into each other. Religious dualism struggles and hopes for a *victory*, a creation or restoration of identity. Rationalism's struggle against the otherness of rebel discourses, non-standard modes of understanding and engagement in the world, can have the excluding energy and hostile passion of dualism. While both have real strength, both have the same weakness: they ignore the realm of the truly contingent and, thus, the experience of the genuinely tragic. They suppress plurality and chance.

Martha Nussbaum's brilliant study in classical ethics and tragedy is invoked to powerful effect here to argue for a conception of the good that is various, mobile, vulnerable, rather than unified and stable.[30] There is a gulf that cannot be crossed between 'first principles', ideals and goods on the one hand, and the 'rough and bloody theatre of history', the realm of actual human choices.[31] Unless this is recognised, theological discourse will simply enshrine the interest of the particular elites who are fluent in it, who set the canonical standards of intelligibility, and will always create and sustain a 'counterworld', a sphere whose darkness and disobedience provide a sort of negative reinforcement of the dominant discourse, and into which can be bundled the non-resolution and provisionality of that dominant discourse. In short, we have a recipe for denial and for oppression, the demonising of the other. In a world of postmodern sensibility, the struggles that matter are not between the clearly good and the rebellious or resistant, but between competing goods and competing powers. We are at once obliged to take stands *against* certain things and to allow that they may have an integrity, a good, proper to them, yet unacceptable *here*.[32] This conviction that not all interests can be harmonised is central to the tragic vision, which accepts 'the inevitability of our involvement in evil'.[33] Tragedy obliges us to 'find every form of conflict and suffering *question-worthy* and *wonder-worthy*'.[34]

Augustine, recognized as the most influential figure in the construction of the western Christian perspective, illustrates precisely the mutual implication of rationalism and dualism.[35] Rationalism allows Augustine to argue against Manichaean dualism and to construct an orderly hierarchy for desire to move upwards to God. But there is a directly moral dissatisfaction with the force of evil that this structure cannot contain; and this finds expression in Augustine's analysis of sin, with its own perverse power, its status as an apparently autonomous force that binds the will. Because sin is manifest in the perversion of the will to the lower elements in creation, these elements take on a sort of moral colouring, and all pleasures connected with the purely bodily order are the objects of suspicion and interrogation. In the post-Fall environment, things that are still good in themselves have become the carriers of moral corruption. Thus, there is, after the Fall, an effectively dualist drama being enacted, even though the beginning and end of the story are dictated by rationalism. In neither context is there room for the tragic. Sands notes Augustine's 'disdain for tragic and comic dramas', and his

117

anxiety about the reaction of readers to his own story: he dreads equally being pitied and being mocked.[36] Behind all this anxiety to secure moral fixity – by the adversarial definition of evil in the present, and the negative account of it in the distant metaphysical horizon – is an anxiety about the maintenance of the threatened dominant position of the male, reasonable will; so that woman, in particular, focuses concerns about evil or rebellion, even though Augustine grants that such rebellion may, in fact, be the effect of the 'higher' agent's failure in the ordering of desire.[37]

Although Sands' discussion of Augustine is brief, and her references often seem to depend on secondary sources, or to relate to a narrow band of Augustine's work, the case is an interesting and challenging one, which does not simply repeat standard feminist charges against Augustine, but allows his schema a degree of moral seriousness and weight. In effect, she is claiming that the tradition of which Augustine is the classical exponent – if not the creator – is preoccupied with what a contemporary critic would call 'closure', a damaging impatience because, whatever the metaphysical good intentions, it is constantly slipping into polarisations of 'the Good' and 'the not-Good' in the present moment; polarisations that encourage the identification of actual agents here and now with the Good and the not-Good, and the projection of failure and lack on to certain classes and categories of existence (matter, woman).

What is interesting here is that what Sands wants to reinforce is, in important respects, exactly what Augustine wants to reinforce: there is no timeless and stable goodness in this world; there is no incarnation of evil. All creaturely good is realised in *time*, and the perfection of goodness exists not as something that issues from a process, but as the eternal standard and direction of creaturely good. However, it is in relation to this last point that the division opens up. Sands seems to want to deny that there is a transcendent measure of good: the good is rather what emerges as a possible, a 'viable', wholeness and balance in the life of moral communities. 'Moral judgements . . . are strategic, contextual judgements about how the diverse goods of life might best be integrated and unnecessary suffering minimised in a particular place and moment'.[38]

We need to look harder at some of Sands' case. The assumption is made that, if there is an uncrossable gulf between ideals and the harsh choices of history, those who articulate ideals and who defend the notion of a transcendent good, are almost bound to become a self-perpetuating elite, surviving by demonizing the 'other' who represents disobedience and disorder. That this has often been true hardly needs saying; that it is the consequence of an Augustinian schema requires more argument to be established. It could as well be said that the practical dualisms of Christian history arise not from too faithful but too careless a reading of Augustine. Part of Augustine's gravamen against both Pelagians and Donatists is to do with their identification of possible states within history as bearers of a goodness that is somehow complete or adequate. The Donatist absolutises the purity of the empirical church; the Pelagian affirms the possibility of keeping the commandments of God. Both take the church out of time, in their different ways. The church which continues to pray 'forgive us our trespasses', is a church whose purity and integrity are inseparable from continuing self-questioning and penitence.[39] And this is because the Good *is* God: the divine self-identity means that the 'ideal' is precisely, in one central sense, not available for realisation. God is not another agent pursuing (successfully, as we pursue unsuccessfully) a proper moral balance. God is not, in any sense, a rival in our universe, so that the divine Good cannot be appropriated by any finite agent as simply identical with its own. If so interpreted, the idea of a transcendent good becomes a decisive *prohibition* against the use of an ideal as the reinforcement of a particular interest. What prevents this itself becoming a claim to a universal and rational perspective is its essentially negative and provisional character: as Augustine insists against the Donatists, the Christian community continues to be immersed in possible and actual sin.[40]

The resolution of historical struggle is, for Augustine, the work of grace and, thus, ultimately a victory never produced by history itself, never the triumph of a moral programme. Augustine certainly fails, in a variety of ways, to spell out what might be needed to make this explicit in such a way as to challenge, discipline or overturn particular bids for the power to exclude or discount; yet the scheme proposed retains a logic that Sands' critique does not wholly answer. If we examine the positive content of what is suggested as an alternative, I suspect that we may find the option collapsing into just the same polar oppositions Sands identifies in the classical account. Say that the Good is, indeed, properly conceived as 'various, mobile and vulnerable': this might mean that the Good is different for different created subjects, to the extent that what is good for one subject is necessarily and permanently at odds with what is good for another; that the Good genuinely differs from circumstance to circumstance, without any 'grammar' of continuity; that the Good of or for certain subjects might simply and finally fail or prove impossible of realisation.

The first reading implies that there are genuine (truthfully conceived) creaturely goods that can be realised only at the expense of the genuine goods of others; a view hard to reconcile with any properly emancipatory ethic, since it is the argument, implicit or explicit, of the slave-master. The second suggests that particular developments might render good what once was not, that torture or racial discrimination might be *made* good by historical changes. The third suggests that there are worldly subjects 'predestined' to final and irredeemable frustration. To appeal to the notion of a viable balance in a community's life as a way of avoiding the Hobbesian consequences of these possible readings (the war of all against all, the *inevitable* non-convergence of creaturely good) will not really meet the case. It assumes that the reconciliation of partial and competing goods is itself a good to be pursued, without qualification, it seems. There is no argument to establish why this good should be exempt from the general prohibition against general goods. An absolutist assumption is being smuggled in under the guise of pragmatism.

Part of the problem comes in the definition of what Sands (or, indeed, Nussbaum) really understands by the tragic. An Augustinian might say that the world *is* tragic, in the sense that our fallen perceptions of the world are so flawed that we are constantly, and inevitably (since the Fall), involved in mistaken and conflictual accounts of our true interests. In so far as the Good, in the fallen order, requires a measure of coercion if total incoherence and fragmentation are to be avoided, *loss* is always bound up with creaturely virtue, even sanctity. And since there is no coercion that can ultimately overcome the perverse will, there are creaturely subjects whose good *is* eternally frustrated, lost souls. However, this frustration is contingent on a history, not intrinsic to the nature of their good. What such an interlocutor could not accept would be a definition of tragic conflict as a *necessary* feature of created order. That would be to return to naked dualism: there is not one Good, therefore there can be no convergence of goods, therefore there is (even if not dramatised in Manichaean terms) irreconcilable cosmic struggle, with no ontological priority accorded to either side. Against this, the Augustinian would have to marshal the saint's own arguments, already considered here, on the grammar of evil in a world created by a good God. In another kind of universe . . . but, for the Christian, there can only be a universe made by a good God; and for such a universe to be at all, the grammar of good and evil must be as Augustine argues. It is not clear whether Sands, for example, accepts any doctrine of a creative origin that can be articulated in anything like traditional Christian terms; and in fairness to her, her book does not pretend to be an essay in Christian dogmatics, and gains much of its moral strength from this standing back from conventionally doctrinal concerns. Nevertheless, I do not believe that an option for the tragic, conceived in terms of necessarily conflictual goods, absolves from attention to the potentially very stark metaphysical implications that begin to arise.

Conclusion

Augustine's account of the character and logic of our discourse about evil is not, by any means, tidy or exhaustive; it is still marked by elements of argument that his theology as a whole is moving beyond or away from. I have tried particularly to put in appropriate perspective the 'aesthetic' aspects of his case. My main concern has been to propose that he was himself right to see this issue as involved with the logic of talk about God. As *Confessions* 7 makes plain, he is engaged in 'de-spatialising' talk about both God and evil: neither has a *place* in the universe, neither is a subject competing with others.

In relation to evil, this means that talking about evil is always talking about temporal processes, the processes we learn to identify as loss or corruption, and that we identify more clearly and truthfully the more we grow in understanding of the whole interlocking pattern of the world's activity. In relation to God, it means that talking about God is always talking about the temporal processes of clarification, reconciliation, self-discovery in love, the processes that lead us beyond rivalry and self-protection; talking about God is the articulation of a self-knowledge that grasps the central dependence of the self, a knowledge of the self as lacking and searching and, thus, as presupposing a goal of desire that exceeds any specific state of affairs in this material world.

Augustine's argument is a pincer movement, driving us to concentrate precisely upon the bloodiness of the world's processes and the obscurity of our decisions, mingling as they do reason and longing, with all the risks attendant on a reasoning that is always interest-bound and a desire that is always haunted by self-obsession. The alternative is, in fact, hard to frame coherently without dissolving the central vision of a God who is able to transfigure our desire and heal our blindness *because* this is a God who has no interest to defend, no limited and self-referring good to promote in negotiation with others. It has become fashionable to promote the idea of a God who is 'really' affected by the world's history, or whose life is, in some rather hard to specify way, bound up with the world's destiny. Augustine's discussions of evil leave us with the question of whether any such God can, in fact, be understood, except as one who has concerns that are other to ours as another inhabitant of a common moral world.

There may be ways of defending the compatibility of this model with the traditional Christian (and Jewish and Muslim) commitment to the divine freedom, and with the doctrine that God creates the world from nothing (and is, therefore, in no way constrained by what is made); but they would have been strange to Augustine. His concern with finding an adequate grammar for evil (not a justification of evil, a rational account of the proportion of evil to guilt, let us say, or a calculus of how much evil is necessary to produce a good cosmic outcome) is, I have been arguing, at every point inseparable from his discovery, as he believes, of the nature of our discourse about God as self-subsistent and therefore without limit, miraculously generous in creation and salvation. If we do not share his understanding of evil as privation, no-thing, no-space, can we in any way share his understanding of God as subsistent and overflowing fullness, no-thing, no-space, the non-competitive other whose freedom makes us free?

Notes

1 Augustine, *ciu.* 11.9.
2 See particularly the Introduction to K. Surin, *Theology and the Problem of Evil*, Oxford, Basil Blackwell, 1986.

3 G. R. Evans, *Augustine on Evil*, Cambridge, Cambridge University Press, 1982, remains a magisterial summary; the chapter on 'Evil, Justice and Divine Omnipotence' in J. Rist's *Augustine: Ancient Thought Baptized*, Cambridge, Cambridge University Press, 1995, is useful, though (surprisingly) does not extensively discuss the logic of evil as privation; D. A. Kress, 'Augustine's Privation Account of Evil: A Defence', *Augustinian Studies* 20 (1989), pp. 109–28, concentrates on this aspect, and offers some rebuttals of recent philosophical critiques; and B. Horne, in Ch. 4 of *Imagining Evil*, London, Darton, Longman and Todd, 1996, gives a very brief but splendidly eloquent and imaginative summary of the Augustinian position.

4 London, Collins, 1966; chs 3 and 4 are a lengthy discussion of Augustine.

5 Minneapolis, Fortress, 1994.

6 Op. cit., pp. 56–8.

7 Op. cit., p. 57: 'For Augustine there was no such thing as bare existence'.

8 Ibid., pp. 58–9.

9 Ibid., p. 59.

10 R. Williams, 'Redeeming Sorrows', in *Religion and Morality*, ed. D. Z. Phillips, London, Macmillan, 1996, pp. 132–48, especially 135–6.

11 The prevalence of the language of seeing and failing to see is notable; see especially 7.1.1–2 (the mind's eye clouded by materialistic images, the failure to be *conspicuus* to oneself), 7.4.6 (seeing that the incorruptible is better that the corruptible), 7.5.7 (materialistic images again), 7.7.11 (the inner light of the mind, blocked by false images), 7.8.12 (God's healing touch reducing the swelling that obscures sight), 7.11.17–15.21 (what the renewed mind sees when it 'looks' at the world) and so on.

12 It is one of the virtues of Evans' study (above, n. 3) that it emphasises this dimension of the problem: evil as *alienatio* of the mind.

13 *Doctr. chr.* 1.4 for the basic distinction of use from enjoyment; 1.31–2 on God's 'use' of us *ad nostram utilitatem . . . ad eius autem tantummodo bonitatem* (for our benefit . . . but only for God's goodness).

14 Ibid., 1.32: God 'makes use' of us for the sake of the exercise of God's own *bonitas*, which is the ground of our existence; so the divine use of us is always to that divine end which is *our* blessedness.

15 *Conf.* 7.1 on God as infinite extension; 7.5 on creation as an immense mass both permeated and spatially exceeded by God.

16 Ibid., 7.12, where Augustine returns to the issue of evil in the wake of learning to 'see' afresh the nature of created being, and understands that corruptibility is not *ipso facto* incompatible with good in some measure.

17 Ibid., 7.13 and 16 on the unavoidable rub of conflict in the 'lower' reaches of creation, which is none the less *conveniens* (fitting) within the whole. The argument is not without obscurity, but the general point seems to be that we do not need 'local' and obvious harmonies at every level of existence in order to believe that the creation is coherent overall.

18 Ibid., 7.18.

19 Hick, op. cit., pp. 61–2.

20 Ibid., p. 62 on pain as 'intrusive'.

21 Of signal importance here is the discussion of loving the Good in others in *trin.* 8.

22 *Ciu.* 19.12–13.

23 Hick, op. cit., p. 83.
24 Ibid.
25 *De natura boni*: see especially 1 and 8; *De Genesi ad litteram*, see for example, 3.16, on beasts of prey.
26 *Ciu.* 11.22.
27 Among many possible instances, see *ciu.* 13.19 and 23; *c. Iul. imp.* 6.39.
28 Sands, op. cit., pp. 2–6.
29 Ibid., p. 3.
30 *The Fragility of Goodness. Luck and Ethics in Greek Tragedy and Philosophy*, Cambridge, Cambridge University Press, 1986 (see especially chs 11 and 12).
31 Sands, op. cit., p. 6.
32 Ibid., pp. 8, 11–12.
33 Ibid., p. 9.
34 Ibid., p. 11
35 Ibid., pp. 17–20.
36 Ibid., p. 19. The passages cited from *ciu.* on Augustine's hostility to drama should be read in context as part of a specifically anti-pagan polemic, concerned with the representation of 'divine' agents as involved in rape or violence. The general conclusion proposed here is poorly supported by these particular texts, and it is not easy to see how they are to be connected to an alleged fear of pity or mockery in Augustine.
37 Ibid., pp. 19–20.
38 Ibid., p. 15; see also p. 136.
39 See, for example Augustine's *ep.* 185.9.39.
40 See, for example, the argument at *bapt.* 2.6 on the 'contamination' of the African church, even in the time of Cyprian, by the communion of the righteous with apostates.

SNARES OF TRUTH

Augustine on free will and predestination

James Wetzel

There is no hedging on predestination in Augustine's letter of AD 418 to the Roman presbyter Sixtus. All human beings inherit the guilt of original sin and are thus of 'one and the same clay of damnation', justly to be forsaken; a select few are destined, nevertheless, to be singled out from common clay and restored to God's favour, not because they have in some way, however meagre, distinguished themselves, but because of God's unfathomable will to redeem.[1] Augustine draws his paradigm case of election from Rom 9, where Paul mentions two famous sons of Israel, Jacob and Esau, and attributes the ascendancy of one over the other to a divine decision, in place before either brother is born. As such, the decision to favour the younger brother, Jacob, could not have been made based on what Jacob deserved, unless God were to have made it based on what Jacob would end up deserving. There is no room for compromise here, insists Augustine, who finds in the appeal to God's foreknowledge an overly subtle attempt to subvert the priority of election over human merit; those who resort to it 'jump off cliffs' in order to evade 'snares of truth'.[2]

Augustine's doctrine of predestination, founded on his premise of unearned election, has been akin to theological dynamite. To preach this doctrine is to invite revolution and retrenchment, license and rebuke. I think especially of John Calvin in the sixteenth century; Jansenius in the seventeenth. There is something potent and potentially destructive in the idea that human redemption is not in human hands; it therefore pays to ask whether Augustine's uncompromising deference to a deity of selective compassion is really the best way of avoiding a bad end and remaining caught up in truth. Not every admirer of Augustine has thought so. Gerald Bonner, for example, seems convinced that Augustinian predestination is a theological dead end: 'Nothing is gained by attempting to defend the doctrine, which remains a terrible one and more likely to arouse our awe than enlist our sympathy'.[3]

At the very least, it must be conceded that Augustine's provocative way of reading Paul disrupts the delicate *pas de deux* of western theism, between ethical self-assertion and religious self-surrender. After AD 397, that is, soon after he has arrived at his definitive reading of Rom 9, Augustine never tires of citing 1 Cor 4:7: 'What part of a good do you have that you have not received?'[4] For the sinner who makes this his petition in his *Confessions*, 'Give what you command, and command what you will,' the answer is clearly, 'no part at all'.[5] In the dance of redemption, it would seem that the human partner arrives empty-handed and lacking in grace; not only does the divine partner supply the grace, God does all the dancing. It is as if sin has drained the human heart of vitality, leaving God to assume (or forsake) a spiritless husk.

'Between predestination and grace,' writes Augustine, 'there is only this difference, that predestination is preparation for grace, while grace is already the giving itself'.[6] If all good is given in the gift, then a prepared heart is a wasteland, barren of good. Where in this emptiness would the redeeming spirit of God meet up with the original goodness of creation? It was never Augustine's intention to attribute to sin, an all-too-human creativity, the power to undo divine creation and rob the soul of its beauty, and yet by fixating on the conjunction of two aspects of predestination, inexorability and selectivity, he risked replacing the vulnerable good of creation with the invincible grace of redemption, a trade of one kind of creation for another. The antithesis between creator and redeemer is so contrary to the spirit of Augustine's confessional theology that it is tempting to dismiss his doctrine of predestination as the late and twisted product of a career overburdened with controversy.

Two considerations should give pause, however, to the friendly amender of Augustine. First, Augustine seemed not to feel the force of the most obvious and persistent objection to his belief in predestination, that it cultivated disbelief in the validity of moral appraisal and, therefore, disinterest in moral improvement. He handed human will, root and branch, over to God. The wisdom set against him was that no one could be good or bad, if no one had a will to be either. Being subject to the will of another is paradigmatic of a lack of freedom.[7] Still, Augustine writes as if being wholly subject to God changes nothing about the urgency of moral striving.[8] I am disposed to believe that Augustine left it largely to his interpreters to discover how his insistence on the priority of grace over virtue could yet retain some motive for ethics, but I remain unconvinced that he offered only dogmatic intransigence to those who held out for a bridge. The amender of Augustine ought to consider whether the burden of misunderstanding is Augustine's alone. Second, even if the doctrine of predestination should prove to be theologically irredeemable, it is not easily excised from Augustine's thought. It was not a late-career innovation, as his loyal opposition had hoped, but, as he himself claimed, a working out of his formative insights into the mystery of redemption.[9] Without the doctrine of predestination, there is no Augustinian theology of grace.

In what follows, I will not be trying to uphold Augustine's doctrine in quite the manner he espoused it. There is much good sense behind Gerald Bonner's sentiment, and I do not want to lose sight of it by serving up too spirited an *apologia*. I begin my defence, then, with an eye towards the most unsavoury parts of Augustine's doctrine. These will turn out to be every bit as unpalatable as his judicious critics have imagined. Nevertheless, the centre holds, and, in the main, I take my inspiration from there. In conclusion, I return to the apparent antithesis between free will and predestination and reconsider the wisdom of Augustine's critics. When his doctrine is viewed from the centre of his vision, it can be seen to accommodate much of the wisdom taken traditionally to oppose it. Augustine was right to be uncompromising, but wrong to be unaccommodating. There is room in his inspiration for a wide diversity of temperament, talent, and insight. In respect of this, I offer an unpolemical defence of predestination.

A mystery misplaced: secret justice

Opposition to Augustinian predestination falls standardly under two rubrics: Pelagian and semi-Pelagian. Pelagianism refers to a loose confederation of theologies taking their name, but not necessarily their inspiration, from the British moralist, Pelagius. Those named for him are more or less united in their dislike of Augustine's doctrine of original sin.[10] Pelagius believed that there was a first sin, and that it had dire consequences, but his reading of Rom 5:12, a prooftext for original sin, differs from Augustine's in limiting the inheritance of sin to physical death, or death of the body.[11] Spiritual death, referring to the soul, is not heriditable and, therefore, we can avoid it if circumstances favour our efforts. For Pelagius, favourable circumstances meant membership in a church that helped its faithful by means of exhortation and example to steel their wills against temptation and commit to a life of virtue. In Augustine's understanding, sin's inheritance is more insidious and correspondingly more mysterious. We are born not only with bodies destined to die, but with hearts disposed to sin. The eruption of sin into human conduct is, for him, a symptom, not a source, of a disease fatal to the soul. Unlike physical diseases, we are morally accountable for soul-sickness, and thus to the doctrine of original sin Augustine appends transmissible guilt.[12] The sin of Adam and Eve is literally everyone's. Although Augustine leaves the mechanism of transmission ultimately unaccounted for, he suggests enough of a connection to sexual intercourse to hand him his reputation as an enemy of sexuality; a reputation he has never quite managed to live down.

The Pelagians were fundamentally at odds with Augustine's theology. Semi-Pelagians, so named long after their day by seventeenth-century controversialists, favoured Augustine over Pelagius, but reacted against what they took to be Augustine's excesses. A number of them played key roles in the monastic movement of southern Gaul, notably John Cassian, abbot of the monastery of Saint Victor in Marseilles. Cassian's thirteenth *Collatio*, though not expressly aimed at Augustine, offers an irenic and elegant alternative to Augustine's numbing emphasis on God's initiative in his later writings against Pelagians.[13] While Cassian never denies that God sometimes seizes upon a wayward heart and, unbidden, sets its straight, he suggests that there is no impropriety in the thought that, at other times, God responds to the heart's petition for help. Regardless of who initiates the relationship, Cassian is mindful of the disproportion of what ensues; whatever the human investment, the divine return far outstrips it. In place of overwhelming grace, Cassian praises grace abounding. In his estimation, the exceptional cases are the ones in which the initial human investment is nil, and even in these there must be a subsequent investment of will in the gift of divine spirit; no one is ever forced to remain with God.

Augustine knew the semi-Pelagians as Massilians, that is, he knew them more for their association with Marseilles and Cassian than for any affiliation with Pelagius. The Massilians came to be known later as semi-Pelagians, but the designation ill suits them; scholars who still use it do so more out of respect for precedent than out of conviction. Much about Augustine had, after all, been praised by Massilian luminaries, in particular his recognition of human debility after original sin and his appreciation for the grace that heals a wounded heart from within. A sizeable number of monks disliked Augustine's apparent elimination of human initiative, as that seemed contrary to their practice of petitionary prayer, but their reservation did not put them halfway along the road to Pelagius.

Granting that 'semi-Pelagian' has been something of a misnomer, there is yet another, far more subtle misconstruing of Augustine's relation to his critics, and this one continues to obscure the motive of his predestinarian sentiments. Massilians may not be centrists in a theological continuum running from Pelagius to Augustine, but nor are they right of centre (taking Augustine as conservative), or left (taking him as radical); the error is to suppose that there is a continuum. On the supposition of continuity, all that really separates Cassian from Augustine is that one reserves a tiny bit of will for human initiative, while the other cuts bait. That is a paltry difference, apt to make Augustine seem inhumane in relation to Cassian's tempered humanism and Pelagius seem, by contrast, rather full of himself. Such a manner of construing difference lends itself to caricature; I doubt that Pelagius had as blithe an opinion of human nature as he has so often been saddled with, and I am certain that Augustine respected the human will (he practically invented the concept).

My alternative to difference in terms of degrees of separation is a shift in perspective. Augustine's negation of the Pelagian ideal of initiative and effort is not the negation of initiative and effort, but a reclaiming of virtue under a new wisdom. Pelagians try to win God's favour with upright resolve and good deeds; Augustine has given up on this, not, I think, because he is too cynical to believe in human virtue, but because virtue makes no sense to him as a means of seducing God. Semi-Pelagians and Pelagians are alike in believing that some good can originate with human beings, and that God, who desires only goodness, will be drawn to it. In that sense, they are on the same road, even if they are far apart. Semi-Pelagians are badly named only because the name understates the degree to which Pelagian conviction has atrophied in them. They have parted company with Pelagius, but they have yet to set out on a new direction. Augustine addresses them with circumspection and without compromise.

The monks of Marseilles received two of the last gasps of his literary output, *De praedestinatione sanctorum* and *De dono perseuerantiae*. Among his major works, only the massive and unfinished harangue against the Pelagian bishop, Julian, post-dates these writings. I confess that I find his two treatises on predestination a tedious pair; Augustine hammers home his conviction that a life redeemed is wholly redeemed in God, from start to finish, but the quality of a such a life, and what one could expect of it, he leaves to the side. If the monks simply had wanted to know what Augustine believed, his replies are ample; they are stingy things, however, for anyone who would like to share in the wisdom of his beliefs.

Perhaps the one redeeming feature of his Massilian rejoinders is his mention in each treatise of the exegetical study he wrote near the beginning of his episcopate, and at the prompting of his friend and mentor, Simplicianus. Book 1 of his replies to Simplicianus deals first with the issue of Paul's persona in Rom 7:7–25, and then with the moral of Jacob's election over Esau in Rom 9:10–29. In *De praedestinatione sanctorum*, Augustine tells the monks that they will find there, in his struggle to fathom the basis of election, a radical change of view.[14] He cites the judgement of his *Retractationes*: 'In resolving this question, I really worked for the free choice of human will, but the grace of God won out'.[15] Augustine further underscores the importance of *Ad Simplicianum* in *De dono perseuerantiae*, where he places his exegetical turn of mind within close proximity of its existential correlate, the description in the *Confessions* of his personal experience of election.[16]

It is not implausible to suppose that, in AD 397 Augustine wrote his *Confessions* out of the impetus of his new reading of Paul and that the conversion he describes so memorably in Book 8 owes as much to exegetical insight as it does to his recollection of an experience more than ten years old.[17] I do not mean to suggest by this that his account is unfaithful to his experience, but more that the meaning of his experience had to wait upon his revision of Paul. *Ad Simplicianum* ends Augustine's attempt of about two years earlier to read into Rom 9 some basis in human worth for God's favouring of one mother's son over another.[18] Back then, election had been of the faithful son, the one who would know not to presume upon his own strength and so would petition willingly for divine aid; in *Ad Simplicianum* the petitioning becomes part of what is given with being elected. Where once there was a human difference, now there is only a distinction in how God calls. Jacob is favoured because God calls Jacob favourably (*congruenter*), so as to bring him irresistibly to faith and a new life. Too bad for Esau; he is called, but not favourably. His heart is never opened.[19] Once Augustine embraces the idea that God is always the source of the soul's desire for God, he never shrinks from it. It awakens him to all he has been given and releases his conversion from its moment: in recollection, the moment fades, but not the grace the moment conveys. In a moment, there is grace enough for a lifetime. The Paul who shuts off Augustine's access to Massilian theology opens his way to the theology of the *Confessions*.

There is a dark side to Augustine's reading of Rom 9. It is Esau. Augustine assumes that because Esau is the son not favoured, he is forever cast off. Leave aside whether this reading fits Paul (it does not); in subscribing to a doctrine of reprobation, Augustine subscribes to the belief that some who feel abandoned by God are, in fact, abandoned by God.[20] These unhappy souls are the damned, the sons and daughters not favoured. The doctrine of reprobation has mixed poison into Augustine's motives for affirming predestination. You do not have to be a Pelagian not to like the taste. His affirmation of reprobation is tragically wrong in two fundamental ways: it assumes that a soul is capable of experiencing the pain of being forsaken by God, and it assumes that God has a motive for inflicting it.

Let me begin with the second part. As of *Ad Simplicianum*, human beings are, for Augustine, a damnable lot, and by the strict imperatives of justice, God has cause to consign every last one of them to perdition. The wonder is that God spares some. God's reprieve of the few and condemnation of the many is in agreement, says Augustine, with 'a certain secret equity, beyond the measure of human reckoning, but there to be observed in the very transactions of mundane human affairs'.[21] The analogy implied is commercial. When an offer of goods or services is something other than the offer of a gift, the willing recipient of the benefit incurs a debt. It is of the essence of equity for a creditor to exact payment and for the debtor to render the same. If, however, a creditor is so moved, he or she may forgive the debt and treat the benefit in question as a gift. There is nothing unfair about forgiving debts, even when the creditor's motive for doing so is mysterious. It is simply an act beyond what we would normally reckon as fair. When the logic of a business transaction is applied to God, it is mysterious, but not unfair, that God forgives the sin of some, and it is within the human measure of fairness that God punishes the sin of others. Augustine sticks to this logic when he defends God's justice to his Pelagian and Massilian critics.

I am not convinced that the analogy between sin and debt is especially strong, but even conceding its force, it strains credibility to think of damnation as settling an account.[22] If human beings have expropriated a life they can rightly have only in God, it stands to reason that God ought to want that life returned. Reprobation is giving up the goods. To maintain his reasoning, Augustine has to deny that the goods forsaken are still good. Such a denial places an enormous burden upon his doctrine of original sin. It must now serve as a warrant for reprobation, a death warrant for those who no longer can pay their debts. All die in Adam, asserts Augustine, but he never explains why Adam's bad debt is everyone else's as well.[23] The mystery is not supposed to be here. We are supposed to be able to see why we are born debtors, fairly owing what we have no hope of redeeming. As a doctrine of redemption, original sin speaks to the darkness of human desire for God, to be broken by God alone. As a doctrine of reprobation, it is a thorough confusion of the laws of commerce, biology, and morality. The only room for a 'certain secret equity' in the doctrine is where Augustine excludes it: where God would discern something redeemable in a humanity human beings have forsaken.

If there is no intelligible motive in justice to move God to withhold grace, then perhaps Augustine should have gone the route of 'double' predestination, where damnation and redemption alike are impenetrable mysteries of divine election.[24] I do not believe that he ever really had this option. The doctrine of reprobation is not an ill-conceived rider to his doctrine of predestination; it is profoundly in contradiction with it. Predestination affirms God's priority as a lover by acknowledging the inspiration behind all human love of God; the doctrine of reprobation subverts this priority by affecting to make a hell out of desire. It would be hell to desire God and never have that desire requited. No one comes to desire God, however, in the absence of God's love. Here, requital is intimated by the very presence of desire. According to Augustine's logic of predestination, there is no pain of separation from God that is wholly without its element of grace.

Reflections on prodigality

Augustine's reputation as a thinker of modern insight rests on his mastery of the psychology of self-contradiction. He found his scriptural epitome of self-contradiction in the voice of Rom 7, who laments: 'I don't know what I am doing, for I don't do what I want, but what I hate I do'.[25] He knew the phenomenon best from his own experience. Most of Book 8 of the *Confessions* details the agony of his irresolution. He cannot will himself to become the person he wants to be, and so he finds himself divided between two wills, or more accurately, between the two contrary inclinations of a wounded will, neither of which has the power to transform and incorporate the other. One inclination chains him to a discredited, but mysteriously seductive, past; the other urges him on to a valued, but mysteriously resistible, future. Since Augustine has no will outside of his will's sorry division, the psychology of Book 8 contributes to the mystery of his divinely inspired resolution.

It took Augustine quite a while to concede that the voice of Rom 7 had to be Paul's own and not that of an adopted persona.[26] His overt motive for making the concession was polemical; against the Pelagian confusion of grace with virtue, and at the risk of impugning the character of a revered saint, Augustine put forth a Paul whose life under grace included self-doubt, internal strife, and a dose of carnal mindedness; failings fatal to the perfection of virtue. Of course, this was a Paul akin to himself and his own experience of grace; the polemical motive of Augustine's reading of Rom 7 had its roots in more basic exegetical and personal imperatives. In *Ad Simplicianum*, where he makes redemption wholly a matter of God's will to redeem, Augustine persists in his habit of assigning Paul a persona in Rom 7; he supposes Paul to speak there in the voice of someone who knows what he should do, but cannot do, who stands in need of divine aid, but has yet to seek it. In Augustine's terminology, this would be the voice of a person bound 'under the law' (*sub lege*), whose one remaining freedom is to turn to God and ask for liberation.[27] Augustine's rereading of Rom 9 will make this persona harder to sustain. When he admits that God's call invokes in the person called both desire for God and consent to it, Augustine erases the boundary between life under the law and law under grace.

It is ultimately not an exegetical imperative, however, that dictates Paul's 'conversion' in Rom 7. Augustine could have re-established the boundary between servitude under the law and freedom under grace by putting a certain spin on irresistible grace, that much-disputed mechanism of predestination. First, he robs life under the law of even its ineffectual love of justice, leaving in its stead fear of punishment; then he marks conversion at the onset of well-directed desire, always the result of an infusion (whether small or large) of divine spirit. The bigger the infusion, the deeper the desire. To some extent, Augustine's dreary doctrine of reprobation pulls him towards a theology of manipulative grace, but his most enduring testimony to life in God holds the line against this drift. Paul under grace, fighting the good fight within, is best represented in what Augustine confesses; whether the representation is finally of Paul himself is perhaps doubtful at best, but it is none the less the only Paul that Augustine could have assimilated at the scene of his conversion.[28] An existential imperative shapes what Augustine comes to hear in the voice of Rom 7, and unless its influence is taken into account, there can be no understanding of his doctrine of predestination.

This imperative, briefly stated, is the imperative of confession: recollect sin and receive grace. In the *Confessions*, Augustine plays upon the intimacy of the connection between sin and the love of God, the former being a kind of parody of the latter. When sin is recollected in confession, the parody is exposed, and the sinner is less subject than before to having to live it out. The premise of Augustine's confessional theology is that grace is already at work in the agonised heart of a reluctant sinner; from there, he looks for the perfection of the work of grace less in sin's transcendence than in sin's thorough transformation into the love of God. In this regard, he differs from most, if not all, of his critics, who allot grace and sin respectively to two contrary worlds of experience, the carnal and the spiritual. Although Augustine is hardly a stranger to the antithesis, he adopts Paul's distinction between flesh and the wisdom of the flesh, and aims his disdain at too great a love of what is bound to die.[29] He avoids making an enemy of the flesh, when he looks into sin's heart and finds there not a diversionary love, competing with the love of God, but love of God unknown to itself and directed toward what has no hope of containing it: the flesh that sin, if unchecked, must inevitably destroy.

The best illustration of the view of sin I am attributing to Augustine comes in Book 2 of the *Confessions*, where he turns his recollection of an adolescent theft into an allegory for sin.[30] Apart from its scriptural allusions and Augustine's analysis, the storyline is simple enough. As part of a company of adolescents in search of amusement, Augustine joins in a night-time trespass of a neighbour's orchard, where he and his cohorts make off with armfuls of fruit taken from a pear tree. They bite into a few of the stolen pears, but throw most of them to pigs. There are two plausible allusions in Augustine's recollection of an otherwise unremarkable adolescent prank. The taking of forbidden fruit recalls the first sin, as described in Gen 2–3; the careless squandering of a bounty recalls the prodigal son of Lk 15, who is reduced by famine and desolate living to envying the pigs he is sent to feed. At first sight, the allusions seem hard to combine. The original man and woman turn from Yahweh in order to have what Yahweh has: wisdom and immortality. The prodigal son wastes what he has been given freely, his share of his father's wealth. A story of theft that takes in both tales is apt to turn on a confusion between taking and receiving. That is a confusion uncommon in theft, but endemic to sin, as is revealed over the course of Augustine's recollection.

He ponders above all else the question of what moved him to thievery. In retrospect, he has an insight into his motives that he surely lacked at the time of his theft. Nothing at all moved him, aside from the sheer delight of transgression: 'I loved my falling away, not for what I was falling toward, but for the falling itself'.[31] The mundane motives of thieving, material advancement and honour among other thieves, have no explanatory force in the recollection. Augustine remembers throwing away the pears, and he does not recall, or does not choose to, the names of his companions. When recollected as sin, the motive behind a theft takes on a more than mundane order of complexity. Augustine concedes that sin is committed for the sake of what may be called 'the most limited of goods' (*extrema bona*), that is, whatever is here today but gone tomorrow, but he adds that sinful desire for goods of this sort is always immoderate; what is transient is coveted as if it were eternal.[32] Sin is its own motive, then, in a negative sense: nothing in the world satisfies the desire behind sin. From a mundane standpoint, sin is desire without end.

There may as yet, however, be an overlooked end in the theft Augustine recollects. Delight in transgression is characteristic of most adolescent rebellions, and most adolescent rebellions have as their aim the expropriation of parental authority, or, at least, parental authority as an adolescent conceives of it. The adolescent Augustine dispenses with what he has in as wilful a manner as he likes. Prodigality is the sign of his new freedom and new authority; parental restraint has been left behind.

Suppose that a pleasurable defiance of adult resourcefulness did at some time move a gang of north African adolescents to waste the fruit of adult labour. That motive, like all the rest, takes on an added gravity when it is mixed up with sin. Theft and prodigality in the mundane sense end in predictable irony. The more you take and waste, the more your life of licence enslaves you to the moderation of others. The prodigal son returns home penniless, expecting to become his father's servant. The irony of sin is deeper and more perplexing. What could the soul take from God and waste, when all the virtues that the soul could covet are inseparable from the divine being?

Augustine speculates that human vice is invariably the counterfeit of divine virtue.[33] What the soul lacks in resource, it makes up in pretence. Fear parades as prudence, ignorance as simplicity, arrogance as self-reliance, envy as the desire to excel. The list goes on. The question, however, is not whether the soul is moved by sin to make a virtue out of a lack, but why. What is the point of stealing virtue from God, or, short of that, of counterfeiting it? Augustine recalls the void in sin; it is the lack in love, the space no mortal beloved can ever fill. Perhaps that lack has to serve as the answer. Sin is the love of nothing. In reality, love of nothing is love's negation, but in pretence, where sin operates, it is God's manner of loving, to love without fear of loss. If the soul can bring itself to love nothing, the soul then has nothing to lose. The motive behind sin is, ironically, the desire to have God's love.

In sin, the profoundest desire of the soul gets perverted into a force of destruction. In seeking invulnerability, the soul loses the substance of divine love – its wholeheartedness – and thus it is driven towards an insane prodigality: to love beyond loss, the soul gives up all that it loves. The insanity lies not only in the divestment, but in having no beloved left to receive it. In practice, sin's counterfeit of God's love is impossible to perfect, for perfection here ends in the void, the undoing of the bonds of creation. The soul that falls away into sin continues to love mortal beloveds, but its attachments lack measure, and so its love goes begging. It wanders about aimlessly in a 'wasteland of need' (regio egestatis).[34]

Why there should be this wasteland is finally a mystery (the mystery of sin's origin), but it is a mystery best shaped by Augustine's sense of predestination. The pre-eminent theme of his Confessions is the persistency of God's love; Augustine often overlooks its presence, and yet the love never leaves him. It gives him his beginning; it draws him towards his end. In the meantime, he wanders about in a self-imposed oblivion, and fear takes him to the edge of one abyss after another. However, whenever he comes to the edge of the abyss fatal to his soul, he finds that he cannot peer over it without knowing he is upheld. The snare of truth that catches him is always some reminder of the love that has preceded his steps. He looks past the emptiness of his heart to what embraces it; there is no exit out of God. That is a hard truth to remember when you are busy trying to steal or win back the love you have already been given.

A mystery replaced: the prodigal heart

Few theologians have had as profound an appreciation as Augustine's for the magnitude of the difference between divine and human orders of being. He opens his *Confessions* on the theme of God's immeasurable greatness, whose variation is his own human puniness. God is boundless, beyond the contentment of heaven and earth. In comparison, Augustine's soul is a hovel in disrepair (*ruinosa*), cramped, dirty, and badly in need of renovation.[35] It is not a likely place for God to dwell. The one nice feature of the place is that it houses desire for God, but even that turns out to be part of an unexpected renovation, under an unlikely new owner. Augustine will not allow his heart to take refuge in even the dubious consolation of a profound longing. Until God awakens it, his desire is dead.

There is a fine line between humility and humiliation, and when Augustine's critics, both loyal and disloyal, fault him for morbid self-criticism, they generally mean to imply that he has crossed the line. You can have a relationship with another person only if you know something of humility; otherwise your ego gets in the way. If, however, you are humiliated instead of humbled, there is no 'you' to enter into a relationship. Massilians and Pelagians had differing understandings of when humility before God became too much of a good thing, but they had common cause in not liking Augustine's scruples about the human will to relate to God. If everything about the soul's relationship to God is God's doing, including the very desire to be in relation, where exactly does the soul surface in its redemption? The Word seems to have become a monologue.

I appreciate this criticism of Augustine and the wisdom behind it. Since I have earlier dissociated predestination from the doctrine of reprobation and all the problems it raises for God's justice, I am now prepared to deal more directly with the issue the criticism raises: free will.

As a criticism of Augustine's commitment to predestination, the claim that he enslaves the will to God is psychologically astute, but theologically misguided. It relies on too close an analogy between interpersonal relations in the human sphere and the soul's relationship to God. For Augustine, God is not a supreme person among other lesser persons, but a wholly other kind of reality. What is anything human to God? Nothing unless God has claimed it first. Augustine allows himself the audacious thought that his desire for God is first of all God's desire for God, because no other alternative conforms to the truth of his existence. He is here because God created him to seek and become part of God, and this despite the fact that a being sufficient unto itself has no motive to create or relate to anything outside of itself. The doctrine of predestination accords a transcendent God a prodigal heart; it is whatever is in God that welcomes back souls drawn from, and enamoured of, the void. In the face of this mysterious divine prodigality (grace), and only in the face of it, is humility endless and human prodigality redeemed.

God's incarnation in Christ gives the mystery its human face and supplies Augustine with his paradigm of predestined humanity, or humanity fully restored to God.[36] Apart from his experience of God incarnate, in whose death and resurrection the body is lost and found, Augustine would have had no awareness of the divine mystery of the flesh. In Book 7 of *Confessions*, he artfully invokes what is lacking in any return to God that is experienced outside of this awareness. The experience he recalls there is of an introspective journey, prompted by his reading of certain undisclosed Platonic writings; in all likelihood they included selections from the *Enneads*, the great work of the Neoplatonic mystic, Plotinus.[37] He follows the admonition of the writings to turn inward, and within himself he encounters the immutable light that is at the source of his own existence. Within this light, he is offered a vision of creation as God sees it, beautiful and unmarred by evil. What is most remarkable about this vision is that Augustine never sees himself in it, and yet he knows he belongs there, as his status as a creature of God is the one certainty he takes from the light.

As a way back to God, the path of introspection ends in paradox. Augustine finds God within himself, but he also finds himself far from God, in a strange place of interior exile (*in regione dissimilitudinis*); it is from there that he has his extraordinary vision of divinely created beauty.[38] After a time, his habit of fleshly love weighs him down and returns him to his familiar world of attachment. His recollection is of having been taken up into a love beyond corruption.[39]

The mystical vision of Book 7 is the high-water mark of Augustine's Platonism. Scholars who have studied it, and it has been a source of great fascination, have generally concluded that the vision fails to take because Augustine's heart was not in it. That is undoubtedly true, and some attention to why it lacked heart will disclose the connection between predestination and the doctrine of the incarnation. The key clue comes in what Augustine reports hearing from on high, while he was trembling alone and awestruck in his place of interior exile. A voice tells him to feed on it as his food, and then adds: 'You will not change me into you, as you do the food of your flesh, but you will be changed into me'.[40] Soon thereafter, the voice identifies itself in the words of the God of exiles: 'I am who I am' (Exod 3:14). It is a frequent theme of the Hebrew Scriptures, and one well familiar to Augustine, that no one sees God and lives. Set within the context of his Platonic adventure, the arrival of the sublime God of Exodus suggests that the God Augustine touches upon in himself is still in some terrifying way wholly other. He cannot take it in and not be consumed. The denouement of his adventure discloses the source of all the difficulty: Augustine continues to identify with a flesh that is foreign to God.

If Augustine were a Platonist in the style of Plotinus, he would have sought the resolution of his difficulty in freedom from all attachment to the flesh. Instead, he sees his way back to God opened in the inspiration of two Pauline imperatives: 'Put on the Lord Jesus Christ and make no provision for the flesh in vain desires'.[41] These words were put before him in the hour of his most desperate self-contradiction, when the pull of old loves and the push of a new vision wrestled within him to a fearsome draw, leaving him, in effect, without power of will. The effect on him, then, of reading Paul's exhortation to a new life was, under the circumstances, little less than miraculous. Light flooded into love; for the first time Augustine found himself able to carry a vision of God in his heart. No longer did God's call threaten him with consumption.

I have long wondered why an exhortation should have been of any comfort or use to Augustine at the very time his will was in abeyance. It seems perverse to demand of a person bound from the inside simply to get over it and get on with it. The ability to 'just do it' is precisely what is lacking. When Pelagius takes up and reads verse 13:14 in his exegesis of Romans, he finds moral exhortation there and with it the expectation of a clean break between the life lived before Christ is put on and the one lived thereafter, a difference between vice and dissolute desire and a life of virtue.[42] I suppose that, for Pelagius, the will to break with sin comes with being freed from having to be held to sin as a punishment. If so, Pelagian wisdom is not to be disparaged out of hand; there is considerable liberation in being forgiven debts of suffering and not always to bad effect. Mercy can be midwife to virtue.

However, whatever the complexities are of the psychological calculus of retribution and pardon, they have no bearing on what binds Augustine prior to his conversion; for he is bound not by guilt but by misguided love. Nor does it add much to imagine him freed by some great infusion of well-turned desire, designed to strengthen his resolve. When Augustine describes his conversion, he speaks of light pouring into his heart, conferring safety (*lux securitatis*).[43] Light is a trope for the wisdom beyond desire. In this second gift of interior illumination, Augustine must have caught sight of the person he lays claim to in confession: the one still roving about in a wasteland of need, but all the while beloved of God and predestined to be welcomed home.

I cannot presume to enter far into this wisdom, but perhaps I can illuminate its surface by turning a different kind of light upon the wisdom held against it. Is love authentic only when it admits of being refused? Many of Augustine's critics have thought so. They believe that where there is no freedom to refuse, there can be no freedom to accept. Put another way, it is wise never to love anything or anyone wholeheartedly; for if you do, you will lose yourself in what you love and disappear. Freedom in loving waits upon a measure of irresolution in the lover, some reserve towards the beloved. Predestination seems to violate this wisdom by locking God and the soul into a relationship of irresistible consummation.

However, there is really nothing in what motivates Augustine's doctrine that would require him to deny the wisdom of a measured love. In fact, the pathology of sin, as he construes it, shows up in disproportionate love. The soul's natural affinity for God, a beloved beyond measure, shipwrecks upon a world unable to contain it. Fear puts a temporary limit on the howling pain of shipwreck by prescribing love of limited aspiration. Little is lost if little is loved. Limits set in fear, however, do not keep. The sin that motivates fear comes eventually to infect it and render it prodigal. Love of limited aspiration degenerates into no love at all and then into love of nothingness. Unmeasured love weds the soul to an abyss.

If it is dangerous to love wholeheartedly in a world where beloveds die, it is no less dangerous to love only a God who is foreign to mortal flesh. The asceticism of bodily hatred is not all that far from the prodigality in sin. Both lack a world in which to love. Augustine gets his world back, or part of his world, along with the promise of the rest, when he puts on the flesh of Christ, for whom love of neighbour and love of God are the supreme and ultimately the same imperatives. Grace conferred by way of incarnation is not some magical recipe for fulfilling the imperatives, but the call to love wholeheartedly in the midst of mortality. We are upheld in our ordinary loves, the very ones we thought made us most vulnerable. Love takes its true measure from faith in love's redemption. Perfect love casts out fear. Then there will be freedom in God.

Conclusion: wholeheartedness

In an early and unfinished exposition of Romans, attempted before the watershed of *Ad Simplicianum*, Augustine identified sin against the Holy Spirit – the one unforgivable sin – as contempt of forgiveness.[44] The human heart imposes a limit upon the divine power to forgive and holds it firm against divine trespass. If you take unforgivable sin to the other side of the watershed, where Augustine has been won over to the idea of God's inexorable, but limited, will to redeem, you will be left to conclude that no sin is unforgivable unless God has lost the will to forgive it; the contempt of forgiveness, and the onus of it, is God's. In contrast to most of Augustine's friendly amenders, I believe that is it far more faithful to him to keep inexorability and remove the limits than the reverse. Without the spectre of reprobation, Augustine's predestinarian theology is relieved of its one unforgivable sin: its presumption to limit God's love.

It may seem that I leave Augustine with a doctrine of universal salvation, the teaching that all souls are redeemed, regardless of their individual disposition or desires. Augustine disliked the moral torpor of the doctrine; I dislike what it must inevitably concede to modern sentimentality about love. Happily, I have not committed him to it. The Augustinian doctrine of predestination is, first and foremost, a doctrine of confession. I can confess to my own redemption but not to yours, and much less to your damnation. The same goes for the church: its communal confession of salvation has no business doubling as a judgement for or against those on the outside. Confession is always in the first person, always addressed to God, and always a mix of joy and sorrow. When I confess to salvation in God, I do so out of the pain of alienation. I may believe, on the contrary, that I am forever lost and met with a fate I deserve, but I cannot make my despair my confession. These truths all belong to humility.[45]

In the end, grace may prove irresistible, but love can never be forced. Augustine knew this. He never expected his world to shake off its chains of fear either quickly or easily. Even a Christian regime could be expected to perpetuate the human tragedy of coercive justice, founded upon fear of retribution and infliction of punishment. The tragedy is not so much that we still have need to punish, but that we have still the desire. In the midst of all this human darkness, Augustine's doctrine of predestination recollects a light of hope: the last word will be the first, God's eternally, and ours when we are ready to receive it within time's covenant. T. S. Eliot put it well, in the confession of poetry: 'In my end is my beginning'.[46] Augustine put it best, in the poetry of confession: 'Restless is our heart until it rests in you'.[47]

Notes

1 *Ep.* 194.2.4; CSEL 57.178: 'una eademque massa damnationis'.
2 *Ep.* 194.8.35; CSEL 57.204: 'Mirum est autem . . . in quanta se abrupta praecipitent metuentes retia ueritatis'.
3 *St Augustine of Hippo: Life and Controversies*, London, SCM Press, 1963, p. 392 (rev. ed., Canterbury Press, Norwich, 1986). In recent work, Bonner's assessment of the doctrine of predestination is more irenic, but no less unsympathetic; see the second part of his masterful Otts Lectures on 'Augustine and Pelagianism,' printed in *Augustinian Studies* 24 (1993), pp. 27–47. In his concluding remarks, Bonner speculates that Augustine held to an 'interior conviction' of predestination, based on his experience of conversion. In my own way, I will be attempting to articulate Bonner's insight.
4 As in *ep.* 194.5.21; CSEL 57.192: 'Quid enim boni habes, quod non accepisti?'.
5 *Conf.* 10.29.40; CCL 27.176: 'Da quod iubes et iube quod uis'.
6 *Praed. sanct.* 10.19; BA 24.522: 'Inter gratiam porro et praedestinationem hoc tamen interest, quod praedestinatio est gratiae praeparatio, gratia vero iam ipsa donatio'.
7 Bernard William makes an excellent case for this paradigm over its alternative,

the lack of freedom involved in being short of choices or opportunities; see especially ch. 6 of *Shame and Necessity*, Berkeley, University of California Press, 1993.

8 *De correptione et gratia* is his most sustained attempt to rebut the claim that predestination renders the practice of moral persuasion otiose.

9 The Benedictine scholar, Dom Odilo Rottmanner, offered one of the earliest and best studies of the theological principles behind Augustine's doctrine of predestination; in calling the doctrine 'Augustinism', Rottmanner rightly underscored the importance of its presuppositions for almost all of Augustine's theologizing. See *Der Augustinismus. Eine dogmengeschichtliche Studie*, Munich, J. J. Lentner, 1892; also available in the French translation of J. Liébaert, 'L'Augustinisme: Etude d'histoire doctrinale', *Mélange de science religieuse* 6 (1949), pp. 31–48.

10 In this supposition, I follow Bonner, 'Augustine and Pelagianism', *Augustinian Studies* 23 (1992), pp. 33–51, especially at p. 35. (This is the first part of his Otts Lectures.)

11 *Pelagius's Commentary on St Paul's Epistle to the Romans*, tr. T. De Bruyn, Oxford, Oxford University Press, 1993, p. 92.

12 Augustine's first nod to the *heriditability* of guilt, as opposed to, say, ignorance or a bad disposition, is *Simpl.* 1.2.16. His expressed use of the term, 'original guilt' (*reatus originalis*), can be found at *Simpl.* 1.2.20; CCL 44.52.

13 *Ioannis Cassiani Collationes* (CSEL 13); an English translation of the thirteenth conference is available in *John Cassian: The Conferences*, tr. B. Ramsey, OP, New York, Paulist Press, 1997, pp. 459–98 (with notes). For Cassian's relation to Augustine, see ch. 4 of O. Chadwick, *John Cassian*, Cambridge, Cambridge University Press, ²1968.

14 *Praed. sanct.* 4.8.

15 *Retr.* 2.1; CCL 57.89–90: 'In cuius quaestionis solutione laboratum est quidem pro libero arbitrio uoluntatis humanae, sed uicit dei gratia'.

16 *Perseu.* 20.52–53.

17 My supposition is not original. For an important precedent, see P. Brown, *Augustine of Hippo, a Biography*, London, Faber & Faber, 1967, the chapter entitled 'The Lost Future'.

18 *Ex. prop. Rm.* 60.

19 *Simpl.* 1.2.13; CCL 44.38: 'Illi enim electi qui congruenter uocati, illi autem qui non congruebant neque contemperabantur uocationi non electi, quia non secuti quamuis uocati'.

20 The Paul of western Christianity is arguably Augustine's invention; Augustine's reading of Romans is especially creative, in goods ways and bad. I recommend one recent and quite brilliant attempt to recover the Paul before Augustine: S. K. Stowers, *A Rereading of Romans: Justice, Jews, and Gentiles*, New Haven, Yale University Press, 1994.

21 *Simpl.* 1.2.16; CCL 44.41: 'Atque ita tenacissime firmissimeque credatur id ipsum, quod deus . . . cuius uult miseretur et cuius non uult non miseretur, esse alicuius occultae atque ab humano modulo inuestigabilis aequitatis, quae in ipsis rebus humanis et terrenisque contractibus animaduertenda est'.

22 The analogy between sin and debt shows up in Mt 6:12, as part of the Lord's Prayer. It is, of course, not my intention to criticize the Lord's Prayer. The strength or weakness of an analogy has to do with its proximity to the literal,

while aptness has to do with how effectively an analogy conveys its intended insight in context. While it may be illuminating to think of sins as debts (as in Mt 6:12), it does not follow that sin is literally, or very nearly, some kind of debt.

23 The issue is tied up with the question of the soul's origin. Is the soul specially created with each individual at birth, or were all souls created with Adam, later to be given their own bodies by way of propagation? Augustine decides not to decide: see *an. et or.* 4.24.38. His best answer to the question is that the soul originates with God, but that one does not help him explain the transmission of original sin.

24 On rare occasions, *an. et or.* 4.11.16, for example, Augustine will write about predestination to eternal death. There is in his reckoning, however, neither divine will to promote sin, nor to single out and condemn particular individuals. There is instead a lack of divine will to save everyone who needs saving. However tenuous the distinction may prove to be, it was very important to Augustine.

25 Rom 7:15, as cited at *Simpl.* 1.1.8; CCL 44.14: 'Quod enim operor ignoro; Non enim quod uolo hoc ago, sed quod odi illud facio'.

26 *C. ep. Pel.* 1.8.13–14.

27 *Simpl.* 1.1.7–14; see *ex. prop. Rm.* 44–46.

28 For the source of the doubt, see the classic argument of K. Stendahl, 'The Apostle Paul and the Introspective Conscience of the West', *Harvard Theological Review* 56 (1963), pp. 199–215. The best account of Augustine's autobiographical use of Paul is P. Fredriksen, 'Paul and Augustine: Narratives, Orthodox Traditions, and the Retrospective Self', *Journal of Theological Studies*, new series, 37:1 (1986), pp. 3–34.

29 *Ex. prop. Rm.* 49.

30 *Conf.* 2.4.9–10.18.

31 Ibid., 2.4.9; CCL 27.22: 'amaui defectum meum, non illud, ad quod deficiebam, sed defectum meum ipsum amaui'.

32 Ibid., 2.5.10; CCL 27.22.

33 Ibid., 2.6.13–14.

34 Ibid., 2.10.18; CCL 27.26.

35 Ibid., 1.5.6; CCL 27.3.

36 *Praed. sanc.* 15.30; *perseu.* 24.67.

37 *Conf.* 7.10.16–7.17.23.

38 Ibid., 7.10.16; CCL 27.103.

39 Ibid., 7.17.23.

40 Ibid., 7.10.16; CCL 27.104: 'Nec tu me in te mutabis sicut cibum carnis tuae, sed tu mutaberis in me'.

41 Rom 13:14 as cited at *conf.* 8.12.29; CCL 27.131: 'induite dominum Iesum Christum et carnis prouidentiam ne feceritis in concupiscentiis'. The Latin word, *concupiscentia*, which I have rendered as 'vain desire', is usually translated as 'lust', or simply 'desire'. In this context, however, I think Augustine clearly intended the connotation of sin, and it is of the essence of sinful desire that it goes begging. Sin can never be satisfied as such. (I make no claims about Paul's meaning.)

42 De Bruyn, *Pelagius's*, op. cit., p. 140.

43 *Conf.* 8.12.29; CCL 27.131.

44 *Ep. Rm. inch.* 21.

45 My understanding of humility and its place in Augustine's theology has been greatly enhanced by the humane argument of G. W. Schlabach, 'Augustine's Hermeneutic of Humility: An Alternative to Moral Imperialism and Moral Relativism', *Journal of Religious Ethics* 22:2 (1994), pp. 299–330.

46 The last line of East Coker, one of the *Four Quartets*. Eliot's quartets are profoundly Augustinian in sentiment. They are arguably this century's greatest poetic expression of the doctrine of predestination.

47 *Conf.* 1.1.1; CCL 27.1: 'inquietum est cor nostrum, donec requiescat in te'. This essay has benefited from the insightful comments of my friend, John Cavadini. He has my thanks once again.

9

AUGUSTINE'S DECENTRING OF ASCETICISM

George Lawless

A recently published book on ascetic behaviour in Greco-Roman antiquity, 'the culmination of an eight-year-long conversation' between the authors, evoked an observation from a reviewer regarding 'the difficulty in defining asceticism that haunts the volume'.[1] Anyone who writes on asceticism in late antiquity knows that definition is more difficult than one might at first suspect. In the case of Augustine, recent criticisms of his asceticism make this task as problematic as it is necessary. Yet paradoxically, these same criticisms, by touching on the points at which Augustine's life and work seem most out of harmony with our modern sensibilities, offer a key with which a tentative description of asceticism in Augustinian terms can best be advanced.

A brief look at some of the recent criticism of Augustine sets out the issues in stark terms. One author has suggested that 'Augustine's ascetic agenda established elite standards of spirituality'.[2] Another critic identified Augustine as 'the man who fused Christianity together with hatred of sex and pleasure'.[3] Furthermore, we are told that an 'escapist version of Christianity', and a 'depreciation of marriage *vis-à-vis* celibacy' characterise much of the bishop's thought.[4] Such criticisms appear to be perennial, almost predictable. In addition, a critique of post-Vatican Council II trends in western Christianity from both an Eastern Orthodox and a western standpoint enumerated the following 'basic distortions': 'real deviations' in the theological trajectory of the last quarter century and western theology generally; a low view of the Incarnation; flight from the world; an estimate of human beings as abject dependants; an individualistic view of salvation; and, finally, low esteem for the sacraments.[5] The transgressor in these areas is Augustine of Hippo. Each of the above criticisms, however, reveals a superficial assessment of complex issues.

Recourse to Augustine's published works on ascetical themes does not, at first, provide us with a clear, comprehensive understanding of his approach.

Apart from a short sermon or treatise favouring fasting as a discipline for all Christians (*util. ieiun.* in CCL 46. 225–41), and his monastic *Rule*, Augustine's only other *ex professo* treatise on an ascetic issue is *The Work of Monks*, written at the request of Aurelius, bishop of Carthage.[6] Moreover, no treatise isolating asceticism as its exclusive, or even principal, theme is to be found elsewhere in Augustine's voluminous *oeuvre*.

In spite of this lack, ascetical concerns appear throughout Augustine's works enabling us to draw a general outline of his approach to the question. While presupposing the necessity of prevenient, or anticipatory, grace of Jesus Christ, asceticism, for Augustine, can broadly be described, first of all, *mutatis mutandis*, in Michel Foucault's phrase as *techniques du soi*, that is, training exercises for care and maturation of the self. In language derived from pagan and Christian authors, Augustine similarly invoked images from human anatomy, from stages of maturation, and from athletic, medical or military metaphors, to articulate the physical, mental components of spiritual training: *exercitatio animi*.[7] As a second feature of its makeup, asceticism required sustained initiatives of body and soul, mind and spirit, that is to say, the cultivation of good habits (*consuetudines*).[8] A learning process, or a core curriculum of doctrines and concomitant praxis (*disciplina*), constituted a third element of ascesis.[9] Finally, there was a twofold aspect, negative and positive, to Christian asceticism. The Pauline verses to which Augustine turned at the bidding of a voice in the garden of his residence in Milan best illustrate this double visage: 'Not in revelling and drunkenness, not in debauchery and licentiousness, not in quarrelling and jealousy, but put on the Lord Jesus Christ, and make no provision for the flesh to gratify its desires' (Rom 13:13–14). Christian ascesis, therefore, was focused primarily on Jesus Christ.[10] In this view, one could say ascesis was inherent in virtually everything the mature Augustine did from the time of his conversion to Catholic Christianity. One of his most succinct formulations of this fact was expressed by him in the words: 'I serve you with my heart and voice and writings'.[11]

Ascetic lifestyles

During the last decade of Augustine's life, Simeon the Stylite (an eponym that came to characterise a form of ascetic living) ascended the first of three pillars on which he was, successively, to spend the remaining two-thirds of his life. Other solitaries likewise inhabited the mountains surrounding the Syrian city of Antioch. The ascetical eremitic excesses of John Chrysostom's early youth, and those of Jerome's early manhood, were undertaken in this Syrian tradition; Augustine's attraction towards asceticism prior to his conversion in the Milanese garden was largely determined by Athanasius's *Vita Antonii* (*conf.* 8.16. 14–15). While the Latin loan-word from the Greek, '*eremita*', hermit, is not attested to in Augustine's voluminous vocabulary, he designated 'conscience' as a 'desert of no small expanse' (*en. Ps.* 54.10), an echo in all likelihood of Athanasius's description of Antony as 'a daily martyr in his conscience'.[12] Before the time of Gregory the Great, no individual in the Latin West was more *engagé* than Augustine of Hippo, whose flight from the world, *fuga mundi*, though essentially spiritual and a matter of the heart, was never a matter for geographical relocation.[13] The bishop of Hippo regarded separation from other people as humanly impossible, altogether incompatible with the social nature of humanity and the exigencies of Christian charity.[14] Jerome's remark to a lifelong friend that on the Day of Judgement, 'Plato with his disciples will be revealed as but a fool', would have been abhorrent to the mind of Augustine at any time of his life.[15] As he lay dying, the bishop of Hippo was reciting a verse of Plotinus and praying the Penitential Psalms.[16]

Both the perfectionism required for a 'servant of Christ' by Jerome, and his idealisation of the Syrian desert near Chalcis as the kind of place most suitable for the practice of asceticism, would have been as unacceptable to Augustine as they were to Jerome's addressee, Heliodorus, who refused to join him in his austere ascetic exercises.[17] Two of the most introspective of men, whose deaths occurred within five years of each other, John Cassian of Marseilles and Augustine of Hippo, were contemporaries. Yet their articulations of *homo interior* and *homo exterior*, in ascetic terms, were vastly different from each other in method, doctrine, design, programme and intensity. Cassian, in contrast, transposed a highly sophisticated eastern ascesis or *techniques du soi* into a western key, while the mature Augustine was chary of rules, whether of rhetoric, prayer or ascesis. In the fourth and fifth centuries, from Spain to the Bosporus and southward to the extremity of Upper Egypt, Asia Minor alone furnished Augustine with like-minded ascetics in the persons of the great Cappadocian Fathers, especially the mature Basil of Caesarea and his brother, Gregory of Nyssa.

In view of the varied ascetic strategies for care of self, cross-culturation, conflicting spiritualities and orthodoxies, and other centripetal pressures of the wider Mediterranean world, the moderate tenor of north African asceticism becomes all the more remarkable a phenomenon. It is attributable largely to Augustine either directly, through his personal intervention, or indirectly, through his influential writings and preaching. Candid discussions between Alypius and Augustine, through the years, on the respective merits of marriage and continence reveal a sensible outlook, which was the response, in part, to an increasing attraction towards virginity as a way of life in Milanese aristocratic circles during the last two decades of the fourth century (*conf.* 6.12. 21–2). As we shall note below, Augustine will add a corrective lens to this perspective. Both Augustine and Alypius exhibit sound judgement, in the meantime, by exhorting Verecundus, an independently wealthy Milanese teacher of grammar (whose wife was Catholic and who himself felt deterred from becoming a Catholic Christian because he was not celibate), to accept the faith in his married status (*conf.* 9.3.5). We do learn of Alypius's treading the icy ground of

Verecundus's estate barefooted, in the winter AD 386/7. However, this stands out as an isolated instance of austere asceticism (*conf.* 9.6.14). No comparable extreme can, to my knowledge, be cited for Augustine; nor does he ever urge such a rigorous regimen upon anyone.

It is one of the many ironies of Augustine's life that the site of his cathedra was called 'Basilica of Peace', since his was an incredibly eventful life and one noted more for its polemical than for its irenic character. The challenging claims and defiant practices of Manichees, Priscillianists, Donatists and Pelagians provided the anvil of controversy upon which the mature Augustine forged many of his perspectives on asceticism.

Manichees

Although he had lived as a Manichaean 'hearer', probably in the house of Constantius at Rome, and had attended meetings of the sect, Augustine knew of no immoral conduct among them.[18] At that time, he also had no immediate experience of how the 'elect' comported themselves.[19] Thus, his subsequent criticisms of their prohibitions against ownership of property, marriage, wine, meat and a variety of fruits and vegetables, are all the more telling.[20] All these proscriptions were mercifully mitigated for the 'hearers', such as himself. There seems to be no reason to impugn the overall accuracy of Augustine's critique of his former co-religionists. Similarly, there is no warrant for faulting the bishop's difference of opinion with Jerome who asserted that Jesus loved John more because of his lifelong chastity and single status.[21] In a heightened hyperbole, Jerome had earlier caricatured the ascetic woman who presented a pallid, sad complexion as 'a pitiful individual, both a nun and a Manichee'.[22] With equal disdain, he spoke of wine as poison for a young girl setting her sights on becoming a 'spouse of Christ'; it was to be consumed by old men only.[23] Augustine, in marked contrast to Jerome, and without taking either for himself, routinely served wine and meat at table in the 'bishop's house', or 'monastery of clerics'.[24] He, again, firmly reproached the Manichaean 'elect' for fasting on Sundays.[25] Like abstinence, fasting became an ally of other ascetic disciplines, such as no meat or wine; no servile work; no sexual intercourse (*signacula oris, manuum et sinus*).[26] These ascetic disciplines remained *de rigueur* for people who preached a Docetic doctrine denying Christ's birth, death and bodily resurrection.[27] The syncretistic tendencies and missionary fervour of the Manichees held out to the masses a universal religion far different from the regional concerns of the Donatists, whose sectarian interests splintered into subgroups of different stripes.

Priscillianists and Cynics

On the basis of extant collateral evidence, we are more richly informed about the Manichees than we are about the Priscillianists.[28] Like the Manichees,

Priscillianists in Spain, by erroneously interpreting Paul's activities at Troas (Acts 20:7), defended the custom of fasting on Sundays (*ep.* 36.12.28–9; *op. mon.* 18.21). Celibacy, voluntary poverty, almsgiving, sexual and dietary abstinence formed a bizarre array of ascetic practises, and combined with arcane liturgical observances. It was a sect that was exceedingly secretive regarding its doctrine and activities. In their view, souls were thought to share the same substance as God, while various parts of the human body, from the head (*Aries*) to the soles of the feet (*Pisces*), were thought to bear resemblance to the twelve signs of the zodiac.[29] Their celebrated exegete, Dictinius, in his *Libra*, found scriptural license for circumstantial lying, even solely for the purpose of concealing the truth (*c. mend.* 3.5; 21.41). Far less fortunate than the Donatists, the Priscillianists had among their ranks no Tychonius to point them in the right direction in terms of explicating the Scriptures. While urging members to take their cue from the practice of Fronto, a Priscillianist monk from Taragona who resorted to bold-faced lying in pursuit of his objectives, Consentius criticised both Augustine and the African hierarchy for leniency in their posture towards Donatist bishops, when tracking down heretics.[30]

In yet another amorphous amalgam, more widely spread than the Priscillianist community within the Iberian church and southern Gaul, it was easy to mistake a philosopher for a monk and vice versa. Most notable in this mix were the ubiquitous Cynics, who rejected outright political authority, private ownership of property, social decorum and marriage, at least in theory (*ciu.* 14.20; 19.1 and 19).

Donatists

In a land where Tertullianic and Cyprianic rigorism refused to remain muted, and women routinely practised asceticism at home, a congeries of disciplinary lifestyles easily took root. The daughter of a local farmer, for example, left the tenant farm where she lived with her parents, abandoning the Catholic catechumenate and becoming baptised a Donatist, in order to wear the attire of a Donatist nun.[31] Augustine, however, refused to encourage a forcible return of the daughter to her Catholic parents (*ep.* 35.4). In reverse direction, two Catholic nuns (it is unclear whether under duress or voluntarily) crossed over to the Donatist camp, and Primus, a Catholic subdeacon, spitefully submitted to rebaptism in that sect (*ep.* 35.2). For Donatists, a populist movement like Priscillianism, the ascetic ideal of martyrdom came within reach of all Christians.[32] As a corrective to such extreme fanaticism, Augustine's refrain, 'it is the reason for the suffering, not the suffering itself', punctuated his more than 100 sermons on martyrdom.[33]

The element of social and political protest cannot be discounted when gauging the fanaticism of the Donatist sub-group known as the Circumcellions, whose violence not infrequently won martyrdom for themselves (*en. Ps.* 132.3 and 4; *ep.* 23.6). In less deadly encounter, the bellicose *agonistici*, a militant brigade of the same group, physically assaulted their victims with wooden cudgels and paraded themselves as a counterpoise to the increasing number of Catholic Christian monks (*en. Ps.* 132.3.4 and 6). Augustine's practical good sense and theological realism admitted to his Catholic congregation that, on both sides of the schism: 'Counterfeit monks live alongside counterfeit clergy and counterfeit laity (*fideles*)' (*en. Ps.* 132.3.4). In an elegantly laconic phrase, the bishop warned his congregants: 'every profession in the church has its phoneys'.[34] Augustine, on the occasion of this remark, was describing the mix of good and bad clerics, monks, nuns and laity in the Catholic Church. Here on earth, he remarked, the church exists as a *corpus permixtum*: 'For the time being the church is lame. It puts one foot down firmly; the other, being crippled, it drags'.[35] Jacob's withered thigh (*s.* 2.9), the threshing floor with its wheat and its chaff, the prostitute of 1 Kings 3:16–28, the murky runoff from both the oil and the wine presses, and other such analogies, furnish for Augustine stark similes and metaphors to express the real world of the church.[36] If, from an ascetic perspective, as the Donatists insisted, the church was a gathering solely of holy people, argued Augustine, then the eucharistic assembly failed to provide any locus for healing and reconciliation.

Pelagians

As for more than a century Donatism had featured institutional holiness and perfection, Pelagianism in its turn personalised them. All the while, Augustine had been insisting to adherents of both of these persuasions that human beings are brothers and sisters.[37] They are not athletic competitors for God's love, holiness and perfection.[38] The following instances represent a few of many where Augustine delineated the fateful rift between genuine asceticism and mere athleticism. 'Better a cripple limping along to God, than the swiftest runner off course; yet cripple, be not proud; the runner may repent, return, and pass you on the way'.[39] Pride, may enjoy the comforts of home in the good works of a holy individual living in a monastery.[40] However, it can also be manifested in the suicides of Lucretia and Cato of Utica (*ciu.* 1.19 and 23). If Celestius and Pelagius had their way, then praying the Lord's Prayer would become an otiose exercise (*perseu.* 7.13), and the cross of Jesus Christ would be eviscerated of all meaning.[41]

Pelagianism brought to light the reluctance on the part of the upper classes in society to dethrone aristocratic ideals that had been entrenched for centuries in the heroes and heroines of ancient Rome. Pelagius' *Letter to Demetrias* (AD 413) anticipated by two years his *De natura* (AD 415), the last self-help book from Christian antiquity. It is partially preserved for posterity in the text of Augustine's *De natura et gratia*.

By the turn of the fifth century, Augustine had already 'decentred' himself by writing his *Confessions*. It had been the custom of north Africans to idolise their bishops. For all time, Augustine decentred all bishops, clergy, monks, nuns, laity, and Christians.[42] He then set himself the task of shifting the terms of asceticism away from the Greco-Roman agenda of nearly 1000 years by accentuating new terms, new issues, an entirely new agenda. Three consecutive treatises, as we shall note below, on work, on marriage and on virginity, in that order, provided enlightening clues for the direction of Augustine's future thought. From the time of his responses to Simplician in AD 396 and concurrent with his writing of the *Confessions*, Augustine's life was shot through with a keen realisation of his dependence upon God's grace. By composing the *Confessions*, he had radically altered and displaced the Greco-Roman philosophical preoccupation with one's own moral capacities. Pelagius was one of the first to perceive this shift, for he was unable to read the *Confessions* as the anti-elitist journal of the soul it purported to be. Its analogous twentieth-century update, the twelve steps of Alcoholics Anonymous, transposes both Augustine's conversion and asceticism into a modern idiom, where the key to spiritual health becomes *confessio*, denial is undone, love, humility, self-knowledge and reciprocal forgiveness become possible of attainment. Contrast, for example, the vertical models of ascesis in Books 7 and 9 of the *Confessions*, and elsewhere (see below, n. 7), with the horizontal magnetic field of temptations and their pull as opposing forces in Book 10, where Augustine's search for God in memory and in the trials of this life are delineated.[43]

Two mirrors of imperfection

Augustine's *Rule* and his *Letter* 189 to Boniface, the personal representative of the emperor, and a prominent military commander and Chief of the Household of Africa (*comes Africae*), offer some illuminating insights into the workings of his mind on the matter of asceticism. Coincidentally, each of these texts is referred to by its author as a 'mirror'.[44] Historically, the prescriptive document, which in the manuscript tradition simply bears Augustine's name, was first designated a monastic rule (*regula*) by Eugippius about a century after Augustine's death.[45] The bishop of Hippo spoke of it as a 'pamphlet' or a 'little book' (*libellus*) (*reg.* 8.2). Surprisingly, some twenty years later *Letter* 189 covers much the same material and is paraenetic rather than prescriptive in tone. Both compositions are significant for their striking textual parallels in vocabulary and thought; similarity in general content; special themes and particular ideas.[46] At least four features common to the two works are noteworthy:

1 the legacy of the Greco-Roman philosophical, that is to say, political, ethical and aesthetic traditions
2 the biblical inspiration

3   the distinctively Christian components
4   the moderate asceticism which constitutes their common substance.

In both texts, Augustine advises against allowing one's surrendering of riches to a community to become a source of self-praise or vainglory, on having entered the monastery or in having continued felicitous enjoyment of them in married life. His views on the ownership of property and use of money, so unlike the argument *De divitiis*, whose authorship has been erroneously attributed to Pelagius, remain steadfastly consistent throughout his life. *Frugalitas*, with its myriad Greco–Roman resonances, was described in Augustine's first extant treatise as 'mother of all the virtues'.[47] At the time, he had not yet been formally enrolled as a catechumen. Some ten years later, he would recommend *frugalitas* to followers of his *Rule*, and twenty years afterwards to Boniface and his family. In both instances, no peculiarly ascetical overlay reveals itself in the bishop's maturing thought. The cultivation of *frugalitas* is simply taken for granted as an identifiable mark of the Christian. Echoes of Cicero's *De officiis* and of Greco–Roman political thought generally are discernible in the bishop's insistence upon caring for the common good of the family, of the larger civic community and of the monastic community.[48] This is in direct contrast to concern for one's personal good.[49] Responsible behaviour towards others, prayer, and the exercise of love, whether in conjugal or in common life, are enjoined as being promotive of growth in holiness. While the concept of order is basic to Augustine's understanding of society, he expresses more concern for the quality of human relationships which establishes networks of individuals: 'Is it walls of a house rather than citizens that identify the city'?[50]

There is in each text a single reference to the eucharist. Augustine's use of the singular form (*sursum cor*) in this connection is consistent with his customary expression of this liturgical phrase.[51] Boniface, his wife, and groups such as those sharing a common religious life are said to function basically as members of the *totus Christus*.[52] This is described by the bishop in *s*. 341.1 as Christ's third manner of presence to and in the world:

1   the pre-existing Word
2   the Word incarnate
3   Christ as head and members.

In the phrase (*sursum cor*), frequently use by Augustine, ecclesial and eucharistic resonances are distinct and loud.[53] The attribute, *coniugalis*, differentiates and qualifies the chastity that is required of Boniface as a married man; in other respects, the requirements of that virtue are the same for the married person as for Augustine himself and his monastic associates. The adherents of the bishop's *Rule* are encouraged to love beauty as something surpassing the confines of corporeal and physical reality. The end of its trajectory, the vision of God as beauty, is the same goal set for Boniface. Augustine's ecstatic words: 'O beauty, ever ancient, ever new'! are widely known.[54] Elsewhere, the Trinity is described by him as 'the most perfect beauty'.[55] From an Augustinian perspective, one may distinguish beauty, truth and goodness, but never so as to separate their transcendental character.

The asking and granting of pardon are substantive issues in both documents. The alacrity with which pardon is to be asked is stressed, as also is readiness to forgive. The fifth petition of the Lord's Prayer, regarding reciprocal forgiveness, is reprised from Chapter 6 of the *Rule* to form part of the last sentence in its final chapter. The sixth petition of the Lord's Prayer relating to temptation (linked, thus, with its seventh petition in the Matthean rather than with the Lukan version), constitutes the final words of the *Rule*.[56] In the *Letter* 189.5 to Boniface, *temptatio*, though matching the conclusion of the *Rule*, is associated with Wisdom 3:5–6, a pairing employed by Augustine to express the constructive uses of temptation through an allusion to the refining of gold by fire (*s*. 62.12).

Apart from the practical exigencies of everyday living in the monastery, as these are enunciated in the *Rule* (decorum at meals, extramural comportment, sensitivity to the special needs of the sick, of individuals from an upper-class way of life, and the like, the lesser necessities pertaining to laundry, library, infirmary, bedding and clothing), we find an extensive overlapping, and virtually identical content, in the *Letter* to Boniface and the *Rule*. These identical contents are: the importance of prayer, chastity proper to one's status in life, love as the basic criterion for performance of good works, heavy accent on mutual forgiveness within the context of the Lord's Prayer, beauty as a fundamental element of asceticism, the single reference to Christ in both writings and, finally, the indispensable dimension of grace.

Both texts reveal fine tuning of indelible elements that underwent progressive refinement within the Greco–Roman ethical heritage handed on to Christianity: love, beauty, frugality, friendship, responsible use of riches, the common good of the political and social orders. In a marvellous melding of Stoic and Christian ethics (*ep*. 189.7), Boniface's *animus*, is, for example, described as *virilis et Christianus*. His service in the military, Augustine assures him, is compatible with Christianity, for peace is the principal objective in waging war. Conjugal chastity and sobriety, however, ought not yield to lust and wine, temptations proverbially linked with soldiering. Augustine and Alypius later advised Boniface to persevere in his military obligations rather than enter a monastery after his wife's death (*ep*. 220.3 and 12). Also worthy of note in Augustine's *Rule* are the respective roles of the 'man in charge', *praepositus* (ten times), and the 'priest', *presbyter* (four times). Apart from the quotidian elements noted above, the sole differentiating mark, therefore, between these two texts is the mode of functioning as a religious superior and priest, concerns extraneous to Boniface's conjugal status. Yet even here, Augustine draws upon the image of a 'father' as applied to the role of the monastic superior.[57]

That the *Rule* was addressed to lay people is too little known and, therefore, often overlooked. While sometimes criticised as being latitudinarian, its message is aimed at directing the path of any group of Christians who wish to enter into a voluntary association (*libenter*, at 12). Its grid of composition is more horizontal than vertical. Lay people are potential ascetics; and use of ascetic means of self-betterment has appealed to many lay people. Asceticism, for Augustine, was basically construed as a means of fostering better human relationships. No easy task! He foresaw *occasional* need for such fraternal correction as spoken of in Mt 18:15–17, and presumed an *incessant* need for reconciliation and reciprocal pardon, as called for by Mt 6:12, in the fifth petition of the Lord's Prayer.[58] To be a Catholic Christian was to be a mendicant.[59]

In his written legacy, Augustine cites Acts 4:32–35, in whole or in part, eighty-two times.[60] Roughly a dozen instances pertain to common life, as it is exemplified within a monastic and/or a clerical context.[61] In marked contrast, some seventy citations of this Lukan pericope relate to Christians generally, apart from any connection with common living as it exists in a monastery. Employing a 'methodology of amplification' (the term belongs to Jaroslav Pelikan, *Mary Through the Centuries, Her Place in the History of Culture,* 1996, p. 25), Augustine extends the thought of the Lukan verses to include:

1 an imaging of the Trinity, with distinctive accents on unity and peace
2 communion among ourselves and with God the Father, as this union is mediated by the risen Christ through the loving activity of the Holy Spirit
3 ecclesial, eucharistic and contemplative dimensions which become actualised in both monastic and married life.[62]

In view of Augustine's seeing the implications of Acts 4:32–35 as reaching all the way to the innermost life of God, we are, accordingly, less surprised to find him extending its application beyond monastic to domestic living. His employing the text more frequently to the latter than to the former, in a ratio of 6:1, shows clearly that he did not consider the acquiring of holiness to be the privilege only of monks and nuns, the preserve, if you will, of a few professional ascetics.

Two citations of Acts 4:35, 'distribution was made in proportion to each one's need', in the first chapter of Augustine's *Rule* and twice later in the text, focus on individual needs and human frailty. Although not within the reach of everyone, frugality ought to be cultivated, he says, gradually. Fasting and abstinence should be contingent upon sound health. In the matter of taking food and beverages, consideration should be given to sick people and convalescents, even to the point of according them a special diet. Similar sensitivity in regard to food, clothes, shoes, mattresses and blankets should be directed towards individual differences deriving from one's social status prior to entrance into the monastery. Conspicuously absent from the *Rule* is any such profile of the ascetic as portrayed in the first section of this chapter. There is a tendency throughout Augustine's text to eschew elitism and self-sufficiency. A non-elitist approach to the *Rule*, therefore, would involve seeing oneself in others, especially in one's enemy, rather than assuming the stance of a poseur who affects a particular lifestyle to impress others. Augustine's much favoured 'wheat and chaff' metaphor is as anti-Manichaean (elect versus hearers), and anti-Pelagian (elitist versus non-elitist) as it is anti-Donatist (saints versus sinners).

A brief note on perfection

In many respects, Augustine's delineation of holiness radiates a hue and a colouration appreciably different from that of John Cassian of Marseilles, his contemporary, and of Benedict of Nursia who lived more than a century later. For example, at a significant juncture in his *Institutes* (4.43), Cassian offers a recapitulation of the ascesis required by monks in their striving towards the heights of perfection (*ad perfectionem summam*).[63] The *ordo*, or sequence, suggested by Cassian is as follows: fear of the Lord (Ps 110:10), salutary compunction of heart, contempt for all possessions, renunciation of one's self and will, humility, mortification of desires, extirpation of vices, the flowering of the virtues and, finally, purity of heart (*Inst.* 4.43).

With its Cassianic resonances, Benedict's language is strikingly similar and as clear as the sound of genuine crystal. For anyone hastening towards the perfection of monastic life (*ad perfectionem conversationis qui festinat*), Benedict recommends the teachings of the holy Fathers as a guide to its very heights (*observatio perducat ad celsitudinem perfectionis*) (*Reg. Ben.* 73.2). In the same epilogue, we read that observance of Benedict's *Rule* is propaedeutic to human efforts towards reaching the loftier heights of doctrine and the virtues (*ad maiora . . . doctrinae virtutumque culmina, Deo protegente, pervenies*).[64]

There is much material to detain us here, but it would take us too far afield. It should be noted, however, that we run the risk also of hasty oversimplification. However, it is pertinent to point out that Augustine's perspectives on the attainment of perfection in categories similar to those of Cassian and of Benedict were restricted to his early years.[65] As observed above, from the time roughly of his episcopal consecration in AD 396, there was in his response to the queries by Simplician on the subject of Pauline exegesis, a paradigmatic shift in the mature Augustine's profound reflections on grace and holiness.[66] While many texts could be cited to demonstrate this trademark of his mature thought, it will be enough to cite the following succinctly characteristic reflection:

'Our holiness itself . . . is such in this life as to consist in the forgiveness of sins rather than in the perfection of virtues. The evidence for this is the prayer of the whole city of God on pilgrimage here on earth. We know that all its members cry out to God, 'Forgive us our debts as we forgive our debtors'. (Mt 6:12)[67]

An appraisal of work and its satisfactions

With his uncompromising honesty and his practical concern for the realities of life, Augustine was not hesitant to place his unique imprint on the monastic tradition regarding the place of work in the attainment of holiness. Of particular interest is his introduction of *otium* or ease, not for its own sake but as a means of pursuing a life of holiness. Also, there is far more to Augustine's critique of refractory and indolent monks than issues of church law or order. The undervaluation of work by pagan Rome had long since been taken for granted. For centuries, the calendar year revealed as many holidays as work days and, while slaves did the work, hordes of parasites, *clientes*, were bought off with 'bread and circuses' (Juvenal, *Satire* 10.81). In contrast to this indolence, everybody worked in both the lay monastery and the monastery of clerics at Hippo (*reg.* 5.2; *s.* 355–6). Among clerics, pastoral care replaced the Stoic concern for the *cura publica*, service to the community. In monasteries of lay people, the labours of carpenters, cobblers, craftsmen, construction workers, farmers, fishermen (Hippo and Carthage were coastal cities), were regarded by Augustine as worthy occupations. He reminds his readers that Saint Paul was both an apostle and a tent maker (Acts 18:1–4; cf. *Io. eu. tr.* 122.2–3). To reject such people or to prevent slaves, either before or after manumission, from entering a monastery would be a 'grievous mistake', *grave delictum* (*op. mon.* 22.25). Practical skills, as well as skills garnered from a liberal education, possessed merit. It is particularly notable, moreover, that both the garden monastery and the monastery of clerics at Hippo had their own libraries.

Written at the turn of the fifth century, *The Work of Monks* constitutes the only free-standing treatise of its kind among ancient Christian writers.[68] Apart from his monastic *Rule*, this lively tract embodies its author's otherwise single book-length reflections on monastic life. This latter composition is more concerned with apostolic discipline, with Pauline precepts and with Paul's public persona as seen in his way of dealing with matters pertaining to the proper functioning of church life.[69] Augustine's use of *disciplina* in his *Rule* concerns itself with protocol relating to the proper ordering of common life, while the range of meanings in *The Work of Monks* reflects the teachings of the New Testament as they may be used in the implementation of the life of monks. In both documents, the bishop's destratification of ancient Roman society resulted in a distinctively creative validation of labour on the basis of strong scriptural warrant from Genesis, on the teaching of Christ and on what was available from Saint Paul. Augustine's versatile appropriation of such words as: *militia / milites Christi / commilitiones / comes / commune–proprium / societas / socius / provinciales / respublica*, as these had application to monastic life, reveals the extent to which a moderate Christian asceticism was being woven into the fabric of late antique culture.[70]

The treatise is both paraenetic and preceptive in tone. While addressing men requesting surcease of manual labour in order to engage in fruitful leisure for reading the very Scriptures which describe work as inherently human, and enhanced all the more by its conjunction with Christian faith, it is rife with irony and irenicism. While urging the monks to derive satisfaction and enjoyment from their work, Augustine also directs them to strive for the common good of the fraternity, to cultivate freedom from attachment to personal possessions and to grow in obedience to God (*op. mon.* 16.19). In a notable text, Augustine himself ruefully laments his own lack of time for manual labour, for prayer, for reading and the study of Scripture (29.37). Pastoral necessities so constantly required of him such surveillance and intervention as we see him exercising, for example, in his effort to protect a certain Ecdicia and her son and husband from becoming, for whatever motive, the prey of itinerant monks (*ep.* 262).[71]

Marriage and virginity

Treatises on marriage and virginity, respectively, followed fast upon the heels of the bishop's reflections on work. Augustine accepted Saint Paul's counsel in 1 Corinthians 7 regarding married couples, (vv. 1–7, 10–16), virginity (vv. 25–35), celibacy as contrasted with marriage (vv. 36–8), and widowhood (vv. 8–9, 39–40). It is easy to understand how one might hesitate to agree with Augustine's views that marriage is a 'hill of lesser blessing' (*virg.* 18.18), continence a 'mountain of greater blessing' (ibid.), that virginity is a 'bright star,' marriage a 'dim star,' in the same sky (*s.* 354.9). In his use of such metaphors to encapsulate Paul's exhortation: *bene facit / melius facit* (1 Cor 7:38), however, Augustine insisted with Paul that both choices were good, yet virginity was superior to marriage. The bishop could hardly be faulted here for agreeing with Saint Paul.

From the two goods of marriage and virginity, Augustine regularly pressed on to another favoured doublet in his thought: the nonpareil Christian virtue of humility versus the one supreme evil of pride. To claim that 'marriage with humility is better (*melius*) than virginity with pride' was axiomatic with Augustine.[72] For him, it was the difference between humble failure and proud achievement. In virtually every instance, the bishop deliberately shifted the emphasis from virginity and marriage to humility and pride, to the extent that even his readers, as he himself acknowledges, were justified in thinking that they were reading a treatise on humility rather than virginity.[73] In a seemingly offhand observation, and a curious turn of phrase,

Augustine referred to virginity as if it had recently become the current vogue.[74] Yet, even here, the bishop warned that 'the pretence of humility is a worse fault than pride'.[75] In a lengthy sermon addressed to a mixed group of *continentes*, he remarked: 'if only we could all just let our thoughts dwell on one thing, charity'.[76] Moments later, he said to these assembled ascetics: 'It's from marriage that human beings are born, it's from pride that angels fell'.[77] He, for this reason, could argue that pride was far and away a greater evil than any misdemeanours associated with human flesh. Near the end of the sermon, Augustine reverted to what is conceivably the basic theme of his mature thought: 'Your chief (Jesus Christ) is humble, and are you going to be proud'?[78]

The biblical figures Susanna (Dn 13) and Joseph (Gen 39), meanwhile, were presented to the preacher's public as exemplifying respect for marital commitment (*s.* 318.2; 359.3). Here, too, there was a hierarchy, with married couples, widows and then virgins being considered in ascending degree of fruitfulness.[79] Also to be noted are the distinct resonances between the Parable of the Sower (Mt 13:4–9, Mk 4:8 and Lk 8:4–18), and these three walks of life where the different situations are aligned. Accordingly, married couples stood on the lower level, upgraded only in the event of martyrdom, while widows held the medial position yielding sixtyfold.[80] The yield of a hundredfold was accorded alternatively to virginity and martyrdom.[81] In this alignment of marriage, widowhood, virginity and martyrdom with the percentage scale suggested by the Parable of the Sower, Augustine noted that, as gifts of God, such blessings were best known and acknowledged by the individuals themselves.[82]

The impenetrability and mystery of the human person is a staple of Augustine's deepest thought: 'Each one carries his own heart, and every heart is closed to every other heart'.[83] An argument for the supreme excellence of martyrdom, meanwhile, was derived from liturgical practices which were sanctioned by church authority.[84] Even so, the bishop does not fail to express his profound admiration for Crispina, martyr and mother of several children.[85] The same holds true for Perpetua, a young mother, and her child (*s.* 280–2), and for Felicity, a slave eight months pregnant at the time of her arrest, who subsequently gave birth to a daughter. There was a time when Peter, though an apostle, was not reputed to be of the same excellence as Crispina, Agnes, Gervase, Protase, Stephen or the boy, Nemesianus.[86]

Such a schematic computation of divine blessings is, of course, facile and out of step with modern sensibilities. However, if one makes allowance for such biblical numbers as though they were the letters of the alphabet scripted for a crossword puzzle, or as the pieces on a chessboard, Augustine can be seen to have used the computation of such blessings in much the same way, seeking to gain partial insight into the mystery of human relationships.[87] After all, numeration had been used similarly in much classical literature and throughout the Bible. Church writers, while attempting to decode their significance and apply them reasonably without becoming flagrantly fanciful, did not always succeed in this latter respect. Such an exegetical strategy, however, offered an intertextual perspective which viewed the Bible as revealing an internal coherence, where love for God and human beings became the chief criterion for its Christocentric interpretation (*doctr. chr.* 3.10.15).

More importantly, in Augustine's mindset, the transitory always succumbed to the eternal.[88] Boniface, for example, was reminded by Augustine of his role as a military officer, that of a Christian seeking eternal peace while facing the prospect of waging war on the battlefield, an outcome which might prove necessary but would not be one of preference.[89] In like manner, married couples were admonished not to grieve over the loss of temporal possessions to an extent that would lessen their looking to the goal of eternal life. Even dedicated individuals afraid to confront evil in an active way for fear of temporal reprisals, attacks upon their reputation and fear for their personal safety acted no differently (*civ.* 1.9). Demetrias was depicted to her grandmother, Anicia Faltonia Proba, and to her mother, Juliana, as a consecrated virgin who, having forsaken marriage that ended with time, had entered into a marriage that would never end. It is in this context, then, that virginity was esteemed as superior to marriage.[90] While there will still be sexual differentiation after the resurrection (*ciu.* 22.17), those gaining heaven 'neither marry nor are given in marriage' (Mt 22:30).

The eschatological element is never wholly absent from Augustine's thought. Human beings were, to him, amphibious creatures, living between the present age and the age to come, and making use of the world as though they were not using it (Jn 17:16; 1 Cor 7:29 and 31).[91] That Christians were resident aliens on pilgrimage was a commonplace in the bishop's preaching.[92] The student of Augustine having even a modest acquaintance with his thought learns that his prose is punctuated with a sort of rhythmic *nunc . . . tunc*, or with his preferred paratactic phrases *in spe . . . in re*, or *fides . . . species*, which signal the near total surrender of the Neoplatonic chain of being to a biblical and eschatological overlay where time is non-repeatable, thereby forcefully articulating both Christian hope and the need of God's saving grace. However, in this time of earthly existence, the home (*domus*) is the plane upon which the most fruitful network of human relationships is operative (*ciu.* 19. 5–8 and 13).

A tentative description of Christian asceticism

In Augustine's case, ascesis got its start with neither a *tabula rasa* nor a vacuum. Asceticism was part of his nature and extraordinary talent, *natura et ingenium*, and indelibly marked by the moderation that characterised the intellectual refinements of ancient Greco-Roman thought; *ne quid nimis* (*doctr. chr.* 2.39.58.). The continuities with so rich a non-Christian heritage seldom receive from scholars the attention they deserve.[93] Augustine staked his strong claim to proprietary rights over such a legacy in emphatic terms: 'In fact, every good and true Christian should understand that wherever he may find truth, it is his Lord's'.[94] At the outset of this chapter, we noted four features of non-Christian ascesis common to all such exercises, and throughout the chapter we cursorily identified many others. The basic elements are:

1 training, *exercitatio animi*
2 the function of habit, *consuetudo*
3 the importance of self-discipline and restraint, *disciplina*
4 both the constructive and renunciatory aspects of such exercises.

For Augustine, Christian asceticism consisted in the cultivation of ways and means, appropriate to one's standing before God, of fostering human relationships and rendering them firm. One has the ability to accomplish such tasks duly through personal effort joined with the grace of Jesus Christ and assisted by the guidance of the Holy Spirit. Prompted by love of God and neighbour, human relations take both their origin and their orientation from divine relations, that is to say, from the trinitarian life of God.[95]

Augustine's optic was that of a single garden in which were found not only the roses of the martyrs but also the lilies of the virgins, the ivy of married couples and the violets of widows (*s.* 304.3). This portrayal occurs only once in the bishop's writings. It is tempting to think that it has much relevance in his thought – notably during the Pelagian controversy – to the kindred metaphor used by St Paul: 'I planted, Apollo watered, but God gave the growth' (1 Cor 3:6).

Notes

1 J. E. Goehring's review of V. L. Wimbush and R. Valantasis, *Asceticism*, New York / Oxford, Oxford University Press, 1995, in the *Journal of Early Christian Studies* 5 (1997), p. 293.
2 K. Power, *Veiled Desire: Augustine's Writings on Women*, London, Darton, Longman and Todd, 1995, p. 233.
3 Uta Ranke-Heinemann, *Eunuchs for the Kingdom of Heaven. Women, Sexuality and the Catholic Church*, tr. P. Heinegg, New York, Doubleday, 1990, p. 75.
4 Ibid. p. 81. See also D. F. Noble, *A World Without Women. The Christian Culture of Western Science*, New York, Alfred A. Knopf, 1993, p. 71, who describes Augustine 'unequivocally exalting virginity over marriage'. A gloss on marriage near the end of his life should give Augustine's critics second thoughts in this regard: 'The good and correct use of libido is not libido'. See *retr.* 2.22.2: 'quoniam libido non est bonus et rectus usus libidinis'.
5 T. P. Verghese, *The Freedom of Man*, Philadelphia, Westminster Press, 1972, p. 55–9. These five criticisms are recycled in K. Leech, *The Social God*, London, Sheldon Press, 1981, p. 25 and pp. 128–35.

6 See n. 68; see also n. 73 regarding Augustine's estimate of his treatise on virginity as a treatise on humility.

7 Among many ascensional or vertical models, so reminiscent of the Platonic tradition, body > mind > God, selected at random from Augustine's writings, we note the following in some of which there is the convergence of ancient Greek philosophical ascesis (*anachoresis eis heauton*, withdrawal and/or *epistrophe*, return to self) and orthodox Christian Catholic theology.

quant. an. 35.79	the ladder of beauty
conf. 7.10.16 and 7.17.23	two 'tentatives d'extase' (Courcelle).
conf. 9.10.23–26	the 'audition' at Ostia where '(t)he persistent Platonic vocabulary is powerful, but does not define the experience'.
	(J. J. O'Donnell, *Augustine, Confessions III*, Oxford, Clarendon Press, 1992, p. 122).
en. Ps. 41.7–8	ardent longing for God
s. 141	on Jn 14:6.
Io. eu. tr. 20.11–13	the vision of God as Trinity
uera rel. 29.52–39.73	'(God) transcends even the mind.'
trin. 8.3.4–5	the good-in-itself, *ipsum bonum*, God.

That Augustine increasingly turned to the Gradual Psalms, 'songs of ascent' or 'pilgrim songs' (Ps 120–134) for yet another understanding of *anabasis*, reveals the extent to which his study of the Bible furnished Judeo-Christian perspectives alongside Platonising models.

8 J. G. Prenderville, SJ, 'The Development of the Idea of Habit in the Thought of Saint Augustine', *Traditio* 28 (1972), pp. 29–99.

9 See *s.* 399 on Christian discipline, where the preacher derives the Latin noun *disciplina* from the verb *disco*, *discere*, and then distinguishes between pagan education and Christian learning. The church is described several times as a 'house of discipline' and a 'school of discipline', with a view to establishing such a programme of instruction in the home. Augustine says: '(Christ's) school is on earth and his school is his own body' (§15). In §12, Augustine relates his message to bishops. See T. J. van Bavel, 'Augustine on Christian Teaching and Life', *Augustinian Heritage* 37 (1991), pp. 89–112.

10 To say: 'It is difficult not to conclude that Augustine did not take the Incarnation too seriously', is erroneous and distorts many perspectives in a recent study. See Power, op. cit., p. 155, and Augustine, *Acad.* 3.20.43. See also G. Madec, 'Christus, scientia et sapientia nostra. Le principe de cohèrence de la doctrine augustinienne', *Recherches augustiniennes* 10 (1975), pp. 77–85; and more recently, *La patrie et la voie: le Christ dans la vie e la pensée de saint Augustin*, Paris, Desclée de Brouwer, 1989.

11 *Conf.* 9.13.37: 'et corde et voce et litteris servio'.

12 Athanasius, *Vita Antonii* 47, versio Evagrii; PG 26.911–12: 'quotidianum fidei ac conscientiae martyrium merebatur'. See also J. J. Gavigan, *De vita monastica in Africa Septentrionali inde a temporibus S. Augustini usque ad invasiones Arabum*, Turin, Marietti, 1926, pp. 95, 200.

13 R. Halliburton, 'The Concept of *"Fuga saeculi"* in St Augustine', *The Downside Review* 85 (1967), pp. 249–61. The people of Hippo, however, did not hesitate to complain of his prolonged visits to Carthage for reasons of pastoral necessity. For Augustine's expressed rejection of flight to solitude, see *conf.* 10.43.70.

14 *En. Ps.* 54.9: 'Non enim a genere humano separatus esse poteris, quamdiu in hominibus vivis'.

15 Jerome, *Epistula* 14.11: 'adducetur et cum suis stultus Plato discipulis', tr. F. A. Wright.

16 Possidius, *Vita Augustini* 28.11 (Plotinus); 31.2 (Penitential Psalms).

17 Jerome, *Epistula* 14.10: 'O desertum . . . O solitudo . . . O heremus . . . '.

18 S. N. C. Lieu, *Manichaeism in the Later Roman Empire and Medieval China. A Historical Survey*, Tübingen, J. C. B. Mohr, ²1992, pp. 173 and 191.

19 Hearsay and second-hand reports (*sed haec audiebamus*), were the source of his information at the time of writing *mor.* 2.19.68.

20 For property, see *mor.* 1.35.78. For marriage, see *c. Faust.* 30.4 and 30.6. For wine and meat, see ibid., 16.31; 20.13; *mor.* 2.14.31–5. For fruits and vegetables see *c. Faust.* 30.5. The motivation for abstinence from vegetables differed between Catholics and Manichees.

21 *Io. eu. tr.* 124.2 and 124.7; see also Jerome, *Adversus Iovinianum* 1.26.

22 Jerome, *Epistula* 22.13: 'miseram et monacham et Manicheam vocant'.

23 Ibid., 22.8: 'vinum / venenum', and ibid., 22.35: 'vinum tantum senes accipiunt'.

24 Possidius, *Vita Augustini* 22.2; Augustine, *s.* 355.2.

25 *Ep.* 36.12.28–9 to the priest Casulanus; *ep.* 236.2 to the bishop Deuterius.

26 Mouth (*mor.* 2.10.19–16.53); hands (*mor.* 2.17.54–64); breast (*mor.* 2.18.65–6).

27 *S.* 183.9.13: 'Omnes haeretici negant Christum in carne venisse . . . Quid miramini, si Manichaei apertissime negant Christum in carne venisse'?

28 H. Chadwick, *Priscillian of Avila. The Occult and the Charismatic in the Early Church*, Oxford, Clarendon Press, 1976, has appreciably narrowed the gap.

29 *Haer.* 70: 'ipsumque corpus nostrum secundum duodecim signa coeli esse compositum'.

30 *Ep.* 11*.25 (Divjak); Consentius to Augustine.

31 *Ep.* 35.4. On Donatist nuns, see *en. Ps.* 44.31, 'haereticae sanctimoniales'; *c. ep. Parm.* 2.9.19, 'sanctimoniales'. Donatist nuns appear to be distinct from the dissolute women who accompanied the circumcellions on their predatory pilgrimages to the shrines of martyrs: *c. ep. Parm.* 3.3.18 and *c. litt. Pet.* 2.88.195. See also Possidius, *Vita Augustini* 10.1: 'velut sub professione continentium ambulantes'. Such Donatists were exhibiting, at least, the pretence of asceticism. See also Tychonius's description of the Circumcellions, and compare it with Augustine's at *en. Ps.* 132.3:

> They wander through the provinces, because they will not permit themselves to stay in one place with brethren, to be of one counsel and to live one in soul and heart after the custom of the apostles: but, as we have said, they roam far and wide and visit the tombs of the saints, as though for the salvation of their souls.
>
> (tr. W. H. C. Frend)

Beatus of Libana is cited from T. Hahn (ed.), *Tyconius–Studien*, Leipzig,

Bonwetsch and Seeburg, 1900, pp. 68–9 (reprinted Aalen, Scientia Verlag, 1971). I owe knowledge of this citation to W. H. C. Frend, 'The *Cellae* of the African Circumcellions', *Journal of Theological Studies*, new series, 3 (1952), pp. 87–9.

32 On 'love as the mother of obedience', and the distinguishing mark between true and false martyrs, see *s. Mainz* 5.17–20 (= *s. Dolbeau* 2.17–20).

33 'Non poena sed causa': *s.* 275.1; 306.2; 306A; 327.1; 328.7.

34 *En. Ps.* 99.13: 'scitote omnem professionem in ecclesia habere fictos'.

35 *S.* 5.8. Hereafter I have generally used Edmund Hill's English translation of Augustine's *sermones ad populum* published in *The Works of Saint Augustine, Sermons*, vols III.1–11, ed. J. E. Rotelle, OSA, New York, New City Press, 1990–7

36 *S.* 10.5–7: An allegorical interpretation of Solomon's judgement regarding the two prostitutes identifies their babies as an eschatological expression of the present and future time(s) of the church. Here also, the runoff from the oil and wine presses, like the wheat and the chaff, are much preferred images of the church.

37 *S.* 399.3; *ep.* 130.6.13: 'There is no one in the human race to whom love is not due, either as a return of mutual affection or in virtue of his share in our common nature'.

38 Book 1 of *doctr. chr.* furnishes the framework and topography of the Christian life: the doctrine of the Trinity; the mission of Christ; the meaning of Jesus' resurrection; the church in pilgrimage; and the love of God and neighbour to which all Christians are summoned. The conclusion to *agon.* 33, offers a résumé of basic ascesis: the introduction, Chs 1–4, delineate its nature as a prolonged conflict with warring elements, while Chs 5–13 propose guidelines for living, and Chs 13–32 integrate that life with doctrine. Such a structure is pervasive in Augustine's writings and preaching. The fact that this latter book was written 'in plain language for brothers with no skill in the Latin language' (*retr.* 2.3), reveals the extent of the bishop's pastoral outreach to people such as he describes in *praed. sanct.* 14.27: 'ab omnibus Christianis, ab omnibus episcopus usque ad extremos laicos fideles, poenitentes, catechumenos'.

39 *S.* 169.15.18: ' Melius it claudus in via quam cursor praeter viam', tr. J. Searle, *Verses from St Augustine or Specimens from a rich mine*, London, Oxford University Press, 1953, p. 5. See also *s.* 141.4.

40 'Pride lurks in good works seeking to destroy them': Augustine, *reg.* 1.7 (tr. R. P. Russell). For the Latin text, see L. Verheijen, *La Règle de saint Augustin I, Tradition manuscrite*, Paris, Études augustiniennes, 1967, p. 420, lines 30–1.

41 Observe Augustine's forceful use of 1 Cor 1:17 and Gal 5:11 in *nat. et gr.*7.7; 40.47; *c. Iul.* 6.11.36; *c. Iul. imp.* 3.31.

42 Note his masterful profile of church membership as a *corpus permixtum* in *en. Ps.* 99, especially at 12–13.

43 *Conf.* 10.28.39–39.64. In sharp contrast, however, 10.40.65 indicates mystical or quasi-mystical vaultings or ascents of Augustine.

44 *Speculum*, a biblical allusion, Jas 1:23–4, much preferred by Augustine: *reg.* 8.2; *ep.* 189.8.

45 G. Lawless, *Augustine of Hippo and His Monastic Rule*, Oxford, Clarendon Press, 1987, p. 124.

46 G. Lawless, 'Il rapporto fra *Regula Sancti Augustini Episcopi* e *l'Epistula* 189 ad Bonifatium', in *Il Monachesimo Occidentale dalle origini alla Regula Magistri*, Studia Ephemeridis Augustinianum 62, Rome, Institutum Patristicum «Augustininianum», 1998, pp. 361–7.

47 *B. uita* 4.31. See S. Barbone, '*Frugalitas* in Saint Augustine', *Augustiniana* 44 (1994), pp. 5–15.

48 *Reg.* 5.2; also 3.5; for Seneca, *Epistula ad Lucilium*, 2.6.

49 1 Cor 13:5, 'non quaerat quae sua sunt', cited at *reg.* 5.2.

50 *Exc. urb.* 6.6: 'An putatis, fratres, civitatem in parietibus et non in civibus deputandam'?

51 M. Pellegrino, '"*Sursum cor*" nelle opere di sant'Agostino', *Recherches augustiniennes* 3 (1965), pp. 179–206.

52 T. van Bavel, *Christians in the World*, New York, Catholic Book Publishing Co., 1980, p. 80, the 'central point'; p. 89, the 'cornerstone' of Augustine's theology.

53 See n. 51.

54 *Conf.* 10.27.38: 'pulchritudo tam antiqua et tam nova'.

55 *Trin.* 6.10.12: 'summa origo est rerum omnium et perfectissima pulchritudo et beatissima delectatio'.

56 *Ench.* 30.115–16 acknowledges no discrepancy in the substantive contents of the Lord's Prayer between Matthew's seven petitions and Luke's five petitions, except the latter's brevity of expression.

57 *Reg.* 7.1 (see Verheijen, op. cit., p. 435, line 217): 'praeposito tamquam patri oboediatur'. Augustine was familiar with the role of the *pater*, among the Desert Fathers (*mor.* 1.31.67). He leaves their function as spiritual director to the *presbyter*, whose principal duties consisted in the teaching of the Scriptures and administration of the sacraments. The overall context of the *Rule*, and its four instances of *presbyter*, sustain such an interpretation, which is also consonant with the fact that the bishop nowhere employs the Latin, *monachus*, in his *Rule*, preferring to describe members of the community as *fratres* (seven times), *famulus dei* (twice) and *vir sanctus* (once). *Servus* is used once in a pejorative sense, *reg.* 8.1, meaning slaves under the yoke of the law. A household slave, in contrast, has earned the affection of the *paterfamilias*, father of the family.

58 Nowhere does Augustine restrict the exercise of fraternal correction (Mt 18:15–17) to life in the monastery rather than the home. Both environments favour its exercise, albeit rarely and with discretion, always, however, within a larger ecclesial context. See *s. dom. m.* 1.20.63; 2.19.64; *exp. Gal.* 56 and 57; *s.* 82.4–15; and *f. et op.* 3.4; 26.48.

59 *S.* 56.6.9: *mendicus Dei* occurs three times; *s.* 61.7.8: 'We are God's beggars'; *s.* 106.4: 'Your soul is begging at your door. . . .'.

60 L. Verheijen, *La Règle de saint Augustin II, Recherches historiques*, Paris, Etudes augustiniennes, 1967, pp. 90–1.

61 For an examination of these texts, see L. Verheijen, *Saint Augustine's Monasticism in the Light of Acts 4:32–35*, Villanova, Pa., Villanova University Press, 1979, pp. 6–81.

62 See Verheijen, *Monasticism*, op. cit., pp. 82–97; M.-F. Berrouard, 'La première communauté de Jérusalem comme image de l'unité de la Trinité. Une des exégèses augustiniennes d'Act 4,32a' in *Homo Spiritalis*, ed. C. P. Mayer, Würzburg, Augustinus-Verlag, 1987, pp. 207–24.

63 John Cassian, *De Institutis Coenobiorum*, CSEL 17/1.78. The full text reads: 'audi ergo paucis ordinem, per quem scandere ad perfectionem summam sine ullo labore ac difficultate praevaleas'. As it stands, the sentence conveys a strong conviction of Stoic self-sufficiency and ascetic self-mastery. Augustine's doctrine of grace would preclude him from framing such a sentence in these terms.

64 *Reg. Ben.*, 73.9. See *La regola di san Benedetto e le regole dei Padri*, ed. S. Pricoco, Fondazione Lorenzo Valla, Turin, Arnoldo Mondadori, 1995, pp. 270–3.

65 See *retr.* 1.19.1–3 commenting on *s. dom. m.* and emending 1.4.11 of that text where he overstated the case for the attainment of order, wisdom and peace in this life and, in the second instance, the following section, 1.4.12, where he expressed the fear of being misunderstood by his readers in this matter.

66 *Simpl.* 1. See J. H. S. Burleigh, *Augustine: Early Writings*, London, SCM Press, 1953, pp. 370–406.

67 *Ciu.* 19.27: 'ipsa quoque nostra iustitia . . . tamen tanta est in hac vita, ut potius remissione peccatorum constet quam perfectione virtutum . . .'. Augustine's first of eight commentaries on the Lord's Prayer was composed about AD 393/4. His final reflections on the Lord's Prayer are found in *perseu.* 2.3–7.15, composed within two years of his death.

68 See Basil's *Regulae fusius tractatae, Interrogationes* 37, 38, 42, passim, and Cassian's *De acedia* in his *De institutis coenobiorum* 10.8–14; 17; 22–3 for less extended accounts of work within a larger context.

69 'Apostolica disciplina': *op. mon.* 28.36; 'in saluberrima disciplina secundum apostolicam normam', *op. mon.* 22.26; 'apostolica et euangelica sententia', 1.2; 'iam more apostolico', 2.3; 'euangelica illa praecepta', 3.4; 'praecepta apostolica', 17.20; 'manifesta apostolica praecepta', 23.30; 'exemplo et praecepto apostolico', 27.35.

70 R. A. Markus, 'Vie monastique et ascétisme chez Augustin', in *Congresso internazionale su S. Agostino nel XVI centenario della conversione, Roma, 15–20 settembre 1986*, vol. 1, Rome, Institutum Patristicum «Augustinianum», 1987, pp. 119–25.

71 For varying interpretations of *Letter* 262, see K. Cooper, 'Insinuations of Womanly Influence: An Aspect of the Christianization of the Roman Aristocracy', *Journal of Roman Studies* 82 (1992), pp. 150–64, at pp. 158–60; and K. Power, op. cit., pp. 111–13, and passim.

72 *En. Ps.* 99.13. See *s.* 354.4.8 and 9; *b. coniug.* 23.30; *uirg.* 44.45 (twice) and 51.52; also *en. Ps.* 75.16.

73 See *uirg.* 51.52: 'Hic dicet aliquis: Non est hoc iam de virginitate, sed de humilitate scribere'.

74 *S.* 304.2: 'nova virginitas'. The time-frame of this sermon roughly coincided with the time-frame of Augustine and Alypius's *Letter* 188 to Juliana, whose daughter Demetrias stunned the Roman aristocracy by deciding against marriage and becoming a consecrated virgin. *Letter* 188 forcefully responded to Pelagius's *Letter to Demetrias*, which was rife with teachings on self-sufficiency and ascetic self-mastery. North African asceticism was tending to follow in the footsteps of Rome and Milan.

75 See *uirg.* 43.44: 'nam simulatio humilitatis maior superbia est'.

76 *S.* 354.6: 'Et utinam possint omnes de una caritate cogitare'.

77 Ibid.: 'De nuptiis homo natus est, de superbia angeli ceciderunt'.

78 Ibid., 9: 'Princeps tuus humilis, et tu superbus'?

79 *S.* 196.2; 208.1; 209.3; 391.6. Also Elizabeth, Anna, a widow, and Mary, the mother of Jesus.

80 See *uirg.* 44.45; 45.46; and elsewhere.

81 Ibid., 44.45; 45.46; and 46.46.

82 Ibid., 44.45; 45.46.

83 *En. Ps.* 55.9: 'quisque cor suum portat, et omne cor omni cordi clausum est'.

84 See *uirg.* 45.46.

85 Ibid., 44.45; *s.* 354.5; *en. Ps.* 120.13 and 137.3.

86 *S.* 286.2. See Hill, op. cit., vol. III.8, p. 76, n. 1.

87 *Trin.* 4.6.10. See E. Hill, *The Works of Saint Augustine*, Part 1, vol. 5: *The Trinity*, ed. J. E. Rotelle, OSA, New York, New City Press, 1991, p. 180–1, n. 40.

88 *Doctr. chr.* 1.38.42; 2.7.10; *Io. eu. tr.* 40.10; *mend.* 18.38.

89 Ep. 189.6: 'necessitas . . . non voluntas'.

90 Ep. 150: Augustine to Proba and Juliana.

91 I borrow this image from Oliver O'Donovan. See also *s.* 9.3–4; 16A.13.

92 *En. Ps.* 55.9: 'omnis homo in hac vita peregrinus est'; *s.* 92.3; all of *s.* 346; 346A; 346B.

93 But see P. Hadot, *Philosophy as a Way of Life. Spiritual Exercises from Socrates to Foucault*, ed. A. I. Davidson, tr. M. Chase, Oxford, Basil Blackwell, 1995, on ancient spiritualities, Christian and non-Christian.

94 Ibid., 2.18.28: 'Immo vero quisquis bonus verusque Christianus est, Domini sui esse intellegat, ubicumque invenerit veritatem'.

95 'In shifting the emphasis from asceticism to the renewal of unspoilt human relationships as the core of monastic life Augustine focused a direction already implicit in the development of fourth-century spirituality'. See R. A. Markus, *The End of Ancient Christianity*, Cambridge, Cambridge University Press, 1990, p. 80.

10

CHRIST, GOD AND WOMAN IN THE THOUGHT OF ST AUGUSTINE

E. Ann Matter

In a lecture given at the Pontifical University of Saint Thomas Aquinas in 1983, Gerald Bonner cited a passage from Book 7 of Augustine's *Confessions* that provides a powerful synopsis of Augustinian anthropology. The passage, in the 1944 translation of F. J. Sheed, says:

> So I set about finding a way to gain the strength that was necessary for enjoying You. And I could not find it until I embraced the *Mediator between God and man, the man Christ Jesus, who is over all things, God blessed for ever,* who was calling unto me and saying: *I am the Way, the Truth, and the Life*; and who brought into the union with our nature that Food which I lacked the strength to take; for *the Word was made flesh* that Your Wisdom, by which You created all things, might give suck to our soul's infancy. For I was not yet lowly enough to hold the lowly Jesus as my God, nor did I know what lesson His embracing of our weakness was to teach. For Your Word, the eternal Truth, towering above the highest parts of Your creation, lifts up to Himself those who were cast down. He built for Himself here below a lowly house of our clay, that by it he might bring down from themselves and bring up to Himself those who were to be made subject, healing the swolleness of their pride and fostering their love; so that the deity at their feet, humbled by the assumption of our cost of human nature; to the end that weary at last they might cast themselves down upon His humanity and rise again in its rising.
>
> *(conf.* 7.18.24).[1]

In Bonner's analysis of this passage, its centrality to Augustine's thought lies in a deeply held conviction that man is made in the image of God, through the mediation of Christ in the Church:

164

Thus he [Augustine] sees the Incarnation as the highest example of divine grace without regard to human merit; he holds that man is incapable of himself of participating in God, and can hope to do so only as a member of Christ's Church.[2]

This is a theological discussion, but one that is deeply rooted in the culture of the Christianity of late antiquity, including concepts of humility and salvation and the intrinsic nature of human existence. It is, therefore, a passage from Augustine, and an understanding of Augustine, that immediately suggests a thorny question: does the 'man' referred to here include Christian women?

Because of Augustine's enormous importance in the development of Christian attitudes towards issues of sexuality, this is a vexed question. The abundant secondary literature on the subject characterises Augustine as both villain and hero, and many works about women in Christian history do not hesitate to load him with a heavy burden of responsibility for the sufferings of Christian women in patriarchy overall. After several decades of feminist scholarship in the history of Christianity, what can we say about the place of women in Augustine's anthropology?[3]

If we begin with a consideration of Augustine's late Roman society, it seems clear that he assumed, comfortably, that women were meant, by the order of creation, to be subordinate to men; that the only legitimate purpose of sexual intercourse is the procreation of children (*nupt. et conc.* 1.4.5; *b. coniug.* 9); and that a woman's purpose in life is to bear children for a man to whom she is subordinate within marriage. In a much-quoted passage, Augustine calls childbirth specifically the 'help' Eve was created to give to Adam: 'If one rejects giving birth to children as the reason why woman was created, I do not see for which other help the woman was made for the man' (*Gn. litt.* 9.5.9). Male domination of women is, therefore, a consequence of the Fall (*Gn. litt.* 9.37.50; *Gn. adu. Man.* 2.11; *ciu.* 14.23; *c. Iul. imp.* 6.26), and the very definition of women's nature (*Gn. litt.* 11.42).

This is the theory Augustine put forth about the theological nature of the abstract category 'woman'; but how does that theory relate to Augustine's experience of women in his own life? He actually had a great many lively and intense relationships with individual women during his lifetime. Any consideration of the topic 'Augustine on women' must also consider the women with whom he interacted on a concrete, daily basis: his mother, Monica, the unnamed companion of his middle years, his sister, and his female correspondents.

Monica was clearly the most significant woman in Augustine's life. Her model of Christian motherhood played a large role in Augustine's meditation on his own life in the first nine books of the *Confessions*. Monica did her best to direct her brilliant and restless son towards the Christian faith, even while he was busy exploring the more philosophical religions of the empire,

165

especially the religious traditions of the Neoplatonists and the Manichaeans. Augustine's tone when speaking of his mother is often rueful, as when he reports the story of the bishop who, after listening patiently to Monica's tearful lament about her wayward son, told her with some vexation: 'Go away from me: as you live, it cannot be that the son of these tears should perish' (*conf.* 3.12.22).

Monica was also an intellectual companion to her son. She followed him from north Africa to the Italian peninsula, and lived with him in Milan. In Augustine's early works, dialogues written at his retreat in Cassiciacum after his conversion, his mother takes part along with friends, disciples, and his son, Adeodatus. Furthermore, it was together with Monica, near the end of her life in a house in the seaport city of Ostia, that Augustine had his most-clearly described experience of mystical transport (*conf.* 9.10.23–27). The 'vision' (or, more accurately, since the entire description centres around what they heard, the 'audition') at Ostia is one of the emotional high points of Augustine's autobiography; not only was it shared with his mother, but the account is embedded in a section of the work that lovingly details his mother's life and death.[4]

Monica's life becomes Augustine's model of a good Christian, a contrast to his own shortcomings. For example, he tells the story of how she was cured from a childhood habit of stealing sips of wine from her family wine cellar by a servant who called her 'boozer' (*conf.* 9.8.18); the taunt stung and she immediately reformed. The power of the chance word is an important theme in Augustine's own spiritual pilgrimage, so his mother's quick response is as much a model as her unflagging devotion to the Catholic faith. Monica's concern for her son's spiritual welfare focused on two intense desires: that he accept Christian baptism, and that he marry a suitable, Christian woman.

In this second goal, Monica came into conflict with the other most important woman in Augustine's life, his companion, usually referred to (although he does not use this term for her) as his concubine. Although Augustine talks about his companion several times in the *Confessions*, he never names her. In fact, he refers to her in the most oblique ways, as *una*, 'one', in the feminine (*conf.* 4.2.2) or 'the one with whom I was used to sleeping' (*conf.* 6.15.25); yet her story stands out as one of the most emotionally ardent of Augustine's relationships. Augustine became involved with this woman in Carthage, during his Manichaean years, at a time when he describes himself as in a state of wandering desire. However restless he was in those days, he says clearly that this woman was the one for him, and that he remained sexually faithful to her (*conf.* 4.2.2).

It was only in Milan, while on the verge of becoming a Christian, that Augustine forced himself to part with this unnamed woman. Convention, rather than morality, motivates this break, especially the desirability of making a good marriage to a Christian woman, Monica's goal. The parting was not easy: on Augustine's side, he says his heart, which had been attached to her, was torn and bled; while she went back to Africa weeping and vowing never to go with another man (*conf.* 6.15.25). She left their young son with Augustine and Monica in Italy. After his companion left, Augustine found himself unable to remain chaste, even in anticipation of marriage, and briefly took another woman, but he never had another sexual or emotional relationship of the intensity of his relationship with his companion. Augustine never did marry; the nature of his conversion was such that he ended up living a far more ascetic life than either he or Monica had anticipated.

After his conversion and his decision to live a celibate life, Augustine maintained a certain distance from women. Augustine's biographer Possidius says that as bishop of Hippo, he never let any woman, not even his sister, stay in his house for fear of scandal (Possidius, *Vita Augustini* 26). It has often been noted that Augustine never cultivated intellectual relationships with learned ascetic women in the way Jerome became friends with Paula and Eustochium at Bethlehem. Nevertheless, he did have women friends; the vast collection of his extant letters includes some important correspondence with women.

Some of Augustine's female correspondents were well-known and important women, such as Melania the Elder and her granddaughter Melania the Younger.[5] He later wrote a treatise about the relationship of Pelagius to the orthodox church in response to a letter from Melania the Younger: *De gratia Christi et de libero arbitrio*. Augustine also corresponded with the consecrated widows Proba and Juliana, a mother and daughter-in-law of a noble Roman family, the *gens* Anicii. One letter to Proba is a discussion of prayer (*ep.* 130), another offers advice for facing adversity (*ep.* 131). He wrote to Juliana in regard to her daughter Demetrias, who had astonished the Roman nobility by consecrating her virginity to God and taking the veil (*ep.* 188). His treatise on consecrated widowhood (*b. uid.*) was dedicated to Juliana.

Other consecrated virgins and widows who were the recipients of letters of spiritual counsel from Augustine include Sapida, a virgin mourning the death of her brother (*ep.* 213); Italica, recently widowed, to whom Augustine wrote about the vision of God in the next world (*ep.* 99); Paulina, in a lengthy reprise on the vision of God and on the equality of men and women in the resurrection (*ep.* 147); Seleuciana about the baptism of St Peter (*ep.* 265); Maxima and Felicia on heretics (*ep.* 264, 208); Florentina on study (*ep.* 266); and Ecdicia, a married woman who had taken a vow of continence, on the difficult problem of her husband's adultery (*ep.* 262). This last letter is especially interesting as a guide to Augustine's view of sexual renunciation. He chides Ecdicia for forcing her husband into a vow of continence against his will, and giving away much of their common property without his consent. While deploring the husband's infidelity and incontinence, Augustine makes it clear that the marriage vows are to take precedence over this quasi-monastic life Ecdicia has taken upon herself. Augustine does not urge Ecdicia to take up sexual relations with her husband again, but he does advise her to apologise to her husband and ask him to return to a life of continence with her.

We know from a passing reference in a letter (*ep.* 211) that Augustine had a widowed sister who became the head of a house of consecrated women in Hippo. When she died, he was asked to help resolve various disputes about authority and monastic life in the community. Two letters from Augustine about the regulation of this community survive: one, to the abbess Felicitas and the priest Rusticus, admonishes the nuns to cease quarrelling (*ep.* 210); the second contains two parts: first, another discourse about the dangers of internal controversy, and, second, a set of rules by which community life should proceed (*ep.* 211.1–4; 211.5–16). The last part of *ep.* 211 is the basic substance of Augustine's monastic rule, although the rule has a very complicated manuscript tradition, including both epistolary and non-epistolary and male and female forms. From Erasmus of Rotterdam on, some scholars have suggested that these letters form the original core of Augustine's monastic rule; that is, that it was written for women first, although the editor of the modern critical edition, Luc Verheijen, argues that the rule was written originally for men and then adapted, as a separate text, for women.[6] In any case, it is clear that Augustine manifested pastoral care for the monastic community with which his sister had been associated.

Augustine's attitudes towards women are, therefore, as complex and contradictory as any of the major theological concepts with which he struggled in his long and eventful life. He certainly accepted the prevailing notions (both Christian and pagan) of his time: that women were subjected to men by the order of creation, and that women's embodiment was the specific focus of inferiority. However, he also maintained a certain type of spiritual equality between men and women, by virtue of the participation of women in the category 'human being' as defined by men. In this limited sense, women are equally in the image of God, and equally able to be in the divine presence in the Resurrection.

Of course, sexuality was never simple for Augustine. In fact, the reality of women's subordination to men is somewhat mitigated within the marriage contract by the 'mutual servitude' of the flesh, that is, the right that spouses can claim over each other's bodies, an idea that derives from 1 Cor 7:4. However, this claim is a tainted power, precisely because sexuality is never an unambiguous good for Augustine. Women have some of the same rights to embodiment as men, but these are not totally to the good; they are reminders of our fallen nature altogether.

Augustine also had ambivalent views about women's power in a physical sense. In comparison to men, women are weak (*Gn. litt.* 11.42.58; *diu. qu.*11). This does not mean, however, that women are incapable of heroics: in a sermon on the Feast of Saints Perpetua and Felicitas (*s.* 282.2.2), Augustine makes it clear that this weakness did not inhibit courage and fortitude in the face of martyrdom. Famous women saints behaved *viriliter*: as men.

On an intellectual plane, Augustine is more critical of women. In several places (*qu.* 1.153; *Gn. litt.* 11.42), he seems to assume women's intellectual inferiority to men; although he does acknowledge that some women (specifically, his mother, Monica) can attain philosophical sophistication (*b. uita* 2.10). We should in no way be surprised to see that, in general, Augustine accepts the belief of his world that men are the measure of creation, and does not address himself more than in passing to the nature of women's inferiority as understood by the subjugation of women to men. This is the formulation of the problem of gender relations that seems most pressing in a modern context, but it is not a topic that attracted much of Augustine's attention.

However, in the realm of the relationship between human beings and God, the locus of Christ's salvific sacrifice, Augustine raises the question of women's essential nature in more disturbing ways and brings us back to the question with which this essay began: simply put, if man is made in the image of God, is woman also the image of God? Augustine's interest in this question resulted in some very problematic theological formulations; these, in turn, have been the subject of lively debate among twentieth-century scholars.

The crucial text is a passage in *De trinitate* in which Augustine seems to say that women are in God's image only when they are considered 'humanity' along with males, but not in some sort of essence as female human beings:

> The woman together with the man is the image of God, so that the whole substance is one image. But when she is assigned as a helpmate, which pertains to her alone, she is not the image of God; however, in what pertains to man alone, he is the image of God just as fully and completely as he is joined with the woman into one.
>
> (*trin.* 12.7.10)

Augustine came to this statement through 1 Cor 11:7, where Paul says that men are forbidden to cover their heads because they are the reflection of God, but women must cover their heads since they are, rather, the reflection of the male. Commentary on this passage of Augustine has focused on the apparent contradiction between the Pauline line followed here and the first creation story, Gen 1:27–8, which states that male and female were created in the image of God. Can Augustine be shown to support both biblical passages?

A number of well-known scholars of early Christianity, including Gerald Bonner, have based their analysis on the fact that, as I pointed out earlier, Augustine was obviously capable of friendship with and respect for women.[7] An emphasis on the demands of Augustine's own asceticism and sexual renunciation, particularly in view of the complicated relationship he had with his companion, the mother of his son, Adeodatus, is at the core of interpretations by other scholars who defend Augustine against charges of misogyny based on the idea that he, as a man of his time, could only be expected to assume women's subordination.[8] Indeed, these scholars have argued that Augustine fought against expected societal norms to insist that women also participate in the category *homo*, and, therefore, in the image of God. Much of his seeming hesitation about women's equality, they claim, can be explained by the fact that, after his conversion, Augustine's relationships to women were marked by the restraint to be expected of an ascetic celibate.

Several explicitly feminist scholars have even gone to the trouble of investigating the roots and nuances of Augustine's relation to and interaction with women *in order* to create a sympathetic portrait. These scholars have defended Augustine largely on the basis of his ultimate assertion of women's spiritual equivalence to men. Kari Elisabeth Børresen's work on the nature and role of women in Augustine and Thomas Aquinas has set a pattern for a scholarship of feminist apologetics for Christian theology.[9] Silvia Soennecken's more recent study of the philosophical and theological resonances (the semantic field) of the major words for 'woman' used by Augustine (*femina*, *mulier*, *coniux*, *uxor*, *matrona*, *virgo*, *virago*, *sanctimonialis*, *castimonialis*, *vidua*, *concubina*, *praelex*, *ministra*, *ancilla*, *famula*, *serva*, *domina*, *mater*, *filia*, *soror*, *germana*, *sponsa*), owes much to Børresen's approach.[10] Both scholars conclude that the problem for Augustine is sexuality, not women, and that, for his culture, Augustine was, in fact, rather positively disposed towards women; he considered women spiritual equals before God and he treated the women he knew with respect.

There is, actually, substantial agreement among these scholars that the key to understanding this passage from *De trinitate* is an assumption of divisions of categories of human existence: first, between body and spirit, then, between the levels of the human mind. At the level of embodiment, the category woman (*femina*, *mulier*) does not participate in the *imago Dei*; but woman as part of the category *homo*, human being, does. Furthermore, the category woman is equated with *scientia*, the active mind, in contrast to the masculine part of the mind, symbolised as *sapientia*, the meditative mind of the wisdom of God. *Scientia* always leads the mind back to creation, so only *sapientia* can truly image God. It is this distinction, Augustine believed, that Paul had in mind.

Therefore, the very particularity of women, not just with regard to incarnate sexuality, but also in the concept of 'the feminine mind', means that women participate in the *imago Dei* only in their status as human beings, not as women. Women are spiritually equal to men, then, but only without regard to the particular characteristics that make them women, for these things are, by the order of creation, inferior and subordinate to the characteristics of humanity attributed to men. This general idea, that the nature of women's inferiority is specifically physical, having to do with female embodiment, is found elsewhere in Augustine's writings (*s. dom. m.* 1.15), as is the assurance that in spirit, and therefore in the Resurrection, women are equal with men before God (*ep.* 147).

It should be no great surprise that this explanation is not at all comforting to another group of feminist historians and theologians, who have taken very seriously the impact that Augustine's views of women have had on the place of women in Christian society. As early as 1977, in their feminist source book of Christian thought, Elizabeth Clark and Herbert Richardson characterised Augustine's views on women as hinging on his negative attitude towards sexual life.[11] Their point is that Augustine's writings on sexuality and marriage, so strongly influenced by his own personal experience, became the basis for Roman Catholic theology on those subjects. Eight years later, in an anthology of writings by the Church Fathers on the subject of women, Clark showcased the obvious texts, with selections from *De Genesi ad litteram*, *De nuptiis et concupiscentia* and *De bono coniugali*, in addition to the *City of God* and *Letters* 262 and 211. Augustine's words are prefaced by brief remarks that highlight the ways in which they influenced later Christine doctrine.[12]

A great deal of scholarship has followed along these lines. Margaret Miles (1979) began mildly, with a study of Augustine on the body, which concluded that he avoided metaphysical dualism (partly in reaction to his Manichaean period), and struggled against the pervasive philosophical or existential dualism of his time to make the body 'the cornerstone of his theology'.[13] A decade later, in a study of the relationship between female nakedness and western Christian theology, Miles is harsher with Augustine. In this study, which focuses on Christian art, Miles emphasises Augustine's discomfort with, and even fear of, women's embodiment, and his counsel that consecrated virgins must avoid any hint of seductiveness.[14]

However, it is perhaps Elaine Pagels who has made the most famous critique of Augustine. Her most widely read book, *Adam, Eve, and the Serpent* (1988) is not specifically about women, but focuses on traditional patterns of gender and sexuality in western culture. Pagels is interested in the cultural implications of the doctrine of original sin, especially the role of the story of the Fall. She lays the blame for Christian sexual repression and misogyny squarely on Augustine. Pagels posits that it is Augustine's pessimistic views of sexuality, politics and human nature that would dominate in western culture, and that 'Adam, Eve, and the serpent – our ancestral story – would continue, often in some version of its Augustinian form, to affect our lives to the present day'.[15] In other words, for Pagels, it is not what Augustine intended, but what he left as a legacy that really counts.

This position – that what is most important about Augustine's views of women is the impact they had on later Christian tradition – is shared by more radical feminist critics such as Rosemary Radford Ruether and Mary Daly. As early as 1968, Daly's analysis of the 'second sex' status of women in the church targeted Augustine, citing passages from *De trinitate*, *De Genesi aduersus Manicheos* and other texts. Daly takes a hard line with Augustine, accusing him of cynicism in the way he blames the evils of 'fallen man' (a category which, of course, includes women) on Eve. She rejects entirely the argument that women can be equal before God spiritually but not in embodiment, claiming that such an understanding of gender makes women less than fully human. Daly's high level of abstraction does not allow for the exclusion of women from any part of God's image or presence because of women's bodies; in the following decade, this point of view would lead her to reject the Christian tradition altogether.[16]

Ruether's systematic feminist theology (1983) reiterates the discussion of women and the image of God in *trin.* 12.7.10, concluding that Augustine is the ultimate source of western Christian patriarchal anthropology.[17] The main problem with patriarchy, Ruether says, is hierarchy, which always leads to the oppression of the subordinated. Ruether's stance is firmly with the oppressed; she believes that Christianity can fulfil its liberating potential only when it rejects the sort of soul/body dualism that Augustine represents for her. Like Pagels, Ruether has been extremely influential in generating other feminist critiques of Augustine, often from those who know his works only second-hand.

The feminist critique of Augustine on women, therefore, is quite varied. Feminist critics have in common a desire to show how Augustine's ideas about the body, marriage, and concupiscence, and, therefore, about women, which may have been appropriate in the fifth century, do not adequately represent the status of Christian women at the end of the twentieth century. Yet, some scholars are motivated to explain why he thought those things, and thus to absolve him of malice; while others call him to task for a legacy of subordination of women in western Christian theology. The most recent analysis of the issue, Kim Power's study of Augustine on women, shows how far the discourse has matured.[18]

Power begins by acknowledging that it is Augustine's cosmos in which his theology makes most sense; in this, she has offered a new vantage point from which to examine the issues. She then painstakingly examines his writings in far more detail than has been done to date, considering many pertinent facets of his culture, for example, the role of slaves. One excellent example of this is the description of Augustine's mother, Monica, in the context of a slave society; 'slave-wife' is the category Power applies. Augustine's enthusiastic praise in the *Confessions* for the way his mother fulfilled her role as wife shows that he accepts and assumes a master–slave relationship as one natural part of the role of women. In a discussion of women and public life, Power points out an important, unexplored, consequence of the relegation of women to the private sphere, an activity in which Augustine participated, particularly in his years as bishop of Hippo. Quoting Robert Markus, Power reminds us that '"privacy", self-enclosure, was the "most insidious form of pride" in Augustine's mature thought'.[19] With such an insight, we can begin to see the subtleties of women's disadvantage in Christian theology and society: forcibly relegated to a state that is in itself inherently sinful.

Power's treatment of Augustine's letter to Ecdicia, in which, as we saw above, he chides a married woman for taking on an ascetic life against her husband's will, is equally illuminating. Power notes that the one element of mutuality Augustine posited in marriage, the mutual obligation to marital sexual relations, here becomes an argument against a woman's self-actuali-sation as an ascetic. Ecdicia, Augustine argues, is ultimately responsible for her husband's adultery, since she drove him to take a mistress. 'Better a sexually active woman who yields the marriage debt to her husband whilst desiring continence, for continence will be imputed to her by God, than a proud and overly bold continent woman who drives her husband into eternal damnation'.[20] Ecdicia is the opposite of a slave–wife, and Augustine does not approve. Although it must be noted that Augustine would undoubtedly direct the same criticism towards a man who abandoned his marriage vows to live a celibate life (as is perhaps evident in s. 9), Augustine's relationship with Ecdicia has special importance for the question of his relationship towards women. Among the many levels of this complicated story, Power notes an indirect confirmation of the status and power of women ascetics. The very fact that this story evoked such a reaction from Augustine suggests the tensions ascetic women were creating in fifth-century Christian society.

Augustine's theology, Power argues, is as culturally constructed as any theology; the final irony is that Augustine, the man who is largely respon-sible for introducing sex into Eden and gender into heaven, could never permit the erotic to symbolise the divine.

As Gerald Bonner has pointed out in the introduction to his major study of the life and controversies of Augustine of Hippo, anyone who dares to add to the mountain of interpretation of this figure must explain exactly what he or she thinks they can add to the picture.[21] Bonner goes on to note that the towering figure of Augustine in western Christianity, and his consequent impact on western society in general, makes it impossible not to keep reinterpreting his thought for each era, and each specific situation. This related challenge and insight are helpful for the dilemma invariably raised by the question of this essay. Did Augustine consider women to be in the image of God, the very humanity assumed by Christ? Yes and no: yes, in the ultimate, abstract theological definition; no, in the practical question of the role of actual women in his culture. In spite of his many close relationships with women, Augustine obviously did not consider the category 'woman' to be equal to the category 'man.' The exception, of course, is the sense in which the term 'man' includes all women; but this is outside of the experience of real live women. Any one woman in her incarnate particularity cannot possibly partake of that deep participation in the divinity described by Augustine in the passage with which I began this chapter.

Does this matter? For those women who have found Augustine used to deny them full participation in the community of believers, it can matter dreadfully. Nevertheless, it is clear that this is an application of the theory that would never have occurred to Augustine; an idea of 'the role of women' unthinkable in his context. The problem that remains is, simply, that Augustine's context is not our own. This essay has tried to point out some of the ways in which the changing Christian community has turned to see whether Augustine, whose understanding of human nature transcends the limits of his place and time, can also tell us something about the humanity of women. Perhaps he simply cannot help us here. However, as we have also seen, as scholars ask the 'woman question' in increasingly more precise and sophisticated ways, they reveal new aspects of the complicated interrelation between Augustine's thought and the context in which he thought. This can only be to the advantage of anyone who shares with Gerald Bonner a sense of the deep and lasting importance of Augustine of Hippo.

Notes

1 G. Bonner, 'Christ, God and Man in the Thought of St Augustine,' in *God's Decree and Man's Destiny: Studies on the Thought of Augustine of Hippo*, London, Variorum, 1987, reprinted from *Angelicum* 61 (1984), pp. 268–9.

2 Ibid., p. 293.

3 See my article 'Augustine and Women', in *Augustine Through the Ages: An Encyclopedia*, ed. A. Fitzgerald, Grand Rapids, Minn., Eerdmans, 1999, pp. 887–92.

4 See J. J. O'Donnell, *Augustine, Confessions III: Commentary on Books 8–13*, Oxford, Clarendon Press, 1992, pp. 127–9.

5 From the evidence of Augustine's letters to Paulinus of Nola and Alypius, *ep*. 45, 124, 125, 126.

6 L. Verheijen, *La Règle de saint Augustin I. Tradition manuscrite, II. Recherches historiques*, Paris, Etudes augustiniennes, 1967. On this topic, see also A. Zumkeller, *Augustine's Rule: A Commentary*, tr. M. J. O'Connell, ed. J. E. Rotelle, OSA, Villanova, Pa., Augustinian Press, 1987; and G. Lawless, *Augustine of Hippo and his Monastic Rule*, Oxford, Clarendon Press, 1987.

7 G. Bonner, 'Augustine's Attitude to Women and *Amicitia*', in *Homo Spiritualis: Festgabe für Luc Verheijen OSA zu seinem 70. Geburtstag*, ed. C. P. Mayer, Würzburg, Augustinus-Verlag, 1987, pp. 259–75.

8 J. A. Truax, 'Augustine of Hippo: Defender of Women's Equality?' *Journal of Medieval History* 16 (1990), pp. 279–99; F. E. Weaver and J. Laporte, 'Augustine and Women: Relationships and Teachings', *Augustinian Studies* 12 (1981), pp. 115–31; T. J. van Bavel, 'Augustine's View on Women,' *Augustiniana* 39 (1989), pp. 5–53; idem, 'Woman as the Image of God in Augustine's '*De trinitate* XII', in *Signum Pietatis: Festgabe für Cornelius Petrus Mayer OSA zum 60. Geburtstag*, ed. A. Zumkeller, Würzburg, Augustinus-Verlag, 1989, pp. 267–88; R. J. McGowan, 'Augustine's Spiritual Equality: The Allegory of Man and Woman with Regard to *Imago Dei*', *Revue des études augustiniennes* 33 (1987), pp. 255–64.

9 K. E. Børresen, *Subordination and Equivalence: The Nature and Role of Woman in Augustine and Thomas Aquinas*, tr. C. H. Talbot, Washington, University Press of America, 1981; idem, 'In Defence of Augustine: How Feminine is Homo?', in *Collectanea Augustiniana. Mélanges T. J. Van Bavel*, ed. B. Bruning, M. Lamberigts and J. van Houtem, Leuven, Institut Historique Augustinien, 1990 [= *Augustiniana* 40 (1990)], pp. 411–28.

10 S. Soennecken, *Misogynie oder Philologie? Philologisch-theologische Untersuchungen zum Wortfeld 'Frau' bei Augustinus*, Frankfurt-am-Main/New York, Peter Lang, 1993.

11 E. Clark and H. Richardson, *Women and Religion: A Feminist Sourcebook of Christian Thought*, New York, Harper and Row, 1977.

12 E. Clark, *Women in the Early Church*, Wilmington, Del., Michael Glazier, 1983.

13 M. R. Miles, *Augustine on the Body*, Missoula, Mont., Scholar's Press, 1979, p. 131.

14 M. R. Miles, *Carnal Knowing: Female Nakedness and Religious Meaning in the Christian West*, Boston, Beacon Press, 1989, citing passages from *ciu.* and *ep.* 211.

15 E. A. Pagels, *Adam, Eve, and the Serpent*, New York, Random House, 1988, p. 150.

16 M. Daly, *The Church and the Second Sex*, New York, Harper & Row, 1968.

17 R. R. Ruether, *Sexism and God-Talk: Toward a Feminist Theology*, Boston, Beacon Press, 1983, pp. 63, 85–7.

18 K. Power, *Veiled Desire: Augustine on Women*, New York, Continuum, 1996.

19 Ibid., p. 235.

20 Ibid., p. 113.

21 G. Bonner, *Augustine of Hippo: Life and Controversies*, Norwich, Canterbury Press, ²1986, p. 10.

11

A CRITICAL EVALUATION OF CRITIQUES OF AUGUSTINE'S VIEW OF SEXUALITY

Mathijs Lamberigts

The German theologian, Uta Ranke-Heinemann, begins the chapter on Augustine in her well-known study *Eunuchs for the Kingdom of Heaven* with the following statement: 'The man who fused Christianity together with hatred of sex and pleasure into a systematic unity was the greatest of the Church Fathers, St Augustine (+430)'.[1] This statement gives radical expression to a frequently recurring criticism of Augustine's view of sexuality, a criticism that has taken a variety of forms over the last several years and that places the blame for the 'scowl' on the face of Western humanity firmly on the shoulders of the bishop of Hippo.[2] In her opinion, the *doctor gratiae* is at the origins of the fact that, until very recently, sexuality *in se* – detached from procreation – was mistrusted within Christendom because it was considered sinful. Sexuality and sin, as it were, called forth mutual associations.

Ranke-Heinemann's criticism is not new, however. As early as Augustine's own time there was much unease concerning his view of sexuality. His younger contemporary, Julian of Eclanum, for example, sharply questioned Augustine's vision of original sin with frequently pointed arguments rooted in the Bible, or based on healthy theological principles, and condemned Augustine's vision of sexuality – closely related to the doctrine of original sin – in no uncertain terms.[3] By the irony of fate, it is precisely thanks to Augustine himself that not only several fragments of Julian's letters and one of his works have come down to us, but also the first six volumes of his *Ad Florum* in their entirety.[4] This essay, therefore, employs criticisms taken from both Augustine's own time and from modern reflection on the topic, although given their courageous character, my preference goes to those criticisms contemporary with Augustine.[5] Julian of Eclanum's bold critique led him to sacrifice a promising church career by sticking his neck out at a point in history when people still had to fight for their convictions. With easy academic consciences, contemporary critics not only call Augustine into question, but also a level of reception ratified and rendered permanent over the centuries. Julian, on the other hand, was reacting to the positions held by an authoritative contemporary who not only had the opportunity to respond, but also had the power to put an end to Julian's career.

Given that Augustine has already responded forcibly to Julian's accusations, and that Julian's objections stand close to those of a number of modern commentators, it seems evident that attention in this essay should be focused primarily on Augustine's responses to Julian's criticisms. Such an option is all the more defensible if one considers that recent studies have tended to criticise the late Augustine, challenging him to defend the position he adopts in works such as *De nuptiis et concupiscentia*, *Contra duas epistulas Pelagianorum*, *Contra Iulianum* and *Opus imperfectum*, all of which were directed against Julian. The aforementioned works contain roughly thirty-three per cent of the instances in which *concupiscentia* (sexual or otherwise), or some expression derived therefrom, is treated.[6] At the same time, the texts in question represent at most ten per cent of Augustine's complete works. Julian's critique, therefore, clearly deserves preferential treatment in the debate, as will become apparent from the following presentation of his various propositions.

For Julian, *concupiscentia* is not a deficiency of nature but rather a quality thereof, a sentiment or feeling.[7] It is perhaps true that the term is not always used univocally, being ascribed in one place to the domain of sensual experience, and treated in another as an intensifying energy.[8] In every instance, however, Julian employs the predicate *naturalis* (see, for example, *Ad Florum* 5.5; PL 45.1435) in relation to *concupiscentia*, and expresses his conviction that it can be directed and controlled by the human mind.[9] In addition, Julian considers sexual *concupiscentia* to be the divinely willed means *par excellence* for the realisation of a successful sexual union, a natural prerequisite for procreation.[10] As a gift of God, sexuality belongs by its very nature to the physical dimension of the human person. In this respect, Julian points to the fact that sexual *concupiscentia* is also to be found in the animal kingdom.[11] Accordingly, if Julian refuses to consider the *concupiscentia carnis* (desire of the flesh) as a consequence of the Fall, then his motivation is both practically and theologically inspired. One would be doing him an injustice if one were to attribute some sort of glorification or defence of *concupiscentia* to Julian.[12] In common with most of his contemporaries, Julian considered a life of sexual abstinence superior to married life and, in line with 1 Cor 7, viewed marriage as a remedy for those who were unable to manage without a partner.[13] What Julian could not accept, however, was that *concupiscentia* had been characterised as having the power to elude the rational and moral autonomy of the human person. As a component of the human body, *concupiscentia* was subject to reason. Indeed, thanks to the gift of reason, which characterizes human persons as *imago Dei* and distinguishes them from animals, human beings are actually able to control their feelings and impulses. Julian was thoroughly convinced that the body was at the service of the mind, and that the mind governed and controlled the body.[14] Moreover, a certain ethical concern had a role to play in Julian's stance. In his view, any understanding of *concupiscentia* as an uncontrollable force against which human persons were powerless might easily be used as an excuse to avoid personal responsibility. Julian, on the other hand, underlined the fact that one could only consider a person guilty if he or she had deliberately violated the prescribed frameworks (unnatural sex, adultery, fornication).[15]

The necessity of this somewhat detailed presentation of Julian's own position will become apparent as I continue. Julian, in fact, is the only contemporary of Augustine who wrote about sexuality in a relatively positive manner, and who dared to confront Augustine's position directly from his own theological–ethical perspective.[16] Against the background of what I have said so far, therefore, I can now present and situate Julian's criticism of Augustine with greater accuracy and clarity.

One of the primary elements of Augustine's position that engendered such strong feelings in his younger contemporary was the fact that Augustine regularly labelled 'desire' as a *vitium*, a weakness characteristic of fallen humanity, a deficiency with respect to the fullness of being for which the devil was responsible.[17] Given the relationship outlined above – physical marriage, sexuality and procreation calling forth mutual associations – Julian concluded that in view of such a negative attitude on the part of Augustine, one could no longer consider the *nuptiae corporales* to be willed by God and one should, therefore, condemn it.[18] Julian also insinuated that, for Augustine, the devil must be the instigator of marriage, the creator of the genitalia, the arouser of men, the impregnator of women and the creator of children.[19] Although Julian's polemic enthusiasm led him to a certain amount of exaggeration, the core of his criticism was, nevertheless, quite serious: what can the value of sexuality within marriage be if it directly refers to the devil, yet, at the same time, is the condition *sine qua non* for the realisation of the physical end of marriage, namely procreation?

A further point of criticism stemming from Julian was his suspicion that the elderly Augustine had remained a Manichaean.[20] Although this accusation was frequently little more than a term of abuse, in the precise context of the discussion on *concupiscentia*, Julian did, nevertheless, present a text which he thought was Manichaean, the so-called *Epistula ad Menoch*, with which he compared Augustine's positions in *De nuptiis et concupiscentia* 1.7–8; 1.13; 1.26 and 2.36.[21] In this work, Augustine proposed that 'lust' was something evil, given that the first human beings had felt it necessary to clothe themselves after the first sin (2.36) because of their woundedness (1.8). The fact that people felt shame with respect to lust was simply proof of its truly evil nature (1.8; 2.36). Augustine also pointed out that, where the *libido* was concerned, the human mind did not enjoy the same supremacy as it did with respect to other parts of the body (1.7). Moreover, sexual desire, for Augustine, did not constitute one of the 'goods' of marriage (1.13). He believed, on the contrary, that all human beings were under the power of the devil, because they had all been born as a result of sexual desire. Julian found a similar position in the *Epistula ad Menoch*. There, too, he found *concupiscentia* condemned, since the devil, via *concupiscentia*, was the creator and master of the human body.[22] In order to establish the negative character of *concupiscentia*, the *Epistula* made a similar appeal to the emotion of shame (see *Ad Florum* 3.177; CSEL 85/ 1.476). Moreover, as Augustine himself had done, Mani made a further appeal to St Paul in order to support his own position.[23] From this point on, the struggle between spirit and flesh was presented as a struggle between good and evil (*malum naturale*) (see *Ad Florum* 3.187; CSEL 85/ 1.487). Julian pointed out that all these elements could be traced in the writings of Augustine: the *concupiscentia carnis* was woven into the human body by the devil; everyone born as a result of such sexual desire is in the power of the devil; *concupiscentia* is a part of human nature. Augustine also refers to the struggle between the flesh and the spirit, arguing that 'desire', in a certain sense, eludes the control of the mind. At the same time, he appeals to Paul's letters to the Galatians (Gal 5:17) and the Romans (Rom 7:18–19) to support his line of thought.[24] It was clear to Julian, therefore, that Augustine continued to be a bearer of Manichaean ideas.

In recent years, a number of additional objections have been added to Julian's none the less serious critique. Augustine has been accused, for example, of supporting the notion that the very experience of sexual desire in itself is already a sin.[25] Given the fact that every human being is confronted with such desire, it has also been suggested that Augustine concluded that the human person had completely lost his or her original power of self-rule and that sexual desire was no longer under his or her control.[26]

How, then, might Augustine respond to such criticisms with respect to the *concupiscentia carnis*? In the present essay, I will focus my attention on the works written against Julian, although I will make frequent reference to passages outside this corpus.[27] In doing so, it is not my intention to present an apology on behalf of the bishop of Hippo, I simply offer the accused a chance to say a word in his own defence.

By way of introduction, a number of elements deserve to be recalled before we examine Augustine's response to Julian's criticisms, with respect to *concupiscentia*, in more detail. In the first place, it is worth noting that there are several forms of *concupiscentia* in Augustine. A first form is termed the *concupiscentia bona* and refers to our desire for the things of the Spirit, a desire which points to that which comes from God, or points to God and is bound up with the very purpose of human existence: a life lived *propter Deum*. With reference to specific biblical texts, this desire is further elaborated as *concupiscentia spiritus* (Gal 5:17b) or as *concupiscentia sapientiae* (Wis 6:21).[28] It is also seen, in essence, as a desire for God's gift of love.[29] A second form is termed the *concupiscentia naturalis*, a desire which he elaborates, for example, as a longing for happiness (*c. Iul. imp.* 4.67; PL 45.1375). Augustine also speaks of the natural desire to marry which, he insists, has nothing to do with the devil, since it is oriented towards procreation and is fully in line with God's command in Gen 1:28, which remains valid even after the sin of Adam (see *ep.* 6*; CSEL 88.33). The desire to have children is an equally natural desire for Augustine, since it is legitimate and honourable, similar to the desire to have good health or nourish and educate our children (*nupt. et conc.* 2.17; CSEL 42.269). Such desires, according to Augustine, belong to the order of nature, which is not the case with respect to the *concupiscentia carnis* (*c. Iul. imp.* 1.68; CSEL 85/1.74; 6.22; PL 45.1551).

With respect to Augustine's view of the *concupiscentia carnis* (in several places, one finds the term *concupiscentia* on its own, but the context makes it evident that one should also read *carnis*, or a derived form thereof), it ought to be underlined that the term alone, without any additional predicate of appreciation, carries negative connotations.[30] It should be emphasised from the outset, moreover, that Augustine regularly speaks of the *concupiscentia carnis* in contexts where it becomes immediately clear that the simple equation of desire with sexual desire would be incorrect.[31] Augustine himself formally lodged a protest on this matter in his controversy with Julian, insisting that every desire of the flesh hostile to the spirit, such as the desire to take revenge, amass money, to do one's own will, or attain fame, and so forth, could be qualified as an aspect of the *concupiscentia carnis*.[32]

With respect to his negative interpretation of *concupiscentia* (*carnis*), Augustine was indebted to the Bible, where both Old and New Testaments spoke repeatedly of sinful desire without necessarily referring to sexual desire.[33] As far as the Old Testament is concerned, one might refer to Exod 20:17 or to Num 11:33; Dt 5:21; Prov 21:25; 23:3 and 6; 24:1; Sir 18:30, among others. A narrative such as that found in Num 11 makes it clear, moreover, that one should make allowances for the fact that sinful desire includes the idea of revolt against God.[34] Augustine would also have called upon the New Testament usage of *epithumia* or *hedone* – both of which had frequently negative connotations – or their derived forms (Mt 5:28; Rom 1:24; 7:7; Gal 5:24; Eph 4:22; 1 Jn 2:16), in order to support his own position, which was in line with that of Tertullian and Cyprian.[35] In response to the accusation that he follows the Manichaeans in calling desire 'bad', Augustine would certainly have reacted by appealing to the Scriptures. The Manichaeans did not have a patent on the negative interpretation of desire, although, on the other hand, they were also certainly not blind to its negative dimensions (*c. Iul. imp.* 3.170; CSEL 85/1.472; 5.30; PL 45.1469).

Of particular importance for Augustine, is the story of the first human beings and their sin in Gen 1–3, within which he frequently emphasises the contradiction between Gen 2:25: 'And the man and his wife were both naked, and were not ashamed', and 3:7: 'Then the eyes of both of them were opened, and they knew that they were naked; and they sewed fig leaves together and made loincloths for themselves'.[36] The original absence of any sense of shame due to the *concupiscentia carnis* is proof of the absence of disorderliness, the result of sin.[37]

When Augustine speaks of the *concupiscentia carnis*, therefore, he is not simply referring to sexuality *in se*, but, in line with Paul, to an aspect of the antinomy between flesh and spirit which was to be found on the level of the disordered soul, and which, given that it had to do with the entire person, was a total experience.[38] Unless his or her spirit was strong enough to resist, the human person tended to strive towards evil.[39] This antinomy had its roots in the disobedience of the first human beings (a *poena peccati*), which had profoundly disturbed the original harmony.[40] The experience of confusion and shame, together with the disobedience of the flesh, was a punishment that revealed what it meant for a human being no longer to be obedient to God.[41]

The revolt of the flesh, or the desire to go one's own way or exert one's own will constituted *indications* that, after the Fall, self-control was no longer an easy matter.[42] This is because the hierarchical order in the human person had been disrupted (not turned upside down!).[43] This disruption led, in turn, to a sense of shame, because the human person, as a reasonable being, was aware that he or she (in Adam) was responsible for his or her own loss of interior harmony.[44] Where fallen humanity was concerned, therefore, the *concupiscentia carnis* inherited negative connotations as a result of a theological motif (disobedience to God).[45] It was a question of a desire, which ultimately strove in its indeterminateness towards the unlawful, that the human person – even under grace – loved what ought to be shunned and shunned what ought to be loved (cf. Rom 7:15,18).[46] All of this constituted a 'law of sin', *lex peccati* (Rom 7:23).[47] Partly in light of the fact that the entire person is involved, I think it best to translate the *concupiscentia carnis* in Augustine as 'sinful desire'.[48] This is all the more fitting given that the desire in question runs counter to the *bonum rationale*, thus explaining why only human beings are confronted with this problem and not animals.[49] As a rational being, the human person realises that he or she ought to take action in the process of unrest brought on by the *concupiscentia carnis*. It is precisely this absence of the will to conform itself to reason, indeed the very necessity for a regulative and remedial intervention on the part of reason, that Augustine repeatedly considered negative in his controversy with Julian and others.[50]

If one takes Augustine's statements seriously, then it becomes clear that whoever would still wish to style him a Manichaean would have to prove that his emphasis on the fact that the phenomenon had to do with the entire person (*cont.* 13.29; CSEL 41.179; see also *c. Iul.* 6.41; PL 44.845) was in conformity with the radical dualism propagated by the Manichaeans.[51] The notion of 'healing', however, provides a useful articulation of Augustine's approach to the question: the human person as such was in need of healing in both body and soul, a concept that would have been completely alien to the Manichaeans.[52] In addition, sufficient attention has been drawn to the fact that one first has to search for Augustine's perspective in Christian Neoplatonism, then in the wider Christian tradition, and only then among the Manichaeans.[53]

It is within this frame of reference, therefore, that Augustine's understanding of sexuality ought to be evaluated. As a particular form of the *concupiscentia carnis*, sexual desire shares in the negative connotations of the whole. It, too, is an evil, a striving which appears as autonomous, heedless of the will and disordered, a source of shame.[54] It is also a movement going its own way in the indifference of lust, in need of the guidance of reason to steer it towards its true purpose: procreation within marriage (*c. iul.* 3.27; PL 44.715). Furthermore, Augustine's own process of conversion, in which his personal struggle with the phenomenon of *concupiscentia* (*carnis*) had a significant role to play, also deserves to be taken into account.[55] As he himself describes it, his conversion can and should also be seen as a renunciation of the active sexual life he had lived for almost thirteen years.[56] With exceptional negativity, his *Confessions* portray his own past, with respect to the desires of the flesh in general, and sexual desire, in particular, as 'mud' (*conf.* 2.2; CCL 27.18), as the defilement of true friendship.[57] He refers to sexual desire as a sickness (ibid., 8.7.17; CCL 27.124), and even quotes his reading of Rom 13:13,

> Let us live honourably as in the day, not in revelling and drunkenness, not in debauchery and licentiousness, not in quarrelling and jealousy. Instead, put on the Lord Jesus Christ, and make no provision for the flesh, to gratify its desires

as a decisive moment in his conversion.[58] His *Confessions* reveal, moreover, that he was aware of an interior conflict: the human person is capable of controlling his or her body, but not his or her self. In the same work, mastery over one's sexuality is also referred to as a gift, a grace from God which empowers the will to choose the good.[59] Personal experience clearly played a role in the establishment of Augustine's position on the matter.[60]

It ought to be emphasised that Augustine's negative evaluation of sexuality is a constant which runs through his entire written corpus, and cannot, therefore, be seen as a characteristic peculiar to the late Augustine alone. It is simply incorrect to conclude that his vision of sexuality was that of an old and passionless man. Reference to sexual desire as an evil can be found in works written as early as *De bono coniugali*, which proposed its proper use within marriage for the purpose of procreation.[61] Likewise, he already considered sexual union between partners for the purposes of satisfying lust as shameful (*b. coniug.* 5.5; CSEL 41.194) and sinful, even though it could be forgiven within the marital context.[62] Throughout his life, Augustine never deviated from his standpoint.[63] Sexuality, for Augustine, apart from procreation, did not belong to the essence of marriage.[64] Sexual union as such was only legitimate within the legal framework of a marriage, which was, indeed, the only context in which children could be afforded legal security.[65] As such, Augustine was fully in line with ancient Roman law, within which he would have been content (and justified) to appeal to Cato, who had refrained from sexual union for purposes other than procreation (*c. Iul.* 5.38; PL 44.807; ibid., 5.46; PL 44.810). On this point, Augustine does not differ, for example, from the Stoic philosopher Musonius Rufus.

Augustine was of the opinion, moreover, that married couples restricted their sexual desires to some degree as part of their engagement with respect to their future children (see *c. Iul. imp.* 5.23; PL 45.1459). Such a motif, however, is absent among those who pursued sexual union for the sole purpose of satisfying their libidinous desires as such. The fact that Augustine speaks at this point of a 'forgivable debt' is partly due to his defective reading of 1 Cor 7:6: '*Hoc autem dico secundum veniam, non secundum imperiam*'.[66] As early as AD 397, he insists in a homily that the man who has sexual union with his wife without a procreative intention is sinning, because he cannot control himself and is going beyond what is prescribed by the law.[67] This belief was rooted in his understanding of the aforementioned Pauline text, upon which he would continue to insist throughout his life.[68] It is true that, as a pastor, Augustine would admit that giving in to sexual desire was justifiable for the sake of fidelity within the marriage, and in order to avoid sins which could not be forgiven.[69] Moreover, he does not neglect to point out that one of the good things of marriage is precisely the fact that it transforms sexual activity rooted in sexual desire into a forgivable sin (*culpa venialis*).[70]

At no stage in his career did Augustine deny the idea that marriage as such was an institution willed by God for the purposes of procreation. On the contrary, he gave it foundation with biblical texts such as Gen 1:28 and 2:24. In agreement with Julian, Augustine viewed the difference between the sexes, sexual union and human fertility as *ex Deo* and thereby deserving of the predicate *naturalia bona*.[71] Julian's allegation that sexual union or marriage were diabolical in Augustine's view is, therefore, unjust.[72] On this point, Augustine is far from the Manichaean perspective, in contrast to which he offered a positive evaluation of the purpose of a legitimate sexual union, namely procreation.[73] From Augustine's perspective, moreover, marriage as an institution guaranteed forgiveness if a person engaged in sexual union for a non-procreative reason. The Manichaeans, on the other hand, condemned marriage and advised their *auditores* only to engage in sexual union at safe moments.[74] With respect to the association of sexual union, at least, with procreation, Augustine is closer to Julian than the latter would have liked to admit (see *c. Iul.* 5.34; PL 44. 805). According to Augustine, moreover, procreation was important for the spread of the Kingdom of God through rebirth in Jesus Christ: Christians were born and engaged in procreation so as to share in the salvation offered by him.[75] It is hard to imagine any Manichaean giving time to such a notion. Such Christocentrism also constituted a point of distinction from the pagans. Their procreative activity as such could also be considered a 'good work', in that it made reference to God's creativity, but from a Christian perspective this was still insufficient, since it was not oriented towards God.[76] Only an activity oriented towards God could be qualified as theologically 'good'. For people to do good in their procreative activity, they had to do so with the intention of conceiving and birthing children who would become children of God and members of Christ.[77] This latter activity should be achieved, of course, through baptism.[78] Only the *concupiscentia carnis*, only the struggle between the flesh and the spirit, only this particular disharmony was labelled bad and viewed as an indication of the incipient presence of original sin.[79]

Augustine also ascribed an important role to reason with respect to sexual desire. Indeed, reason was capable of making use of the evil of sexual desire in the proper manner (*gr. et pecc. or.* 2.39; CSEL 42.197–8). The reasonable appropriation of sexual desire for procreative purposes was precisely what constituted the correct motivation. In such instances, sexual desire became a procreative means at the disposal of married, rational beings. In all other instances, however, the same rational beings found themselves 'at the disposal' of their own sexual desire, as it were, because they sought nothing other than to satisfy their lust for its own sake.[80] According to Augustine, the person who made proper use of sexual desire within marriage bore no guilt, nor was he or she in the service of the devil as Julian had maintained (*c. Iul. imp.* 5.13; PL 45.1443; ibid., 6.23; PL 45.1557). While it was evident to Augustine that the person who followed the right intention, due to the faculty of reason, was innocent, it was equally evident that a person who sought to satisfy his or her sexual desires via adultery, for example, was guilty of sin because they refused to do what they were capable of doing: saying no to their sexual impulses (see *c. Iul.* 4.39; PL 44.758; ibid., 5.60; PL 44.817).

It would be incorrect, for that matter, to suggest that, for Augustine, the very experience of a sexual impulse was already a sin.[81] Such a statement would have to ignore the fact that as far as Augustine was concerned, even where fallen humanity was concerned, freedom continued to be possible and could be actualised, by the grace of God, in so far as it oriented itself towards the good. It was never Augustine's intention to undermine the moral responsibility of the human person, or to abolish it. It is true that, since the first sin of Adam, humanity had lost the theological *libertas boni* that Adam had once possessed. As believers, however, human persons still retained this real, although relative freedom (*c. Iul. imp.* 6.11; PL 45.1520), which could be actualised within the basic structure of the human will as *liberum arbitrium*. Augustine was unable to accept that the human person had lost the *liberum arbitrium*. For him, free will was innate to human beings and could not be lost. It was ultimately a question of the human will to happiness.[82] This co-natural, inalienable and immutable will belonged, as Augustine would repeatedly stress, to the essence of the human person.[83] Augustine had to defend himself so frequently on this point that it comes across as somewhat strange when commentators state that free will for the bishop of Hippo was lost due to the Fall.[84] Where *concupiscentia* was concerned – whatever form it took – Augustine's position implied that once under grace (*sub gratia*), the human person had the potential to grow, in transcending and gaining victory over his or her irrational desires. If Augustine defined the *concupiscentia carnis* as a *lex peccati*, then his purpose was to show that it was an incitement to sin. In order to speak of an actual sin, however, the assent of the rational human person was still necessary. If desire is still termed a sin, then it has to be understood in the figurative sense: desire understood as sin because it origi-nates in sin and tends towards sin.[85] The *concupiscentia carnis* is no more and no less than an impulse to sin. It only leads to actual sin, however, when a human person gives in to it.[86] If a person says no to his or her unruly desires then that person is being moved to desire (*concupiscere*) by the spirit (*spiritu*) against the *concupiscentia carnis*, in which event there can be no talk of sin (see, for example, *c. Iul.* 4.66; PL 44.771).

In contrast to Julian and a number of modern critics of Augustine (for example, Pagels 1998 p.113), the bishop of Hippo held that although *concu-piscentia* was a disordered impulse, it could still be resisted.[87] Furthermore, it never led to sin if a person stood up to it.[88] He resolutely rejected the claim that with his understanding of an insuperable *concupiscentia carnis*, he had opened the door for immoral behaviour.[89] At the same time, he considered it the duty of every believer who desired to grow in faith to resist sexual desire.[90] Grace had a crucial role to play in the struggle, given that it worked in a liberating and beneficial way for the human persons.[91] Partly due to the dynamic interplay between their own efforts and God's help, such persons pleased God all the more as they struggled against sinful desires (*c. Iul.* 2.5; PL 44.676). Human persons are capable of this because they have received the gift of love and because they are moved by a 'spiritual delight' (*spiritalis delectatio*). Grounded in these gifts, they are able to reduce gradually the intensity of their sinful desires in a growing process of renewal.[93] Ultimately, they receive final healing *as a reward* after death.[94] Such a notion is certainly far from the final destruction of matter as proposed by the Manichaeans.[95] One should take good note of the fact that Augustine does not shy from tersely reminding his readers that a significant number of his contempo-raries, often not without enormous effort, had succeeded in the struggle against the *concupiscentia carnis* (see *c. Iul. imp.* 6.7; PL 45.1513). Even the very way he describes the potentiality for progress in the conflict with sinful desires – a fact insufficiently recognised by his critics, in my opinion – clearly teaches us that we ought to situate the *concupiscentia carnis* in a theological-ethical context.

It is also necessary to underline the fact that Augustine's position is far less strict than one might be led to believe if one focuses too much on his concentrated approach. Ambrose, his spiritual father, or Jerome, his contemporary, had both clearly made an issue of sexuality.[96] Indeed, for both Fathers, it would have been unthinkable to suggest that sexuality belonged to the original essence of the human person.[97] Such was not the case for Augustine. As far as he was concerned, there was actually nothing wrong with the *concupiscentia carnis* in itself, that is, detached from the situation of humanity before and after the Fall. In contrast to a number of Greek Fathers and to Jerome, Augustine certainly no longer considered sexuality and procreation to be a consequence of the Fall from the writing of *De Genesi ad litteram* (AD 401–14) onwards.[98] Prior to the Fall, it was also possible that the *concupiscentia carnis* existed, although it would have been in harmony with the will, a function for the well-being of the body, or an aid to procreation.[99] On this point, the late Augustine had even changed his mind in favour of a potential presence of sexual desire in paradise![100]

It goes without saying that Augustine lived at a time when ascesis, virginity and abstinence were widely propagated. Examples of asexual marriages are legion: Paulinus and Therasia, Turcius Apronianus and Avita, Melania the younger and Pinianus are perhaps the best known examples. Certainly where Augustine was concerned, the resultantly troubled vision of sexual desire was partly due to his reading of Paul (especially 1 Cor 7), and to his own experience with sexuality, which was firmly rooted in the traditional conviction that the choice of marriage was inferior to a life of abstinence.[101] It seemed to make more sense to Augustine that a person should make a radical break with sexual desire, rather than make proper use of it within marriage. Sexual desire – clearly present during sexual union – was a disturbing force running counter to reason, a sign of the fact that all people are born with original sin, an experience which elicited shame and characterised the time after the Fall as marked by sin, suffering and death. Sexual desire was something to be avoided at all costs, rather than exploited, however legitimately.

Before I conclude, I would like to focus on another aspect of Augustine's struggle with desire in general, and sexual desire in particular. For the bishop of Hippo, desire sought its own way and its own fulfilment, and, as such, it ran counter both to the meaning and purpose of human existence (obedience to God) and to the very thing that, for Augustine, constituted a human being as a human being, namely, reason. Desire, with all its irrationality, disorderliness and pursuit of that which is not God, is constituted, therefore, as a *malum* precisely because it does not and will not refer to God. The central concept in Augustine's evaluation of *concupiscentia* is the criterion of faith. Since desire as such distracts the human person from his or her true purpose and, in a certain sense, commands the entire person, it cannot be from God but must belong to the world of the flesh, which is at war with the spirit. The world of the flesh incorporates everything that encourages the human person to place his or her own will above the will of God.[102] Such a theological point of departure has to be taken into account if one is to do justice to Augustine's discussion of (sexual) desire. If one accepts, together with Augustine, that true fulfilment can only be found in the *spiritualis delectatio*, then one cannot avoid recognising that the struggle of the human person against sinful desire prevents him or her, to a greater or lesser extent, from enjoying this intelligible beauty (*c. Iul.* 4.11; PL 44.741–2). It is perhaps due to the irrational tension which exists in the human person that the unimpaired contemplation of the spiritual values is no longer without difficulty. Where the purpose of humanity – life in and for God – hindered by *concupiscentia*'s ungodly aspirations, such *concupiscentia* certainly cannot be good and, as such, it would be better neither to make use of it nor to 'know' it than to use it properly for the sake of procreation. It is for this reason that Augustine had the highest regard, at least on this question, for a life of *Christian* abstinence, within or without marriage (see, for example, *c. Iul. imp.* 4.122; PL 45.1418).

It must also be evident, therefore, that every form of sexuality outside marriage was formally rejected by Augustine. On this level, however, he is on the same wavelength as his predecessors and is in a position to draw good arguments from the Scriptures to defend himself.[103] Up to the present, no author has criticised this aspect of Augustine's teaching, and I therefore leave it undiscussed.

Of course, one is forced to agree with the critics that sexuality for Augustine received a negative evaluation, and that qualifications of sexual activity as sinful and diabolical are at odds with modern day sentiments. At the same time, however, it is also possible to view such things as polemical exaggerations uttered in the heat of debate. In an undated homily, Augustine explains what he understands as daily sin: uttering a harsh word, untempered laughter and other such similar trifles. Curiously enough, he includes going to bed with one's spouse for non-procreative purposes in his list. The latter sin, however, in line with the aforementioned, can be wiped away by the daily giving of alms (see *s.* 9.18; CCL 41.143–4), or by daily prayer (*s.* 179A. and 229E; MiAg. 1.679 and 1.469). In light of this, it would be hard to accept that to concede to sexual desire within marriage was something terrible. We can add, moreover, that those who lived a life of abstinence were also considered guilty if they were to dwell on sexual pleasure with a certain degree of gratification, even when they never indulged the intention of giving in to it (*c. Iul.* 2.33; PL 44.696).

One might ask, in conclusion, whether the fact that the discussion between Julian and Augustine was a discussion between two clerics has not been too quickly overlooked. It is well known that Augustine was very strict with himself and his clergy at the level of sexual desire. At the same time, however, he continued to defend marriage as something good. Expressions such as 'the filth of marriage' never crossed his lips.[104] His rather strongly worded dispute with Julian was a dispute between colleagues in the ministry and was not intended for the people in the pews.[105]

In any case, one has to agree that, for Augustine, the fallen human person had not completely lost his or her freedom, nor was he or she the powerless prey of the *concupiscentia carnis* which was already a sin. As a believer supported by grace, the human person was capable of transcending the *concupiscentia carnis* and making daily progress in his or her struggle against it. It is clear, finally, that in contrast to the belief of the Manichaeans, Augustine did not view the *concupiscentia carnis* as an element of corrupt matter, but rather as affecting the entire person, in so far as he or she is wounded in both body and soul. For Augustine, therefore, the *concupiscentia carnis* was far more than a material instrument at the uncomplicated service of procreation as Julian had opined.[106] On this point, at least, one can say that Augustine was neither a Pelagian nor a Manichaean.[107]

Does what we have said so far infer that Augustine's understanding of sexuality was '*sine peccato*'? Our present day positive sentiments with regard to sexuality would certainly force us to answer no. Augustine and his contemporaries, however, did not believe in sexuality as an enriching factor in the marriage relationship.[108] He was firmly rooted in a tradition – partly confirmed by the Bible – in which the satisfaction of sexual desires as an end itself was rejected.[109] Nevertheless, one would be doing him too great an 'honour' if one were to elevate Augustine alone as the Father of the whole of western history's dealings with sexuality.

Notes

1 U. Ranke-Heinemann, *Eunuchs for the Kingdom of Heaven. Women, Sexuality and the Catholic Church*, tr. P. Heinegg, New York, Doubleday, 1990, p. 75 = *Eunuchen für das Himmelreich. Katholische Kirche und Sexualität*, Hamburg, Hoffmann und Campe, 1988, p. 81.

2 See, for example, M. Müller, *Die Lehre des hl. Augustinus von der Paradiesesehe und ihre Auswirkung in der Sexualethik des 12. und 13. Jahrhunderts bis Thomas von Aquin*, Regensburg, Pustet, 1954, p. 20 and *passim*; K. Flasch, *Augustin. Einführung in sein Denken*, Stuttgart, Philipp Reclam jun., 1980, pp. 209–12.

3 See, for example, my 'Julian of Aeclanum: A Plea for a Good creator', *Augustiniana* 38 (1988), pp. 5–24, at pp. 5–8 (including further bibliography) for an introduction to this interesting figure.

4 Accordingly, the often-noted remark that we only have fragmentary evidence with respect to Julian's contribution to the controversy is incorrect, as E. A. Clark, among others, points out in 'Vitiated Seeds and Holy Vessels: Augustine's Manichaean Past', in her *Ascetic Piety and Women's Faith. Essays on Late Ancient Christianity*, Lewiston / Queenston, 1986, pp. 291–349, at pp. 291–2. See also J. Mausbach's highly accurate, *Die Ethik des heiligen Augustinus*, vol. 2, Freiburg im Breisgau, ²1929, pp. 18–9; and S. Kopp, *Aurelius Augustinus. Schriften gegen die Semipelagianer*, Würzburg, Augustinus-Verlag, 1955, p. 25.

5 A well-structured survey of Julian's various criticisms of Augustine can be

found in Clark, 'Vitiated Seeds', op. cit.

6 For the term *libido*, or one of its derivatives, the figure is forty per cent and for *voluptas* it constitutes twenty per cent. The percentages in question are taken from the Cetedoc Library of Christian Latin Texts (CLCLT) database. As we know, the term *libido* is a classical Latin word while the term *concupiscentia* is a Christian term with a broad, and mostly negative, biblical usage. In this regard, see G. Bonner, 'Libido and concupiscentia in St Augustine', *Studia Patristica* = Texte und Untersuchungen 81, Berlin, Akademie-Verlag, 1962, pp. 302–14, especially pp. 304–9.

7 With regard to Julian's understanding of the first person and his sin, see M. Lamberigts, 'Julien d'Éclane et Augustin d'Hippone: deux conceptions d'Adam', in B. Bruning, M. Lamberigts and J. Van Houtem (eds), *Collectanea Augustiniana. Mélanges T. J. Van Bavel*, Leuven, Institut Historique Augustinien, 1990 [= *Augustiniana* 40 (1990)], pp. 373–410, especially pp. 373–82.

8 See, for example, *Ad Turbantium*, frg. 295; CCL 88.390; *Ad Florum* 4.27; PL 45.1352; and 4.69; PL 45.1378–9.

9 See *Ad Turbantium*, frg. 116; CCL 88.366; see also frg. 233; CCL 88.383.

10 See *Epistula ad Romanos*, frg. 10; CCL 88.397; *Ad Florum* 4.40; PL 45. 1360.

11 The examples are legion; see, for example, *Ad Turbantium*, frg. 41.45; CCL 88.350–1; *Ad Florum* 2.39; CSEL 85/1.191; ibid., 3.182; CSEL 85/1.481; ibid., 4.67; PL 45.1377; ibid., 5.5; PL 45.1435. See also in this regard, M. Abel, 'Le Praedestinatus et le pélagianisme', *Recherches de Théologie ancienne et médiévale* 35 (1968), p. 16; P. Langa, *San Agustín y el progreso de la teología matrimonial*, Toledo, Seminario conciliar, 1984, p. 254.

12 Thus M. Meslin, 'Sainteté et mariage au cours de la seconde querelle pélagienne. Saint Augustin et Julien d'Éclane', *Études carmélitaines* 31 (1952), pp. 293–307, at p. 297. See, however, *Ad Florum* 3.142; CSEL 85/1.447; ibid., 5.16; PL 45.1449. See also A. Bruckner, *Julian von Eclanum. Sein Leben und Seine Lehre. Ein Beitrag zur Geschichte des Pelagianismus*, Leipzig, Akademie-Verlag, 1897, p. 140; Lamberigts, op. cit., pp. 16–9.

13 See, for example, *Ad Turbantium*, frg. 197; CCL 88.379; frg. 49; CCL 88.49; frg. 63; CCL 88.356; frg. 84; CCL 88.362. A similar position can be found, for example, in Ambrose, *De virginibus* 6; PL 16.206ff.; *De virginitate* 6; PL 16.286ff.

14 See, for example, *Ad Turbantium*, frg. 233; CCL 88.383; see also frg. 116; CCL 88.366; *Ad Florum* 4.59; PL 45.1374–5.

15 See, for example, *Ad Turbantium*, frg. 45.48; CCL 88.351; frg. 62; CCL 88.356; frg. 135–6; CCL 88.368–9; frg. 194, 198; CCL 88.378–9.

16 A presentation of the indirect critique of individuals such as Cassian would take us beyond the scope of the present article.

17 For Augustine's position on the question see, for example, *nupt. et conc.* 2.9.21; CSEL 42.273.

18 This criticism can be found repeatedly in Julian's work. See, for example, *Epistula ad Romanos*, frg. 2; CCL 88.396; *Ad Florum* 1.62; CSEL 85/1.58; ibid., 1.65; CSEL 85/1.63; ibid., 4.77; PL 45.1382–3.

19 *Ad Turbantium*, frg. 257; CCL 88.386 contains all the above mentioned accusations in one place; see also, for example, *Epistula ad Romanos*, frg. 3; CCL

88.397; *Ad Turbantium*, frg. 36; CCL 88.349; *Ad Florum* 2.228; CSEL 85/1.329.

20 See, for example, *Ad Turbantium*, frg. 1; CCL 88.340–1; frg. 15; CCL 88.343; frg. 62; CCL 88.356; frg. 66b; CCL 88.357; frg. 78; CCL 88.360; frg. 184; CCL 88.377; frg. 186; CCL 88.186, etc. Lack of space prevents me from offering a more detailed presentation of Julian's knowledge of Manichaeism. Suffice to say that during a trip to Carthage he met Honoratus, a Manichaean not unknown to Augustine himself; see *Ad Florum* 5.26; PL 45.1464. With respect to Honoratus, see A. Mandouze, *Prosopographie de l'Afrique chrétienne (303–533)*, Paris, CNRS, 1982, p. 564. In addition, Julian also seems to have been familiar with a work of Serapion of Thmuis directed against the Manichaeans; see N. Cipriani, 'L'Autore dei testi pseudobasiliani riportati nel C. Iulianum (I, 16–17) e la polemica agostiniana di Giuliano d'Eclano', in *Congresso internationale su S Agostino nel XVI centenario della conversione (15–20 settembre 1986)*, vol. 1, Rome: Institutum Patristicum «Augustinianum», 1987, pp. 439–49.

21 See *Ad Florum*, 3.166ff.; CSEL 85/1.469ff.; see also in this regard G. J. D. Aalders, 'L'Épître à Menoch, attribuée à Mani', *Vigiliae Christianae* 14 (1960), pp. 245–9. With respect to Julian's accusations, see also Clark, op. cit., especially pp. 304–15.

22 See *Ad Florum* 3.74; CSEL 85/1.475; 3.180; CSEL 85/1.480. With respect to the accuracy of this position, see J. van Oort, 'Augustine and Mani on *concupiscentia sexualis*. Some Remarks', in *Augustiniana Traiectina*, ed. J. den Boeft and J. van Oort, Paris, Etudes augustiniennes, 1987, pp. 137–52, especially pp. 140–5.

23 The text appeals to Rom 7:19; 9:16; Gal 5:17, 19, 22; see *Ad Florum* 3.177; CSEL 85/1.477.

24 Although the limits of space prevent me from offering more detail, it should be noted that Julian, at least in these passages, also points to the differences between Augustine and the Manichaean text; see, for example, *Ad Florum* 3.180–2; CSEL 85/1.480–1.

25 See E. Pagels, *Adam, Eve, and the Serpent*, New York, Random House, 1988, p. 111, with reference to *pecc. mer.* 2.22.36; CSEL 60.108.

26 See Pagels, op. cit., pp. 113 and 131.

27 The present article will not deal with the idea of marriage as a *societas*, a notion so important to Augustine. On this question, see the excellent study of D. G. Hunter, 'Augustinian Pessimism? A New Look at Augustine's Teaching on Sex, Marriage and Celibacy', *Augustinian Studies* 25 (1994), pp. 153–77.

28 See *nupt. et conc.* 2.23; CSEL 42.275; ibid., 2.52; CSEL 42.308; *c. Iul.* 4.17; PL 44.746; *ciu.* 14.7; CCL 48.422; see also A.-M. La Bonnardière, *Biblia Augustiniana. A. T. Le livre de la Sagesse*, Paris, Études augustiniennes, 1970, pp. 103 and 280.

29 Thus *c. ep. Pel.* 2.17; CSEL 60.479; ibid., 2.21; CSEL 60.482.

30 See *en. Ps.* 118.8.3; CCL 40.1687. For the use of *concupiscentia* and *libido* in Augustine, see, for example, G. Bonner, 'Libido', op. cit.; idem, 'Concupiscentia', in *Augustinus-Lexikon*, vol. 1, ed. C. Mayer, Basel, Schwabe, 1994, cc. 1113–22 (with further literature); J. van Oort, 'Augustine on Sexual Concupiscence and Original Sin', in *Studia Patristica*. Papers presented to the Tenth International Conference on Patristic Studies held in Oxford 1987, vol.

22, ed. E. Livingstone, Leuven, Peeters, 1989, pp. 382–6; J. M. Rist, *Augustine. Ancient Thought Baptized*, Cambridge, Cambridge University Press, ²1995, especially pp. 320–7.

31 See, for example, *en. Ps.* 136.19; CCL 40.1977; *s.* 2.3; CCL 41.12; *ep.* 95.6; CSEL 34/2.511; 175.2; CSEL 44.655; *retr.* 1.19.1; CCL 57.56; ibid., 1.23; CCL 57.67; ibid., 1.24; CCL 57.72.

32 *Ciu.* 14.15; CCL 48.438–9. See also E. Schmitt, *Le mariage chrétien dans l'oeuvre de saint Augustin. Une théologie baptismale de la vie conjugale*, Paris, Etudes augustiniennes, 1983, pp. 102–4. See also *c. Iul. imp.* 4.28; PL 45.1352.

33 See Bonner, 'Concupiscentia', op. cit., cc. 1114–5.

34 See G. Mayer, אָוָה , *Theologisches Wörterbuch zum Alten Testament*, vol. 1, Stuttgart/Berlin/Köln/Mainz, Kohlhammer, 1970, cc. 145–8, at c. 148.

35 See G. Stählin, επιθυμια, *Theologisches Wörterbuch zum Neuen Testament*, vol. 2, Stuttgart, Kohlhammer, ²1960, cc. 911–28, especially 920–8; F. Büchsel, ἡδονη , in *Theologisches Wörterbuch zum Neuen Testament*, vol. 3, Stuttgart, Kohlhammer, ²1957, cc. 168–72. K. E. Børresen, 'Patristic Feminism: The Case of Augustine', *Augustinian Studies* 25 (1994), pp. 139–52, at pp. 148–9, rightly points out that to read 'sola pars scripturae' is not enough. See also Bonner, 'Concupiscentia', op. cit., c. 1115 (with further literature), for Augustian's own position, in line with Tertullian and Cyprian.

36 For the version employed by Augustine, see B. Fischer (ed.), *Vetus Latina*, vol. 2, *Genesis*, Freiburg, Herder, 1951, pp. 55–6 and 62.

37 See *c. Iul. imp.* 3.74; CSEL 85/1.404.

38 *C. Iul. imp.* 4.69; PL 45.1379; see also *c. Iul.* 5.28; PL 44.802; ibid., 5.16; PL 44.793; ibid., 5.41; PL 44.845. See also N. Cipriani, 'Una teoria neoplatonica alla base dell'etica sessuale di S. Agostino', *Augustinianum* 14 (1974), pp. 351–61; P. Fredriksen, 'Beyond the Body/Soul Dichotomy. Augustine on Paul against the Manichees and the Pelagians', *Recherches augustiniennes* 23 (1988), pp. 87–114, especially pp. 105–14; Rist, op. cit., p. 120.

39 *C. Iul. imp.* 6.9; PL 45.1514. Although the senses were also considered part of this desire, the process of desire as such implied something more than the senses; in this regard see *c. Iul.* 4.65–6; PL 44.769–70; ibid., 6.56; PL 44.856; *c. Iul. imp.* 4.27; PL 45.1352; ibid., 4.29; PL 45.1353; ibid., 4.47–9; PL 45.1366–7; ibid., 4.53; PL 45.1370. See also in this regard, E. Samek Lodovici, 'Sessualità, matrimonio e concupiscenza in Agostino', in *Etica sessuale e matrimonio nel cristianesimo delle origini*, ed. R. Cantalamessa, Milan, Vita e pensiero, 1976, pp. 212–72, especially pp. 249–51.

40 See, for example, *c. Iul.* 5.12; PL 44.790; *c. Iul. imp.* 1.47; CSEL 85/1.34–6.

41 *Nupt. et conc.* 1.7; CSEL 42.218; see also ibid., 1.24; CSEL 42.237; ibid., 2.14; CSEL 42.266; *ciu.* 14 brings all this together in a very succinct manner. It should be noted here that, for Augustine and his predecessors alike, it was an obvious fact that people ought to obey God as a duty and source of happiness. For Augustine and the majority of the Fathers, it was also a matter of logic that disobedience with respect to God had to lead, in one way or another, to some form of punishment; in this regard, see the well-documented conclusions of J. Gross, *Entstehungsgeschichte des Erbsündendogmas. Von der Bibel bis Augustinus*, Munich / Basel, 1960, Reinhardt, pp. 254–5. The fact that Augustine differed less from his predecessors on the question of *concupiscentia* than is often assumed

has been clearly demonstrated by P. Burnell, 'Concupiscence and Moral Freedom in Augustine and Before Augustine', *Augustinian Studies* 26 (1995), pp. 49–63.

42 *Nupt. et conc.* 1.7; CSEL 42.219; see also *c. ep. Pel.* 1.32; CSEL 60.450.

43 See *c. Iul.* 3.39; PL 44. 722; ibid., 4.3; PL 44. 738; ibid., 5.32; PL 44. 804.

44 See, for example, *nupt. et conc.* 1.8; CSEL 42.219; ibid., 1.24; CSEL 42.237; ibid., 2.14; CSEL 42. 266; ibid., 2.16; CSEL 42.268; ibid., 2.36; CSEL 42.290; ibid., 2.52; CSEL 42.308–9; ibid., 2.54–5; CSEL 42.311–2; *c. ep. Pel.* 1.33; CSEL 60.450; *c. Iul.* 4.82; PL 44.781; *c. Iul. imp.* 3.184; CSEL 85/1.483; ibid., 4.37; PL 45.1357; ibid., 4.43; PL 45.1363. See also F.-J. Thonnard, 'Pudeur, révolte des sens et lois psychologiques', in *Premières polémiques contre Julien* [= BA 23], Paris, Desclée de Brouwer, 1974, pp. 671–5.

45 See, for example, *nupt. et conc.* 1.7; CSEL 42.218; ibid., 2.14; CSEL 42.266. Other qualifications of 'desire', such as wound, sickness, infection, evil, should also be associated with the idea of punishment due to the Fall.

46 For a detailed commentary on Rom 7 as Paul's personal witness to his Christianity (Augustine's position since AD 418), see *c. ep. Pel.* 1.13–25; CSEL 60.433–5. The literature on Augustine's use of Rom 7 is boundless; an outstanding survey can be found in M.-F. Berrouard, 'L'exégèse augustinienne de Rom 7,7–25 entre 396 et 418 avec des remarques sur les deux premières périodes de la crise «Pélagienne»', *Recherches augustiniennes* 16 (1981), pp. 101–95.

47 *Nupt. et conc.* 1.25; CSEL 42.237; ibid., 1.28; CSEL 42.241; ibid., 1.30; CSEL 42.241; *c. Iul.* 4.2; PL 44.737; *c. Iul. imp.* 4.69; PL 45.1379; see also *c. Iul.* 4.7; PL 44.739; ibid., 6.50; PL 44.852; *c. Iul. imp.* 1.71; CSEL 85/1.82.

48 In all respects, Augustine himself makes a clear distinction between perception as such and a perception that has its origins in a sinful desire; see esp. *c. Iul.* 4.65; PL 44.769–70; see also ibid., 6.56; PL 44.856; *c. Iul. imp.* 4.29; PL 45.1353; ibid., 4.47–8; PL 45.1366; ibid., 4.53; PL 45. 1370. See also Schmitt, op. cit., pp. 102–4.

49 It constitutes a problem for rational human beings but not, for example, for animals in which the *bonum rationis* is absent; see *c. Iul. imp.* 4.58; PL 45.1374; see also ibid., 2.122; CSEL 85/1.253; ibid., 4.37; PL 45.1357; ibid., 4.38; PL 45.1359; ibid., 4.39; PL 45.1359–60; ibid., 4.43; PL 45.1362–3; ibid., 4.56; PL 45.1372; ibid., 5.8; PL 45.1436; ibid., 5.20; PL 45.1453; *c. Iul.* 4.74; PL 44.776. See also Y. de Montcheuil, 'La polémique de saint Augustin contre Julien d'Éclane d'après l'Opus imperfectum', *Recherches de science religieuse* 44 (1956), pp. 193–218 and 215; F. Refoulé, 'Misère des enfants et péché originel d'après saint Augustin', *Revue thomiste* 63 (1963), pp. 341–62 esp. 352; A.-M. Dubarle, *Le péché originel. Perspectives théologiques*, Paris, Cerf, 1983, pp. 37–8.

50 See, for example, *nupt. et conc.* 1.1; CSEL 42.212; ibid., 1.6; CSEL 42.217–18; ibid., 1.7; CSEL 42.218–9; ibid., 1.8; CSEL 42.219–20; ibid., 1.9; CSEL 42.221; ibid., 1.13; CSEL 42.226; ibid., 1.18; CSEL 42.230; ibid., 1.19; CSEL 42.232; ibid., 1.24; CSEL 42.237; ibid., 1.27; CSEL 42.239; ibid., 2.14; CSEL 42.266; ibid., 2.16; CSEL 42.269; ibid., 2.17; CSEL 42.270; ibid., 2.18; CSEL 42.271; ibid., 2.20; CSEL 42.272; ibid., 2.22; CSEL 42.275; ibid., 2.23; CSEL 42.275; ibid., 2.26; CSEL 42.279; ibid., 2.29; CSEL 42.283; ibid., 2.36; CSEL 42.290; ibid., 2.37; CSEL 42.291; ibid., 2.42; CSEL 42.296; ibid., 2.52; CSEL

42.308–9; ibid., 2.53; CSEL 42. 310; ibid., 2.54; CSEL 42.312; ibid., 2.55; CSEL 42.312; ibid., 2.59; CSEL 42.316; *c. ep. Pel.* 1.33; CSEL 60.450; *c. Iul.* 3.26–7; PL 44.715–6; ibid., 3.38; PL 44.722; ibid., 3.42; PL 44.723; ibid., 4.40; PL 44.741; ibid., 5.30; PL 44.803; *c. Iul. imp.* 3.184; CSEL 85/1.483; ibid., 4.37; PL 45.1357; ibid., 4.43; PL 45.1363; ibid., 4.63; PL 45.1376; see *b. coniug.* 10.11; CSEL 41.203; ibid., 16.18; CSEL 41.210–1. See also de Montcheuil, op. cit., pp. 205–6; Thonnard, op. cit.

51 For an excellent introduction to the problem, see G. Sfameni Gasparro, 'Natura e origine del male: alle radici dell'incontro e del confronto di Agostino con la gnosi manichea', in *Il mistero del male e la libertà possibile: lettura dei Dialoghi di Agostino*, ed. L. Alici, R. Piccolomini and A. Pieretti, Rome, Institutum Patristicum «Augustinianum», 1994, pp. 7–55.

52 See, for example, *c. Iul.* 6.53; PL 44.854; *c. Iul. imp.* 3.167; CSEL 85/1.470; see also L. Scheffczyk, *Urstand, Fall und Erbsünde. Von der Schrift bis Augustinus*, Freiburg / Basel / Wien, Herder, 1981.

53 See W. Geerlings, 'Zur Frage des Nachwirkens des Manichäismus in der Theologie Augustins', *Zeitschrift für katholische Theologie* 93 (1971), pp. 45–60, at pp. 58–9.

54 *Nupt. et conc.* 1.1; CSEL 42.212; ibid., 6–9; CSEL 42.217–21; ibid., 1.13; CSEL 42.226; ibid., 1.18; CSEL 42.230; ibid., 1.19; CSEL 42.232; ibid., 1.24; CSEL 42.237; ibid., 1.27; CSEL 42.239; ibid., 2.14; CSEL 42.266; ibid., 2.17–18; CSEL 42.270–1; ibid., 2.20; CSEL 42.272; ibid., 2.22–3; CSEL 42.274–5; ibid., 2.26; CSEL 42.279; ibid., 2.29; CSEL 42.283; ibid., 2.36–7; CSEL 42.290–1; ibid., 2.42; CSEL 42.296; ibid., 2.52–4; CSEL 42.308–12; ibid., 2.59; CSEL 42.316; *c. Iul.* 3.26–7; PL 44.715–16; ibid., 3.38; PL 44. 722; ibid., 3.42; PL 44.723; ibid., 4.7; PL 44.739; ibid., 6.50; PL 44.852; ibid., 4.10; PL 44.741; ibid., 5.30; PL 44.803. See also de Montcheuil, op. cit., pp. 205–6.

55 My deficient knowledge of psychology does not permit me to react to Flasch (op. cit., p. 49), who proposes that pathological elements were involved here.

56 In this regard, see P. Brown, *The Body and Society. Men, Women and Sexual Renunciation in Early Christianity*, New York, Columbia University Press, 1988, pp. 393–5.

57 *Conf.* 3.1.1; CCL 27.27; see also *conf.* 6.12.22; CCL 27.88, and the description of his personal interior struggle between the flesh and the spirit in *conf.* 8.5.10–11; CCL 27.119–20.

58 *Conf.* 8.12.29; CCL 27.131. A glance at Book 10 shows, in addition, that when Augustine speaks of 'the flesh' he is also thinking of eating and drinking.

59 *Conf.* 8.11.27; CCL 27.130; ibid., 10.29.40; CCL 27.176.

60 Indeed, the late Augustine was to note that abstinence was more difficult for those who had had some sexual experience than for those who had never 'known' it; *c. Iul.* 6.55; PL 44.855.

61 *B. coniug.* 3.3; CSEL 41.191; other examples can be found in, for example, *pecc. mer.* 1.57; CSEL 60.56; *nupt. et conc.* 1.8; CSEL 42.220; ibid., 2.36; CSEL 42.290; *c. ep. Pel.* 1.33; CSEL 60.450; *c. Iul.* 3.15; PL 44.709; ibid., 3.30; PL 44.718; ibid., 3.41; PL 44.725; ibid., 3.50; PL 44.728; ibid., 3.52–4; PL 44.729–30; ibid., 4.6–7; PL 44.739; *c. Iul. imp.* 2.45; CSEL 85/1.195; ibid., 3.183; CSEL 85/1.482; ibid., 5.17–18; PL 45.1451.

62 *B. coniug.* 6.6; CSEL 41.195; see also, for example, *b. uid.* 4.5; CSEL 41.308–9; *ciu.* 21.26; CCL 48.797.

63 See, for example, *nupt. et conc.* 1.1; CSEL 42.212; ibid., 2.25; CSEL 42.278; *pecc. mer.* 1.57; CSEL 60.56–7; *gr. et pecc. or.* 2.38–45; CSEL 42.196–203; *ep.* 6*.3–8; CSEL 88.32–8; *c. Iul. imp.* 2.45; CSEL 85/1.195; ibid., 2.122; CSEL 85/1.253. In this regard, see also Schmitt op. cit., pp. 51–3, 193–4; Langa, op. cit., pp. 265–7; E. A. Clark, 'Adam's Only Companion: Augustine and the Early Christian Debate on Marriage', *Recherches augustiniennes* 21 (1986), pp. 139–62, at p. 149.

64 *B. coniug.* 10.11; CSEL 41.203; see also ibid., 13.15; CSEL 41.207; *nupt. et conc.* 1.16; CSEL 42.228; *c. Iul.* 3.30; PL 44.718.

65 *Nupt. et conc.* 1.5; CSEL 42.215; ibid., 1.8; CSEL 42.219; ibid., 1.11; CSEL 42.223; ibid., 1.17; CSEL 42.229; ibid., 2.19; CSEL 42.271; ibid., 2.37; CSEL 42.291; ibid., 2.54; CSEL 42.311; *c. Iul.* 3.30; PL 44.717; ibid., 3.43; PL 44.724; *c. Iul. imp.* 5.23; PL 45.1459; see also Schmitt, op. cit., p. 265. For children's legal security, see *c. Iul. imp.* 6.30; PL 45.1582.

66 'I say this by way of concession, and not as a commandment'. Although Augustine was also familiar with the reading 'secundum indulgentiam'; see *mor.* 1.78; PL 32.1344; *spec.* 31; CSEL 12.212.

67 See 'Sermons inédits de saint Augustin prêchés en 397, E. Sermo de Bono Nuptiarum', ed. F. Dolbeau, in *Revue Bénédictine* 92 (1992), pp. 267–97, at pp. 278–80. With respect to the *tabulae* spoken of in this text, see M. Marin, 'Le 'Tabulae Matrimoniales' in S Agostino', *Siculorum Gymnasium* 29 (1976), pp. 307–21; O. M. Péter, 'L'image idéale du mariage et de la filiation à Rome', *Revue internationale des droits de l'Antiquité* 38 (1991), pp. 285–331.

68 See, for example, *doctr. chr.* 3.27; CCL 32.93; *b. coniug.* 6.6; CSEL 41.195; ibid., 10.11; CSEL 41.202–3; *b. uid.* 3.5; CSEL 41.308–9; *s.* 51.22–3, *Revue Bénédictine* 91 (1981), p. 37; *ep.* 6*.7; CSEL 88.37; *ench.* 21.78; CCL 46.92; *nupt. et conc.*1.16; CSEL 42.228–9; *c. ep. Pel.* 1.33; CSEL 60.450; ibid., 3.14; CSEL 60.502; *c. Iul.* 3.30; PL 44.718; *c. Iul. imp.* 4.29; PL 45.1353. See also Lodovici, op. cit., pp. 243–5.

69 *B. coniug.* 11.12; CSEL 41.203–4; *b. uid.* 3.5; CSEL 41.308–9; *ep.* 6*.7; CSEL 88.37; *ench.* 21.78; CCL 46.92.

70 *Nupt. et conc.* 1.16–17; CSEL 42.229; *c. Iul.* 3.43; PL 44.724; see also A. Zumkeller, *Aurelius Augustinus, Schriften gegen die Pelagianer*, vol. 3, *Sankt Augustinus, Der Lehrer der Gnade*, Würzburg, Augustinus-Verlag, 1977, p. 429; D. Covi, 'El fin de la actividad sexual según San Agustín', *Augustinus* 17 (1972), pp. 47–65, especially pp. 60ff.

71 The following references are a mere sample from among the many: *nupt. et conc.*1.23. CSEL 42.236; ibid., 2.14; CSEL 42.265; ibid., 2.16; CSEL 42.269; ibid., 2.23; CSEL 42.275; ibid., 2.36; CSEL 42.290; ibid., 2.42; CSEL 42.296; ibid., 2.53; CSEL 42.310; *gr. et pecc. or.* 2.40; CSEL 42.198–9; *c. Iul.* 3.14; PL 44.709; ibid., 3.60; PL 44.732–3; *c. Iul. imp.* 4.10; PL 45.1344; ibid., 4.118; PL 44.1412.

72 See protests in, for example, *c. Iul.* 4.4; PL 44.738; ibid., 4.34; PL 44.756; ibid., 4.38; PL 44.757; ibid., 4.49; PL 44.762; *c. Iul. imp.* 5.7; PL 45.1437.

73 See *nupt. et conc.* 2.36; CSEL 42.290; *c. Iul.* 3.15–16; PL 44.709–10; ibid., 4.7; PL 44.739; *c. Iul. imp.* 4.115; PL 45.1409; ibid., 4.117; PL 45.1411; ibid.,

5.23; PL 45.1459; ibid., 5.24; PL 45.1461; see also Müller, op. cit., p. 29–30; Schmitt, op. cit., pp. 265–6.

74 See, for example, Clark, 'Adam's Only Companion', op. cit., pp. 146–7; ibid, *Ascetic Piety*, op. cit., pp. 319–20.

75 See, for example, *b. coniug.* 19.22; CSEL 41.216; *pecc. mer.* 2.45; CSEL 60.116; *nupt. et conc.* 1.5; CSEL 42.215–16; ibid., 1.19; CSEL 42.231; ibid., 1.27; CSEL 42.240; *c. ep. Pel.* 1.10; CSEL 60.431; *c. Iul.* 3.66; PL 44.736; *c. Iul. imp.* 1.62; CSEL 85/1.58; ibid., 1.109; CSEL 85/1.128; ibid., 6.12; PL 45.1523; *s.* 260D.2; MiAg 1.500; *s.* 317.3; PL 38.1436; *s.* 370.4; PL 39.1659; *ep.* 202A.8; CSEL 57.313; *ench.* 14.49; CCL 46.75–6.

76 *Nupt. et conc.* 2.54; CSEL 42.311; *c. Iul.* 4.36; PL 44.757; ibid., 4.38; PL 44.758.

77 *Nupt. et conc.* 1.5; CSEL 42.215–16; ibid., 1.19; CSEL 42.231; *c. ep. Pel.* 1.11; CSEL 60.431; *c. Iul.* 4.3; PL 44.737–8; ibid., 4.39; PL 44.758; ibid., 4.49; PL 44.763; ibid., 5.41; PL 44.808; see also D. Covi, 'Valor y finalidad del sexo según San Agustín', *Augustinus* 17 (1972), p. 183.

78 *Nupt. et conc.* 1.5; CSEL 42. 215; ibid., 1.9; CSEL 42. 220–1; ibid., 1.19; CSEL 42.231; *c. Iul.* 4.50; PL 44.763. See also Schmitt, op. cit.

79 See, for example, *c. Iul.* 3.18; PL 44.711; ibid., 4.49; PL 44.763; ibid., 4.65; PL 44.770; *c. Iul. imp.* 2.59; CSEL 85/1.207. That original sin and the *concupiscentia carnis* do not coincide is already apparent from the fact that the guilt due to original sin is wiped out by baptism while the *concupiscentia* as such continues to exist. Augustine himself, moreover, makes a clear distinction between both concepts; see, for example, *nupt. et conc.* 1.25; CSEL 42.237–8; ibid., 1.27; CSEL 42.240; ibid., 2.15; CSEL 42.267; ibid., 2.20; CSEL 42.272; *c. ep. Pel.* 1.27; CSEL 42.445; *c. Iul.* 6.47; PL 44.849; ibid., 6.73; PL 44.868; *c. Iul. imp.* 2.42; CSEL 85/1.193; ibid., 2.71; CSEL 85/1.215.

80 See Lodovici, op. cit., pp. 261–2.

81 See Pagels, op. cit., p. 111; van Oort, op. cit., p. 386.

82 *C. Iul. imp.* 6.11; PL 45.1520; *c. Iul. imp.* 6.12; PL 45.1524; see also ibid., 6.26; PL 45.1565–6; *c. ep. Pel.* 1.5; CSEL 60.425; ibid., 2.9; CSEL 60.468; see also *ciu.* 22.30; CCL 48.862ff. A massive amount of literature has been written on the distinction between *libertas* and *liberum arbitrium*. M. Huftier, 'Libre arbitre, liberté et péché chez saint Augustin', *Recherches de théologie ancienne et médiévale* 33 (1966), pp. 187–281, continues to be the primary study; see also F. Clodius, 'El libre albedrío según el "Opus Imperfectum" de san Agustín', *Anales de la Facultad de Teología* 13 (1961), pp. 5–51; F.-J. Thonnard, 'La notion de nature chez saint Augustin, Ses progrès dans la polémique antipélagienne', *Revue des études augustiniennes* 11 (1965), pp. 239–65; A. Mengarelli, 'La libertà nelle opere antipelagiane di S Agostino', *Sapienza* 29 (1976), pp. 73–81; F. J. Weismann, 'The Problematic of Freedom in St Augustine: Towards a New Hermeneutics', *Revue des études augustiniennes* 35 (1989), pp. 104–19. See further H. Staffner, 'Die Lehre des hl. Augustinus über das Wesen der Erbsünde,' *Zeitschrift für katholische Theologie* 79 (1957), pp. 385–416, which underlines the fact that, for Augustine, the human person was unable to find his or her own happiness within, precisely because he or she was made for God (p. 397). See further in this regard *ciu.* 12.9; CCL 48.363–4; ibid., 13.2; CCL 48.385–6; ibid., 19.25; CCL 48.696. I have the impression that a writer such as Flasch (op. cit., pp. 189–90) does not do

justice to the aforementioned (and other) texts when he proposes that the human person as human person is not free. He pays too little attention, moreover, to the theological perspective within which Augustine discusses the relationship between *libertas* and *liberum arbitrium*. See G. Madec's pertinent critique in, 'Sur une nouvelle introduction à la pensée d'Augustin', *Revue des études augustiniennes* 27 (1982), pp. 100–11, especially p. 109.

83 See *c. Iul. imp.* 5.38; PL 45.1474; ibid., 6.12; PL 45.1524; ibid., 6.25; PL 45.1565.

84 See Pagels, op. cit., pp. 99, 105, 107, 109, 120. See my reaction: 'Augustine, Julian of Aeclanum and E. Pagels' *Adam, Eve, and the Serpent*', *Augustiniana* 39 (1989), pp. 393–435, especially pp. 396–407.

85 *Nupt. et conc.* 1.25; CSEL 42.238; *c. Iul. imp.* 1.71; CSEL 85/1.84.

86 See the clear examples in *c. Iul.* 4.66–7; PL 44.770–1; see also *nupt. et conc.* 2.58; CSEL 42.316; *c. Iul. imp.*6.3; PL 45.1511; ibid., 6.6; PL 45.1511.

87 I wonder whether it is not possible to speak of a widespread philosophical conviction with respect to the *motus inordinatus* of the *concupiscentia carnis*. See the association made by Augustine with the Neoplatonists in *ciu.* 14.19; CCL 48.441. Even Plato himself was familiar with the idea; see *Laws* 2.660b; 8.840e. At the same time, it is worth noting that when Augustine speaks of this sexual impulse he repeatedly refers to the Scriptures: *c. Iul.* 3.27; PL 44.716 (Rom 7:18b); ibid., 5.30; PL 44.803 (Rom 7:18b); ibid., 6.40; PL 44.844–5 (Gal 5:17); *c. Iul. imp.* 1.68; CSEL 85/1.75 (Rom 7:18).

88 E. Pagels, *Adam, Eve and the Serpent*, New York, Random House, 1998. See, for example, *c. Iul.* 2.33; PL 44.696–7; ibid., 4.34; PL 44.756; ibid., 4.73; PL 44.775; *c. Iul. imp.* 3.185; CSEL 85/1.484; ibid., 3.187; CSEL 85/1.490; ibid., 3.212; CSEL 85/1.504; ibid., 4.10. PL 45.1344; ibid., 4.57; PL 45.1373; ibid., 4.61; PL 45.1375; ibid., 4.67; PL 45.1378; ibid., 5.15; PL 45.1436; ibid., 5.16; PL 45.1449. The list could be extended without difficulty. In any event, it is clear that Augustine is speaking in earnest when he states that the human person is capable of successfully resisting this sinful desire.

89 *C. Iul.* 3.65; PL 44.735–6; ibid., 5.32; PL 44.804; see also ibid., 3.39; PL 44.722; ibid., 5.24; PL 44.799; ibid., 5.27; PL 44.801.

90 *C. Iul.* 2.3; PL 44.673; ibid., 2.5; PL 44.675; see also, for example, ibid., 3.49; PL 44.727; ibid., 6.47; PL 44.849--50; ibid., 6.50; PL 44.852; ibid., 6.53; PL 44.853; ibid., 6.62; PL 44.860–1.

91 For grace as 'liberating' see *c. ep. Pel.* 1.18; CSEL 60.440; as 'beneficial' see, for example, *c. Iul.* 2.5; PL 44.676; ibid., 2.9; PL 44.680; ibid., 5.65; PL 44.820; ibid., 6.20; PL 44.829; *c. Iul. imp.* 1.70; CSEL 85/1.78; ibid., 2.218; CSEL 85/1.330; ibid., 4.57. PL 45.1373; ibid., 6.8. PL 45.1514.

92 For the gift of love, *c. Iul.* 5.32; PL 44.804; ibid., 5.56; PL 44.815; ibid., 6.41; PL 44.845–6; ibid., 6.71; PL 44.866; *c. Iul. imp.* 2.71; CSEL 85/1.215; ibid., 2.137; CSEL 85/1.262; ibid., 2.140; CSEL 85/1.264; ibid., 2.233; CSEL 85/1.347; ibid., 6.15; PL 45.1535. For spiritial delight, see *c. ep. Pel.* 1.17; CSEL 60.440.

93 See especially *nupt. et conc.* 1.28; CSEL 42.240; *c. Iul.* 2.7; PL 44.678; see also *nupt. et conc.* 1.30; CSEL 42.242; ibid., 1.32; CSEL 42.244; ibid., 1.33; CSEL 42.245; ibid., 1.56; CSEL 42.248; *c. Iul.* 6.41; PL 44.845; ibid., 6.50; PL 44.852; ibid., 6.56; PL 44.856; ibid., 6.60; PL 44.859; *c. Iul. imp.* 3.71; CSEL

85/1.403; ibid., 4.57; PL 45.1373; ibid., 6.8; PL 45.1514.

94 See *c. Iul.* 6.50; PL 44.852; see also ibid., 4.3; PL 44.738; *c. Iul. imp.* 6.7; PL 45.1512.

95 See van Oort, op. cit., pp. 385–6.

96 See P. Brown, 'Sexuality and Society in the Fifth Century AD: Augustine and Julian of Eclanum', in *Tria corda, Scritti in onore di A. Momigliano*, ed. E. Gabba, Como, New Press, 1983, pp. 49–70 and 67ff.; idem, *Body and Society*, op. cit., pp. 341–86.

97 Brown, *Body and Society*, op. cit., pp. 399–400.

98 See Hunter, op. cit., pp. 166–7.

99 See *c. Iul.* 4.69; PL 44.773; see *c. Iul.* 3.57; PL 44.732; *nupt. et conc.* 2.59; CSEL 42.317–8; *c. ep. Pel.* 1.34–5; CSEL 60.450–2; *c. Iul. imp.*1.68; CSEL 85/1.75. See also Zumkeller, op. cit., p. 471; Clark, *Ascetic Piety*, op. cit., p. 293.

100 *C. ep. Pel.* 1.34; CSEL 60.450–1; *c. Iul.* 4.57; PL 44.765; ibid., 4.62; PL 44.768; *c. Iul. imp.* 1.68; CSEL 85/1.75; ibid., 1.70; CSEL 85/1.79–80; ibid., 1.71; CSEL 85/1.83; ibid., 2.39; CSEL 85/1.191. See Lamberigts, 'Julien d'Éclane', op. cit., pp. 388–91 (with additional bibliography).

101 See Hunter, op. cit., pp. 155–6 (with additional literature).

102 *Gn. litt* 10.20; CSEL 28/1.324; *ciu.* 14.3; CCL 48.416–8.

103 Besides the tractate *adult. coniug.*, see, for example, *b. coniug.* 4.4; CSEL 41.191–3; ibid., 6.6; CSEL 41.194–5; ibid., 8.8; CSEL 41.198–9; *nupt. et conc.* 1.27; CSEL 42.239; *c. Iul. imp.* 5.17; PL 45.1450; ibid., 5.17–18; PL 45.1450–1; ibid., 5.20; PL 45.1453; see also A.-M. La Bonnardière, 'Adulterium', *Augustinus-Lexikon*, vol. 1, ed. C. Mayer, Basel, Schwabe, 1986, cc. 125–37.

104 See Jerome, *Adversus Jovinianum* 1.26; PL 33.274A.

105 Brown is correct in this regard, see *Body and Society*, op. cit., p. 397.

106 Gross, op. cit., p. 312.

107 See G. R. Evans, 'Neither a Pelagian nor a Manichee', *Vigiliae Christianae* 35 (1981), pp. 232–44.

108 Brown, *Body and Society*, op. cit., p. 402.

109 In this regard see P. Wilpert, 'Begierde', *Reallexikon für Antike und Christentum*, vol. 2, Stuttgart, Hiersemann Verlag, 1954, pp. 66–78, especially pp. 74–6.

Part III

WE ARE THE TIMES

(Augustine, *Sermon* 80.8)

12

'TEMPORA CHRISTIANA' REVISITED

Robert A. Markus

To help understand the religious transformation of the Roman world, Gerald Bonner once made use of a distinction between two classes of persons: those 'well disposed towards the Christian faith and to the Church, who could even adhere to them quite firmly, but who nevertheless still clung to the old faiths to a greater or lesser degree'; and 'sincere converts who, while accepting Christianity for better or worse, continued to retain some of their old customs and habits of thought'.[1] The distinction, he thought, is often not easy to apply; the hallmark of the latter group was their readiness to accept baptism or martyrdom, indicating the readiness of a person 'to commit himself to Christ, even if he did not fully comprehend the Christian faith and its implications'. Many churchmen around AD 400 would have concurred. Martyrdom or baptism were, indeed, the decisive marks of a Christian; but now that the age of the persecutions was a distant memory, and martyrdom, or willingness to undergo it, no longer a test of Christian commitment, baptism seemed, to many, a net of too coarse a mesh to catch the 'authentic Christians' among those who were Christian in name, but not in reality. Bonner rightly saw a clue here to the the process of 'Christianisation' of the Roman world: for the dividing line between 'pagan' and 'Christian', always liable to shift, was especially unstable at the end of the fourth century and early in the fifth.

The generation of Christians that grew up in these decades was caught up in a conflict: between a sense that they were witnessing a decisive turning point in the Christianisation of the empire, and an opposed sense of the persistence of ancient habits of thought and pre-Christian styles of living. Augustine, to take the best documented example, lived through the culminating phase of the government's legislative repression of paganism, of heresy and dissent. The religious legislation of Theodosius I inaugurated with the emblematic *Cunctos populos* of AD 380 – placed in due course at the head of Justinian's Code – gathered momentum from 391, the year of Augustine's ordination to the priesthood.[2] The legislative achievement of the Christian emperors was to be retrospectively summed up in the Theodosian Code eight years after Augustine's death.[3] His working life coincided, almost exactly, with the legal establishment of Christian orthodoxy as the empire's official religion.

Augustine can, of course, never be taken as representative. He was the most thoughtful of those who tried to take the measure of what had been achieved in the course of a century of rule by Christian emperors, and his assesment of the 'Christian times' is very far from being uncontroversial.[4] This study seeks to reconsider Augustine's evaluation of the official Christianisation of the empire. It is gratefully offered to that fine Augustinian scholar, Gerald Bonner.

'Tempora christiana'

Christians believed that Christ had conquered the powers of the gods once and for all. However, it was only in the fourth century, since the time of Constantine's conversion, that that victory was made manifest; and especially, so many of Augustine's contemporaries thought, in these most recent times, in the reign of Theodosius and his sons, when the idols were being finally broken, the temples destroyed. The 'Christian times' that Christians welcomed as the fulfilment of divine purpose, seemed, to anxious and resentful pagans, the beginning of their troubles.

There is general agreement that the phrase the 'Christian times' (*tempora christiana*) bore a variety of meanings for Augustine. He certainly used it to refer to the very recent times – beginning in the early 390s – during which the imperial initiatives for establishing Christianity gathered momentum; but the phrase could also refer to the longer stretch of the empire's history since the conversion of Constantine, or even to the whole period since the incarnation.[5] The 'Christian times' are clearly an elastic concept in Augustine's usage, and must be interpreted according to the context. However, it is not the meaning Augustine attached to the phrase that is of importance for us, but his attitude to what it stood for. What we need to scrutinise is how Augustine portrays the *tempora christiana* when he evidently has in mind the most recent period, from the 390s, of the legal enforcement of Christian orthodoxy and the repression of paganism and heresy.

In line with what he learned at his mother's knee, Augustine saw the historical career of the church as fulfilling the predictions of the Old Testament prophets. The 'full history' of our salvation to be taught to catechumens, he advised the deacon Deogratias, should start with the creation story and come down to 'the present times of the church'.[6] Later in the same work, he runs through the items that such a 'full history' might include: from Abraham down to the incarnation and earthly life of Christ and the first preaching of the Gospel – to which Augustine gives pride of place here – with a brief final mention of the conversion of the kings who had previously persecuted the Church, and the trials of the Church by heresy and schism.[7] This follows the lines of what had impressed him as a recent convert: the persecutions, the time of 'so much blood, so much fire, so much suffering by the martyrs', then the emergence from persecution, followed by the present time – the 390s – when the Gospels are being read all over the world, expounded by clergy, heard with veneration; a time when many are turning from wealth and worldly honours to dedicating their whole life to God, when in town and country the 'the whole human race almost with one voice' praises Him.[8] We should note that Augustine lumps together the age of the persecutions with the glorious present (to contrast them with 'yesterday's intoxication', with things such as haruspication). This refusal to single out the recent history of the empire's Christianisation among the events in which the prophecies can be seen fulfilled is even more striking in the passage from the *De catechizandis rudibus* (above, n. 7). From the time of his ordination to the last books of the *City of God*, the church's whole history was the fulfilment of the prophecies. In the eighteenth book, he began to round off the history of the two cities with the prophecies predicting the incarnation, the passion and death and the resurrection of Christ, the calling of the gentiles and the history of the church, its spread, its suffering in the persecutions, the heresies that shadowed its growth, its mixed composition until the Last Judgement (18.27–37, 49–54). Towards the end, having reached his own day, he mentions the most recent events in Africa: the arrival of the imperial officials in Carthage in AD 399 to destroy the temples and break up the idols, inaugurating the subsequent huge growth of the church in the following thirty years that Augustine went on to mention.[9] The whole sequence is designed to set forth the variable fortunes of the church's history, as predicted by the prophets. Good and bad are as inextricably mixed in the church's history, as in its members. Augustine is simply asserting that it has all been prophesied.

This is, in fact, a commonplace in Augustine's writings and preaching, and entirely unremarkable.[10] What is more remarkable is a distinctly different feature to be found in some of his writings, all of the 390s and the opening years of the fifth century. In one of the earliest of his psalm commentaries, Augustine commented on the verse 'let all my enemies be ashamed and very much troubled; let them be turned back and confounded very speedily' (Ps 6:11): 'very speedily' (*valde velociter*) is to be referred either to the desire of the speaker expressing the wish, or to the power of Christ who is converting with such speed (*tanta temporum celeritate*) the idolatrous peoples who had been persecuting the church to the faith of the Gospels'.[12] As a prophecy, the verse refers to the present time, and in the present, to the remarkable speed of Christianisation. Augustine's language suggests that he is thinking not of the gradual Christianisation during the ninety years since Constantine's conversion, but to its sudden acceleration since 391. It was only a short step from reading the whole history of the period since the incarnation in prophetic terms, to giving the most recent times, from the 390s, a privileged status in that history. In the years 400–5, Augustine seems to have been very prone to this, and to triumphant celebration of the Christianisation of the empire in these years. He will single out the paucity of the remaining pagans, the rapidity of their conversion through the measures of the Christian emperors.[13] In fulfilment of the prophecies, God is calling the kings of the earth to His service; the idols have been, or are being, uprooted and the nations gathered from the ends of the earth to the worship of Christ. 'The whole world has become a chorus praising Christ' (*en. Ps.* 149.7).[14]

Such passages are very unlike those in which Augustine affirms the general truth that the history of the church has been predicted by the prophets: its sufferings, its sinfulness, its victory. They interpret a highly particularised moment in its history, in prophetic terms. *This*, what is being played out before our eyes, the breaking of the idols and the conversion of the nations, is God's work, predicted by the prophets, carried out through the work of the Christian emperors.[15]

The theme crops up repeatedly in the sermons recently discovered and edited from a Mainz manuscript by François Dolbeau. They constitute an important part of the dossier, containing, as they do, a number of variations on the theme. A brief survey will be useful:

Mainz 5: (AD 404/5?).[16] Augustine comments on the rule of the Christian emperors: let nobody say, he preached, that now that the emperors are Catholics the church suffers no persecutions. The Devil is not asleep, he is still going about seeking whom he may devour (§ 15).

Mainz 9: probably of the years 403–6.[17] Augustine refers to the breaking of idols now, the disappearance of pagans by conversion to Christianity: but qualifies this success by remarking on the many Christians who live immorally (*male viventes*: §§ 8–9).

Mainz 12: on the Second Coming (403–4?).[18] Augustine undertakes to enumerate 'as many things from the beginning of time down to today' as he can find prophesied in the scriptures; the many things fulfilled exclude doubt concerning what is still left to be accomplished (§ 3; also § 6).[19] He then lists the fulfilled prophecies of the Scriptures, on the same lines as he does in the *De catechizandis rudibus* (above, n. 7). Near the end of the sermon, he speaks of the complaint of pagans of the *mala tempora*, *dura tempora*, *molesta tempora* that we are living through; let them mend the times by mending their ways (instead of seeking security in the shows); let us allow ourselves to be healed by Christ, that great physician (*medicus ille magnus*: §§ 14–15).

Mainz 13: companion piece to 12 (403–4?).[20] Augustine again takes up the pagans' complaint about the badness of the times 'since the times began to be Christian' (*ex quo tempora Christiana esse coeperant*: § 13). However, he says, read your own ancient authors to discover what disasters happened before; and then ask yourself whether times were better when theatres and amphitheatres were built, or now, when they are being destroyed? This is the time of the olive-press; do not complain of being pressed harder in Christian times than before: do not blame Him who comes to test us (*discernere*: §§ 14–15).

Mainz 54: (403–4?).[21] Augustine reminds his congregation that a few years ago they were pagans, now they are Christians. It has all been foretold, and it has all happened very suddenly; so believe that the remaining prophecies will also be fulfilled (§ 16).

Mainz 60: (399–405?).[22] Aimed against the Donatists, again resorts to the argument that the prophecies have been fulfilled in the conversion of the pagans. Let the heretic believe what has been prophesied for the church just as the pagans have to believe what has been prophesied about idols (§ 5).

Mainz 61: (399–409; 404?).[23] 'Thousands of years ago these things were predicted' (§ 20): the context suggests that Augustine is here thinking of Christ's incarnation and its sequel: the martyrs and the crop of believers that has grown from their seed (§ 19). Augustine places particular weight on the prophesied victory of the church, secured by the blood of the martyrs (§§ 24–5) and now by the conversion of kings: *et hoc factum est*.

It is not easy to draw any clear conclusion from these sermons, not least because some of them (like some of the other relevant sermons) cannot be, or at least, not precisely, dated.[24] The first two (Mainz 5 and 9) contain a mild reminder that the recent Christianisation has not disposed of all evils; of the rest, four (Mainz 12, 54, 60 and 61) contain the argument that, as the prophesied conversion of pagans has been (in large part) achieved in our times, its completion (and/or the reconciliation of heretics and schismatics) and the unification of the church will soon follow. The impending, very near, future is associated with the very recent past, to become a kind of specious present. Without detailed discussion of each passage, the sermons confirm the range of possible meanings borne by the phrase *Christiana tempora* and suggest that the 'mood of heady optimism' came to a climax in the years immediately following 399, lasting to about 404, and trailed away from about 405.[25] As I have argued at tedious length in my book *Saeculum*, not only does it vanish completely, but the *City of God*, especially in its later books, is concerned to undermine the theological foundations that had sustained the post-Theodosian euphoria that Augustine had briefly shared with so many of his contemporaries. The perspective in which Augustine saw the Theodosian age shifted drastically. It no longer seemed to him the definitive establishment of Christianity, a firm narrative closure of the previous age and the start of a new stage in the history of salvation.

The Christianisation of the empire came to seem starkly ambiguous. Again and again, when Augustine alludes in later works to the prophecies of the conversion of rulers and that of peoples subject to them, he is careful to deflate any sense of jubilation they might encourage. Thus commenting on Ps 72:10–11 ('The kings of Tharsis and the isles render him tribute . . . all the nations shall serve Him'), he says the kings' tribute is the gift of the people brought within the communion of the church by their authority; but he immediately catches himself: 'not as if the persecuting kings had not also brought their gifts, without knowing what they were doing, in immolating the holy martyrs'.[26] The kings' service of Christ, far from securing the church's glory, constitutes 'a greater and more insidious temptation'.[27] Or he will see the real Christianisation of the empire postponed to some distant future: 'the city which gave us birth according to the flesh [Rome] survives; if only it were also spiritually reborn!'.[28] The legislation, coercion and repression of the emperors are quietly devalued in the homogeneity of these 'last times'; efforts to spread the Gospel are balanced by the perversity with which it is despised.[29] We cannot confidently predict even that the persecutions have finally come to an end.[30] Anything is possible; the Bible gives no clues, and, concerning the future, we can only make our uncertain human conjectures. Contemporary history is powerless to provide landmarks and signposts. The whole myth of the Theodosian Christianisation of the empire is now revealed to Augustine as a mirage.[31]

'*Tempora constantiana*' and '*tempora christiana*'

Augustine, having at first shared unquestioningly the euphoria of his contemporaries, was alone among them when he came to discard it unequivocally. The contrast, for example, with the views held by Orosius on the future of the empire and of Christianity, is well known.[32] Thanks to Françoise Thélamon's magisterial study of Rufinus' *Ecclesiastical History*, we are now also in a position to give sharper relief to Augustine's view of the *tempora christiana* by comparing them with Rufinus'.[33] Rufinus, writing in the opening years of the century, aimed to meet Christian needs analogous to those Augustine was soon to address when he settled down to write the *City of God*. Rufinus hoped to comfort the Christians of Aquileia, especially their bishop Chromatius, in their anxieties over the gathering storm of barbarian invasion. The thrust of the account of the fourth century that he appended to his translation of Eusebius' *Ecclesiastical History* is this aim to give comfort in difficult times. His history is the narrative of the victory of Christianity; its events are *signa uirtutis*, signs revealing God's power. It is a sacred history (*une histoire sainte*): it aims to show 'how God's design for the world manifests itself in events'.[34] In the expansion of the church 'during the time of Constantine' (*temporibus Constantini*) Rufinus saw proof of God's intervention in history through the acts of his elect.[35] The struggle against paganism and the triumph of Christianity are, for Rufinus, evidence of the church's vitality: they are 'clear proof of the construction of God's kingdom across the vicissitudes of human history'.[36] The actual reigns of Constantine and of Theodosius have a 'particular value' in Rufinus' history: they frame the period of its definitive Christianisation, and a stretch of time in which the church is exposed to trials by bad emperors and heretics.[37] Julian's aborted plan to allow the temple to be rebuilt at Jerusalem brought Rufinus' first book to its climax. In his monstrous arrogance, Julian had sought to reverse what God had made irreversible. 'By seeking in vain with all the means at his disposal to wipe out the empire's Christianisation, he proved that it was irreversible.'[38] Rufinus' second book opens with the Christian emperor Jovian, *confessor et depulsor erroris*, and ends with the final and definitive triumph of Christianity: Theodosius' miraculous victory at the River Frigidus.[39] Rufinus presents the victory as the reward of *pietas*, granted in answer to prayer and foretold by prophecy; but he does more, giving it a far more than episodic significance: it is set in the 'framework of two rival religious systems' as a victory of Christianity and orthodoxy over *superstitio* and idolatry.[40]

Rufinus' history asks for *une double lecture*: it is at once a narrative of the great deeds (*res gestae*) of human beings and the record of God's miracles (*mirabilia Dei*).[41] In a manner that Augustine could never have adopted, and, finally, radically rejected, it was a sacred history, revealing God's purposes in human actions and in the history of His people. In inviting Chromatius and his Aquileian congregation to read the signs of the times and to see in them the *mirabilia Dei* accomplished, Rufinus was indeed giving them comfort in their anxieties: through the history of the church from Constantine to Theodosius, God had secured its victory. There was no possibility of going back.

Augustine's radical agnosticism about God's purposes in human history allowed no comfort on such lines. There could be no guarantee of conclusive victory; the Theodosian achievement itself (which Augustine was ready enough – following Rufinus – to appreciate) stood under a final question mark.[42] The future, like the present, remained inscrutable. All that the Christian could know with certainty was that at the end Christ would return to gather his faithful from the four corners of the world into His Kingdom. And the time of that was known to Him alone.

When Augustine became disillusioned about the collective, legal and institutional Christianisation of the empire, he fell back on a more personal need for renewal. In a sermon preached probably around 410 he said, 'Bad times, hard times: this is what people keep saying; but let us live well, and times will be good. We are the times: such as we are, such are the times'.[43]

As the 'Christian times' are revealed to be illusion – illusory as an end of paganism, illusory as the beginning of a new Christian era – so the past was revealed as still powerful in the present, the achievement of genuine Christianisation still far in the future, and destined necessarily always to remain so. Augustine and his fellow bishops thus came to see the problem of Christianisation in terms of a struggle of Christianity against the inert weight of an ancient, unconverted world, and, in doing so, to redefine the 'dominant Christian narrative of Christianisation'.[44]

Additional note on the meaning of 'tempora christiana'

In his survey of Augustine's usage, Goulven Madec distinguishes four senses the phrase could bear in his writings:

1 'objectively and in general': the whole period of the Christian era since the birth of Christ
2 'objectively and in particular': the period since the 'conversion' of Constantine, or, more strictly, the period of the legal enforcement of Christianity (by the Christian emperors).

From these, Madec distinguishes two other senses, labelled 'subjective':

3 the period vilified by pagans in their complaints about the evils suffered by the Empire in consequence of its Christianisation (which could be either the whole period since Constantine, or, more specifically, the Theodosian period) and
4 the period envisaged by Christians elated by the victory of Christianity and the defeat of paganism as providential.[45]

As he remarks, the meanings are not mutually exclusive and can shade into each other. Madec surveys forty-one passages from Augustine, together with a few others, from more or less contemporary writers. We need not follow him in his analysis of all these passages; the meaning of most of them is not at issue. I single out the more interesting texts and those whose interpretation seems to raise a problem as to Augustine's meaning or his evaluation of the *tempora christiana*.

1 *De uera religione* 3.3[46] Here, Augustine contrasts the time of the ancient philosophers, when even Socrates worshipped idols (2.2) with the 'Christian times', in which the true worship has been revealed. This clearly suggests that these times began with the coming of Christ; as the sequel (4.6–7), however, goes on to show, Augustine slides from this to giving *tempora christiana* its sense (2) or (3), the time of the empire's Christianisation: for an

ancient philosopher returned from the dead would now find the temples deserted and the churches full. It may be that he had the most recent times of the legal enforcement of Christianity in mind, when the churches were being filled; if so, he does not specifically say so. The passage seems to illustrate all four senses and the ease with which they can slide into one another.

2   *De consensu euangelistarum* 1.26.40[47] The coming of the peoples from the ends of the earth to worship God, and the breaking of the idols foretold by Jeremiah (16:19), is being fulfilled, and being fulfilled now, before our eyes. This could hardly refer to anything but the most recent and literal breaking of the idols and the subsequent filling of the churches. Augustine's vocabulary is heavily loaded; the language is reminiscent of the account he gives in the *City of God* 18.54 (*templa euerterunt et simulacra fregerunt*) of the imperial officials' repressive measures in 399 and the sequel. Like the passage above from *De uera religione*, this passage clearly refers to the time of Christianisation; like it, it is elastic in its application to the post-Constantinian or the Theodosian era; with, however, a much stronger suggestion of the more determined effort to repress paganism of the 390s; *ecce nunc fit*: it is happening now.

3   *Enarratio in psalmos* 80.1[48] Like Tertullian (*Apologia 40*), and echoing his words, Augustine says Christians have always been blamed for troubles. 'When you hear blasphemers prattle arrogantly saying that evils abound *temporibus Christianis*, you know they like to say this, and you know the proverb which, though old, began *temporibus Christianis*: 'God refuses rain: look for the Christians' The *tempora Christiana* are clearly the evil times complained of by pagans; perhaps very recent, perhaps less recent.

4   *Epistula* 111.2[49] Augustine, again answering complaints about the evils that happen in Christian times, recalls Lk 12:47–8 ('That servant who knew his master's will but did what deserves a beating) and answers:

> What wonder then is it if in Christian times this world should receive a heavy beating, like the servant who knew his master's will and yet doing what is worthy of punishment receives a heavy beating? They [the pagans] take note of the energy which is devoted to preaching the Gospel, but they fail to take note of the perversity with which it is despised.

The *tempora christiana* again are evidently the time complained about. What, however, is interesting about the passage is the last sentence: Augustine is undermining the whole force of the argument about *tempora christiana*, saying these (and all) times are a mixture of good and bad; the Gospel is both preached and spurned. The letter is probably to be dated late 409, and the sentence reflects Augustine's disillusion with the idea that the *tempora christiana* (in whatever sense: probably the Theodosian years) have achieved any definitive Christianisation.

It is hardly necessary to refer to the many passages in which Augustine takes up the pagan disparagement of the *tempora christiana* as bad times, times of trouble and suffering, of crumbling and destruction, of decline and fall.[50] The theme is common in the sermons Augustine preached in the aftermath of the Gothic sack of Rome in 410, and abounds in the pages of the *City of God*. It may well be that pagan complaints about Christian times (sense (3) above) – which certainly pre-date the fall of the City in 410 – helped to form the sense Augustine attached to the phrase. Such complaints were concentrated on the Theodosian epoch, and will thus have helped to narrow the reference of Augustine's *tempora christiana* to this recent period. However, there is no need to assume they – and Augustine's 'rétorsive' remarks – must always bear a narrowly and rigidly defined time-reference: it is rather that the pagans, and like them, Augustine, saw the Theodosian period as the climax of the 'Christian times', which gave the phrase its focal and typical meaning without confining it to the twenty years in question.

Notes

1 'The Extinction of Paganism and the Church Historian', *Journal of Ecclesiastical History* 35 (1984), pp. 339–57, at pp. 348–9; he was endorsing the distinction made by C. Guignebert, 'Les demi-chrétiens et leur place dans l'Église antique', *Revue de l'histoire des religions* 88 (1923), pp. 65–102. On 'semi-Christians', see my reservations in *The End of Ancient Christianity*, Cambridge, Cambridge University Press, 1990, p. 8.

2 *C.Th.* 16.1.2; *C.J.* 1.1.1.

3 This is not intended to imply that legislation and coercion played a decisive part in the Christianisation of the empire. For important reservations, see P. Brown, *Power and Persuasion in Late Antiquity: Towards a Christian Empire*, Madison, Wis., University of Wisconsin Press, 1992, and his *Authority and the Sacred: Aspects of the Christianisation of the Roman World*, Cambridge, Cambridge University Press, 1995, especially Ch. 2.

4 The argument of my *Saeculum. History and Society in the Theology of St Augustine*, Cambridge, Cambridge University Press, ²1988, Ch. 2, has been called into question by G. Madec, '«Tempora christiana»: expression du triomphalisme chrétien ou récrimination païenne?' in *Scientia Augustiniana: Studien über Augustinus, den Augustinismus und den Augustinerorden. Festschrift Adolar Zumkeller*, ed. C. P. Mayer and W. Eckermann, Würzburg, Augustinus-Verlag, 1975, pp. 112–36. I consider his arguments in the Additional Note at the end of this essay.

5 Madec, op. cit., pp. 112–3, refers to H.-I. Marrou, *Nouvelle histoire de l'Église*, Paris, Seuil, 1963, pp. 1 and 361; A. Mandouze, 'Saint Augustin et la religion romaine', *Recherches augustinennes* 1 (1958), pp. 187–223, at p. 214, n. 133; P. Courcelle, 'Propos anti-chrétiens rapportés par saint Augustin', *Recherches augustiniennes* 1 (1958), pp. 149–86, at pp. 180–1.

6 *Cat. rud.* 3.5.

7 *Cat. rud.* 27.53.

8 *Vera rel.* 3.5; see, for example, *s.* 22.4; *en. Ps.* 32.3.9.

9 *Ciu.* 18.54: 'templa euerterunt et simulacra fregerunt'. This is the only dated historical report Augustine gives in *ciu.*

10 Several examples are given by Madec, op. cit., pp. 134–5. What they show is that the cases of fulfilled prophecies are either confined to the Apostolic Church (calling of gentiles, spread over the nations), or valid in general and undifferentiated terms (persecution, glory, sin, failure) of the whole period of its history. Madec – bafflingly – writes, 'C'est peut-être au détriment de la cohérence de sa théologie de l'histoire [why should it be?]; mais c'est ainsi' (p. 135).

11 I summarise here my conclusions in *Saeculum*, op. cit., pp. 30–8.

12 *En. Ps.* 6.13 (AD 392).

13 *Cons. eu.* 1.14.21.

14 See also *cons. eu.* 1.32.50–34.52; 26.40; *en. Ps.* 62.1; *s.* 328.5.5; *c. Faust.* 13.7; 13.9; 22.76. With reference to outlawing of heretics, see *en. Ps.* 59.2 (*ecce nunc*).

15 On this, see A. Mandouze, op. cit., pp. 218–20. On Augustine's 'prophetic viewpoint', see P. Brown, 'Saint Augustine's Attitude to Religious Coercion', *Journal of Roman Studies* 54 (1964), pp. 107–16 (reprinted in his *Religion and Society in the Age of Saint Augustine*, London, Faber & Faber, 1972, pp. 260–78 at p. 267). Most recently, Goulven Madec has suggested that Augustine adopted this type of argument in response to pagan polemic:, 'Le Christ des païens d'après le *De consensu euangelistarum* de saint Augustin', *Recherches augustiniennes* 26 (1994), pp. 3–67, at pp. 28–32.

16 *Revue des études augustiniennes* 38 (1992), pp. 63–79.

17 Ibid., 39 (1993), pp. 411–20.

18 Ibid., pp. 73–87.

19 For parallels, see Dolbeau's note on this at ibid., p. 75.

20 Ibid., pp. 97–106.

21 Ibid., 37 (1991), pp. 271–88.

22 Ibid., pp. 42–52.

23 Ibid., pp. 58–77. It is noteworthy that this sermon was preached with pagans present within the congregation.

24 The *terminus ante quem* of the sermons is AD 412. It is, however, likely that most of them, perhaps all, were preached well before that date. The sermons considered above all seem to have been preached before 406, possibly by 404.

25 Brown, 'St Augustine's attitude', op. cit., p. 267.

26 *En. Ps.* 71.13.

27 *Perf. iust.* 15.35.

28 *S.* 105.6.9.

29 *Ep.* 111.2.

30 *Ciu.* 18.53.1; see Markus, *Saeculum*, op. cit., p. 54.

31 On all this see Markus, *Saeculum*, op. cit., pp. 27–44.

32 It has been much studied, notably by T. E. Mommsen; for references, see ibid., pp. 31, 54, 161–4.

33 F. Thélamon, *Païens et chrétiens au IVe Siècle. L'apport de l'«Histoire ecclésiastique» de Rufin d'Aquilée*, Paris, Etudes augustiniennes, 1981. The relationship between Rufinus' *Historia ecclesiastica* and Augustine's *City of God* would still repay investigation. For a beginning, see Y.-M. Duval, 'L'éloge de Théodose dans la *Cité de Dieu* (V.26.1)', *Recherches augustiniennes* 4 (1966), pp. 135–79, and P. Courcelle, 'Jugements de Rufin et d'Augustin sur les empereurs du IVe siècle et la défaite

suprème du paganisme', *Revue des études anciennes* 71 (1969), pp. 100–30.

34 Thélamon, op. cit., p. 26.

35 Rufinus's *tempora Constantini* present a parallel to Augustine's *tempora christiana*, not least in being flexible in its chronological application:

> Situer un évènement religieux *temporibus Constantini*, c'est l'inscrire dans un temps doté d'une qualité religieuse particulière, tant il apparaît avec le recul et à la lumière des évènements postérieurs, comme une nouvelle étape dans l'économie du salut. Constantin, premier empereur chrétien, mérite par sa *pietas* des conquêtes tant d'ordre spirituel que d'ordre temporel: le *religiosus princeps* sanctifie en quelque sorte son époque. Réciproquement, la réussite de l'action missionaire apparaît à son tour comme un signe de la qualification religieuse particulière d'un temps que Dieu choisit pour intervenir dans l'histoire des hommes.
>
> (Thélamon, op. cit., p. 35)

36 Ibid., 159.

37 Ibid., p. 62.

38 Ibid., p. 309; see the whole section at pp. 281–322.

39 Ibid., p. 309–22.

40 Ibid., p. 316.

41 Ibid., p. 468–70.

42 See above, nn. 25–31.

43 *S.* 80.8.

44 Brown, *Authority and the Sacred*, op. cit., p. x. His first lecture is concerned with the slow changes of mentality by which this dominant narrative came to be flanked, in the Latin world, by a considerably less euphoric attitude: by a view of Christianisation that was prepared to linger less on the supernatural victory of Christ and more on the weight of the pagan past within the Christian present. (ibid., p. xi). In another paper, I intend to consider the models of Christianisation that came to take the place of Augustine's assurance about the Theodosian epoch as that collapsed.

45 Madec, '"Tempora christiana"', op. cit., pp. 114–15. Madec's classification confuses the distinction of periods with that of the attitudes adopted towards them. In my *Saeculum*, op. cit., I also failed to distinguish two questions as clearly as necessary: a) what time-stretch is referred to by *tempora christiana*? and b) what attitude to them – in whatever sense the phrase occurs – does Augustine express? I thus evidently conveyed the impression that the mere use of the phrase implied a 'triumphalist' view on Augustine's part. Madec rightly considers that no value-judgement is expressed in the mere use of the phrase (except his numbers 6 and 7; see below), but he does not consider the evidence on b): what was Augustine's attitude to the official enforcement of Christian orthodoxy in the *tempora christiana*, when this phrase was taken to refer to the Theodosian age? As A.-M. La Bonnardière wrote, 'La "Cité terrestre" d'après H.-I. Marrou', *Saint Augustin et la Bible*, ed. A.-M. La Bonnardière, Paris, Beauchesne, 1986, pp. 387–98, at pp. 396–8, I sought to make a historical, not a philological observation on Augustine's views.

46 Madec, '"Tempora christiana"', op. cit., p. 117, no. 3, whose interpretation follows the same lines as mine.

47 Madec, '"Tempora christiana"', op. cit., p. 119, no. 6, who comments on this text along with *cons. eu.* 1.16.24 (no. 4); 1.23.35 (no. 5); 1.33.51 (no. 7). I omit these latter texts from consideration because their sense is not at issue. On *cons. eu.* 1.26.40, Madec remarks (pp. 119–20):

> on ne saurait nier qu'Augustin se réjouisse de la victoire du chris-
> tianisme et de la déroute du paganisme; et je serais tenté de dire qu'il
> le fait en bon chrétien de son temps. Mais je doute qu'il convienne de
> déceler cet accent triomphaliste dans l'expression *tempora christiana*
> comme telle. Peut-on dire qu'elle désigne la période de la répression
> légale du paganisme? Oui, à condition d'associer ce fait au phénomène
> de l'expansion universelle du christianisme.

In his conclusion this is one of the two texts of which Madec writes, 'on pourrait, à la rigueur, soupçonner quelque accent triomphaliste' (p. 133).

48 Madec, '"Tempora christiana"', op. cit., pp. 121–2, no. 8: notes the parallel with *ciu.* 2.3, and concludes that the passage 'déborde manifestement l'âge théodosien et probablement l'ère constantinienne' (p. 122). This may or may not be the case; it is clear, however, that the meaning the phrase bears here is whatever the pagan objectors have given it (= 3).

49 Madec, '"Tempora christiana"', op. cit., pp. 122–3, no. 9: Madec gives 409 as its date, which is probably right. However, he mistakes the point I made about it: 'about this time', that is, around AD 410 (Madec mistakenly thinks I dated this letter to after the fall of Rome), Augustine began to see through the 'mirage of the fulfilment of the prophecies *temporibus Christianis*'. This was the point I made (*Saeculum*, op. cit., p. 41), as it is now: not that Augustine thought that prophecies were no longer being fulfilled (as Madec goes on, rightly, to observe at p. 123), but that good and bad equally are being fulfilled; it is the euphoria about the official Christianisation that is gone.

50 Madec, '"Tempora christiana"', op. cit., pp. 123–8, nos 10–22. There is no substantial disagreement on these. Of nos 11–14, Madec observes: 'Ces sermons révèlent, comme le dit R. A. Markus, l'amertume des accusations païennes.' (p. 126). They are agreed to bear sense (3). There are, of course, many more passages on these lines, especially in *ciu.*; the theme, and sometimes the phrase, also crops up in the sermons discovered by F. Dolbeau. See *s. Mainz* 12 = *s. Dolbeau* 5, in *Revue des études augustiniennes* 39 (1993), pp. 73–87 (§§ 14–15: *mala/dura/-molesta tempora*); *s. Mainz* 13 = *s. Dolbeau* 6, in *Revue des études augustiniennes* 39 (1993), pp. 97–106 (§ 13: evils said to have come *ex quo tempora Christiana esse coeperant*; § 15: *torcular/pressurae* now, *temporibus Christianis*). Equally, it is agreed that Madec's no. 23 (*ciu.*, Breuiculus 18.47) refers to 'the whole period since the incarnation'. Madec adds: 'Mais il convient aussi de noter qu'Augustin ne remet pas en cause la notion de *tempora christiana*. Pour lui c'est un fait; l'époque est chrétienne (sens 2)' (p. 129). However, although Madec concedes in respect of two texts (see above, n. 47) that 'on pourrait, à la rigueur, soupçonner quelque accent triomphaliste' (p. 133), he wishes to minimise the contrast between Augustine's enthusiastic endorsement and his disillusion.

13

THE RHETORIC OF
SCRIPTURE AND
PREACHING

Classical decadence or Christian aesthetic?

Carol Harrison

Henri Marrou's classic book, *Saint Augustin et la fin de la culture antique* (Paris, 1948) initiated what was to prove a far-reaching and influential debate concerning Augustine's relation to late antique literature and culture. Its subsequent, rather unconventional appendix, or – in Augustinian fashion – *Retractatio* (Paris, 1949), in which Marrou sought to amend, revise and temper some of his original opinions, is a measure of the liveliness of the debate that followed its first publication. Was Augustine simply a typical product of late antique culture – *un homme de la décadence* – someone whose education, work and written style betrayed all the marks of an overripe culture, a culture which had, as it were, gone to seed; its preoccupation with eloquent presentation largely obscuring any attention to content and truth? Or was he one of the first representatives of a new Christian culture, in which style was sacrificed on the altar of truth, and concern for eloquence was strictly subordinated to a desire to instil the message of the gospel? Of course, Augustine, like all the Church Fathers, belonged to both cultures. The question really was, and is, just how far he achieved, or failed to achieve, the difficult, almost amphibious movement, between them. How far was classical culture left behind? How much of it was taken up, adopted, transformed? How was this done? Can we speak of an emergent, distinctively Christian culture? What sort of culture was this?

These questions have reverberated throughout Augustinian scholarship for almost half a century. In this essay, I would like to examine some of their most recent echoes, as they touch upon the still sensitive issue of the literary, aesthetic value of the Christian Scriptures and preaching upon them. In this respect, the questions are still being discussed, the subject still sensitive and Augustine still criticised, largely because of unresolved tensions in his own work and practice. These tensions are perhaps nearest the surface in Book 4 of *De doctrina christiana*. This work, on Christian exegesis and preaching, which was begun in AD 396 (Book 1–3.35.51) but completed only in 426/7 (the rest of Book 3 and Book 4), was tremendously influential throughout the Middle Ages.[1] It was central to Marrou's thesis and has received an extraordinary amount of attention in the last decade or so, largely in relation to questions of language and hermeneutics.[2]

The dates of the work are significant: 396 was the year in which Augustine became Bishop of Hippo. From entering the priesthood in 391, he had been conscious of his lack of knowledge of the Christian Scriptures and had taken serious measures to remedy this.[3] The fruits of his reflections are recorded in Books 1–3 of *De doctrina christiana*, which are a general discussion of what it is that motivates the exegete, what he seeks to find in Scripture – in both cases, love of God and neighbour (1) – how he should go about interpretation; what tools he needs for the task – here, Augustine discusses the exegete's debt to classical culture and its disciplines (2.19.29–42.63) – how to interpret the language of Scripture. In Book 4, written near the end of his life, he turns to the question of preaching; of how to express, to communicate the message of Scripture.[4] We therefore find him attempting to come to terms with the Christian practice – or art – of public speaking, or rhetoric.

In a sense, Book 4, written so late on, seems to mark Augustine's coming full circle. If late antique culture was defined by anything it was the art of rhetoric, the art of public speaking, of teaching, moving and persuading an audience. All education – the liberal disciplines or arts – were simply a preparation for this, the highest achievement, the most desirable and influential profession of late antique culture. And Augustine, as we know, had followed this well-trodden path to advancement to become the municipal rhetor of Milan, the imperial capital, before his conversion in 386. From 391, and for the rest of his life, he was to be similarly involved, as a priest and bishop, in the art of speaking: in teaching, preaching, and advising his congregation. In Book 4, he is able to reflect on a lifetime's experience of the art of public speaking although, of course, the texts and audiences changed rather dramatically during its course. Here, more than at any other point in his work, the meeting of classical and Christian cultures is seen in all its complexity, and Augustine is more than aware of the need to articulate the nature of their relation.

His main concern in Book 4 is to discuss how the Christian teacher or preacher should go about expressing the message of Scripture. The discussion proceeds almost entirely within the frame of classical rhetoric, in order to evaluate its aims, practices and rules and their usefulness for the Christian preacher. Augustine obviously regards it as a norm, a yardstick, an unavoidable rule against which Christian practice is to be evaluated and defined.

This should not surprise us. Rhetoric, like classical culture in general, could not simply be dispensed with, ignored or rejected as wholly irrelevant and inappropriate. Religions and communities have cultural contexts; cultures evolve. Christianity was inextricably, unavoidably, linked with, formed by and understood within the parameters of classical culture. However, Augustine's attempt to come to terms with his own, and western Christianity's, cultural context has been severely criticised. He is held to be too narrow, too utilitarian and reductivist in his rejection of various aspects of classical culture, especially in Book 2.[5] There is some justification in these criticisms, at least in respect of what Augustine has to say when writing theoretically (though it is worth remembering that other Christian Fathers were much more vehement in their rejection of classical culture, and that, in practice, Augustine's theories are often somewhat modified). On the other hand, and it is this that I would like to develop further, he is blamed for too freely and willingly adopting its criteria and techniques – its literary artistry – in order to engage the interest and delight of his listener, with unfortunate results. His figurative, allegorical exegesis, most especially, is frequently criticised in this respect for its artificiality and arbitrariness.[6] Eloquence which aims to please seems to take precedence, for some of Augustine's critics, over content; the means of expression over the true meaning of the passage. It was for precisely these reasons that the most popular rhetorical school of Augustine's day, the Second Sophistic, was criticised, not least by Augustine himself. So why does he use its techniques? In this essay, I would like to demonstrate that Augustine is keenly aware of, and highly sensitive to, these criticisms; that he both articulates them, appreciates their force, and seeks to counter them by attempting to justify his own practice, and that of the biblical authors. I will argue that some of his justifications are more convincing than others.

Most of the answers are found in Book 4 of *De doctrina christiana*, which I will address shortly. Before that, a number of general observations need to be made. First of all, we have noted the cultural significance of rhetoric: it carried with it social respect, prestige, power, authority. In this sense, Christianity could not ignore it; rather, it was an important instrument in establishing its own position within society.[7] Secondly, the Fathers themselves were products, educationally and socially, of late antique culture. They naturally adopted its methods of understanding and communication in order to frame and preach their new Christian identity, however critical they were of it in theory (indeed, we often find them using classical rhetoric to inveigh against it!).[8] Furthermore, they justified their practice by appealing to Scripture, a rather disappointing, strange, somewhat crude and badly written text (especially in its Latin translation), which they rendered acceptable, both to themselves and its pagan critics, by reading it according to classical exegetical practices, such as allegory (the technique pagans used to make their own classics, Virgil or Homer, relevant and acceptable).[9] The scriptural account of the Israelites spoiling the Egyptians of their treasure proved to be a useful model for the Fathers to apply to their own use of classical culture (Exod 3:22; 12:35–6). The Egyptians derived their treasure from the prophets, from divine illumination, and to take over and deploy parts of it for Christian use was really, therefore, simply restoring it to its rightful owners.[10] Thus, the Fathers justified their use of classical culture and, in particular, its defining characteristic: its use of eloquence.

In Book 4 of *De doctrina christiana*, Augustine cautiously, and, at times contradictorily, attempts to define just what the Christians' use of eloquence should be: what *its* aims, practices and rules are in relation to, and in contradistinction to, classical practices. At times, they follow the same path, motivated by the same aims; at others, the fundamental principles of the one are seen to be in opposition to the other; in some instances, they follow the same practices for different ends. Augustine moves rapidly between acceptance, rejection and modification of classical eloquence. The argument is, therefore, far from straightforward, but, as I suggested earlier, this probably has more to do with the unresolved tensions – even at this late stage, near the end of his life – within Augustine's own person and mind, between his past, but still enduring, educational and intellectual formation, and his present identity as a Christian bishop. The biggest tension seems to lie in what he has to say about what I have called 'rhetoric' in the title of this essay, but which should properly be described in Augustine's terminology as *eloquentia*, eloquence: the linguistic or literary artistry of the written or spoken word. Arguments for its usefulness, indeed its indispensability, are juxtaposed throughout Book 4 with arguments for its irrelevance and redundancy in Christian exegesis and preaching.

For example, Augustine is at pains to demonstrate that the Christian Scriptures can be analysed according to the rules of classical 'eloquence', and that they will not be found wanting in this respect; 'For where I understand these authors, not only can nothing seem to me more wise than they are, but also nothing can seem more eloquent' (4.6.9). The exercise is a rather artificial one. Passages from 1 Corinthians and Amos are subjected to a thoroughly classical critique, in terms of *caesa*, *membra* and *circuitus*; their ornaments, figures and expressions are detailed, as it were, to show their pedigree. Later on, in a similar vein, Augustine betrays an educated rhetor's niggling concern that the authors of Scripture lack the rhetorical ornament of rhythmic closings. Perhaps, he suggests, this is the fault of their translators, or perhaps – and he has to admit that he thinks this more likely – they avoided them themselves. The fact worries him, so much so that he rather desperately resorts to the suggestion that if someone skilled in rhetoric rearranged their endings by changing a few words here and there, they could then be shown not to lack anything that is 'so highly regarded and taught in the schools of grammarians or rhetoricians' (4.20.41). Furthermore, he appeals to Jerome, who had found rhythmical metre in the prophets. Then, perhaps realising these concerns are inappropriate for a Christian bishop, he concedes that although he does not himself neglect rhythmical endings in so far as they can be used moderately, it pleases him to find them only rarely in the authors of Scripture.

How much does this stance owe to Augustine's sensitivity to pagan criticism, and to his own desire to make the Scriptures palatable to himself and other refined, educated minds? He openly admits that the former is indeed a matter for concern: 'I am ashamed to be tainted by this boasting when I discuss these things in this way', he writes at the end of his rhetorical analysis of Paul, 'but ill-informed men are to be answered when they think to condemn our authors, not because they do not have, but because they do not show that eloquence which such men love too well' (4.7.14). However, his sensitivity to criticism is obviously stronger than his shame: in the next paragraph, he proceeds to analyse Amos, according to classical rules, to defend himself from the criticism that he has chosen Paul because he is the only eloquent speaker Christianity possesses!

Nevertheless, his embarrassment continues to surface: he is more than tacitly aware that what he is doing might be perceived as a rather decadent selling-out to pagan critics and the over-refined sensibilities of an educated, cultured rhetor, in a manner which is inimical both to the aims, and the methods, of the biblical writers. His analyses of both the passage from 1 Cor and Amos are immediately followed by very similar retractations: he is at pains to make clear that the eloquence he finds in Scripture is not contrived or deliberate, but is, rather, the natural, spontaneous accompaniment of words that are true: 'like wisdom coming from her house (that is, from the breast of the wise man) followed by eloquence as if she were an inseparable servant who was not called' (4.6.10). And following the Amos passage:

> But a good listener warms to it not so much by diligently analysing it as by pronouncing it energetically. For these words were not devised by human industry, but were poured forth from the divine mind both wisely and eloquently, not in such a way that wisdom was directed towards eloquence, but in such a way that eloquence did not abandon wisdom.
>
> (4.7.21)

When he turns to examine how Christian authors have used the most elaborate and extravagant 'grand style' of rhetoric (as opposed to the subdued or moderate styles), he is likewise careful to modify any impression that they might have deliberately and consciously worked on their style as a sort of decoration for what they have to say; rather, it is attributable to an unconscious enthusiasm, to an 'ardour of the heart', to the inherent force of the things being discussed, rather than careful choice (4.20.42). So, the biblical authors are indeed eloquent – naturally and unconsciously – even though they did not mean to be!

This attempt to exonerate the authors of Scripture, or those who preach upon it, from being overly concerned with decadent rhetorical eloquence, is also evident in the passages where Augustine discusses how eloquence is to be acquired. He is quick to point out, at the very beginning of Book 4, that he will not be giving the rules of eloquence he learnt in the secular schools; not that they are not useful in the service of truth, but that they are to be learnt elsewhere. Besides, methodical study of rules, he quickly points out, is of secondary importance. What is more important is the unconscious acquisition of eloquence that occurs when one reads, or hears, it in a text or speech which one is reading for other purposes: for *what* is said, rather than *how* it is said. This happens in the natural course of study of ecclesiastical literature or of Scripture (4.5.7), and in the practice of writing, dictating or speaking upon them. Here, eloquence is not a matter of rules; the rules are observed *because* someone is eloquent, they are not applied so that they might be eloquent (4.3.4). It is rather like the way a child acquires language: the child is not taught to speak, but learns by hearing and practice. Similarly, a boy does not need to learn the art of grammar if he grows up and lives among men who speak correctly (4.3.5).[11]

Eloquence is, therefore, not a matter of rules, it is not directly learnt, but somehow picked up intuitively and unconsciously. Indeed, it is very much a gift: the preacher is effective 'more through the piety of his prayers than through the skill of his oratory' (4.15.32). It is not acquired, but given.

The above arguments, which I have suggested arise from Augustine's ambiguous attitude towards classical rhetoric and its use in a Christian context, and which serve, to a large extent, to distance the Christian preacher and writer from deliberate, direct, conscious use of it – while still holding onto the idea that Christianity possesses rhetorical eloquence, are in fact the arguments of classical rhetors themselves. They too, while formulating, teaching and analysing according to rules, taught that rules do not lead to eloquence; that eloquence is better acquired by reading and listening to the classics; that it naturally accompanies truth; that it is a gift. These observations were, no doubt, made from experience and used to defend the practice of rhetoric in the face of long-standing criticism, especially from the philosophers who viewed it with distrust and distaste. How could it be said to teach the truth when its primary concern seemed to be to utilise rules of speech in order to please, to delight and to persuade the listener merely of a plausible opinion – of what might seem to be true (*verisimiliter*) – in other words, 'the ability to persuade without teaching'?[12]

It might, therefore, be argued that, in Book 4, Augustine is continuing the defence of rhetoric – in this context, Christian rhetoric – against its detractors. He is aware of the criticisms that have been made of classical rhetoric, and of the arguments deployed by classical authors to counter these, and can be seen using them on two fronts. First, to demonstrate that Christian literature and preaching *is* rhetorical, against pagan criticisms that focused on its lack of literary sophistication. Second, to defend its use against the criticisms that were commonly made of classical rhetoric, and especially of the Sophists, or the Second Sophistic of Augustine's day, that it was merely verbal fireworks, a technical display of virtuosity performed to please and, thus, to sway its hearers, whatever its relation to truth or the good. What he seems to want to say is that Christian literature *is* rhetorical, in a way that takes up the best of classical practice but is not subject to its failings.

This becomes evident if we examine the ways in which Augustine distinguishes the Christian practice of rhetoric from classical practice, and especially from Cicero.[13] Unlike the arguments discussed above, in which he was concerned to demonstrate that Christianity does indeed possess rhetorical eloquence, Augustine is less wavering, and far more forceful in his criticisms of classical 'eloquence' and the way in which Christian eloquence diverges from it.

In Chapter 12, Augustine refers to Cicero's classic definition of the three aims of rhetoric: to teach (*docere* or *probare*), to delight (*delectare* or *conciliare*) and to move (*movere* or *flectere*: Cicero, *Orator* 21.29). For Cicero, as for all classical rhetors, teaching and delight were subordinate to the ultimate goal of persuasion. After all, rhetoric's primary forum was the law court. Augustine, however, reverses these aims: the first and determining aim, the ultimate goal of the Christian preacher, is to teach. Delight might, indeed, be useful in this context to persuade the listener of the truth and move him to act upon it – I will return to this later – but Augustine can see that, in fact, this need not always be the case. Sometimes the bald, unadorned statement of the truth is sufficient to move the listener to act upon it. It is pleasing in itself, and causes the hearer to act upon it, precisely because it is the truth (4.12.28). In a sense, it is the substance of what is said, the content, that is pleasing and motivating, rather than the manner and style in which it is expressed. As Augustine observes of the preacher:

> In his speech itself he should prefer to please more with the things said than with the words used to speak them; nor should he think that anything may be said better than that which is said truthfully; nor should the teacher serve the words, but the words the teacher.
>
> (4.28.61)

Thus, in sharp contrast to how rhetoric was popularly perceived, he subordinates eloquence to truth, a desire to please to clarity and concern that one be understood (4.8.22–9.23), to the extent that, if a word in good Latin is obscure or ambiguous, the preacher should not be afraid to use vulgarisms instead (4.10.24). In this sense, Christianity can be seen to overcome the philosophers' criticism of rhetoric in teaching its own understanding of the truth, and might well claim to be the true philosophical rhetoric (just as it claimed to be the true philosophy).

It is because of his overriding emphasis on teaching the truth, that, in examining the three styles of rhetoric – the subdued to speak of small matters, the temperate to speak of moderate concerns, the grand to speak of matters of import – Augustine inclines in favour of the subdued as the basic style to be adopted by the Christian preacher. This style most easily lends itself to teaching. The simple exposition of the truth of the faith should, as we noted above, be sufficient in itself to move and persuade. Writing on the equality of the Holy Spirit with the Father and the Son, for example, Ambrose, Augustine notes, uses the subdued style, for 'the thing discussed does not need verbal ornaments, nor motions of the affections to persuade, but evidence as proof' (4.21.46). Augustine recommends the employment of the other two styles, which were usually associated with delight and persuasion, respectively, only when they also further the aim of teaching: to praise and to persuade of what is taught. Thus, the great truths of the faith, which would ordinarily demand the grand manner, are best taught in the subdued manner, praised in the temperate manner and instilled for acceptance and action in the grand manner.

As in his demonstration of the rhetorical eloquence of the Scriptures, Augustine provides scriptural and patristic illustrations of the use of the three styles, in accordance with his revised recommendations as to their use (4.20.39–21.50). The three styles complement each other and are best varied and intermingled in a single passage (4.22.51–23.52), so as not to tire the hearer. However, in his relative evaluation of them Augustine has introduced a radically new note that overturns classical practice – while still, as is often the case, using its terminology – and has more in common, once again, with the philosophical critics of rhetoric. The unadorned, unarmed, naked truth (albeit with a certain uncontrived beauty, and a few unostentatious rhythmic closings, not, of course, deliberately sought, but, rather, in some way natural) comes forth to 'crush the sinews and muscles of its adversary and overcomes and destroys resisting falsehood with its most powerful members' (4.26.56). Augustine cannot entirely give up his predilection for the old 'eloquence'!

The ethical dimension of rhetoric, that had been effectively sidelined by the rhetors of Augustine's day, but very much emphasised by the philosophers, is also made central in Augustine's observation towards the end of Book 4 that 'the life of the speaker has greater weight in determining whether he is obediently heard than any grandness of eloquence' (4.27.59). His life is, as it were, as eloquent a witness to the truth as his words; but if his life is a lie it undermines the force of his words (4.29.62).[14]

However, it is not when Augustine is attempting to demonstrate the eloquence of Christian literature, nor when he is desperately trying to show that this eloquence is somehow 'natural', unintentional and uncontrived, nor when he is at pains to criticise classical rhetoric and to set it in contradistinction to Christian aims and practices, that he is at his most convincing. Rather, it is when he turns to actually *justify* his use of rhetoric, to explain why it is necessary and effective for the Christian writer and preacher, that what he says seems most cogent, ingenuous, and true to his own experience. The key term here is one which recurs frequently in Book 4: delight or *delectatio*. In this context, it refers to Cicero's second aim of rhetoric – to please or delight – which follows teaching, and, by engaging the listener's assent, enables the speaker to persuade and move them to act upon what has been taught:

> But if those who hear are to be moved rather than taught, so that they may not be sluggish in putting what they know into practice . . . there is need for greater powers of speaking. Here entreaties and reproofs, exhortations and rebukes, and whatever other devices are necessary to move minds must be used.
>
> (4.4.6)

It also belongs to the second style of rhetoric – the moderate or temperate style – which similarly aims to render what is said 'sweet' or pleasing, before the grand style moves the listener to consent. Ever conscious of criticism, Augustine warns that the speaker must not go too far: rather unusually, he chooses to illustrate his call for restraint with the work of another, otherwise venerated, African Father, St Cyprian. Referring to an especially flowery, somewhat over-the-top passage: 'Let us seek this place; the neighbouring solitudes offer a refuge where the wandering tendrils of the vines twine through loaded trellises with pendulous interlacings so as to make with a leafy roof a woody colonnade' he comments, 'that sweetness of discourse is not pleasing in which, although no iniquity is spoken, trivial and fragile truths are ornamented with a frothy nexus of words' (4.14.31).[15] The proper and acceptable use of the moderate style is not to evoke pleasure in rhetorical eloquence, as was almost exclusively the case among classical rhetors, but understanding of, delight in, love of, and obedience to the truth that is taught by means of it. (4.25.55; 4.26.57). It is in this sense, I think, that we can speak of a Christian aesthetic, a new Christian literary culture; one in which rhetoric holds as central a place as it did in classical culture, but where it is transformed from a practice that primarily aims to please and persuade, to one which aims to inspire love of, and the practice of, the truth.

This assertion should make more sense if we investigate the theological presuppositions on which it is based. First, the Fathers held that Scripture, unlike the works of classical culture, expressed the truth. This is what they believed the authors of Scripture were seeking to express, this is what the exegete seeks to find and what the preacher, in turn, attempts to teach. Augustine therefore distinguishes between *res* and *signa*, things and signs, in Book 1 of *De doctrina christiana*, in order to make clear what it is the exegete is dealing with: the *res* of the faith – God, the Trinity – expressed in the *signa* of Scripture. The interpretation of the exegete, like Scripture itself, has one end, one goal: the love of God and of one's neighbour in God.[16] In other words, love of the truth. How *signa* work to express this truth is discussed in Books 2 and 3; how they are to be *used* to express this truth is, as we have seen, the subject of Book 4.

Here I must stop to underline the special status Augustine attributes to Christian revelation – including Scripture and preaching – which enables him to make the confident distinctions in *De doctrina christiana*. Although language was a possibility in man's pre-lapsarian state, it was not a necessity: Adam and Eve enjoyed a direct and intuitive grasp of the truth in their minds and had no need for language to convey, or mediate it, for them.[17] They were inwardly refreshed by a fountain of truth. After their fall in pride, however, the situation we are now all too familiar with came about. Having turned away from inward illumination, from the fountain that welled up within, we are now dependent on truth which is mediated to us in words, in language; we can look for refreshment only to the rain that falls from the dark clouds of human doctrine and preaching.[18] So language, to some extent, is a result of the Fall: it forms a veil which obscures, distances, hides the truth from fallen man, whose eyes are no longer able to gaze upon its brightness. It separates and distances one man from another; it is essentially arbitrary; it can dissemble, misrepresent, be misunderstood. The variety of languages is the result of Babel, of pride.[19]

In *To Simplicianus*, Augustine presents his first sketch of fallen man as a *massa peccati*; of 'one lump in which the original guilt (of Adam) remains throughout'.[20] All people are implicated in Adam's sin; all deserve punishment; all are afflicted by concupiscence so that their wills are impotent to do anything but sin. That some do the good, that some are saved, can only be attributed to God's grace.[21] When something delights us, so that our wills are redirected and moved to do the good, this is wholly due 'to the inspiration of God and to the grace he bestows'. And delight does not appear here as just one example among others of how God works to motivate us towards the good. Rather, it is crucially important: 'the will itself can have no motive unless something presents itself to delight and stir the mind'.

Furthermore, it is the notion of delight that transforms Augustine's very negative picture of language after the Fall, to make it one of the key ways in which God reveals himself to fallen man, in a manner which inspires his delight, and, therefore, pleases and moves him, so that he loves and performs the good. Before re-evaluating what we have discovered about the role of delight in rhetoric in Book 4 of *De doctrina christiana* in this new theological context, a little more needs to be said about the interrelation of delight and love, for it is here, I think, that the key to interpreting what Augustine has to say there lies.

Here we enter upon a number of interrelations or synonyms:

- truth is beauty
- we can only love beautiful things[22]

- we only love that which delights us[23]
- love, desire and delight (*dilectio, desiderium* and *delectatio*) are synonymous
- love is the weight of the soul and orders the soul[24]
- to enjoy (*frui*) something is to cling to it with love for its own sake; to use (*uti*) something, however, is to employ it in obtaining that which you love [25]
- an ordered love (*ordinatam dilectionem*) enjoys only God, and loves everything else for the sake of God (*propter Deum*), or enjoys them in God (*frui in Deo*), or uses them with delight (*cum delectatione uti*).[26]

The two latter are a sort of transitory, rather than abiding, love and delight (*quadam dilectione et delectatione*), 'so that we love those things by which we are carried along for the sake of that toward which we are carried'.[27] Furthermore, we are only moved to act by that which inspires our love and delight: 'there is no devotion, no good life, unless it also be delighted in and loved'.[28] These insights are perhaps summed up in the famous passage from Augustine's sermon on John 6:44 , 'No man cometh to me except the Father draw him'. He writes:

> You are drawn, not merely by the will, but what is more, by pleasure. What is it, to be drawn by pleasure? 'Delight in the Lord, and he shall give you the requests of your heart' (Ps 37:4) . . . Moreover if the poet had leave to say, '*Trahit sua quemque voluptas*', not necessity, but pleasure; not obligation, but delight; how much more strongly ought we to say that a man is drawn to Christ, when he delights in truth, delights in blessedness, delights in righteousness, delights in everlasting life, all of which Christ is?
>
> (*Io. eu. tr.* 26.4)

In the light of these theological principles, we should not be surprised to find Augustine at pains to demonstrate the rhetorical eloquence of Scripture in Book 4, or to find him enthusiastically recommending the use of the rhetorical techniques of classical culture to the preacher in order to render the truth he teaches beautiful, delightful, love-worthy. If truth is beautiful; if beauty is delightful; if delight is the way in which God chooses to orient the fallen will towards Himself, there is nothing artifical, arbitrary, misleading, superfluous or decadent about describing Scripture as a work of literature, or using rhetoric to preach. To seek out the beauty of Scripture, to make preaching aesthetically pleasing, is, rather, to do full justice to their subject matter and to make it accessible.

There is a sort of hermeneutical circle here: love is the hermeneutical principle of Scripture; delight is that which inspires love; beauty is that which inspires delight; truth is that which inspires beauty; what man loves is the truth. It is, therefore, essential for Augustine that Scripture be shown to be beautiful, be made delightful, if its true end is to be attained. This is not a concession to its refined, cultured critics, or to his own sensibilities, but is, rather, the keystone of a 'Christian aesthetic' which recognises that God has chosen to motivate the fallen will to the true and good through the delight occasioned by His beautiful revelation of Himself, and this includes, centrally, Scripture and preaching.

Thus, Scripture becomes that difficult entity: a work of literature. In his interpretation of it, we see Augustine coming to terms with the 'fallenness' of language, its obscurities, ambiguities, difficulties – and Scripture has more than its fair share of these – by making them something positive, indeed, something literary, artistic, fashioned in order to arouse fallen man's interest, (positive) curiosity, aesthetic delight. It meets him at an affective, rather than a rational level, and demands imagination, intuition and aesthetic sensitivity if its message is to become clear.[29] As Marrou comments in the *Retractatio* we mentioned at the beginning of this paper:

> If Holy Scripture is not just the history of sinful humanity and the economy of salvation . . . if it is also this forest of symbols that through the appearances of figures suggests to us these same truths of the faith, one must have the courage to conclude that God is also a poet himself: To manifest himself to us he chose a means of expression which is also poetic, which brings into play one of the conceptions of poetry that reason and human culture have developed.
>
> (Marrou, op. cit., p. 648)

As well as a general Baudelairean tendency, one presumes what Marrou has in mind includes the fact that Scripture was thought to be inspired, to possess different levels (literal, spiritual), that it uses imagery, allegory, figures, poetry and parables as well as betraying the more formal traits of rhetorical artistry which Augustine demonstrates in Book 4 of *De doctrina christiana*.[30] Scripture signifies as language, but is sacramental as the inspired word of God. Thus, the difficulties and obscurities inherent in language overcome human pride, inspire humility, and cultivate a healthy sense of his limitations. They veil, honour and guard the truth, meeting readers at their different levels, with their different approaches, to inspire, exercise, attract and delight them, so that its meaning and its mystery might both be grasped and desired in its fullness.[31] Thus, Scripture became a work that could stand its ground against pagan literature and satisfy the cultured sensibilities of the educated (including the Fathers).[32] Much more importantly however, it became the means whereby God reorients and inspires the wills of the faithful, whatever their erudition (or ignorance), so that they can delight in the truth of the faith and realise the one thing necessary: love of God and neighbour.

A large proportion of the Fathers' exegesis takes a homiletic form. They generally interpreted Scripture, not in the manner of modern, academic, biblical scholars (though, of course, one only has to think of Origen or Jerome to realise that this discipline was not wholly absent from their work), but as pastors intent on expounding the text for the benefit of their congregations. It is in this context that the preacher's use of rhetoric finds its place. We noted Augustine's somewhat ambiguous attitude towards it and his careful adoption, and to a large extent, transformation, of it in a Christian context; not least because, like Scripture, it proved to be the best means of reorienting the will of fallen man to move him to delight in the truth, goodness and beauty of the Christian revelation and to act upon it. This essay is not, however, the place to demonstrate Augustine's rhetorical artistry: his use of verbal ornaments, figures, allegory, parables, metaphors, imagery, puns, proverbs, assonance, rhythm, word-play, antitheses, parallelism, *abundantia*, rhythmic closures and so on.[33] We might simply note that, as one might expect, it was influenced by classical, Cynic-Stoic, Sophistic and ecclesiastical or scriptural forms, and that practice does, indeed, usually follow theory (with a few gratuitous rhetorical excesses): what we find is a distinctive 'Christian aesthetic', shaped by the desire to teach and to move the listener to delight in and love the truths of the faith.

In conclusion, I would like to investigate a little futher just what it is that makes Augustine's literary aesthetic distinctively Christian. We have already noted the distinctive concern with truth and clarity, the priority of teaching, the role of delight in relation to the fallen will, and of love of God and neighbour; all of which characterise this aesthetic and set it apart from classical practice. Two further observations might be made.

The delight occasioned by Scripture or the preacher is not, as in classical practice, to be taken as an end in itself. Delight in the artistry of the preacher, or the literary form of Scripture, is meant to inspire love that points beyond them, to their inspiration and source, that is, to love of God. In other words, what ultimately matters is not the aesthetic form, the words themselves, or the style used, but their content, their meaning, their intention or inspiration, and this can only be found in God himself.[34]

This insight is the key to Augustine's defence of the apparent crudity and simplicity of Scripture, of his attempt to reconcile the divergent accounts of the four evangelists, of his acceptance of a plurality of meaning, of his use of allegory, of his positive approach to the difficulties, ambiguities and obscurities of Scripture. It enables him to tolerate and explain the obscurities and difficulties of the text at a literal level, but also to develop a literary aesthetic that makes sense of Scripture's ability to point beyond itself by engaging man's delight and love for what it says. The text itself, with all its apparent contradictions and difficulties, is both secondary to and instrumental in leading the interpreter to seek its inspiration and truth. Moreover, there is no divorce between style and substance, words and meaning, signs and signification in a Christian context, because, as we saw, the former are sacraments of the latter. In this sense too, then, the former cannot be taken as ends in themselves, as they perhaps were in classical practice, but are to be 'used' so that their truth can ultimately be 'enjoyed'.

> The plenitude and end of the law and of all the sacred Scriptures is the love of a Being which is to be enjoyed and of a being who can share that enjoyment with us . . . That we might know this and have the means to implement it, the whole temporal dispensation was made by divine providence for our salvation. We should use it, not with an abiding but with a transitory delight, like that in a road, or in vehicles, or in other instruments, or, it may be expressed more accurately, so that we love those things by which we are carried along for the sake of that towards which we are carried.
>
> (*Doctr. chr.* 1.35.39)

The inconclusive, open-ended, eschatological nature of Augustine's attitude to language and literary artistry is, therefore, grounded in his theological understanding and interpretation of them, and sets him apart from classical theory and practice.

The final point I would like to discuss relates to the social, cultural aspect of what we have termed 'Christian aesthetics'. What I mean by this is the way in which the language of the Christian faith, as it is found in Scripture and the words of the preacher, both demonstrates and lends itself to the formation of a distinctive culture and community in which it can operate effectively.

As we have seen above, the heart of the Christian faith, as it is found in Scripture and preaching, is love of God and neighbour. It is this love that defines and unifies the Christian community, not least because it enables communication between fallen men to take place. This is a note that is frequently sounded throughout Augustine's work. In the prologue to *De doctrina christiana*, he observes that, 'charity itself, which holds men together in a knot of unity, would not have a means of infusing souls and almost mixing them together, if men could teach nothing to men' (6). It is a point orchestrated most fully, however, in *De catechizandis rudibus*, On Teaching the Uninstructed. An awareness of language as a result of the Fall is not far from the surface of this work. Augustine first discusses the discouraging frustrations and difficulties of the preacher who may not feel inclined to speak, but who must, nevertheless, labour to articulate his understanding of the faith, and descend from an inward enjoyment of the truth to find words suitable to the level of his hearers (who are themselves all too prone to fail to grasp, or be moved by, what he says). He then gives the example of Christ's descent to man in love. This ought to be the true motive of the preacher's efforts: the more inspired by love his discourse is, the more irresistibly it finds its way into the heart of the hearer (10.15). What matters is not so much what the preacher says, but his state of mind, whether he takes pleasure and delight in what he is saying. If he does, he will be heard with pleasure, for 'so great is the power of sympathy', Augustine acutely comments in Chapter 12:

> that when people are affected by us as we speak and we by them as they learn, we dwell in one another and thus both they, as it were, speak in us what they hear, while we, after a fashion, learn in them what we teach.

De catechizandis rudibus might aptly be described as a treatise on the nature of love: it is love that ought to form the preacher's attitude and words; love that forms the subject of his discourse, and is the central lesson of Christian history as it is narrated in Scripture and expressed in the Church; love that the discourse inspires and that motivates man's actions. Love, therefore, informs the nature, practice, content and goal of exegesis and preaching.[35]

Like any other linguistic, interpretative community, the Christian community is determined by its acceptance of certain customs, traditions, conventions, authorities and texts.[36] These possess validity and value precisely because they are accepted and agreed upon.[37] Thus, words signify because there is agreement as to what they mean; conversely, they determine the nature, practice, and self-understanding of the community as they become traditional, authoritative, customary. As we have seen, Christianity's distinctive emphasis on the practice and rhetoric of love in its Scriptures and preaching enabled it to create a linguistic community in which the central message of the faith could be both understood and communicated so that it was then practised and lived. In other words, the central message of love of God and neighbour was interpreted and preached in such a way that it inspired and moved the hearer to love: and we have seen that eloquence, rhetoric, an artistic, affective, 'delightful' use of language in Scripture and preaching was central to this process. We cannot, therefore, underestimate the social and cultural function of exegesis, and, particularly, preaching in the formation of a Christian society. It is in this context, more than any other, that Christian rhetoric finds its justification and defence.

Of course, the same might be said of classical rhetoric. In the course of this essay I have suggested a number of ways in which Christian 'rhetoric' is distinctive and diverges from classical theory and practice. Above all, I have tried to defend it against the criticism of being simply a regrettable manifestation of the worst excesses of classical decadence. Having done so, I am perhaps free to admit, in conclusion, to the obvious overlap between the two: in Augustine's own personal history and identity, and in his work and preaching. He did not leave his past behind, as it were, and try to root out any traces of it in his new Christian identity; he was too well aware of the futility of such a task, and of the pervasiveness, importance and usefulness of secular culture, even for Christianity, to make such an attempt. Rather, he attempted to come to terms with secular culture, to appreciate but also criticise, to assimilate but also reject, in other words, to 'convert' it to his use, just as he had done in his own person.[38] It is in this respect that we can read *De doctrina christiana* Book 4 with full seriousness.

Notes

1 The text used throughout is CCL 32. One hesitates to give any summary of what *De doctrina christiana* is actually about, since it has been the subject of so much debate: see F. X. Eggersdorfer, *Der heilige Augustinus als Pädagoge und seine Bedeutung für die Geschichte der Bildung*, Freiburg im Breisgau, Herder, 1907; H.-I. Marrou, *Saint Augustin et la fin de la culture antique*, Paris, E. de Boccard, 1938; E. Kevane, 'Augustine's *De doctrina christiana*: A Treatise on Christian Education', *Recherches augustiniennes* 4 (1966), pp. 97–133; and most convincingly, L. Verheijen, 'Le *de doctrina christiana* de saint Augustin: Un manuel d'herméneutique et d'expression chrétienne avec, en II,19 (29)–42 (63), une "charte fondamentale pour une culture chrétienne"', *Augustiniana* 24 (1974), pp. 10–20.

2 See, for example, the fine collection of essays and extensive bibliography in D. W. H. Arnold and P. Bright (eds), De Doctrina Christiana: *A Classic of Western Culture*, Notre Dame, Notre Dame University Press, 1995.

3 He asked his bishop, Valerius, for time to study the Scriptures, and from 395 onwards wrote a series of works on Paul, especially Romans.

4 For suggestions as to why there is such a gap in the composition of this work see C. Kannengiesser, 'The Interrupted *De doctrina christiana*', in Arnold and Bright (eds), op. cit., pp. 4–14.

5 For the criticism of being 'narrow', see G. Bonner, '*Vera lux illa est quae illuminat*: The Christian Humanism of Augustine', in *Renaissance and Renewal in Christian History*, ed. D. Baker, Oxford, Blackwell, 1977, p. 14. For 'reductivist', see C. Schäublin, '*De doctrina christiana*: A Classic of Western Culture?', in Arnold and Bright, op. cit., p. 53.

6 M. Comeau, *Saint Augustin: Exégète du quatrième évangile*, Paris, Beauchesne, 1930, Ch. 6; J. Finaert, *Saint Augustin rhéteur*, Paris, Société d'édition 'Les Belles Lettres', 1939, p. 94; R. J. O'Connell, *Art and the Christian Intelligence in Saint Augustine*, Oxford, Basil Blackwell, 1978, p. 146; R. A. Markus, 'World and Text I: Augustine', in *Signs and Meaning*, Liverpool, Liverpool University Press, 1996, p. 12.

7 P. Brown, *Power and Persuasion in Late Antiquity*, Madison Wis., University of Wisconsin Press, 1992; A. Cameron, *Christianity and Rhetoric of Empire*, Berkeley /Los Angeles, University of California Press, 1991, p. 123.

8 See the example given by G. Clark, *Augustine: The Confessions*, Cambridge, Cambridge University Press, 1993, p. 77.

9 What is known as the *Vetus Latina*, is an extremely literal, early third-century Latin translation of the New Testament and Septuagint. It is extant in a large number of versions which are in the process of being collected by the Institute at Beuron.

10 *Doctr. chr.* 2.40.60–1. See also 2.18.28.

11 The gender-exclusive language is Augustine's, not mine; girls were not usually educated to the same degree as boys in his day.

12 Plato, *Gorgias* 454e. Note the contrast Plato draws between eloquence basd on plausibility and philosophical eloquence founded on the truth that it aims to

teach. See E. L. Fortin, 'Augustine and the Problem of Christian Rhetoric', *Augustinian Studies* 5 (1974), pp. 85–100.

13 For a discussion of Augustine's use of Cicero, see Fortin, op. cit.; A. Primmer, 'The Function of the *genera dicendi* in *De doctrina christiana* 4', in Arnold and Bright (eds), op. cit., pp. 68–87.

14 For commentary, see G. Howie, *Educational Theory and Practice in Saint Augustine*, London, Routledge and Kegan Paul, 1969, pp. 232–9.

15 Cyprian, *Ad Donatum* 1. See Augustine's comments on the similar rhetoric of the Donatist bishops in *Cresc.* 4.2.

16 *Doctr. chr.* 1.35.39; *ep.* 55.21.38; *s.* 350.2.2. He cites Rom 13:10 and 1 Tm 1:5, that 'love is the plenitude and end of the law', and Mt 22:37–40, that the double commandment of love 'contains all the law and the prophets'.

17 *Gn. litt.* 11.28.43.

18 *Gn. adu. Man.* 2.4.5–5.6

19 *En. Ps.* 54.11; *s.* 266.2.

20 *Simpl.* 2.17

21 Ibid.

22 *Mus.* 6.11.29–30; 6.13.38.

23 *S.* 159.3.

24 *Conf.* 13.9.10. See *mus.* 6.11.29.

25 *Doctr. chr.* 1.4.4.

26 For *frui in Deo* see ibid., 1.26.27–27.28. For *cum delectatione uti*, see ibid., 1.33.37, in relation to Philemon 20 where Paul writes 'may I enjoy thee in the Lord'.

27 Ibid., 1.35.39.

28 *Spir. et litt.* 3.

29 See V. Gillespie, 'Mystic's Foot: Rolle and Affectivity', in *The Medieval Mystical Tradition in England. Papers read at Dartington Hall, July 1982*, ed. M. Glasscoe, Exeter, Exeter University Press, 1982, pp. 199–231.

30 See M. Moreau, 'Sur un Commentaire d'Amos 6,1–6', in *Saint Augustin et la Bible*, ed. A.-M. La Bonnardière, Paris, Beauchesne, 1986, pp. 313–23.

31 See C. Harrison, *Revelation and Beauty in the Thought of Saint Augustine*, Oxford, Oxford University Press, 1992, pp. 81–95; and H.-I. Marrou, op. cit., pp. 488–94 for references and a discussion of Augustine's practice of allegory.

32 For Augustine's awareness of this problem and his recommendation of this sort of exegesis to meet it, see *cat. rud.* 9.13; *ep.*137.1.3–5.18.

33 See C. Mohrmann, *Etudes sur le latin des chrétiens*, vol. 2, Rome, Edizioni de storia e letteratura, 1961; Finaert, op. cit.

34 See R. D. Williams, 'Language, Reality, and Desire in Augustine's *De doctrina christiana*', *Literature and Theology* 3 (1989), pp. 138–50.

35 See *mor.* 1.17.31: 'It is love that asks, love that seeks, love that knocks, love that reveals, love, too, that gives continuance in what is revealed'.

36 See R. A. Markus, 'Signs, Communication and Communities in Augustine's *De doctrina christiana*', in Arnold and Bright (eds), op. cit., pp. 105–24, to whom I am indebted for these insights.

37 *Doctr. chr.* 2.24.37.

38 These observations are inspired by J.-C. Fredouille, *Tertullien et la conversion de la culture antique*, Paris, Etudes augustiniennes, 1972.

14

AUGUSTINE'S SECULAR CITY

Robert Dodaro

'I need not describe the power of patriotic love (*caritas patriae*), for you know it already; it alone could justly take precedence over affection for our parents'. So begins Nectarius, an elderly resident of Calama, in a letter addressed to Augustine, the Catholic bishop of Hippo Regius, some 65 km northwest.

> If a good man's service of his home town had any limit or terminus, then by now I might deserve to excuse myself worthily from my duties to it. On the contrary, though, one's affection and gratitude for one's city grows as each day passes; and the nearer life approaches to its end, the more one desires to leave it flourishing and secure. That is why I am delighted before all else to be conducting this discussion with a man who is thoroughly well educated.[1]

Nectarius is a pagan and a former official in the imperial civil service.[2] The 'discussion' that he opens with Augustine concerns the recent outbreak of ferocious, anti-Christian violence in Calama, his home town. On 1 June AD 408 and on two successive days a week later, rioting between devotees of a local pagan cult and the city's Catholics seriously disrupted the peace. As Augustine later recounts the incident, violence first broke out when Possidius, the city's bishop and a close friend, intervened to impede certain rites connected with an unspecified pagan festival. During the ensuing confrontation, stones were hurled at the bishop's church as a reprisal for his interference. When, eight days later, in accordance with established legal procedure, Possidius lodged a formal complaint over the incident with the municipal officials, his church was again attacked, and, on the following day, was stoned a third time, looted of valuables and set ablaze. One of the members of his church was killed in the conflict, and Possidius himself narrowly escaped assassination by hiding from the mob, perhaps in his own house (*ep.* 91.8). Not all the criminal acts were committed by pagans; a number of Christians either failed to render assistance when the church was burning, or participated in the looting (*ep.* 104.9).

Possidius knew that, in attempting to prevent the pagan rites from being observed, he was acting in full accord with a recent edict of the Emperor Honorius, addressed to Africa during the previous year, which reiterated a ban by the Emperor Theodosius in AD 391 against pagan religious ceremonies, such as public processions and festivals, and gave Catholic bishops the right to intervene against them. Honorius charged imperial officials with enforcing these edicts and protecting the Catholic church against interference from pagans.[3]

In this first of his two letters to Augustine, Nectarius acknowledges that serious crimes had been committed against the church, and that harsh penalties could thus lawfully be applied to residents who were convicted of related, illegal activities, because they either participated in the violence or did not act to prevent it. He writes to Augustine in loyal response to an urgent request of the municipal council, but also out of sympathy with the city's pain, in the hope that the bishop will accept a settlement for damages suffered by the church, and that he will intercede with imperial officials to reduce the harshness of whatever criminal penalties (*supplicia*) they might contemplate against the city's inhabitants.

Sometime before the end of June, Augustine visits Calama and meets separately with groups of Christians and pagans, the latter at their own request, in an effort to gather information about the incidents and impart counsel (*ep.* 91.10). Returning to Hippo Regius, he receives Nectarius' letter in July and responds to it immediately and at length (ep. 91). He assures the city's representative that, although the matter is not his to decide, he will strongly urge that no one in Calama suffer the death penalty or any physical torture, but that penalties be restricted to heavy fines. He warns, however, that in order for this Christian leniency to be shown, the fines may have to be applied more indiscriminately than if judicial investigations were undertaken to distinguish more clearly the guilty from the innocent. Such interrogations could not be carried out lawfully without the application of torture, and neither Augustine nor Nectarius wished this to happen (*ep.* 91.9). An additional reason for Augustine to welcome a more widespread application of fines against the city's residents is that he suspects members of the municipal council not only of failing to prevent the unlawful festival, and the ensuing violence against the church, but even of actively encouraging them.[4] Because many of these councillors are wealthy landowners, he hopes the fines will punish them in a way that leads them to true repentance, and serve as a warning to municipal councils elsewhere in Africa that anti-Christian violence will not be condoned.[5]

Some time passes before Nectarius writes in response to Augustine.[6] When he does so, he objects to the latter's suggestion of serious fines as punishment on the grounds that 'a life of poverty produces endless misfortune', and that many would rather die than face such stark, material deprivation (*ep.* 103.3). He points out that those Christians who have confessed criminal involvement in the affair (possibly in open court before a magistrate), and who are undergoing penance (*poenitentia*) within the church, have already been exempted from any penalties. If, by publicly confessing and repenting of their sins, Christians can justly be spared civil punishments, why cannot the same leniency apply to pagans? Nectarius takes little notice of Augustine's earlier assurances that he will urge imperial officials to avoid inflicting capital punishment or torture, and voices his fear that innocent, non-Christian residents who are subjected at random to torture in this matter will be enraged at the sight of self-confessed, but unpunished, Christian criminals (*ep.* 103.4).

Augustine's reply opens with his repeated assurance that he will intercede with imperial officials to prevent the application of capital punishment or physical torture in the pursuit of justice at Calama, and he invites Nectarius to make him aware of any such occurrences should they arise (*ep.* 104.1 and 5). However, he insists that substantial fines ought to be applied against those who may have been involved, even indirectly, in the crimes committed against the church, because their extravagant wealth is used to support pagan religion and to oppose Christianity (*ep.* 104.5). By continuing to do so unpunished, they might incite pagan aristocrats in other cities to follow their example. Augustine clearly has the wealthiest landowners in mind here. He does not wish them to be reduced to begging, but demands that they be stripped of superfluous wealth (*ep.* 104.6). He defends the practice of excusing those Christians from civil penalties who publicly confess their crimes and submit themselves to penance, and of not extending this same leniency to non-Christians, on the grounds that Christians who do penance will be forced, thereby, to take time to reflect deeply upon their misdeeds, while non-Christians, for whom a public confession and apology is an expeditious, judicial formality, will not do so. Aside from deterring other cities from following the violent example of Calama, the only goal of punishment in this case is conversion of heart. True sorrow for grave crimes cannot be mass produced in a short period of time. Conversion requires a gradual process of interior reflection that allows the soul sufficient time to recognise itself uncomfortably in its misdeeds.[7] Thus, its aim is to reshape desire at the heart of the individual. Augustine does not believe that the church's practice is unjustly discriminatory toward non-Christians. If Nectarius were sincerely concerned for his city's best interests, he would be more anxious over the lack of true conversion of heart than he is in mitigating the very penalties which alone may produce such conversion (*ep.* 104.5–10).[8]

The politics of confession

The four letters constituting the correspondence between Nectarius and Augustine have attracted the attention of a recent critic of Augustinian political thought. Writing in *The Augustinian Imperative*, William Connolly comments on the Calama affair as one among many illustrations of Augustinian political authoritarianism and intolerance of religions other than his own brand of Catholic Christianity.[9] Although Connolly concerns himself only briefly with the specific issues between Nectarius and Augustine, he examines them in conjunction with similar applications of political thought drawn from a range of the bishop's pastoral activities, including his attitudes to pagans, his treatment of women and his opposition to heretical groups such as Manichaeans, Donatists and Pelagians.[10]

Connolly's is a sweeping, well-reasoned and penetrating indictment of the philosophical and theological underpinnings of Augustine's political thought, and it pays close attention to the role of moral conversion accompanied by confession of sins. As such, it deserves to be taken seriously by Augustinian scholars. He develops his analysis of what he terms the 'Augustinian imperative' through readings of Friedrich Nietzsche and Michel Foucault, and develops a highly original critique which none the less runs parallel at points to those of other scholars from Hannah Arendt to Elaine Pagels.[11] Discussing the case Connolly makes thus enables one to address, in a limited fashion, a cluster of criticisms aimed at the more troubling foundations of Augustinian political thought.[12] I propose to do this by briefly summarising some of the features of Connolly's critique that seem the most compelling, and then by discussing them in the context of Augustine's debate with Nectarius over the best ways to care for the city.

To begin with, Connolly describes 'the Augustinian imperative' as:

> the insistence that there is an intrinsic moral order susceptible to authoritative representation. This imperative, in turn, is linked to an obligatory pursuit: the quest to move closer to one's truest self by exploring its inner geography. Although neither the imperative nor the pursuit is susceptible to full realisation, each provides an indispensable complement to the other in the Augustinian world.[13]

The 'imperative' in Augustine's political thought is, therefore, moral in nature and derives from religious faith in a single, omnipotent God who creates the universe and endows it with a specific order rooted in God as the principle of goodness. It conceives of morality in terms of 'obedience to transcendental command' and 'attunement to an intrinsic design' (p. xviii). Connolly recognises that Augustine is neither the first nor the last in history to formulate this imperative; the outstanding reason for studying it at work in his thought lies in the success of the tactics by which the bishop 'installed these themes in the heart' of western culture, in spite of strong opposition from a number of significant forces inside and outside the church of his day. Connolly holds out the hope that, by becoming more aware of the operation of these themes in the 'consolidation of any ethic, including one that we may endorse, we might . . . become more ethical with respect to the tactics of

morality' found in Augustine (pp. xvii–xviii). In saying this, he acknowledges that western culture in general, and American political culture in
particular, have assimilated much of Augustine's authoritarian 'politics of
morality', but also that, while awareness and reform of Augustine's legacy is
warranted, not everything in his thought ought necessarily to be rejected in
the name of today's (post-)Nietzschean, democratic, pluralist political
consensus. Connolly thus seeks to 'disturb Augustinianism from an ethical
perspective that is both indebted to it and at odds with it' (p. xviii). The
Augustinian tactics of concern to Connolly centre on the political consequences of the bishop's confessional theory and practice.[14] I shall, therefore,
limit my discussion to Connolly's understanding of them as structures aimed
at reinforcing patterns of political control and exclusion.

Connolly is drawn to confession as a tactic in Augustine's political
thought because of its rhetorical power in constructing and reinforcing the
foundations of a transcendent moral order which seemingly lie beyond
narcissism, but are actually a manifestation of it. By this reading, the divine
moral order to which Augustine voices commitment is an order he creates
through confession of his own sinfulness (classically in his *Confessions*), and
then imposes upon his church and beyond it. Through his writings and
preaching, the personal experience of radical conversion and the confession
that enables it, dynamics that form the heart of his own theology, become
paradigmatic for the determination of a just social and political order (pp.
44–8). Because this conversion experience can be objectified and narrated
through confession, because God's omnipotence can be confidently felt
behind it as the source of tranquillity for a divided will, and because the
processes involved can successfully be imitated, no other religious system
than his, with its foundation in confession and conversion, can guarantee
access to an enduring personal good in the form of salvation of the soul, and,
therefore, no other system can produce a public good in the form of peace in
the city. Connolly chides Augustine for being bimodal when he should be
polymodal, for universalising his own conversion experience and, thus,
excluding the possibility that other forms of religious life (Jewish, Platonic,
Pelagian) might equally produce just social and political orders. This
religious exclusivity, however, is inevitable, as Connolly sees it, because the
confessional mode through which Augustinian conversion takes place stands
beyond scrutiny; the self-abasing humility which it performs acts rhetorically
to blind the soul to its own self-aggrandising fictions, and moments of self-
doubt, when they occur, are resolved through repetition of confession (pp.
44–7, 60–7).

As an example of the projective possibilities of Augustinian confession,
Connolly seizes on *Confessions* 3.8.16, where Augustine bemoans his captivity
to sexual lust and identifies God as the 'fountain of life', the 'sole and true
creator and ruler of the universe', who cleanses him from his evil ways and
frees him from his chains once he has submitted himself to God by an act of

'humble devotion'. Connolly argues that, in this text, Augustine '*defines* his god through confessing to it':

> From within Augustine's faith this sounds like a contrite confession to god of its own power, sovereignty, goodness and grace set within an appreciation of the role that contrite confession plays in drawing the faithful closer to this god. From a position outside Augustinian faith, these same words sound like the cultural production of a divinity by the persistent confession of the specific attributes it must have.
>
> (Connolly, op. cit., p. 45)

Thus, Connolly asks whether Augustine's divinity really does free him from lust or whether, in making his confession, he is fashioning a 'god' according to the attributes he most ardently seeks in divinity: an omnipotent source of goodness capable of bestowing an eternal salvation that includes temporal liberation from sexual desires of this sort. Any personal failure in this regard that Augustine experiences after his confession only causes him to repeat the confession, rather than question its theoretical foundations. The moral authority and intrinsic moral design for the universe which Augustine attributes to God are thus reinforced through repeated confessions of sins.

For Connolly, the 'contribution' of Augustine to western political thought is summed up in his having successfully institutionalised this personal form of confession and exported it throughout the western church and empire. This generalisation of confession and its moral foundations constructs and reinforces an identity for Catholic Christianity, which, at the same time, constitutes and then underscores differences between this form of the Catholic church and 'pagan' or 'heretical' groups defined as outsiders to it. The latter thus become political rivals to the peace offered by Augustine's church. His political legacy to western history is to have handed down the specific *pattern* of identity/difference that arises from confession.

Connolly traces this pattern as it is found in Augustine's dealings with a series of internal and external threats to the social control confession secures. In *ep.* 211, he sees Augustine reacting against a challenge to the authority of the superior of a monastery of nuns within his city, by accusing the women of an arrogance and rebellion rooted in pride. By Connolly's analysis, Augustine's reiteration of minutely detailed, monastic rules involving self-scrutiny which he imposes on the community both *produces* the desire for the illicit object or behaviour at issue, and *enables* the confession of sin that the rules themselves have produced. The system that these two functions represent thus reinforces the arbitrarily imposed rules that govern the monastery. For example, Augustine's prohibition of nuns receiving letters or small gifts from men both creates the 'sin' of receiving letters and gifts, and provides the opportunity for the rule's reinforcement through confession of the sin by the offending nun:

Whenever anyone has gone so far in misconduct as to receive secretly from any man letters or small gifts of any kind, if she confesses the matter freely, pardon her and pray for her. If however, she is detected and proved guilty, she is to be rather severely corrected according to the judgement of the priest or superior.

(*reg.* 4.11)[15]

Connolly asks:

What is going on here? New thoughts, desires, temptations, and acts are being created through the authoritative practice of confession. Sin is produced to enable confession; confession is pursued to disclose and correct sin. Is the inward self being uncovered? Or is it being manufactured by a particular conjunction of rules, desires, and the confessional imperative?

(Connolly, op. cit., p. 70)

Connolly detects in Augustine's monastic rules an 'authoritative network of confessional morality' consisting in:

meticulous specification of rules, the production of sinful desires, the obligation to confess, a network of mutual surveillance among equals, a system of punishments, the manufacture of the inward self, and the confession of a divine source hovering over the entire complex.

(Connolly, op. cit., p. 71)

He further observes in these monastic rules the universalising of the confession and conversion processes that Augustine underwent in his own attempt to gain freedom from the 'rebellious desires' of a divided will. Moreover, the rules embody a hierarchical, authoritarian social control rooted in sororal correction, a form of systematic and voyeuristic surveillance whereby sisters in community practise vigilance over each other's chastity, confronting one another or reporting infractions of the rules to higher superiors who then employ punishments in order to induce confession and behavioural correction on the part of the wayward. Here again, Connolly points out that, paradoxically, the rules produce the effect they were intended to thwart: the roving, unchaste eye that Augustine fears in nuns who might fix their gaze longingly on men is transformed into the roving, unchaste eye of the sister on the lookout for infractions of the rules by her companions in the monastery (p. 71–2).

If the Augustinian 'politics of identity' applied within the church requires an arduous and delicate effort at maintenance, the Augustinian 'politics of difference' governing relations with those outside the church demands even stiffer forms of coercion equally grounded in a confessional practice. The generalisation of Augustine's own conversion experience carries with it the projection of that conversion – and of the personal confession with its construction of an interior self which formed its core – onto the whole of the society which surrounded him. Pagans, Jews, and even groups of Christians (Donatists, Pelagians and other 'heretics') are challenged to defend their claims of access to true wisdom and the highest good on the basis of a comparison with the truth claims of Augustine's brand of Catholic Christianity. The terms on which this challenge and the comparison which it involves are based provide the key issue for Connolly in Augustine's exchanges with Nectarius. Connolly observes this affair as one of a number of examples of the Augustinian 'politics of difference' at work in constructing paganism as an inferior religious system and, hence, one which has to be controlled and even suppressed by political means.

With regard to Calama, Connolly asserts that the terms with which Augustine couches his charges against Nectarius' colleagues 'presuppose the objectivity of the Augustinian order and the justice of the law against celebrating pagan holidays'. Augustine at no time admits the possibility that pagan religion might be regarded as offering a way into sacred mysteries and a coherent view of salvation alternative, but not inferior, to Christianity. Moreover, while he ignores the extent to which his own religion borrows heavily from Platonism, he is certain that non-Christian forms of faith cannot produce the level of moral good which the city requires for its security. Augustine's policy toward Calama represents a 'gentle war of difference' because it firmly excludes capital punishment or physical torture, but it is none the less intended to suppress pagan cults. Suppression, however, is not the only goal of Augustine's politics. For Connolly, Augustine's correspondence with Nectarius represents the bishop's attempt once again to construct paganism as a religious system with a theology and an accompanying moral order inferior to what is found in Christianity. Connolly would have us note how, in his arguments against Nectarius, Augustine continually shapes the content of pagan religion to fit his interpretation of it by comparing it negatively with the content that he also provides for a superior, because Christian, moral order. This Augustinian insistence upon differences between Christianity and paganism enables him rhetorically to create two discernible religious and moral systems, and to exaggerate their differences in favour of the former (pp. 76–7).

This peculiar feature of Augustine's approach to theologies other than his own is also exemplified in his dealings with heretical Christian groups, especially with adherents of 'Pelagianism'. Heresy, like paganism, is 'indispensable to the Augustinian system' because, by providing the experience of alterity or difference in religious outlook, it shores up his conception of "true religion", the Christian identity which he associates with confession and conversion as he understands these processes' (p. 78).[16] Definitions of different religious viewpoints as 'other', as morally inferior or even harmful to salvation, enable the exclusion of threats which appear within Augustine's system from 'a dangerous line of reflection latent within' it. Thus, Augustine first senses the Manichaean doctrine of two competing forces, good and evil, as an internal challenge arising from his own Catholic insistence on the omnipotence of the God to whom he confesses two wills, good and evil, and, thus, as a threat to the theoretical foundation of the conversion process which he believes confession fosters. Manichaeism must, therefore, be defined and suppressed as a heresy. A similar logic obtains for Pelagianism. Long before he heard the teaching of Celestius and Pelagius, he felt aspects of their doctrine within himself as the impulse to believe that he and all Christians should be able to exercise total self-control over their wills. This 'temptation' threatened his own conviction in the necessity of repeated confession as an ongoing process of enabling the will to be healed through an extended moral conversion. Connolly thus stresses that, for Augustine, both of these heretical tendencies of thought (along with Donatism) also exist as internal challenges to the hegemony of confession of sins in the construction of a superior moral order. He deals with the threats these alternative ways of thinking represent by continually re-constituting them as heresies even after they have been formally defined by the church and expelled as such.[17] This repeated re-constitution of heresies keeps them outside the boundaries of the interior self so that they do not re-constitute themselves inside as temptations to think differently about God and salvation.

Connolly suggests, finally, that Augustine's need to ward off threats to the centrality of confession and conversion in his account of salvation arises from a related need to manage anxiety, in particular, the anxiety of death. Augustine claims in the *Confessions* that the philosophical approach to good and evil suggested by Epicurus appealed to him as a young man, and that the sole defect he found in it lay in its rejection of immortality and of the eternal rewards and punishments an individual earns before death (p. 82).[18] Because belief in an afterlife plays no role in Epicurus' thought, his philosophy lacks the 'internal pressure to construct heresies' out of adversarial positions. Connolly judges Augustine's affirmation of an afterlife complete with a system of rewards and punishments to be a 'narcissistic insistence' which forms yet another theoretical foundation to the Augustinian imperative's unique claim on salvation.

As mentioned earlier, Nectarius argues that his clients at Calama are prepared to make a full, public confession of their involvement in unlawful violence against the church in exchange for the same leniency that Christians, who have made a similar, public confession, enjoy (*ep*. 103.3). Augustine refuses the offer, and, by Connolly's analysis, he does so because the pagan confessions would not have been instruments of their conversion, since they are not able to form these individuals in the identity of the true faith (p. 85). Hence, confession and the self-knowledge it allegedly produces are not efficacious for Augustine unless they reinforce belief in his concept of an omnipotent God, and in the possibility of an eternal salvation earned exclusively by means of repeated confessions of sins committed against a divinely-established, intrinsic moral order. It is in this light that Connolly understands Augustine's reply to Nectarius:

> Now it is true, as you write, that repentance wins mercy and atones for the offence itself. But it is only that sort that is undertaken by true religion, with the future judgement of God in mind; not the sort that is displayed (or feigned) before human beings, just for the occasion, to free their ephemeral lives from immediate fear of trouble for the moment, rather than to cleanse the soul of its misdeeds for eternity.
>
> (*ep.* 104.9).[19]

Connolly concludes his argument by venturing that western political cultures have paid a high price to sustain the Augustinian imperative in its many reincarnations since the fifth century. Had Augustine been able to conceive of God in less absolute and omnipotent terms, he might have been able also 'to oppose a rival position actively while refusing to define it as heretical' or, as we might add in the case of non-Christian religions, without discrediting their intrinsic value. Such a reformed understanding:

> exposes uncertainties, undecidabilities, and ambiguities in the opposition without pretending to do so from a ground that is solid, intrinsic, or incontestable. It affirms the element of paradox within which it works. It resists and counters its adversaries without striving to eliminate them.
>
> (Connolly, op. cit., p. 89)

Confession in historical context

Although Connolly admits that his criticisms of Augustine's political applications of confession stem from modern and contemporary philosophers such as Nietzsche and Foucault, he still fails to situate Augustine within an accurate historical perspective, both in terms of early Christianity and the philosophical and religious traditions of late antiquity. There are three points in his critique in which the lack of historical perspective is most pronounced: the absolute character of the authority of those Christian doctrines which were shared by both Catholic and heretical groups, the question of religious tolerance in late antiquity and the widespread diffusion of Christian and non-Christian spiritual traditions regarding confession and moral conversion.

As with many modern critics of Augustine, Connolly isolates him from the theological givens of the Christian religion of his day, as if he were singularly responsible for their authority. However, doctrines concerning divine omnipotence, the resurrection of the body, the last judgement and an eternal afterlife were commonly and forcefully defended by Christian writers throughout the patristic period, prior to and following Augustine.[20] Nor did all 'heretical' groups oppose such convictions. No Donatist, Pelagian or Arian Christian in good standing within his or her own religious community would have conceived of a universe without an omnipotent God presiding over an intrinsic moral order.

With regard to religious tolerance, historians today who look in late antiquity for this evolving, typically modern phenomenon more frequently note the lack of a theoretical foundation for it in any branches of ancient religion, Christian or non-Christian.[21] While agreeing with this judgement, Peter Brown cautions that in order to evaluate religious intolerance in late antiquity with an historically accurate viewpoint, we need to pay far greater attention to the ways in which education and breeding (*paideia* and decorum) established codes of conduct for the negotiation of religious practice among the social and political elite of the era, and to pay less attention to philosophical debates and to the character of imperial legislation. Brown argues that, in effect, the practical religious intolerance experienced at large may have been less harsh and comprehensive than the written sources seem to suggest.[22] By this reading, the outbreak of religious violence at Calama, while not without parallel, may depict more the exception than the norm for relations between Christians and pagans.[23]

Finally, Connolly's analysis of the Augustinian imperative may too easily imply Augustine's unique responsibility for having first integrated confession of sin with the acquisition of self-knowledge before an omnipotent God functioning in an intrinsically ordered moral universe. In creating this impression, Connolly fails to locate Augustine within broader Christian spiritual traditions which he inherited at the same time that he influenced both their evolution and diffusion through the western Church and empire. To grasp this point it is sufficient to examine the role of Ambrose, the bishop of Milan who instructed and baptised Augustine into the Catholic church (AD 387), in forming the latter's views on the importance of confession of sins for acquiring the self-knowledge requisite for a sincere and efficacious moral conversion.[24] Yet such themes are also found within earlier Christian and non-Christian writers; Ambrose and Augustine are the heirs to a number of ancient, interdependent Jewish, pagan (Platonic, Stoic, Neoplatonic) and Christian traditions concerning a spiritual and moral 'attention to oneself' (*prosoche*) which includes the practices of minute examination of conscience, confession, conversation with a spiritual director, self-vigilance or 'watch of the heart' (*nepsis*), contemplation, rules of life (*kanones*), self-mastery and the absence of passions (*apatheia*).[25] Connolly acknowledges that Augustine does not invent the moral imperative (p. xvii), but his account lacks the historical foundation from which a comparison of the 'Augustinian' imperative can be made with those contemporary philosophical and religious approaches to confession and conversion with which it interacted.

The point of these observations concerning a lack of historical foundation to Connolly's argument is not merely to identify antecedents to Augustinian confession in other philosophical or religious movements. One of the values in joining a comparative historical study to Connolly's philosophical enquiry is to achieve a deeper understanding of the differences arising between Augustine's views and those of his contemporaries, concerning confession and its role in the construction of an interior self. Viewed from a comparative perspective, Augustine's debates with pagans such as Nectarius over the public good to be produced by repentance are not simply occasions for rehearsing philosophical arguments over the moral advantages obtained through conversion to the 'true God'. They reveal significant divergences concerning the structure and quality of virtues such as contrition, repentance and forgiveness as they apply to the moral growth of individual citizens, to their reconciliation with each other and, thus, to the promotion of the public good. It is precisely the character and centrality of these debates which are obscured for us without serious, interdisciplinary enquiries into competing Christian and non-Christian forms of philosophy and spirituality, and the consequences of these rivalries upon civic life in Augustine's day.

We would like to know the full extent to which Augustine borrowed from spiritual practices or approaches to virtue among various Platonic, Stoic or Roman schools of thought aimed at nurturing civic order and peace. How did he combine these borrowings with various orthodox Christian forms of spirituality (prayer and meditation, fasting, almsgiving, periodic sexual continence), some of which were also derived at an earlier point in history from Jewish, Manichaean, Neoplatonic and other non-Christian practices? How ought we to distinguish the Christian practice of generosity as, for example, in almsgiving, from contemporary, non-Christian manifestations of civic virtue such as evergetism?[26] Connolly has done us the service of focusing his study of Augustine's anti-pagan and anti-heretical polemics narrowly on the negative political consequences of the authoritarian and coercive features of Augustinian confession. Yet, by neglecting to look at the dynamics of confession and conversion historically, he restricts their motivations in Augustine to the philosophical *a prioris* bound up with what he views as theological dogmatism, a belief in an omnipotent God and a system of rewards and punishments in an eternal afterlife.

Reading Augustine's critique of non-Christian or 'heretical' spiritualities with greater historical awareness of the comparative philosophical and religious issues at stake does not produce an interpretation of Augustinian confession as any less authoritarian or coercive than Connolly judges it to be, and certainly does not provide a justification for this shadow side to the political consequences of Augustinian theology. Yet, such an interpretation might tell us, with greater specificity, the nature of Augustine's criticisms of alternative spiritual practices aimed at moral improvement, and thereby alert us to the dangers which he perceived in them for the promotion of the public good.

Confession and the rhetorics of empire

Turning back to the letters exchanged between Nectarius and Augustine with this comparative approach at interpretation in mind, and re-examining Augustine's rejection of his pagan interlocutor's proposals for reconciliation in the city, it is possible to locate the key to their differences. This lies not in a lofty debate over 'true religion' (although traces of this argument are also found there), but in the nature of the virtue mentioned in the statement with which Nectarius opens the discussion and which is quoted at the beginning of this essay: affection and care for one's own home town (*caritas patriae*).[27] In turning to this closer reading of the correspondence, we find, interspersed within the debate over which sanctions to apply to the perpetrators of the recent violence, a second debate over philosophical and religious sources for civic virtue.

Cicero, clearly the source for Nectarius' expression of devotion to patriotic love, praised the virtue as the 'road to heaven and to those gathered there'.[28] Nectarius' sentiment is thus expressive of classical Greco–Roman religious traditions concerning the sacred character of the city. To care for the city in terms of these traditions is to embrace the concept of a corporate bonding between its inhabitants and local gods as a guarantee of honour and security. By deftly opening his challenge to Augustine on the grounds of *caritas patriae*, Nectarius implicitly accuses the repressive imperial legislation of seeking to destroy the traditional religious foundation for his city's welfare (*ep.* 90).

To the municipal councillors at Calama whom Augustine suspected of collusion in the anti-Christian violence, and on whose behalf Nectarius appealed to the bishop for intercession, the support of the Catholic bishops for imperial policies aimed at supplanting local religious rites with Christian worship appeared as harmful indifference and, perhaps, outright hostility not only to pagan religion as such, but to the security and prosperity of the city which the cults were intended to foster.[29] In our own day, American 'civil religion' remains as powerful a political force as it is almost imperceptible to those under its spell, and yet it fails to approach the magnitude of fusion between religious and civic life in antiquity.[30] Nectarius opens his appeal to Augustine, not only as a bishop, but as 'a man who is thoroughly well educated', thereby indicating his hope that the latter's familiarity with the Latin literature bearing the traditions of his forefathers will enable him to sympathise with so reasonable an appeal on behalf of the city (*ep.* 90).

In his initial rejoinder to Nectarius, Augustine indicates that he understands his well-intentioned interlocutor's anxiety but suggests that the Christian religion is not unconcerned with the welfare of the secular city, even in terms of the temporal peace and security so vital to its local patrons. He then comes right to his point: given the recent events, patriotic love for Calama demands the reform of those persons responsible for the violence which divides it. Augustine picks up Nectarius' allusion to Cicero's devotion to love of the *patria* in *De re publica*, and responds that, for the Roman philosopher, care for the city was rooted in civic virtues, especially as practised by political leaders whose example was to have provided a model for other citizens (*ep.* 91.2–3). Augustine's intention is clear; he does not wish to browbeat Nectarius over the superiority of the Christian religion, but to compare its capacity to promote social reconciliation with that of pagan philosophy and religion, in this instance as represented in the writings of Cicero.

Augustine thus turns to Cicero to make his point that the presence of temples and statues at Calama dedicated to pagan divinities and to the cultic observances, such as festivals, which these gods receive does nothing to promote the public good, but, in fact, deters it. In *De re publica*, Cicero eschewed the gods as moral exemplars and located the source of Roman virtue in the *viri optimi*, in those political leaders such as Gaius Laelius 'Sapiens', Quintus Aelius Tubero and Quintus Mucius Scaevola Augur, speakers in *De re publica* noted in Roman political thought as outstanding in civic virtue (*ep.* 91.3–4).[31] In taking note of this preference in Cicero, Augustine also implies that the proper place to observe civic virtue at work is in the models offered by each religion or philosophical system to exemplify it.

Nectarius understands Augustine's strategy when he next writes to the bishop. This second exchange of letters (*ep.* 103–4) demonstrates a deeper engagement of the issues between the two men. Following Augustine into a discussion of Cicero's *De re publica*, Nectarius reminds the bishop that pagans, too, have a conception of a heavenly city, the destiny of those political leaders who, during their lives, demonstrate the best care for the well-being of their homeland (*optima cura de salute patriae*).[32] The former civil servant's self-representation in his letters to Augustine might be taken as conforming to the portrait of Cicero that he offers: a life wholly dedicated to public service in the law in order to 'save the lives of countless fellow-citizens', and, in old age, the contemplation of a future life in the heavenly homeland (*ep.* 103.1).[33] Brief as his remarks are here, Nectarius' retort to Augustine reaches deeply into the heart of Ciceronian and Stoic civic spiritualities, with their emphases on the love of one's city and the pursuit of justice within it.[34] As to Augustine's observation that worship of the local, traditional deities has produced violence in the citizens of Calama, Nectarius' response implies a dialectical outlook on history; the view that peace frequently arises out of violence (*ep.* 103.2).

It is also at this point, that the political objectives of confession and conversion come to the fore in their discussion. Nectarius argues for a continuity between his own, traditional Roman civic values and those of the Christian religion. Does not Augustine, as a bishop, support the poor, care for the sick and do whatever is possible to relieve the long-term suffering of those who live in his city? In offering this service, how do his aims differ from those of non-Christians who care for the same needs? Augustine demands the repentance of those responsible for the anti-Christian violence at Calama. In response, Nectarius asks him why, if those who were involved 'throw their arms around your feet and beg for pardon', do you judge them unrepentant and still require their impoverishment as punishment? By appeal to what notion of virtue can leniency justly be granted to Catholic but not to pagan penitents (*ep.* 103.3)? Nectarius' oratorical and legal training is clearly in evidence; yet the philosophical and religious challenges to Augustinian Christianity implicit within his argument are not without foundation. Augustine charges that pagan cults produce violence, not virtue. But where in Augustine's politics is the mercy in which the Christian religion prides itself? If pagan cults are to be judged by their fruits, why should the Christian religion not be judged by its own?

Connolly will not accept Augustine's response to this paradox. The argument that Catholics have agreed to enter into a penitential process designed to produce true conversion, while the proposed, public apology of the pagans would be perfunctory, collapses too easily into the exclusivist claim that only a confession offered to the 'Christian' God can produce true repentance and, therefore, true social reconciliation. For Connolly, Augustine's disparagement of Nectarius' arguments for alternative sources of civic virtue in ancient religious and philosophical traditions, such as Cicero's, stems from the bishop's religious chauvinism.

Nectarius grounds his appeal in a Stoic ethical logic akin to the reasoning behind general amnesties: all sins are equal; if one group is pardoned for participation in violence, all parties should be pardoned equally (*ep.* 103.3). However, Augustine is certain that the Stoic principle of the equality of all sins, if applied to Calama, would result not in an amnesty, but in massive, indiscriminate retaliation (*ep.* 104.17).

In effect, Augustine reminds Nectarius that Roman imperial officials locate their ideals in statesmen such as Marcus Aurelius, Seneca and Cicero, each of whom was influenced by an eclectic combination of Stoic ethical traditions and Roman patriotism, and in military heroes such as Marcus Atilius Regulus, Mucius Scaevola, Marcus Curtius, the Decii and Scipios, whose lives exemplified the courage which these ancient traditions promote.[35] His point is that the administration of justice by imperial officials which Calama fears and against which Nectarius implores him to intercede, consists for the most part in a harsh insensitivity, and not in the more compassionate, Christian justice which he would like to instil in these officials (*ep.* 104.15–16). Mindful of the emphasis that Stoic philosophers placed upon love and friendship between neighbours as the core values behind civic harmony, he none the less reminds Nectarius that they classically disparage mercy as a vice because it stems from an undisciplined, sentimental reflex in the soul and not from an unbiased act of reason.[36]

Although Stoic and Ciceronian ideas are explicitly mentioned in the letters exchanged between Nectarius and Augustine, the references are not of a sufficient length to permit further exploration of the respective arguments. However, Augustine enlarges his criticism of Stoic understandings in the *City of God* (especially at 9.4–5, and 14.9), a work begun five years after the Calama affair. In the *City of God*, Augustine locates the cause for his rejection of commonplace understandings of spiritual freedom within the moral and spiritual self-mastery that the ancients believed could be attained by individuals who practised spiritual disciplines, including philosophy itself, the spiritual discipline *par excellence*.[37] Augustine's view of the interior, confessing self as inherently weak and, therefore, permanently vulnerable to fear and other seductive emotions thus radically challenges what he takes to be the conventional attitudes of ancient philosophical traditions (including most of Christianity), because in one form or another they espouse a rational self-control through which the mind, to a greater or lesser extent, represses such sentiments in order to attain freedom. Augustine mistrusts this freedom and prefers the quality of mercy that results from a self-knowledge deepened through confession of moral and spiritual failure, because it produces a compassion for other sinners that arises out of a recollected experience of moral weaknesses commonly shared by human beings.[38]

He would not deny that pagan writers evoked the ideal of mercy or clemency toward Rome's enemies. Thus, he recalls Sallust's judgement, in the *Bellum Catilinae*, that the Romans 'preferred to pardon rather than to avenge the wrongs' committed against them, as well as Vergil's well-known axiomatic reminder to Roman leaders of their legacy 'to spare the conquered and beat down the proud' (*ciu.* 1.6).[39] Yet he judges that this classical, Roman outlook on mercy derived from a sense of oneself as morally 'other', qualitatively different, superior to the enemy, criminal or sinner. In effect, Augustine substitutes Nectarius' Stoic view that pardon should be extended to everyone who sins because all *sins* are equal, with his own view that human beings ought to pardon each other because all are equally *sinners*. True forgiveness thus arises out of an identification with the other as sinner, an identification that would not be possible unless it were produced by the searching self-examination and confession which rejects the possibility of ever completely overcoming personal moral failure in this life. To see this point, one only has to notice how closely the sins Augustine confesses about himself as a bishop mirror those confessed about his youth. At *Confessions* 10.35.56, he prays that God drive away from him vestiges of an earlier attraction (*curiositas*) to signs of divine activity in sacrilegious practices such as astrology. In terms of pride, he acknowledges that 'the temptation to want veneration and affection from others' may still exercise some hold on him as bishop (*conf.* 10.36.59–60). He admits being less concerned when another is unjustly criticised than when he is so treated (*conf.* 10.37.62). In Augustine's view, Stoic mercy stems from a form of *apatheia* which suppresses self-doubt and anxiety, and thus ruthlessly severs in the soul any continuity between one's present behaviour and the temptations and moral failures committed in one's past.[40]

Following the logic of his analysis from an individual into a social context, it becomes clear that what is at stake for Augustine's conception of civic virtue is nothing less than a reformation of the Roman heroic ideal away from the illusions of moral victory and self-possession which it promotes. Thus, Augustine assures Nectarius:

> There is no moment when it is not fitting and proper to discuss how we may please God. In this life it is either impossible, or at least extremely difficult, to fulfil this so perfectly that no sin at all remains in a person. That is why we must abandon all hesitation and take refuge in his grace.
>
> (*ep.* 104.11)[41]

Written three years in advance of his first introduction to Pelagius' thought, this passage from Augustine's letter to Nectarius adumbrates the central issues of that final theological conflict of his life. In the *City of God* Augustine opposes ancient philosophies and spiritualities, Jewish, Platonic, Peripatetic, Stoic, Epicurean, Manichaean, Roman, Ciceronian, Neoplatonic and Pelagian, in which he finds moral autonomy and self-perfection set out as attainable goals in this life. Furthermore, he subtly aligns the assumptions grounding these spiritual programmes with the classical goal of ancient philosophy: to rationalise or otherwise repress fear of death. Crucial in his opposition to such philosophical therapies is his acceptance of a legitimate, ongoing role for fear of death as a means of redirecting the soul's attention away from the illusion that it might impose and maintain order over assorted self-destructive longings, fantasies and fears.[42]

Connolly is right to see in passages such as the above an Augustine tenaciously clinging to an *apologia pro vita sua*: a divided will operating in a condition of moral dependence upon an omnipotent God from whose grace any attempt to escape through spiritual self-perfection constitutes blasphemy. Augustine would reply to Connolly that these alternative approaches to spiritual progress, 'ways' (*uiae*) as he calls them in his letter to Nectarius (*ep.* 104.12), nurture in their practitioners a hidden, insidious form of pride. This pride consists in an over-estimation of the human capacity to eliminate any trace of personal, moral weakness, and thus fear of death.[43] His remarks about pride can often seem sermonic and out of place to modern ears, as if he were sternly lecturing his monks on the necessity of avoiding worldly vanities. However, for Augustine, this form of pride acts as an interior, self-congratulatory rhetoric, firmly persuading the soul away from the determination to imitate the models of personal heroism incorporated into accounts of Roman history and philosophy.[44] Reading the *Confessions* together with the *City of God*, one understands that, for Augustine, these examples of heroic virtue amplify within the soul the rhetoric of glory which permeates the empire through myriad cultural and religious forms and institutions. They thereby fuel the political fantasies and ambitions of ruling elites from smaller cities, such as Calama, to the imperial capitals at Rome and Constantinople. For Augustine, the spiritual liberation that the soul requires in order to govern the city justly consists in a freedom from such interdependent rhetorics, because true pardon and reconciliation, both of which are essential to social justice, can only be produced between individuals who continually recognise themselves as sinners in need of God's pardon. The cultivation of this interior self and its aptitude for reconciliation are, therefore, threatened by philosophies that insist upon the possibility of an accomplished, autonomous moral and spiritual perfection.

Political culture and the *Confessions*

Paradoxically, for one concerned to criticize the political implications of the *Confessions*, Connolly filters out of the text the multiple layers of self-examination, confession and repentance which are most directly related to the political aspects of the bishop's earlier education and life. As with most scholars who venture interpretations of the *Confessions*, he reduces its moral concerns to impulse gratification and control, in particular in relation to sexuality, thereby missing the predominance of the political aspects of confession that the text highlights. Deception, career ambition and social reputation clearly overshadow sexual excess as the most serious moral issues at the heart of a conversion struggle that culminates in Augustine's rejection of a career as public orator for Milan and propagandist in the court of the Emperor Valentinian II.[45] Reading the *Confessions* with attention to both sets of rhetoric mentioned above, self-mastery and imperial glory, opens up Augustine's confession as a method in political self-examination, one based not simply in the public renunciation of unjust actions and orientations such as lying, careerism and greed for wealth and fame, but in an exploration of their subtle, imperceptible growth in the soul as a result of external, social and cultural influences arising from parents, patrons, teachers, friends and colleagues, literary *exempla* and the dramatic arts, public games and festivals, education and initial career success. Against the cultural and ideological pull fostered within this environment, Augustine's confession alerts his soul to the masked forces that lure it into an uncritical subservience to the deceptions required for empire maintenance. He thus painstakingly details a youth spent first unconsciously absorbing, and only later detecting, an education in the 'adult games' (*negotia*) of dissimulation which he ultimately plays out in the imperial court.[46]

He provides one of a number of illustrations of this irony in his observation that parents naturally punish their sons for distracting themselves from schoolwork by their attendance at the public games. Such parents hope that, forced to avoid the games and apply themselves faithfully to their lessons, their sons will one day enjoy a level of wealth commensurate with that of the city's elite. Yet these parents fail to realise that, should their sons succeed at acquiring sufficient wealth, they will be obliged by their social status to put on the same kinds of public entertainment whose deleterious moral and intellectual consequences cause such alarm among good parents generally (*conf.* 1.10.16). Augustine aims this particular criticism in part at the effects which the tangible display of wealth and prestige exhibited by the city's elite exercises upon parents eager to promote their children's early career preparation. In this way, too, such parents blindly accede to civic traditions and institutions allied with municipal patronage, and thereby unknowingly reinforce the cultural and political hierarchies that these traditions and institutions embody.[47]

With a similarly critical purpose in view, Augustine recalls that his own elementary education at Thagaste stressed grammatical rules concerned with the correct pronunciation of words such as *homo*, but neglected to teach the divine laws urging love of human beings. This irony was compounded in rhetorical studies at schools in Madaura and Carthage, where rhetoricians sought to perfect in law students the verbal tactics through which they would one day win legal prosecutions, while they neglected to impart to these same students any moral foundation for ensuring that their skills in debate would not cause innocent persons to be condemned to death (*conf.* 1.18.29). By the time Augustine enters the murky world of political image management within the imperial court at Milan, he and his audiences are already culturally prepared to accept the inevitable predominance of distorted, because artificially optimistic, reports of imperial accomplishment over more sober analyses and prescriptions for civic life and security (*conf.* 6.6.9; 8.6.13). Hence, a broad, cultural emphasis on grammatical and rhetorical formalism over truth and virtue provides him with the thread connecting his account of his education with that of his brief career as a teacher of rhetoric and imperial panegyrist, and links these personal experiences with his analysis of the political and social ills which beset late Roman imperial society.

Complaints of the extent to which the vices and weaknesses of influential citizens injure the commonwealth are not lacking in Greek and Roman political writings. Plato famously decries the specious effect of the poets' lies about the gods on the education of the young, within his more general treatments of the harmful consequences of rhetorical influences on the *polis*.[48] Aristotle, Cicero and Seneca, to name only a few ancient philosophers, provide additional social criticism directed at the detrimental consequences on the public good of personal moral failings commonly associated with disordered human passions, in particular, the commonplace triad of possessions, pleasure and power (*auaritia, luxuria, ambitio*).[49] Yet unlike the ancient ethical writing it at times consciously echoes, Augustine's *Confessions* personalises while it explores at greater depth the soul's interior struggle to gain awareness of its captivity to external influences, and rejects the seductive premise that such weaknesses, and the self-deception that inevitably disguises their presence, might be rooted out of the soul.

Connolly criticizes Augustine's insistence on the need to resort to repeated confession of sins as a means of shoring up his moral universe against threats from within himself. He asks whether Augustine uncovers an interior self through confession, or whether he manufactures one. A reading of the *Confessions* attentive to the manner in which the form of self-examination contained therein requires exposure of the soul's gradual and undetected political formation forces a reformulation of Connolly's question. The text shows that both 'uncovery' and 'construction' of a selfhood are interrelated processes and depend upon the soul's ability to gain at least liminal awareness of the ways and extent to which its core ideals, aspirations, attachments, fears, fantasies and motivations are constantly compromised by the plethora of social, cultural and, therefore, political forces from which the self can hardly be abstracted, even when it attempts through asceticism to flee social and political involvements entirely. In this respect, each of us remains, for Augustine, 'deceivers and deceived'.[50]

Augustine's confessional imperative thus cannot be evaluated in an intellectual or social vacuum, as if moral imperatives other than his were not continually bearing down on the soul, enticing it to embrace illusory images of spiritual freedom. Repeated confession of sins and an accompanying, necessary belief in the soul's complete inability to establish moral autonomy serve neither to 'uncover' nor 'construct' an interior selfhood in absolute terms, but to ward off the threat to spiritual freedom which lies in a misplaced confidence in autonomy and self-mastery as achievable spiritual conditions, and which thus make the self God's potential rival as the sole dispenser of the gift of pardon.

Turning once again to the form of pagan cult which Nectarius defends at Calama, the reasoning behind Augustine's objections to the proposal to accord pagan repentance the same recognition that he willingly offers to Christians extends deeply into the way he conceives *caritas patriae*. True love for one's city requires a shared understanding of the nature of reconciliation among individuals who accept that the spiritual arts of penitence – self-examination, confession, prayer for pardon and forgiveness of others, especially of enemies – constitute the essence of civic virtue, of *pietas*, and, thus, the heart of patriotism.[51] Such penitence will only be efficacious for the just rule of the city when it draws its subjects away from concern with the fantasy of moral and spiritual autonomy and perfection, and towards the freedom to live interiorly as citizens in God's *ciuitas*. In this pilgrim city, the only human achievement worthy of praise is the prayerful search for, and acceptance of, pardon as a divine gift, and the only noble political action lies in the reciprocal exchange of that gift with one's neighbours. It is in this way that eschatology and history are joined in Augustine's political thought. Finally, pardon will be effective only when it involves an identification with the other as sinner, a bonding arrived at through the realisation of an interior self which earnestly seeks out the history of its own ongoing collusion with injustice.

Augustine carries these images of reconciliation into his conception of eucharist as an act of worship which, as distinct from pagan cults and philosophies, attempts neither to ward off cosmic or political threats to the security of the city, nor to achieve, through a contemplative purification of the soul, an interior peace which masks complicity with injustice, but to locate the centre of secular peace and civic well-being in a divine pardon which is humbly received and shared with others. They alone receive and give this gift who understand that they cannot compete with God for holiness or justice.[52]

William Connolly and others before him claim that within Augustine's confessional tactics lie the seeds of an authoritarian, coercive politics. Less apparent to scholars today is a different Augustinian legacy also centred on the politics of confession, one capable of offering at least a partial antidote to the ideological pull of statehood, race, philosophy and religion, class and national security: the absolute refusal to deny one's own or one's party's role in a shared responsibility for the breakdown of comity. In this regard, the upshot of Augustinian political thought is that it will always be exigent for individuals as well as social groups, to seek the reflection of their own images in those of their enemies, and to seek to be reconciled with those images. In so far as Augustine opposes any philosophical insistence on the possibility of moral and spiritual perfection, he articulates a view of confession capable of promoting a paradoxically lasting, because necessarily ongoing, social reconciliation.

Published accounts of the public atonement for the massacre at Thessalonika which Theodosius I performed at Milan in AD 390 offer Augustine a portrait of the emperor as penitent, an icon of political leadership prepared to achieve peace through the politics of confession. The contrast which he draws in the *City of God* (5.26) between the humility displayed by Theodosius and the desire for glory that characterised the real political aims of traditional Roman leaders also describes the conflict in perspectives that colours his discussion with Nectarius.[53] It is fair to observe that Augustine preferred Theodosius to other emperors because of his strong Catholic beliefs and virulent opposition to the enemies of the church. However, the overriding factor in his appraisal of Theodosius stems from his view that, while the judgements and actions of rulers will always be subject to sin, they none the less retain the capacity to promote the public good to the extent that they are free to renounce their own longing for glory by openly recalling in thanksgiving the gift of pardon.[54]

Notes

1 Augustine, *ep.* 90: Nectarius to Augustine; CSEL 34.426:

> Quanta sit caritas patriae, quoniam nosti, praetereo. sola est enim, quae parentum iure uincat affectum. cui si ullus esset consulendi modus aut finis bonis, digne iam ab eius muneribus meruimus

> excusari. sed quoniam crescit in dies singulos dilectio et gratia
> ciuitatis, quantumque aetas fini proxima est, tantum incolumen ac
> florentem relinquere patriam cupit, idcirco gaudeo primum quod apud
> instructum disciplinis omnibus uirum mihi hic est sermo institutus.

The English translation of this text and of the other letters between Augustine and Nectarius, which I have at times modified slightly, is by E. M. Atkins, in R. J. Dodaro and E. M. Atkins (eds), *Augustine: Political Writings*, Cambridge, Cambridge University Press, forthcoming. A fuller commentary on this correspondence is offered by H. Huisman, *Augustinus' Briefwisseling met Nectarius. Inleiding, tekst, vertalung, commentar*, Amsterdam, J. Babeliowski, 1956. On the notion of 'love of one's home town' see R. Lane Fox, *Pagans and Christians*, San Francisco, Harper and Row, 1986, p. 55–63.

2 It is not known what rank or position he held. J. R. Martindale, *A Prosopography of the Later Roman Empire, Volume II: AD 395–527*, Cambridge, Cambridge University Press, 1980, p. 774, s. v., Nectarius 1, suggests that he may have been the *defensor civitatis* for Calama, but this cannot be proved. Huisman, op. cit., pp. 9–20, believes that Nectarius served outside of Calama. C. Lepelley, *Les cités de l'Afrique romaine au bas-empire, I: La permanence d'une civilisation municipale*, Paris, Etudes augustiniennes, 1979, p. 291, regards Nectarius as a member of the municipal council (*curia*) at Calama.

3 *C. Th.* 16.5.43; *C. Th.*16.10.9 = *C. Sirm.* 12, dated 15 November 407. At the same time, Honorius decreed the transfer to the Catholic church of properties used for religious assemblies by pagans, Jews and heretics, among them Donatists, Manichaeans and Priscillianists. It is rare to have documented accounts of the application of such edicts; the mere record of an imperial decree from this period does not always mean that it was known to, or enforced by, local officials. On this and other problems of interpretation of collections of imperial constitutions in general, see A. Cameron, *The Later Roman Empire, AD 284–430*, Cambridge Mass., Harvard University Press, 1993, pp. 26–9.

4 See *ep.* 91.8. There are three statements in this section of the letter that indicate the reasons for this suspicion on Augustine's part:

1 no municipal councillor acted to prevent the pagan festival
2 on the third and worst day of the violence, attempts by Catholics to dissuade the rioters by threats of legal action were undertaken in vain, because church members had been denied their legal right to record their complaints in the municipal records (*acta*)
3 when officials did finally intervene on the third day, the violence was curtailed, a fact which shows that if the municipal councillors (*primates*), had intervened either before the outbreak of the disturbance or immediately after its onset, greater violence and death could have been avoided.

Later (§ 10), Augustine closes this letter by reiterating the necessity of deterring other cities from following the example of Calama. He may have in mind an earlier case at Sufes in the African province of Byzacena, where, in AD 399 anti-Christian violence also followed close on the heels of an imperial edict, in this case, one which ordered the proconsul of Africa to remove statues of idols from pagan temples. Augustine wrote shortly thereafter, accusing the city councillors of Sufes of complicity in the violence (see *ep.* 50).

5 C. Lepelley, *Les cités de l'Afrique romaine au bas-empire, II: Notices d'histoire municipale*, Paris, Etudes augustiniennes, 1981, pp. 97–101, argues that the issue, for Augustine, may lie in a rivalry between some African municipal councils and the authority exercised over matters of religion by imperial officials. To the extent that pagan, aristocratic members of municipal councils sympathised with local pagan cults, they may have ignored the imperial prohibitions and their enforcement by imperial officials. See also the helpful remarks of B. Ward-Perkins, 'The Cities', in *The Cambridge Ancient History*, vol. 13, *The Late Empire, AD 337–425*, ed. A. Cameron and P. Garnsey, Cambridge, Cambridge University Press, 1998, pp. 371–410, especially pp. 392–403.

6 At *ep.* 104.1, Augustine claims that he did not receive Nectarius' second letter (*ep.* 103) until 27 March 409, eight months after replying to him the first time (in *ep.* 91). However, he also acknowledges Nectarius' claim not to have received his first reply for a long time.

7 This is part of what Augustine intends at *ep.* 104.9 as the 'fruitful pain of repentance' (*poenitentiae dolor fructuosus*).

8 It never becomes clear to us either by what authority, or in what precise rôle Augustine becomes involved in a matter that did not occur within his own episcopal jurisdiction. However, we do not hear of any party objecting to his involvement, least of all Nectarius, who claims at *ep.* 90 that he welcomes it, because he believes that he finds in Augustine a Catholic bishop who is educated in the liberal arts, and who is accustomed both to showing mercy to the guilty and to protecting the innocent. Even allowing for flattery on Nectarius' part, in neither of the two letters he writes to the bishop about the matter (*ep.* 90; 103) does he challenge either the grounds for Augustine's involvement in the affair, or the latter's presentation of the facts of the case. Instead, he clearly expresses a desire for the bishop's intervention as an intercessor with imperial officials.

9 *A Reflection on the Politics of Morality*, Newbury Park, Cal./London/New Delhi, Sage Publications, 1993.

10 Connolly treats two specific cases in regard to women. The first is Augustine's *ep.* 211.1–4, traditionally known as the *Reprimand to Quarelling Nuns* (about which see my discussion below, n. 15), and his *ep.* 262 to Ecdicia. The latter case is briefly discussed by E. Ann Matter in 'Christ, God and Woman in the Thought of St Augustine', published elsewhere in this volume.

11 See especially H. Arendt, *Between Past and Future*, New York, Penguin, 1958, pp. 143–72 and E. Pagels, *Adam, Eve and the Serpent*, New York, Random House, 1988.

12 See also the criticisms along these lines offered by R. Joly, 'Saint Augustin et l'intolérance religieuse', *Revue belge de philologie et d'histoire* 33 (1955), pp. 263–94; and K. Deschner, *Kriminalgeschichte des Christentums. I. Die Frühzeit: Von den Ursprüngen im Alten Testament bis zum Tod des hl. Augustinus (430)*, Reinbek bei Hamburg, Rowohlt, 1986, pp. 462–530.

13 Connolly, op. cit., p. xvii. Hereafter, references to Connolly's book will normally be indicated in the text by page numbers placed in parentheses.

14 See ibid., p. 87: 'Augustinian politics presupposes the confessional imperative and the confessional imperative constitutes the core of Augustinian politics'.

15 English translation by G. Lawless, *Augustine of Hippo and his Monastic Rule*, Oxford, Clarendon Press, 1987, p. 114. See also *ep.* 211.11. However, the opinion of most

scholars since Verheijen's 1967 critical study of Augustine's monastic legislation is that the *Reprimand to Quarrelling Nuns* (*ep.* 211.1–4) and the feminine version of Augustine's monastic rule (*ep.* 211.5–16) were joined to each other at a time later than their original dates of composition to form what has come down to us in the manuscript tradition as *ep.* 211. See L. Verheijen, *La règle de saint Augustin, II. Recherches historiques*, Paris, Etudes augustiniennes, 1967, pp. 203–4, and idem, 'La Règle de saint Augustin: L'état actuel des questions (début 1975)', *Augustiniana* 35 (1985), pp. 245–7, who also cautiously attributes the *Reprimand* to Augustine. Verheijen, *Saint Augustine's Monasticism in the Light of Acts 4,32–5*, Villanova, Pa., Villanova University Press, 1979, p. 70, suggests that the nuns at Hippo Regius were already in possession of the feminine version of the *Rule* before he sent the *Reprimand* to them, but Lawless, op. cit., pp. 153–4, cautions against concluding too much on this point from 'the slender base of textual evidence' mustered by Verheijen. While these historical points challenge Connolly's assumption that Augustine despatched the monastic rule for women as an integral part of his written reprimand to them, I do not believe that the textual questions raised by Verheijen damage Connolly's case.

16 Connolly cites *conf.* 7.19.25: 'In fact the refutation of heresies causes what your Church thinks, and what sound doctrine holds, to stand out. "For there must be heresies, so that those who are approved may become manifest among the weak"' (1 Cor 11:19). See CCL 27.109: 'Improbatio quippe haereticorum facit eminere, quid ecclesia tua sentiat et quid habeat sana doctrina. Oportuit enim et haereses esse, ut probati manifesti fierent inter infirmos'.

17 On Augustine's role in procuring the condemnation of Pelagius and Celestius as heretics, see G. Bonner, *St Augustine of Hippo. Life and Controversies*, London, SCM Press, 1963, pp. 328–46; P. Brown, *Augustine of Hippo, a Biography*, London, Faber and Faber, 1967, pp. 353–64; O. Perler with J.-L. Maier, *Les voyages de saint Augustin*, Paris, Etudes augustiniennes, 1969, pp. 328–45; O. Wermelinger, *Rom und Pelagius. Die theologische Position der römischen Bischöfe im pelagianischen Streit in den Jahren 411–32*, Stuttgart, Anton Hiersemann, 1975; C. Pietri, *Roma Christiana. Recherches sur l'Eglise de Rome, son organisation, sa politique, son idéologie de Miltiade à Sixte III (311–440)*, Rome, Bibliothèque de l'Ecole française d'Athènes et de Rome, 1976, pp. 1222–44; J. P. Burns, 'Augustine's Role in the Imperial Action Against Pelagius', *Journal of Theological Studies*, new series, 30 (1979), pp. 67–83; F. G. Nuvolone and A. Solignac, 'Pélage et Pélagianisme', in *Dictionnaire de Spiritualité*, vol. 12:2, Paris, Beauchense, 1986, cc. 2889–942, and M. Lamberigts, 'Augustine and Julian of Aeclanum on Zosimus', *Augustiniana* 42 (1992), pp. 311–30.

18 See *conf.* 6.16.26.

19 See CSEL 34.588:

> Nam et paenitentia, sicut scribis, impetrat ueniam et purgat admissum sed illa, quae in uera religione agitur, quod futurum iudicium dei cogitat, non illa, quae ad horam hominibus aut exhibetur aut fingetur, non ut a delicto anima purgetur in aeternum, sed ut interim a praesenti metu molestiae uita cito peritura liberetur.

20 See B. E. Daley, *The Hope of the Early Church. A Handbook of Patristic Eschatology*, Cambridge, Cambridge University Press, 1991; C. W. Bynum, *The Resurrection*

of the Body in Western Christianity, 200–1336, New York, Columbia University Press, 1995, pp. 1–114.

21 See especially P. Garnsey, 'Religious Toleration in Classical Antiquity', in *Persecution and Toleration*, ed. W. J. Shields, Oxford, Clarendon Press, 1984, pp. 1–27, who argues soberly that standard modern views of religious toleration found no place among either Christians or pagans in late antiquity. See also F. Paschoud, 'L'intolerance chrétienne vue et jugée par les païens', *Cristianesimo nella Storia* 2 (1990), pp. 545–77, who suggests that fourth-century pagans were as intolerant as Christians. However, A. H. Armstrong, 'The Way and the Ways: Religious Tolerance and Intolerance in the Fourth Century', *Vigiliae Christianae* 38 (1984), pp. 1–17, finds fourth-century emperors generally tolerant.

22 *Authority and the Sacred. Aspects of the Christianisation of the Roman World*, Cambridge, Cambridge University Press, 1995, pp. 29–54: 'The Limits of Intolerance'.

23 See, too, the careful discussion of this relationship with particular reference to Augustine offered by R. A. Markus, *The End of Ancient Christianity*, Cambridge, Cambridge University Press, 1990, pp. 27–43, 107–23. A helpful orientation to the general difficulties concerning the evaluation of 'paganism' during this period is also provided by G. Bonner, 'The Extinction of Paganism and the Church Historian', *Journal of Ecclesiastical History* 35 (1984), pp. 339–57.

24 See, for example, Ambrose, *De paenitentia*; CSEL 73/7.117–206; *De apologia prophetae Dauid*; CSEL 32/2.299–355, but also those sections of *De obitu Theodosii* (§§ 28, 34); CSEL 73/7.369–401, concerning the public penance performed by the Emperor Theodosius I following the massacre of citizens at Thessalonika in AD 390. See also A. Fitzgerald, *Conversion Through Penance in the Italian Church of the Fourth and Fifth Centuries. New Approaches to the Experience of Conversion from Sin*, Lewiston, N.Y., Edwin Mellen Press, 1988, pp. 209–15; and R. Gryson, 'Introduction', in Ambroise de Milan, *La Pénitence*, Sources Chrétiennes 179, Paris, Cerf, 1971, pp. 15–50.

25 I refer the reader to the account of Christian and non-Christian sources for the historical evolution of these 'spiritual exercises' offered by P. Hadot, *Philosophy as a Way of Life*, ed. A. I. Davidson, tr. M. Chase, Oxford, Blackwell, 1995, pp. 126–44, and now idem, *The Inner Citadel: The Meditations of Marcus Aurelius*, tr. M. Chase, Cambridge Mass., Harvard University Press, 1998. An excellent treatment of comparative spiritualities in late antiquity is found in A. H. Armstrong (ed.), *Classical Mediterranean Spirituality. Egyptian, Greek, Roman*, New York, Crossroad, 1986. I shall be citing the 1989 edition (London, SCM Press). For a clear discussion in this volume of spiritual direction as conceived of in antiquity, see the essay by I. Hadot, 'The Spiritual Guide', pp. 436–59.

26 On the general question, see R.-A. Gauthier, *Magnanimité: L'idéal de la grandeur dans la philosophie païenne et dans la théologie chrétienne*, Paris, Vrin, 1951; P. Veyne, *Le pain et le cirque. Sociologie historique d'un pluralisme politique*, Paris, Editions du Seuil, 1976, in particular pp. 341–67. The English translation of Veyne's book is abbreviated from the original. Comparative studies of pagan evergetism and Christian charity or generosity are still relatively new in the literature. See P. Brown, *Power and Persuasion in Late Antiquity. Towards a Christian Empire*, Madison Wis., University of Wisconsin Press, 1992, pp. 71–117; A. Giardina, 'Carità eversiva: le donazioni di Melania la giovane e gli equilibri della società

tardoantica', in *Hestíasis. Studi di tarda antiquità offerta a Salvatore Calderone*, vol. 2, Messina, Sicania, 1986, pp. 77–102; M. Le Glay, 'Evergetisme et vie religieuse dans l'Afrique romaine' in *L'Afrique dans l'occident romain (Ier siècle av. J. C.–IVe siècle ap. J. C.)*, Rome, Ecole française de Rome, 1990, pp. 77–88; A. Fraschetti, 'Melania, la santa', in *Roma al femminile*, ed. A. Fraschetti, Rome / Bari, Laterza, 1994, pp. 259–85. Useful in a general way, but not as focused on the comparison is D. Janes, *God and Gold in Late Antiquity*, Cambridge, Cambridge University Press, 1988. See also Lane Fox, op. cit., pp. 52–63; Lepelley, *Les cités . . ., I: La permanence*, op. cit., pp. 298–303.

27 See n. 1.

28 See Cicero, *De re publica* 6.16.16: 'via est in caelum et in hunc coetum eorum'. In this same passage Cicero ranks love for one's country above love for parents and relations ('magna in parentibus . . . in patria maxima'). See also Cicero, *De officiis* 1.57; *De partitione oratoriae* 25.8.

29 See especially Lepelley, *Les cités . . . I. La permanence*, op. cit., pp. 358–9.

30 A good introduction to these issues is offered by A. Wardman, *Religion and Statecraft among the Romans*, Baltimore/London, Johns Hopkins University Press, 1982. See also, R. Gordon, 'From Republic to Principate: Priesthood, Religion and Ideology', in *Pagan Priests, Religion and Power in the Ancient World*, ed. M. Beard and J. North, London, Duckworth, 1990, pp. 179–98.

31 Augustine repeats this point to Nectarius at *ep.* 104.6. See also his discussion of these Roman leaders at *ciu.* 2.9 and 14.

32 The expression is from Cicero, *De re publica* 6.28.29.

33 The sentiment is common in Stoic literature. In addition to Cicero, *De re publica* 6, see, for example, Seneca, *De otio* 4, and the discussions by Gauthier, op. cit., pp. 129–30, and M. Schofield, *The Stoic Idea of the City*, Cambridge, Cambridge University Press, 1991, pp. 93–103.

34 Brief, but helpful remarks are found in M. Colish, *The Stoic Tradition from Antiquity to the Early Middle Ages. I: Stoicism in Classical Latin Literature*, Leiden, E. J. Brill, 1985, pp. 38–41, on general political thought, and pp. 94–5, on Cicero.

35 On Augustine's readings of these Latin authors, see H. Hagendahl, *Augustine and the Latin Classics*, 2 vols, Göteborg, Acta Universitatis Gothoburgensis, 1967. On his knowledge of Cicero, see also M. Testard, *Saint Augustin et Cicéron*, 2 vols, Paris, Etudes augustiniennes, 1958; idem, 'Cicero' in *Augustinus–Lexikon*, vol. 1, ed. C. Mayer, Basel, Schwabe & Co., 1986–94, cc. 913–30. See also J. J. O'Donnell, 'Augustine's Classical Readings', *Recherches augustiniennes* 15 (1980), pp. 144–75. On Augustine's regard for the place of Marcus Atilius Regulus in Roman history and folklore, see *ciu.* 1.24; 1.15.1–3; 2.23.1; 2.29.1; 3.18.1; 3.20; 5.18.2. *Ciu.* 5.18 offers the best account of Augustine's appreciation of Roman military heroes. However, see my discussion of Augustine's critique of these traditions in R. Dodaro, 'Il *timor mortis* e la questione degli *exempla virtutum*: Agostino, *De civitate Dei* I–X', in *Il mistero del male e la libertà possibile (III): Lettura del* De civitate Dei *di Agostino*, L. Alici, R. Piccolomini and A. Pieretti (eds), Rome, Institutum Patristicum «Augustinianum», 1996, pp. 7–47, at pp. 18–28.

36 See, for example, Seneca, *De clementia* 2.5; Cicero, *Tusculanae disputationes* 3.9.20. Augustine offers a fuller and more nuanced exposition of this argument at *ciu.*

9.5, where he points out that the Stoic philosopher Epictetus found room for mercy within the soul of the sage, provided that it did not diminish his strength of determination to act on the basis of reason, and not sentiment.

37 On these latter points, the arguments marshalled by P. Hadot, *Philosophy*, op. cit., are fundamental, and overwhelmingly convincing.

38 In arriving at this position, Augustine owes much to Ambrose, as I have suggested. See above, n. 24.

39 See Sallust, *Bellum Catilinae* 9.5; Vergil, *Aeneid* 6.853. At *ciu.* 1.6, Augustine observes a lack of testimony from pagan historians that such mercy had, in fact, been shown to Rome's enemies.

40 It may be that Augustine has Cicero, *Tusculanae disputationes,* in mind as his model of Stoic reflections on mercy. On this point, see Dodaro, 'Il *timor mortis*', op. cit., pp. 18–28.

41 CSEL 34.590:

> Nullum enim tempus est, quo non deceat et oporteat agere, unde deo placere possimus; quod in hac uita usque ad eam perfectionem impleri, ut nullum omnino peccatum insit in homine aut non potest, aut forte difficillimum est; unde praecisis omnibus dilationibus ad illius gratiam confugiendum est.

42 Augustine thus claims a usefulness for fear of death in promoting justice or holiness (*usus iustitiae*) within the individual soul. See especially *ciu.* 9.4–5; and 14.9.2, along with Dodaro, 'Il *timor mortis*', op. cit., and idem, 'Note sulla prensenza della questione pelagiana nel *De civitate Dei*', in *Il* De civitate Dei. *L'opera, le interpretazioni, l'influsso*, ed. E. Cavalcanti, Rome, Herder, 1996, pp. 245–70. Further detailed treatment will be found in my forthcoming book, *Language and Justice in Augustine's City of God*. On philosophy as therapy for fear of death, see the conclusions of P. Hadot, *Philosophy*, op. cit., pp. 93–101, 241–3.

43 Among the non-Christian *uiae* which Augustine examines in his writings, theurgy offered him perhaps the greatest difficulties at criticism. As an admixture of Platonic and Neoplatonic contemplation and esoteric religious ritual, theurgy offered a theology and sacramental practice which paralleled and rivalled that of the Christian religion, in part, because by the fifth century the two religious systems actively borrowed from each other. Augustine's criticisms of theurgy occupy a good part of his discussion in *ciu.* 10, and are treated seriously in the recently discovered *s. Dolbeau* 26.36–63. See R. Dodaro, '*Christus sacerdos.* Augustine's Preaching Against Pagan Priests in the Light of *S. Dolbeau* 26 and 23', in *Augustin Prédicateur* (395–411), *Actes du Colloque International de Chantilly (5–7 Septembre 1996)*, ed. G. Madec, Paris, Etudes augustiniennes, 1998, pp. 377–93, especially pp. 383–93, along with my remarks in 'Il *timor mortis*', op. cit., pp. 33–42. However, Augustine's criticisms apply generally to Porphyrian theurgy and not to Iamblichean, about which we cannot say that he knows anything except Iamblichus' name (*ciu.* 8.12), even though this form of theurgy was practised and promoted during Augustine's youth by the Emperor Julian (AD 361–3). Iamblichus places responsibility for the initiation of the ecstatic union on the divine side of the mediation and warns theurgists against presumption on their powers. See G. Shaw, *Theurgy and the*

Soul. The Neoplatonism of Iamblichus, University Park, Pa., Pennsylvania State University Press, 1995, pp. 111–3. It would be enlightening to know how Augustine might have reacted to Iamblichus' account of theurgy. In spite of recent scholarly interest in Christianity's understanding and appropriation of pagan theurgy, the present state of research remains inadequate to the tasks which evaluation of Augustine's criticism requires. We do not yet understand the social and religious contexts in which theurgy exists in Augustine's day, the relationship between theurgy and other spiritual practices such as confession, between theurgy and other philosophical schools or religious and civil communities. Thus, too, in spite of the Emperor Julian's open profession of, and institutional support for, Iamblichean theurgy, we still cannot draw meaningful conclusions about its complex relationship to Roman patriotism. Important, initial researches into this question are being advanced by D. O'Meara, 'Evêques et philosophes-rois: Philosophie politique néoplatonicienne chez le Pseudo-Denys', in *Denys l'Aréopagite et sa postérité en orient et en occident*, ed. Y. de Andia, Paris, Etudes augustiniennes, 1997, pp. 75–88; idem, 'Vie politique et divinisation dans la philosophie néoplatonicienne', in ΣΟΦΙΗΣ ΜΑΙΗΤΟΡΕΣ *"Chercheurs de sagesse". Hommage à Jean Pépin*, ed. M. O. Goulet-Cazé, G. Madec and D. O'Brien, Paris, Etudes augustiniennes, 1992, pp. 501–10; idem, 'Aspects of Political Philosophy in Iamblichus', in *The Divine Iamblichus. Philosopher and Man of God*, ed. H. Blumenthal and E. Clark, London, Bristol Classics Press, 1993, pp. 65–73.

44 Marcus Atilius Regulus offers such an example. Compare Augustine's discussion of this Roman hero (for texts, see above, n. 35) with Cicero, *Tusculanae disputationes* (ed. G. Fohlen, Paris, Les Belles Lettres, 1970) 5.5.12–5.7.20, especially 5.5.14, and my discussion in 'Il *timor mortis*', op. cit., pp. 22–8. On Roman models of heroic courage, see H. Litchfield, 'National *exempla virtutis* in Roman Literature', *Harvard Studies in Classical Philology* 25 (1914), pp. 1–71; and G. Achard, *Pratique, rhétorique et idéologie politique dans le discours* optimates *de Cicéron*, Leiden, E. J. Brill, 1981.

45 See C. Lepelley, '*Spes Saecvli*: Le milieu social d'Augustin et ses ambitions séculières avant sa conversion,' in *Atti del congresso internazionale su s. Agostino nel XVI centenario della conversione*, vol. 1, Rome, Institutum Patristicum «Augustinianum», 1987, pp. 99–117, together with P. Brown, *Augustine*, op. cit., pp. 65–72. B. Stock, *Augustine the Reader. Meditation, Self-Knowledge and the Ethics of Interpretation*, Cambridge, Mass., Belknap Press of Harvard University Press, 1996, in a recent and otherwise intriguing treatment of self-knowledge and conversion in Augustine, offers another instance of the wholesale neglect of these themes in the *Confessions*.

46 The reference to 'adult games' (*negotia*) is found at *conf.* 1.9.15.

47 See the works cited above at n. 26.

48 See Plato, *Republic* 2 (376e–385c) on lies told about the gods.

49 G. Lawless, '*Auaritia, luxuria, ambitio, Lib. arb.* 1, 11, 22: A Greco–Roman Literary Topos and Augustine's Asceticism', in *Il monachesimo occidentale: dalle origini alla* Regula Magistri, XXVI Incontro di studiosi dell'antichità cristiana, Rome, Institutum Patristicum «Augustinianum», 1998, pp. 317–31, skillfully demonstrates Augustine's dependence upon pagan, Latin classical authors in his discussions of this triad of vices.

50 See *conf.* 4.1.1. The specific reference is to Augustine's tenure as a teacher of

rhetoric while still searching for the truth of himself in the Catholic church. However, as mentioned above, Augustine speaks in Book 10 of the *Confessions* about his continuing self-deception as a bishop at the time of the composition of the work. He implies there that ongoing confession is necessary in order to hold this reality clearly before his conscience. For further references and discussion, see my article 'Loose Canons: Augustine and Derrida on their Selves', in *Of God, the Gift and Postmodernism*, ed. J. D. Caputo and M. J. Scanlon, Bloomington, Ind., Indiana University Press, forthcoming.

51 In Dodaro, 'Il *timor mortis*', op. cit., I explain in greater detail what I see as the links between *uera pietas*, *uera iustitia* and penance in the terms discussed here. Although she does not discuss penance in Augustine from this perspective, A.-M. La Bonnardière, 'Pénitence et réconciliation des pénitents d'après saint Augustin', *Revue des études augustiniennes* 13 (1967), pp. 31–53; ibid., 13 (1967), pp. 249–83; and ibid., 14 (1968), pp. 181–204, offers the best overall treatment of penitential theory and practice in Augustine's writings and episcopal ministry. See also A. Fitzgerald, 'Penance', in *Augustine Through the Ages: An Encyclopedia*, Grand Rapids, Mich., Eerdmans, 1999, pp. 640–6.

52 Thus, eucharist offers a political symbol of the social reconciliation achieved once and for all through the divine pardon accomplished in the death of Christ, the one true priest. This theme is especially clear in *s. Dolbeau* 26, but is also key to Augustine's discussion of eucharist at *ciu.* 10.4–5. See my articles, '*Christus sacerdos*' op. cit., and 'Il *timor mortis*', op. cit., at the respective pages cited in n. 43.

53 See *ciu.* 5.12–26, together with R. Dodaro, 'Eloquent Lies, Just Wars and the Politics of Persuasion: Reading Augustine's *City of God* in a "Postmodern" World', *Augustinian Studies* 25 (1994), pp. 77–138, especially pp. 89–94; and idem, 'Note sulla presenza', op. cit., pp. 261–70.

54 See *ciu.* 5.26 in conjunction with the portrait of the ideal (*felix*) emperor at *ciu.* 5.24. I have drawn out these themes in the articles indicated in n. 53.

INDEX

DATE DUE

5/11/14			
DEC 1 1 2015			